GALUT

The Modern Jewish Experience

Paula Hyman and Deborah Dash Moore, *editors*

GALUT

Modern Jewish Reflection
on Homelessness and Homecoming

ARNOLD M. EISEN

INDIANA UNIVERSITY PRESS
BLOOMINGTON AND INDIANAPOLIS

Manufactured in the United States of America

Library of Congress Cataloging-in-Publication Data
Eisen, Arnold M., 1951–
Galut : modern Jewish reflection on homelessness
and homecoming.
(The Modern Jewish experience)
Bibliography: p.
Includes index.
1. Jews—Diaspora—History of doctrines. 2. Judaism
—Doctrines. 3. Zionism—Philosophy. 4. Israel and
the Diaspora. I. Title. II. Series: Modern Jewish
experience (Bloomington, Ind.)
BM613.5.E57   1986   296.3   85-45763
ISBN 0-253-32550-1

1   2   3   4   5   90   89   88   87   86

For Ace

Integrity, however, compels us to state that
for the many who today tarry for new
prophets and saviors, the situation is the
same as resounds in the beautiful Edomite
watchman's song of the period of exile that
has been included among Isaiah's oracles:
"He calleth to me out of Seir, Watchman,
what of the night? The watchman said, The
morning cometh, and also the night: if ye will
enquire, enquire ye: return, come." The
people to whom this was said has enquired
and tarried for more than two millennia, and
we are shaken when we realize its fate.
—Max Weber
"Science as a Vocation"

No creatures to my knowledge live in such
wide dispersion as we dogs, none have so
many distinctions of class, of kind, of
occupation, distinctions too numerous to
review at a glance; we, whose one desire is to
stick together—and again and again we
succeed at transcendent moments in spite of
everything—we above all others live so
widely separated from one another, engaged
in strange vocations that are often
incomprehensible even to our canine
neighbors, holding firmly to laws that are not
those of the dog world, but are actually
directed against it. How baffling these
questions are, questions on which one would
prefer not to touch. . . .
—Franz Kafka
"Investigations of a Dog"

CONTENTS

ACKNOWLEDGMENTS

Preoccupation with *galut* or Jewish homelessness comes naturally in the Jewish homeland. The newspapers report regularly on Soviet Jews who wish to come home but cannot. Israelis who have chosen to "descend" from the Land into voluntary exile provoke widespread criticism and no little anxiety. As I write, Ethiopian Jews newly arrived in their promised land wonder publicly just who and where they are. West Bank settlers, by contrast, seem utterly confident of their homecoming and its imperatives, bending government policy in its name and vilifying opponents as prisoners of a retrograde "galut mentality." *Exile* is a term of opprobrium in the Jewish state intended to overcome it. Concern with exile is encountered at every turn. It reminds Israelis of where they sit, by calling to mind the image of where they would sit still had the Zionist revolution not reversed the current of two thousand years of Jewish history and brought them home.

These pervasive societal concerns were made compelling to me through personal conversation. Israelis are not shy in asking diaspora Jews to join their homecoming. Nor are they reticent in wondering how one could possibly prefer exile, even among the "fleshpots" of America, to the renewed wholeness of Jewish life in the Land. Their questions, posed to a student of modern Jewish religious thought, provoked others no less arresting. How had it come about that Israeli and American Jews had already developed, a mere four decades into statehood, such vastly different perceptions of each other and the history they share? And how was it that a traditional religious vocabulary, crucially influenced by the experience of exile, had come to play such a central role in the self-description of a homecoming still largely secular? What could it mean for Jews to come home and yet fail to achieve the redemption identified by their tradition with return to Zion? And what could exile mean when it smiled upon Jews with the benevolence of America? The traditional vocabulary seemed incongruous with the present realities that it is called upon to legitimate and even explain. I therefore resolved to examine it up close, the better to clarify and perhaps contribute to the current debate concerning the meaning of exile and of overcoming exile, now that Jews have and have not come home.

I am grateful to Ari Elon for initiating me into conversation on these themes over a decade ago, and for continuing my education in the intervening years with persuasiveness and passion; grateful too to those who took up these issues with me in later stages of this manuscript's development, particularly Janet Aviad, Arye Carmon, Paula Hyman, Aviezer Ravitzky, and Michael Rosenak. I am also greatly indebted to the colleagues and friends who read the manuscript in whole or in part, thereby enabling me to venture beyond areas in which I am expert and pose questions I would otherwise not have considered: Janet Aviad, Baruch Bokser, Eliezer Diamond, Edward Greenstein, Paul Mendes-Flohr, Alan Mintz, Wayne Proudfoot, Aviezer Ravitzky, Alvin Rosenfeld, and Robert Somerville. The readings and ideas presented in this study were tested and refined in discussion with a study circle of Ha-Magshimim, a class at the National Havurah Summer Institute, regular meetings of the Continuing Seminar on Zionist Thought in New York City, the audience of the 1985 Aaron Roland Lecture at Stanford University, and a graduate seminar in the Department of Jewish Philosophy at Tel Aviv University. My sincere thanks to all.

I would also like to acknowledge the assistance of the Lady Davis Fellowship Trust, which provided the postdoctoral grant that made possible much of the research for the work; the Van Leer Jerusalem Foundation and its director, Yehuda Elkana, for use of the most comfortable library in which I have ever worked; and Naomi Goldberg, Vivian Shaw, and Rina Werber, who patiently typed successive drafts of the manuscript and bore with the pressure of my deadlines.

I am grateful to Oxford University Press for permission to quote from Max Weber's essay "Science as a Vocation," which appears in the anthology *From Max Weber: Essays in Sociology*, edited by Hans Gerth and C. Wright Mills; and to Schocken Books for permission to quote from *The Complete Stories* of *Franz Kafka*, edited by Nahum N. Glatzer.

My late teacher Uriel Tal inspired this research, both through his own work on the subject and by the example of his conviction and commitment. May his memory continue to be a blessing.

"Finally, the most beloved": my wife, Adriane Leveen, contributed to my thinking on these issues still more directly. Her comments and criticism, from the first public presentation of my ideas to the final reworking of the manuscript, have been invaluable. But I am more grateful still for the homecomings which she has made possible for me in two countries, amid our shared continuing education in the many dimensions of Jewish homelessness.

A. E.

Jerusalem

Rosh Hashanah, 1985

INTRODUCTION

In the beginning, there was exile. God had hardly put the seal upon His perfect order, the Book of Genesis tells us, when His creatures incurred eternal punishment for disrupting it. Paradise had not even begun to be a home when the parents of us all were cast out of it, never to return. They proceeded in their exile to the true beginning of the world, *our* beginning, which lay to the east of Eden; to the round of work and childbearing, love and culture, death and imperfection, which constitutes human life upon the earth.

The loss and leaving of home stamp all the narratives of Genesis—from Cain the perpetual wanderer, through Abraham's departures for Canaan and beyond, to the final descent into Egypt. Indeed, they predominate throughout all five books of Moses. God's people Israel, conceived in Egyptian exile and born in the wilderness of Sinai, spends the remainder of Exodus, Leviticus, and Numbers in extended desert wanderings. Even the marvelous promise of home conveyed by Deuteronomy is overwhelmed at the book's conclusion by the threat of renewed homelessness. So it is with the rest of the Bible, particularly in the writings of the prophets. So it has been with Jewish reflection ever since.

Paradise, it seems, has never preoccupied the Jewish imagination nearly so much as exile. As if they could exorcise the terrors of dispersion by giving them a name, generation after generation of Jews has returned to the depiction of its alien people on the run. There was comfort in the knowledge that one's sufferings had been shared by the ancestors. There was, too, a modicum of explanation. If exile had been ordained by God Himself as the lot of His chosen people, there was honor and purpose in apparent disgrace. If exile would end only with the coming of God's Messiah to all the world, the millennia of waiting could be endured and lent significance. In the meantime, Jews oriented themselves in their dispersions by reference to the Center which they had left behind, even as they imagined their homecoming to the Land in mirror images of the exile they knew all too well from experience. And what they knew, they passed on. Each generation's experience of exile was shaped in large part by the reflection of previous generations, itself cast in an inherited mold. "What occurred to the ancestors," said a medieval commentator, "is a sign for the children." It was a lesson in what was to be, and in how to bear and overcome it.

This tradition of reflection has remained unbroken even in modern times. Nowhere have the lessons of exile and homecoming been pondered more keenly, or more paradoxically, than among Zionists who sought to harness the tradition in order to bring it to an end—through the profoundly anti-traditional enterprise of homecoming. Even today, with homecoming accomplished, the tradition of reflection on galut has by no means lost its hold. Israelis ponder it along with classical Zionist "commentaries" to find the key to their troubled return to the Land. What can it mean for Jews to come home, impelled by their tradition, if what they find and build there falls far short of the fulfillment stored up in every traditional promise of return? American Jews turn to the same sources for help in justifying and comprehending their own ambivalent relation to the Center. What does exile mean if the majority of the Jewish people have freely chosen it over life inside the Land? Today as always Jews grasp their continuing homelessness primarily in terms of homecoming, and their Land in terms of exile. The tradition has prevented many well schooled in the meaning of human exile upon God's earth from calling their new nation among the nations by the simple (but for Jews messianic) word *home*.

The countless personal conversations in both America and Israel which drew me to these issues are part and parcel of the lively and often acrimonious debate which the success of Zionism has engendered among Jews concerning the possible and proper contemporary meanings of exile and homecoming. Israelis, my own friends and teachers among them, are fond of arguing that exile remains exile, for all that it now goes by the honorific *diaspora*. American Jewry like previous galut communities is either doomed to destruction or barren of creativity or both. The claim that "America is different," so the Israelis observe, rings hollow in the light of similar claims made for exilic communities of the past, every one of which eventually proved a tragic delusion. The fate of American Jews will be the same—a sentence which seems to follow as inexorably as biblical justice from the crime that they have committed in failing to act upon or even recognize the fact of their homelessness at the very moment of Jewish homecoming. America is not "different," it is exile. Only Israel can be home.

Many American Jews, likewise including my own friends and teachers, reject both claims. They invoke traditional sources in order to remind Israelis that homecoming has always meant far more than physical return to the Land of Israel. And they offer a reading of Jewish history and contemporary Jewish experience that effectively denies the centrality of the Land in Jewish life, past or present. The traditional concept of exile is inapplicable to contemporary American realities, they insist. Nor can Israel be called home. The pretensions in this regard heard regularly in Jerusalem should be attributed to the obvious insecurities of Israeli life, the country's desperate need for immigrants, and the understandable effort to legitimate a homecoming called severely into question by the refusal of most diaspora Jews to join it. America is far from exile, rather as much a home as Jews could hope for. Israel is home in a different sense—but it is not Home. Claims to the contrary must be judged premature until the Messiah comes and makes them good.

I have over the years found myself on both sides of this conversation: an

"Israeli" among American Jews, an American among Israelis; at once in exile and at home among both. The present study developed out of a search for middle ground. I wanted, first, to examine the classical sources concerning exile and homecoming brandished by all parties to the modern debate, invoked by nearly all to legitimate their positions, but rarely if ever seen whole. Seeing them whole, I trusted, would enable me to gauge the influence which the traditional sources had exercised both upon the founders of Zionist thought and upon current debate. Turning to the former, I found that the influence of the Bible and the rabbis was decisive. The notions of homecoming which guided the Jewish return to the Land were shaped crucially by inherited pictures of homelessness. Where Jews were going was constantly explained by reference to the exile they were leaving behind. Turning to contemporary debate over the meaning of galut and homecoming, I found that it too simply cannot be comprehended apart from the classical sources still misread or read partially in an effort to make sense of a situation which is unprecedented for Jews—and so in desperate need of precedent. The tradition is indispensable to that effort: particularly the idea of galut—the norm of Jewish existence which the Jewish state seeks to overthrow.

This study presents the results of that working through of sources, classical and modern. It is my hope that it sheds useful light on the contemporary discussion and its roots; my hope, too, that it may enrich the age-old Jewish conversation to which it attends.

I believe that the contemporary debate, like the State of Israel which occasioned it, is of more than merely Jewish concern. It is no coincidence that Max Weber invoked Isaiah's prophecy of return to Zion at the conclusion to "Science as a Vocation," an essay devoted to the loss of ultimate meaning in the modern "disenchanted" world. Neither is it mere accident that the nightmares and parables of Franz Kafka, the product in part of the exile he felt so keenly and portrayed with unmatched power, have become preeminent in our own generation's reflection about its "wide dispersion," alienation, and "strange vocations"; the vehicle for "questions on which one would prefer not to touch" and which are asked nonetheless, again and again. The Nobel laureate for literature in 1980, speaking for his countrymen and his age, described the obligations of the poet to truth and memory in terms of exile and homecoming which derive from the Hebrew Bible and echo the convictions of the rabbis.[1] The growing literature of political exiles, like the growing number of stateless refugees, seems an ironic commentary on the oft-expressed sense of the world's most privileged citizens that they, too, are not at home—and would wish to be, above all else.

It is in that context that the Israelis have returned to Zion, thereby challenging far more than the historical wisdom that such a thing could never be done. The wandering Jews, the very symbols of "rootless cosmopolitanism" in the Christian West, have come home. They have made deserts bloom, in the shadow of the Holocaust. They have leaped confidently, in faith, at a time when so many feel "weightless" in the wake of God's passing. They have played a role in making others refugees. Neither the Jews' own vision of Jewish exile and homelessness, it would seem, nor that of the Western world, can long remain unaffected. Having examined the former in detail, I will conclude the study with brief consideration of the latter, prompted by suggestions from Weber and Kafka. Authentic Jewish discourse in our day largely stands at one remove from this larger conversation over exile and homecoming, for reasons which I shall analyze. Homecoming has entailed a certain isolation, imposed both from within and from without.

My method in this study has been determined by the centrality to Jewish thought and experience of the issues which it probes. To write a history of Jewish exile is to write the history of the Jews—witness Yehezkel Kaufmann's magisterial *Golah Ve-Nekhar* (Exile and estrangement, 1929–30), still the finest work on the subject.[2] To trace the idea of galut through the manifold Jewish experience which gave rise to it, or the hundreds of texts in which that experience has found expression, is to follow the entire course of Judaism. I have, of necessity, been doubly selective in focus.

First, I have concentrated on the single concept of galut, though I have conceived it broadly, in line with the classical sources in which it originates. I have left to one side the integrally related ideas of messianism, Zionism, destruction (*ḥurban*), and the Land of Israel, all of which have been treated thoroughly and recently elsewhere.[3] Exile has until now been examined extensively only in Kaufmann's work and in Yitzhak Baer's *Galut* (1936, 1947),[4] a passionate survey of the Jews' wanderings and longings for Zion. It still requires intense and systematic scrutiny.

Second, I have been selective in the classical and modern sources chosen for analysis. Rather than present the development of the concept of galut in all its permutations, I focus in Part One of the study upon three "moments" or "stations" in that development especially crucial to all the rest. The picture of political and metaphysical exile furnished by the narratives of Genesis; the counterimage of homecoming put forth by Deuteronomy and routed in chapter 28 by the curses of the *tokheḥah* (reproof); and the struggle by the rabbis, once the Romans had made Jews exiles inside *and* outside their Land, to contain exile within the sacred order of Torah—these are the stages in the history of the concept of exile (logical even more than chronological "moments") most determinative of its future development and most important to the modern reflection analyzed in Part Two. I examine them through the reading and analysis of selected texts, taking as my rabbinic texts the mishnaic and talmudic tractates Avodah Zarah. It is not that the four particular texts selected are necessarily representative of the whole (though I believe that in significant measure they are), nor that they are most often cited by later thinkers (though we will find them cited frequently). I wish rather to expose the reader to the importance of three stages in the development of galut for later reflection, and that significance is best appreciated if we proceed like Jewish thought itself through the discipline of reading and commentary. Significance lay and was discovered, over the centuries, in the exposure of texts to present experience and the reading of present experience through texts—a process which our own reading of Genesis, Deuteronomy, and Avodah Zarah will continue. My treatment of the modern and contemporary debates proceeds in a similar fashion: through a focus upon leading thinkers and central texts. The aim throughout is to understand and contribute to those debates, by working through the sources and ideas from which they have derived.

Chapter One, then, unpacks the narratives in Genesis in which we first encounter the themes and imagery that will dominate all subsequent Jewish reflection on galut. Not yet at home in their promised homeland, the patriarchs wander to and fro upon its surface, making their peace with the powers that be as they go. The political and metaphysical dimensions of homelessness are joined in these narratives, never again to be separated in Jewish reflection until the modern period. Sexual and political powerlessness are likewise linked—from Sarah's encounter with Pharaoh to Joseph's, from the banishment of Isaac to the rape of Dinah. Home, in Genesis, is a place remembered and revisited, but never really known.

In Chapter Two our subject is Deuteronomy, the most sustained and coherent imagining of home that one finds in Jewish tradition. Deuteronomy is the developed positive image of the negative presented in Genesis. As Israel prepares to cross the Jordan, Moses tries to conjure up a picture of the life awaiting his people on the other side, if only they choose to live it. His rhetoric—a poetry of law—seeks to soar to the heights demanded by the unique possibility which it holds out, both to Israel and the world. Yet here too the imagination of home is overpowered by the specter of homelessness. Curse routs blessing; home remains unachieved, and incompletely imagined. However, as we will see in the chapter's conclusion, it was that very combination of vision and the knowledge that vision would fail which provided comfort and meaning to succeeding generations—when, after a relatively brief homecoming, Israel once more found itself in exile.

Chapter Three examines the mishnaic tractate Avodah Zarah ("Idol worship") and its talmudic commentary. Israel had regained its homeland from the Babylonians, only to lose it once more—this time to the Romans. The Jews were exiles inside the land of Israel as well as outside it, and so the rabbis struggled to delimit a Jewish time and space amid a once-holy Land now utterly defiled—upon an earth which God Himself was forced to wander as an exile. No place was any longer holy, no locus of meaning any longer existed, to be inhabited or pointed to. Such was the world's condition in *ha-zeman ha-zeh:* "this time"—*all* time, all history, until the Messiah's coming to take Israel home. Deprived of the sacred center, the rabbis pointed to it all the more insistently, even as they enabled Jews to live their lives—with God—outside it. They fantasized the discomfiture of their enemies, gave vent to their fears of death and temptation, and rehearsed again and again the unanswerable question of why God had allowed His Land, His people, and His world to sink to the degraded state of exile. This rabbinic reflection formed the basis for medieval developments, philosophical and kabbalistic, sketched at the chapter's close. It also contained the seeds for the spiritualization and politicization of the concept of *galut* which occurred in the wake of the Jews' expulsion from Spain. These in turn laid the ground for the modern developments which are our concern in Part Two—the attempt by the Zionist "founders and sons" to overcome the entire line of thinking set forth thus far, by putting an end once and for all to the wandering and dispersion which had occasioned it.

Neither Ahad Ha'am nor Theodor Herzl could renounce that tradition of reflection entirely, though neither could embrace it without reservation. The former, examined in Chapter Four along with other preeminent cultural Zionists, sought to translate Jewish *faith* to secular *culture* and so to revive the flagging "spirit" of the Jewish people. The problem of the Jews, Ahad Ha'am concluded sadly, had no solution. He could not bring them home. But the problem of Judaism could be overcome—if only the people focused its energies upon rebuilding the Center in which it had first come to life. The establishment of a Spiritual Center in the Land, to serve a people who would continue to live outside it, was all the homecoming that could be hoped for. Succeeding cultural Zionists, chiefly Martin Buber and A. D. Gordon, sought to bring Ahad-Ha'am's problematic notion of the Spiritual Center down to earth—the real earth of the Land then being reclaimed. They also attempted to infuse it with Jewish religious commitment beyond the bounds of Ahad Ha'am's soberly rational agnosticism. The latter effort, crucial to the understanding of the Jewish state as a "return," dominates contemporary Israeli discussion of homecoming, as the former dominates debate between Israel and its American diaspora. Cultural Zionism's agenda has succeeded in attaining this preeminence, one might say, because its original vision failed. Jews chose to concentrate body as well as spirit in Zion—seeking and finding a higher synthesis than Ahad Ha'am could bring himself to dream.

Herzl, on the other hand, has failed because of his success. His brilliant translation of age-old Jewish longing for return from exile into the modern "state-idea," powered by international capital and a healthy dose of real-politik, left disciples such as Jacob Klatzkin and Yehezkel Kaufmann with a twofold task, considered in Chapter Five. They had to demonstrate that Herzl's secular messianism would indeed solve the Jewish problem, rather than prove a recipe for despair. To that end they embarked on an analysis of anti-Semitism and assimilation and a "negation of the diaspora" still crucial to Israeli self-perception. Second, they had to show that Herzl's *Judenstaat* would be Jewish in more than name only; that the tradition against which political Zionists rebelled in order to bring Jews home could somehow undergird the new state which they constructed. The "Jew" and the "Hebrew," past and future, could be one. This issue too stands at the forefront of current Israeli discussion; then as now there are those who are not convinced that the merger can be accomplished.

I turn in the second part of the chapter to one of the most brilliant doubters and critics of political Zionism: Franz Rosenzweig, who saw in the attempt to make Jews "like all other nations" the abandonment of Israel's unique destiny. To congregate in a Jewish state, or settle for a Spiritual Center, was to squander the gift of eternal life. Exile was an integral part of Jewish existence. Homecoming as the Zionists intended it was impossible.

Only religious Zionists, convinced that God Himself stood behind the return to the Land, could marry the extremes represented by Herzl and Rosenzweig. Thesis and antithesis would come together in the highest synthesis of all. Homecoming could go forward, for the Messiah was on the way. The heirs of Rabbi Abraham Isaac Kook, the preeminent exponent of messianic religious Zionism, have far louder a voice in the definition of contemporary Israel than those of Herzl. "Normalization" has proven a pipe-dream; and the goal of statehood, once achieved, is no longer self-legitimizing. Political Zionism could bring Jews home but not supply the meaning of their being there, and precisely this is what contemporary Israelis seek above all else.

Chapter Six considers the three leading contenders for the definition of Jewish homecoming. Orthodox religious Zionists unanimously bless the Jewish state as the "beginning of the flowering of our redemption," perceiving divine approval in its establishment and maintenance. They differ, however, on how imminently the Messiah's arrival can be expected (a dispute which carries with it profound political consequences) and on when and to what degree traditional Jewish law or *halakhah* should become the law of the modern Jewish state. Secular thinkers such as Amos Oz and A. B. Yehoshua, dismayed that the ideological initiative seems to rest in the hands of a retrograde and dangerous Orthodoxy, have been hard-pressed to formulate secular Herzlian or Ahad Ha'amist alternatives. They too want their new state to be a homecoming, its establishment a return. But they are uncomfortable with the exilic tradition that makes it such. They seek a state Jewish in more than name or population, but reserve the right to "pick and choose" among the tradition's elements and varieties—hardly the road to an authentic Israeli Jewish culture, and not at all what Ahad Ha'am had in mind. The heirs of cultural Zionism, meanwhile—Gershom Scholem and Eliezer Schweid chief among them—have sought a middle path between normalization and Orthodoxy. The search has so far met with little success. Such thinkers are looking for what no Jew has ever found: a revolutionary homecoming which is nevertheless continuous with the past that it overthrows and leaves behind. The contradiction inheres within Zionism itself. Israelis occupy the unprecedented space between homecoming and redemption, and yet seek to make ultimate sense of it with the help of Jewish tradition. The sense of true homecoming as a result eludes them.

A large part of their effort to define home consists in negation of the ever-present alternative: diaspora. Imagination of homecoming, now as always, proceeds through over-vivid contrasts with exile. The Promised Land takes shape, now as in Deuteronomy, against the background—never to be forgotten—of Egyptian bondage. Chapter Seven examines the varieties of this Israeli attack on the viability and legitimacy of American Jewish life and then turns to the diaspora's self-defense, which draws on a conception of exile and homecoming first formulated by Solomon Schechter and Mordecai Kaplan. American Jewish thinkers concede that Israelis have come home in a political sense, but argue that so too, in a different way, have American Jews. They recognize that (in Abraham Heschel's words) "Miami Beach is galut," but aver that so too, in a way, is Tel Aviv. In short, Israel *is* the Spiritual Center, but that centrality is robbed of the consequence claimed for it by Israelis. American Jews are centered rather on their own "spiritual aliyah" (again Heschel's term): a regimen available now as ever wherever Jews congregate to observe God's Torah.

In the final section of the chapter I argue that this division between Israel and diaspora carries over into contemporary Jewish thought as a whole. Heschel, Joseph Dov Soloveitchik, and Emil Fackenheim—three of the generation's preeminent thinkers—all see the Land in a context determined by where they sit, outside it. The split between Center and periphery, Israeli and American Judaism, has already gone far beyond the definition of exile and homecoming. It reaches to the very definition of Jewish commitment in our time.

The conclusion represents an initial attempt to bridge this split, insofar as that is possible, as well as to span the equally wide gap separating contemporary Jewish and non-Jewish discourse on homelessness and homecoming. The classical sources examined in Part One are instrumental in this effort. They are liberating in their analysis of the Jewish and human conditions where the polemical arguments all too often are narrow and constricting. The tradition is deep precisely because it is broad, always considering the Jewish people in its uniqueness in terms of humanity as a whole. An encounter with these sources which bears in mind several hints from Weber and Kafka—students of the particular face of exile in our century—helps us to understand why the certainties sought by Israelis and diaspora Jews alike have proven so elusive. To say we are not at home, but somewhere else, is a truism. The underlying conviction of this study is that traditional Jewish sources concerning exile and homecoming, through their refinements and complexity, enable us to say a good deal more.

One lesson can be stated at the outset. The concept galut has always had both a *political* dimension—the perils of statelessness, the disabilities of the alien—and a *metaphysical* dimension: a function of our brief sojourn as human beings on God's earth. Deuteronomy teaches nothing if not that homecoming means far more than conquest or settlement of the Land. Rather the Land will "spew forth its inhabitants" at God's command if they fail to establish upon it the ideal political order meant to make possible metaphysical fulfillment heretofore unknown. The rabbis of the Mishnah and the Talmud, robbed of that fulfillment not only outside of the Land but within, recalled Jews in their many dispersions to the Center—the real estate of human beings on the earth—and directed their efforts and imaginings toward true homecoming.

It will not do, in the presence of such subtleties, to argue that traditional notions of galut are inapplicable in contemporary America. The rabbis' understanding of the difficulties involved in carving out Jewish time and space inside a larger culture, hostile or at best indifferent to that effort, is more relevant now than we would wish. Nor will it do, given the lessons that exile can mean a life in service to the highest and that a homecoming which means less than this is no homecoming, to claim that "until the Zionist revolution, Jews were forced to hover in the heavens, like figures in the paintings of Chagall,"[5] or that "Israel in essence had no history during its exile—this in fact is the significance of galut."[6] As if there were no groundedness, no life, no *home*, in the "round of work and childbearing," of service to God through His commandments, wherever it may occur; as if history were only, or even fundamentally, activity in the arena of world politics or the field of battle. Clichés of this sort cannot survive sustained and serious encounter with what galut and its opposite—always far less satisfactorily described—have meant to Jews for centuries.

Before proceeding to those sources, two final methodological reflections on their interpretation. First, no interpretation of any text, particularly a biblical or rabbinic text, can ever claim to be complete or authoritative. I have of course attempted no such finality here. However, despite the "seventy faces" which every verse of Torah is said to present to its serious students, I believe that the distinction between the *pshat*, or "literal" meaning of the text, and more open-ended imaginative or homiletical readings known as *drash* remains workable and worthwhile. One person's *pshat*, of course, may be another's *drash;* what Genesis "really meant" by the story of Dinah, or the Mishnah by its demarcations of prohibited and permitted, will forever elude us. Nevertheless, I have everywhere sought the *pshat* (or rather a *pshat*), hoping, with the help of traditional and modern commentators and scholars (cited in the notes), to capture the surface meaning insofar as this can be encompassed within my limited set of concerns. All classical sources and most modern sources cited in this study are easily available in English. Citations to the classics are included in the body of the text. The reader is urged to open their pages and follow along.[7]

Second, it has not been necessary for the purposes of this study to enter into scholarly disputes over when, or by whom, a particular text was written or edited. We can similarly leave aside the question of whether the events described in biblical or rabbinic sources ever took place, or whether the texts examined here represent any "consciousness" other than those of their own particular authors. The point, again, is to grasp the several "moments" in the development of the idea of galut most crucial to the normative rabbinic tradition that directed Jewish life for close to two millennia as well as to the modern corpus which has responded to that tradition, even in rebellion. I have taken up modern issues of authorship and historicity in the notes, where I have also undertaken a dialogue with the classical Jewish commentators. In general, neither the modern scholars nor the classical commentators touch my concerns directly.[8] That E. A. Speiser can account for the "wife-sister" stories in Genesis by reference to ancient Near Eastern law,[9] or Michael Astour ascribe Genesis 14 to a Deuteronomist who borrowed from and satirized seventh-century B.C. Babylonia,[10] is relevant to this study but peripheral to the business at hand. That the Jewish commentators largely ignore the passages that I examine is testimony to their apologetic concerns, as well as to the role of Zionism and social science in shaping the questions which I, unlike them, have asked.[11]

My hope is that this working through of the sources, and the further readings which it may provoke among its readers, can assist our generation's troubled but privileged reflection on galut. That reflection cannot but be troubled, for homelessness continues the lot of Jews and others. The shadow of recent destruction looms too large. And yet it is privileged reflection nonetheless, for Jews most of all, because it takes place at the hour of homecoming. Galut can now be considered, as it is in this study, from the vantage of a partially rebuilt Jerusalem.

Part One

I

NOT YET HOME
GENESIS

Rashi, the greatest of Jewish biblical commentators, begins his own gloss of Genesis by citing the astonishment of an earlier rabbi that the book forms part of the Torah at all. Why should the Torah begin—at the Beginning? What does God's revelation of commandments to Israel have to do with stories of paradise and flood, tribal wars and family intrigue? Why not begin, instead, with the heart of the matter: the first commandment given Israel, celebration of the Passover sacrifice—which comes only in chapter twelve of the Book of Exodus!? The answer, given our concern in this study, is especially instructive. The Torah begins at the Beginning so that if the nations of the world should ever say to Israel, "You are thieves—you have conquered the lands of the seven nations [of Canaan]," the Jews can reply: "All the earth belongs to God. He created it, and gave it to whomever He saw fit. By His will he gave it to them, and by His will He took it away from them, and gave it to us."

Two aspects of Rashi's commentary demand our attention at once.[1] First, it teaches us that Genesis, by beginning at the Beginning, establishes the place of Israel in the order of God's creation. "Why Genesis?" raises the more fundamental question "Why Israel?" Why, in other words, did God have recourse to the apparently arbitrary choice of one man and his descendants as the instruments with which to realize His plans for all of creation? Could God not have proceeded more directly—and more successfully!—to His goals? Genesis answers this question for us, Rabbi Isaac suggests, by recounting the series of human failures, tracing the lineage of generations and degenerations, which led God to seek the education of His creatures (and thus the perfection of His world) through Israel. In understanding why Israel got its *eretz*, its homeland, we come to understand why the *eretz*, the earth, got Israel.

We notice immediately, however, that when Rabbi Isaac wrote this *midrash*, and certainly when Rashi quoted it, Israel did *not* have its Land. God had apparently taken it from the nations, "given it to us," and then taken it away again, to give to others! The relevant argument would seem to be, *not* the nations' denial of Israel's right to what it has, but rather Israel's reassertion before any who will listen of its right to what it does not have—and its denial of the *absolute* right of other nations to the lands which they occupy, by God's grace, for the time being. The biblical text in this reading provides reassurance far more than legitimation. It does not depict a world in which each nation, like Israel, is at home upon its assigned portion of God's earth. Rather it shows us a world in which Israel is not at home—and neither, in a very real sense, is anyone else.

Rashi and Rabbi Isaac thereby remind us, indirectly to be sure, of the theme which dominates the book of Genesis: the wandering and expulsion, homelessness and estrangement, which begin at the very exit from the Garden. Genesis develops this theme of exile in three distinct stages that correspond to the divisions of the narrative framework itself. In the first, as the text rushes through the generations from Adam to Noah and from Noah to Abraham, we encounter the *existential* or *metaphysical* dimension of exile. We see what it is to be a human being upon the earth, in universal terms unconcerned with a still nonexistent Israel. The narrative's second stage begins with Abraham's move west into Canaan (followed immediately by the first of the patriarchs' many descents into Egypt!) and concludes with the final and fatal descent of Jacob and his sons into Egypt, instigated by the final and most protracted famine which Genesis describes. In these chapters we come to know the *political* dimension of exile: the life of the alien, the "stranger in a strange land," recounted through the story of one family's interaction—political, economic, religious, even sexual—with the peoples among whom it wanders and resides. Political and metaphysical galut are brought together in the text's third stage: the climactic story of Joseph's meteoric rise to power in the land of Egypt, which ironically leads directly to the four hundred years of Israelite slavery in Egypt that God had foretold to Abraham. We who read Torah as a whole know that Israel will finally inherit a land in which to be at home. Genesis leaves Israel, however, in the only state that the book knows: homelessness. I shall try to analyze that condition by examining passages from each of the three stages in turn.

The Mark of Cain

We begin at *our* beginning: the expulsion from the Garden. Because Adam and Eve listened to the serpent rather than to God, their relation to God's earth has been utterly disrupted. Note the terms of their punishment: "Cursed be the ground (*adamah*) because of you. In anguish shall you eat of it all the days of your life. Thorns and thistles shall it bring forth for you . . . until you return to the ground, for from it you were taken. For dust you are, and to dust you shall return" (3:17–19). Humanity had been placed upon the earth "to work and watch over it" (2:15).[2] We were meant to supervise a natural order in which we, like the streams and fish and plants, had a part.

All this is now changed, and the punishment takes the form of a struggle between humanity and the earth from which both suffer. The earth is "cursed," in opposition to the blessing which it originally enjoyed, blessing in its primary connotation (cf. 1:22) of fertility. Now the earth shall sprout only thorns and thistles, and only with the greatest human effort will it provide food for man. Earth and humanity still need each other, but they shall be locked in struggle until they are reunited, in death. Whether Adam and Eve had been meant to be immortal, or only learn of their mortality once "their eyes are opened," is not important here. What matters is that images of death and estrangement now dominate a narrative previously given over to images of life abundant. Finally, and most crucially, Adam and Eve are forever banished east of Eden, "to till the soil from which [humankind] was taken"—"taken" in three senses: birth, alienation, and exile.

Things were not meant to be this way. Humanity was to have found its place on earth among the other creatures created on the sixth day. Through the earth which it worked and tended, humanity would have related to God in heaven—that heaven created, along with the earth, at the very beginning. Each of us would have related to the *eretz*, and so to God, through the particular plot of ground (*adamah*) for which we cared, its topmost layer of dust being both our origin and our destination.[3] Now, however, a corrupted humanity having corrupted the earth, we must relate to earth and to God in full awareness of all that separates us from them. Adam and Eve come before God together, as guilty members of a shared culture.

This outcome, of course, is far from entirely negative. Human life in any other form than the one initiated with the expulsion is inconceivable to Genesis, as to us. Indeed, the human partnership with God to which Genesis and the remainder of the Bible call us is premised on the consciousness and freedom which, in this myth of Paradise, come only from our first parents' disobedience. This paradox is the principal source of the text's profundity and power. What should not have been done, once having been done, leads to all that is most noble and most miserable, all that human beings fear and treasure, all that they know as life. The home which would have stifled us had we stayed there and precluded all human creativity—our eternal Parent watching every move—is instead a place which we can recall fondly and with great longing, secure in the knowledge that we can never go back. The way of the world starts to the east of Eden.

The punishment meted out to Cain in the very next chapter of Genesis (4:10–17) develops directly from that incurred by his parents.[4] The ground had been cursed because of Adam and Eve. Now, because Cain forced it to swallow the blood of his brother Abel, Cain shall be "cursed from the ground."[5] Whereas his parents were condemned to struggle with the earth in order to bring forth their daily bread, Cain is told that his struggle to do the same will prove futile. They were banished from Eden. He is cast out from everywhere, a ceaseless wanderer (*na'va-nad*) who can settle only in the "land of Nod"—the land, that is, of "wandering," located even further to the east of Eden.[6] The punishment is indeed "too great to bear." As if metaphysical exile "from off the face of the earth" as well as from "God's face" were not enough, Cain will also suffer the political exile of the alien denied the protection of his clan. "Anyone who meets me may kill me." God therefore agrees to become Cain's sole protector, the potential avenger of his blood. Cain leaves God's presence, enters on his endless wandering, fathers a child, and founds a city. Civilization has begun.

Banishment from home and estrangement from the earth are established here, at the very outset of things, as the two principal components of divine punishment. The punishment fits the crime. Adam and Eve avoid God's demanding presence by hiding and are cast out from Him; Cain evades God's knowing question with a lie and will never be privileged to speak to God again. Banishment is fixed as the mark of shame appropriate to a sinner. It is as if distance from the sacred center, the place where God is wont to walk, confers a covering that hides those who are not worthy to be seen. Once again the curse proves something of a blessing. It provides the saving distance between humanity and God in which we manage to exist, as sinners, on His earth. Yet the curse remains a curse, further estranging us from God, the earth, and each other. Cities, farming, music, "tools of copper and iron," all follow from Cain's murder of his brother—human culture developing inextricably, so it seems, with homelessness.

The final punishment which concerns us follows in detail the pattern now established. Before examining it, however, we need to review the events which led humanity to build the Tower of Babel and God to destroy it. A few individuals during the ten generations separating Adam from Noah did "call on the name of the Lord" (4:26) and "walk with God" (5:24), but in general the picture is one of corruption and disharmony. The so-called "sons of God" "see" beautiful women and take them. God on the other hand "sees" how great is humanity's wickedness, how pervasive its evil, and decides to begin creation all over again. What is striking is that humanity too seems dissatisfied with this state of affairs. Noah, the individual selected by God to be the progenitor of the renewed species, is given the name Noah (that is, "comfort") by his father in the hope that he will "provide us relief from our work and from the toil of our hands, out of the very soil which the Lord placed under a curse" (5:29). The wish is fulfilled, though like many human wishes (so the text wishes to say) not in the manner intended. Rather the earth which had become corrupt (*va-tishahet*) before God is utterly destroyed (*hineni mashhitam:* cf. 6:11–13). This punishment departs from the pattern by exaggerating it—so utterly dividing man from the earth and destroying them both that a new beginning can emerge from the cleansing.

Starting over, God is less demanding. He now realizes that the "devisings of man's mind are evil from his youth" (8:21) and promises never again to curse the earth because of him. The new blessing builds compromise into a covenantal order no longer said to be "very good" (compare 9:1–7 with 1:28–

31). Where Adam and Eve had been vegetarians, Noah and his progeny can eat meat, thereby alienating man from other creatures and placing "the fear and dread" of humanity upon "all the beasts of the earth and all the birds of the sky." We are solemnly warned (9:6) to exact punishment from murderers, in the tragic recognition that only such dissuasion will suffice; only fear implanted in us by Heaven can prevent our spilling of human blood. How far we have come from Paradise, then, even with this new beginning. The estrangement which began in the Garden, and continued with Cain, is now nearly complete. Human beings now stand divided from God, the earth, other creatures and each other. Without God's promise never again to destroy this imperfect order (8:22, 9:16), one feels life would have been literally—as Cain said—unbearable.

It is perfectly understandable, then, that Noah's descendants should "crave a name for ourselves, lest we be scattered on the face of the earth" (11:1–9). A name is a place in the order of things, the gravity or weight that ties one firmly to the earth. A name, in this text, defines who one is—first of all to oneself. Without such grounding, one might be carried off by the winds, precisely the fear of the tower builders: "else we shall be scattered all over the world." In a situation of near-total estrangement, they seek to cleave to one another, to hold on so tightly that all even speak in the same language, the better to assert whatever collective human power there can be on the earth. But that intention, for reasons not clear from the text, runs counter to God's. It may be that He regards congregation in one place as antithetical to His wish that the species "be fertile and increase and fill the earth" (9:1). The text seems not to encourage the possible reading that God is somehow threatened by the endeavor. "Nothing that they propose to do will be out of their reach" seems rather a statement that conflation into one people and one language is out of keeping with humanity's best interests as God alone understands them.[7] He confounds the builders' speech and sentences them to the very *dispersion* which they had feared. It is as if God understands the need for security and community which drove the builders, but intervenes to say: this is not the way. Babel, significantly, lies to the west of previous settlements (11:2)—that is, on the way back from the wrong direction, but not quite "there." The proper way follows in the text at once, after a connecting genealogy: Abraham's migration to Canaan, where he is to achieve the "great" name sought by the tower builders, and, because he does God's bidding, a blessing.

Babel, then, concludes a cycle, exhausting the options that human beings could know in the absence of the turn of events which begins with Abraham. Even he and his descendants do not escape the insecurity, wandering, homelessness, dispersion, and estrangement encountered thus far. They settle, rather, for something less than home, strengthened by the promise that home will be theirs one day and by intermittent contact with the God who has promised it to them.

Political and Sexual Alliances

It is not Abraham but his father Teraḥ who sets out for Canaan, but in completing the journey which his father had interrupted by settling in Haran, Abraham goes forth from his "father's house" as well as from his "land and birthplace" precisely as God has ordered. This break with his own previous biography marks as total a break with all past human history as Adam's exit from the Garden—a parallel signified in the text by the triumphal return of the word *blessing*. The text does not so much use that word as bathe in it. Abram, as he is still called, will be blessed by God, will be a blessing, will be blessed by all the families of the earth, and will see God bless all those who bless him. The blessing, moreover, will take its original form—fertility of crops and livestock, goods aplenty—as we see in the immediate fulfillment which follows on Abraham's descent because of famine to Egypt. There, for reasons to which we will come momentarily, he is said to acquire "sheep, oxen, asses, male and female slaves, she-asses, and camels" (12:16)—a very tangible blessing indeed.

The sojourn in Egypt, coming a mere five verses after the initial arrival in the promised land, drives home the fact that Abraham does not settle in his new land but rather wanders it.[8] He goes as far as Shekhem, builds an altar, moves to the east of Bethel, builds another altar, journeys to the Negev "by stages," and then descends to Egypt—whence he will return, "proceed by stages" back to Bethel, and only then, having separated from his nephew Lot because the land could no longer support their many flocks, "come to dwell at the terebrinths of Mamre which are in Hebron," where he builds a third altar. Even there he lives like a nomadic shepherd, in tents. He does not work the land but roams upon its surface, driven by the need of his flocks to nibble at the soil. He is in fact the very picture of a driven man, though the text is silent about what moves him. One senses that he is learning from these wanderings the precarious terms under which human beings enjoy ownership of God's earth.

Genesis is not nearly so reticent when it comes to the relation of Abraham and his descendants to the peoples among whom they dwell—relations in which, necessarily, political and sexual threads intertwine. Take, for example, the three "wife-sister" narratives,[9] the first of which (12:10–20) occurs immediately after Abraham's initial encounter with the land and describes his very first encounter with non-Israelites since pledging fealty to God.[10] Lest the Egyptians among whom he is sojourning kill him out of desire for his beautiful wife, Abraham instructs Sarah to say that she is his sister. She does so, is spotted by Pharaoh's courtiers, and is taken to the royal palace, while Abraham, as brother of the bride, is plied with the "sheep and cattle" previously mentioned. Pharaoh, in contrast to all this blessing, is punished by God for his unknowing (attempted?) adultery. He then reproves Abraham for concealing the fact that Sarah is his wife and "sends him away" under armed escort. Abraham takes with him all that he has acquired through the ruse, "very rich in cattle, silver and gold" (13:2).[11]

In the next occurrence of this motif (chapter 20), Abraham is sojourning closer to home: on the border between Egypt and Canaan, in a place called Gerar (perhaps a pun on *ger* or alien).[12] This time the "gentile" king, Avimelekh, is granted a warning by God in a dream, explicitly before he had "approached her." Affirming Avimelekh's lack of blame, God instructs him to restore Sarah to Abraham and, "since he is a prophet," to request his intercession. "Why did you do this?" Avimelekh demands of Abraham. "You have done to me things that ought not to be done." Abraham replies that he thought, "surely there is no fear of God in this place, and they will kill me because of my wife. And besides, she is in truth my sister, my father's daughter though not my mother's; and she became my wife."[13] Avimelekh showers still more herds and slaves upon him, invites him to settle in Gerar wherever he pleases, and, observing that "God is with you in everything that you do," soon offers Abraham a pact of friendship.

The final occurrence of the drama—this time enacted by Isaac and another Avimelekh of Gerar—demonstrates the general applicability of the dilemma of blessing to all of the blessing's inheritors.[14] This time Avimelekh does not take Rebekah into his household, but rather looks out his window and sees Isaac fondling her (the verb is a pun on Isaac's own name). "What have you done to us! One of the people"—a euphemism for himself?[15]—"might have lain with your wife, and you would have brought guilt upon us." The king does not reward Isaac, although he orders his nation not to molest Rebekah. Yet Isaac nonetheless sows seed and reaps a hundredfold. Demonstrably, "the Lord blessed him," and so "the man grew richer and richer"—until he excites the envy of his hosts, who stop up his wells and ask him to leave. "For you have become too big for us."[16] Yet the interaction does not end there (vv. 26–31). Avimelekh one day appears with the chief of his army. "Why have you come to me," Isaac demands, "seeing as you hate me and have sent me away from among you?" Their answer is equally blunt. "We now see plainly that the Lord has been with you and we thought: Let there be a sworn treaty between us . . . that you will do us no harm. . . . From now on, be you blessed of the Lord!" Indeed, as an ally at a safe distance, Isaac's blessing could bring them only good. Their hatred is overcome by his usefulness. Isaac too agrees to the pact despite his hatred of them—what choice does he have, after all, with Avimelekh's military chief standing before him?—and the Philistines "departed from him in peace."

The pattern of patriarchal relations to host peoples is nearly fixed. Its elements bear enumeration.

1. Nonpartners to the covenant are suspected of immorality, primarily in matters of sex. Abraham's concern that idol worshippers could not be trusted to be moral is both common xenophobia and the start of a chronic, even pervasive, theme in Jewish sources of all periods.

2. Partners to the covenant are visibly blessed—that is, prosperous. Isaac sows and reaps "a hundredfold."

3. Outsiders to the covenant recognize the patriarchs' unique enjoyment of God's favor and despise them for it. Avimelekh, even when judged innocent, even after being visited by God in a dream, must nonetheless go on bended knee to the man who is not blameless in this situation, "because he is a prophet," and ask him to intercede with God! His own direct appeal would not be sufficient. "How can they not despise us?" the Hebrew text seems to say. "God is so palpably with us, and not with them."

4. And yet it is with them that Israel must live. It cannot be at home in its own land—God has decreed it so—and therefore must suffer the consequences of living as a stranger among the peoples whom it "blesses." The hosts either allow the patriarchs to live among or near them, thereby benefiting all concerned, and perhaps even form a pact of friendship at a safe distance; or

5. They take Pharoah's option, both in chapter 12 of Genesis and later, in the Book of Exodus, and expel those whom God has made "too big for us." The patriarchs enjoy both the divine protection which renders this mode of relation with the natives necessary (otherwise the hosts would simply oppress and exploit their guests) and the blessings—the wealth—which render such alliances efficacious.

6. Finally, the patriarchs are forced by these far from ideal circumstances into moral compromise. In contrast to the apparent sincerity of Avimelekh's plea to God, Abraham stammers in recourse ("And besides . . .") to the technicality that he had married a member of his own family who therefore could be counted as his sister. He has been caught in a lie—the least of the transgressions to which Israelites will be led by their lack of possession of the land, large numbers of people, and the power which these two confer.

The lack of possession is nicely revealed in the story of Abraham's purchase of Makhpelah, the cave in which he buries his wife Sarah. One can live in the land, "sojourn" there (cf. 17:8), without possessing it. To die in it, however, one needs an *ahuzah*, a holding, and so when Sarah dies, Abraham must negotiate the purchase of a grave property (*ahuzat-kever*) in which to "bury my dead from before me."[17] In a loving and lengthy recital of the negotiations, the text recounts Abraham's purchase of "Ephron's land in Makhpelah, facing Mamre—the field with its cave and all the trees anywhere within the confines of that field" (23:17). The detail is justified, for this is the only piece of land for which money ever changes hands between patriarchs and hosts in Canaan, with the exception (33:19) of the "parcel of land" on which Jacob pitches his tent near Shekhem.[18] Abraham's descendants will one day possess the land, so God promises, but in the meantime all they possess is one field on which to pitch a tent and the ground in which they return to God's earth. To the end, the text refers to Makhpelah as "in the field of Ephron son of Zohar the Hittite" (cf. 25:9, 50:13). The land which really belongs to Israel—here we recall Rashi's midrash—never really belongs to them.

Because it does not, the pattern of political and sexual relations described thus far only intensifies as the patriarchs' stay in the land continues. Two episodes in particular illustrate the art which the Israelites were forced to master. In the first (chapter 14) Abraham joins an alliance of local kings to rout invaders from the north who had just defeated the local alliance and in the process had taken his nephew Lot among their booty.[19] Abraham uses his 318 retainers to mount a guerrilla attack on the invaders, employing what little leverage he has to maximum advantage. He thereby earns the gratitude of his hosts, makes God's blessing manifest once more, and gains title to all the territory which he has liberated—the Promised Land of Israel.[20] Our attention is also directed to the fact that Abraham refuses to keep the booty which he has captured, graciously giving up what his meager power in relation to the local kings would never have permitted him to keep in any case. His prudence does not go unrewarded.[21]

The story of Dinah (chapter 34) reveals the consequences of *imprudence* and brings together, as no other episode in Genesis, the political and sexual consequences of residing as a small minority in other peoples' land. All three generations of patriarchs had managed to cultivate the careful distance from their hosts initiated by Abraham, apparently mixing with them as little as possible. The Israelites had joined their *adamot* to adjacent properties only in the two cases of Abraham's purchase of Makhpelah and the purchase by Jacob which now occasions Dinah's abduction. Intermarriage with their neighbors was out of the question.[22] What then are the Israelites to do when the son of the local chieftain rapes Jacob's daughter, then falls in love with her—and asks his father to arrange a union. "Give your daughter to us, and take our daughters for yourselves," he proposes to Jacob and his sons. "You will dwell among us, and the land will be open before you; settle, move about [alternatively: "trade"][23] and acquire holdings in it." Shekhem, the suitor, offers to "pay whatever you tell me." The proposed price is steep: if the locals agree to circumcise every male among them, "we will dwell among you and become as one kindred." The terms are accepted. The chief and his son return home, report to their townsmen, convince them of the advantages of the deal ("would not their cattle and substance and all their beasts be ours?") and, together with all the men of the city, undergo circumcision. Then, "on the third day, when they were in pain, Simeon and Levi, two of Jacob's sons, brothers of Dinah, took each his sword, came upon the city unmolested, and slew all the males. . . . The other sons of Jacob came upon the slain and plundered the town, because their sister had been defiled," seizing all the wives, children, and wealth of the city. Jacob's reaction is instructive. "You have brought trouble on me, making me odious among the inhabitants of the land . . . my men are few in number, so that if they unite against me and attack me, I and my house will be destroyed." To which the brothers reply: "Should our sister be treated like a whore?"

We note the occurrence of all the motifs of interaction already described. An act of Canaanite passion for a daughter of Israel disturbs the fragile equilibrium of established relations between "Israelites" and "Gentiles," and forces a new, less satisfactory, resolution. Sarah had received a "covering of the eyes" that served to conceal, by compensating for, her disgrace. In the case of Dinah, however, amends cannot be made. She has been defiled, and her shameful exposure serves to expose Israel's "nakedness" among the surrounding population. Jacob, moreover, cannot consider seriously the Canaanites' eminently reasonable, if self-serving, offer of alliance. He cannot settle and acquire holdings in this land, let alone intermarry, even if the financial consequences were not the loss of possessions to the host population that the latter expected. Partners to God's covenant cannot think of becoming one with people quite happy in their paganism. In making their offer, then, Jacob's sons either intended from the start to carry out their brutal attack or were counting on the fact that the Canaanites "will not listen to us and become circumcised, and we will take our daughter and go." Once the offer is accepted, they have but two choices: to swallow their pride, bear the shame of their weakness, and perhaps leave themselves open to future humiliations of the same sort; or to take revenge and suffer the consequences—perhaps counting on the protection which had been afforded their father and great-grandfather, and which indeed comes to rescue them here. "A terror from God fell on the cities round about, so that they did not pursue the sons of Jacob" (35:5). They have no choice, these children of the blessing.[24] God has set it up this way, and even He gets entangled in the skein, compelled to sanction—by His protection of the murderers—an act which shocks us (and, I think, the text) by its brutality. It is as if a God who works in history must take it as it comes, trapped in the dynamics which He Himself has set in motion. Even He comes to play a role in the demanding sexual politics of homelessness.[25]

Lords and Servants

In Joseph we come to the master practitioner of these politics of the alien; with his story all the elements of homelessness introduced thus far, both political and metaphysical, are gathered up and brought to a haunting climax. Once again the narrative takes us down to Egypt, speeded on its course thereafter by yet another famine. Once again an Israelite is sexually desired by a foreigner and demonstrates before a pagan king that he possesses divine blessing. Joseph, despised by his brothers because he is especially beloved of their father (37:4), only reenacts, within the family, the situation of the Israelites as a whole among the nations. They too are tolerated by their brothers on earth, despite resentment of their Father's special love, out of a combination of interest and fear; they too must bear the consequences, when their brothers' prudent restraint is overwhelmed by anger. Joseph rises from his pit to power beyond even his own ambitious dreams, and certainly beyond that of any other partner to the covenant. Yet the story does not end there. Genesis concludes with the foreshadowing of the slavery that Joseph's very success and blessing call forth. What goes up, in the political world that Israel plays in, must someday come down.

The ups and downs to which Joseph himself is subject are endemic to Pharaoh's court. One day the king is angry with two of his courtiers and throws them into prison. Another day—his birthday—he for no reason whatsoever "lifts the head" of his cupbearer, restoring him to favor, and "lifts the head off of" his baker, impaling him upon a pole (40:20–22). The pun highlights the farce. How can anyone survive and even thrive in such a setting? By keeping one's wits, seizing any opportunity which comes along, making oneself indispensable—and enjoying God's blessing. Joseph prospers.

He enacts the role assigned him in three discrete arenas. In Potifar's house, he is so manifestly successful, God is so visibly with him, that Potifar places him in charge of all he owns. As a result, he and his household and fields are blessed. Were Joseph's responsibility not complete, the resultant success could not have been attributed to him and him alone—and so to God. In prison the pattern repeats itself exactly. The chief jailer takes a liking to Joseph, puts him in complete control, and once again God is "with Joseph" and makes him successful. Finally, when Pharaoh sees the wisdom of Joseph's clever suggestion that a man "of discernment and wisdom" be given total charge of the land of Egypt in order to prepare it for the famine, Joseph is given that complete control and once more is able to demonstrate God's blessing. "So Joseph collected produce in very large quantity, like the sands of the sea, until he ceased to measure it, for it could not be measured" (41:49).

The moving story of Joseph's reconciliation with his brothers is less relevant here than the events (47:1–27) which follow their settlement, at Pharaoh's order, "in the choicest part of the land of Egypt," sustained by Joseph at a moment when "there was no bread in all the world, for the famine was very severe."[26] Joseph first amasses all the currency of Egypt in payment for the rations which he distributes. Then, the next year, the Egyptians beg, "give us bread, lest we die before your very eyes, for the money is gone." Joseph provides them with bread "in exchange for all their livestock." In the third year the Egyptians can offer only themselves and their lands. Joseph accepts, thereby "acquiring you and your land for Pharaoh." A fifth of every Egyptian's earnings would now belong in perpetuity to Pharaoh. Joseph also has the population "removed to cities, from one end of Egypt's border to the other." All of Egypt now belongs utterly and completely to its monarch, thanks to the divine blessing attendant on his chief minister. The text is brutally honest about his role in their enslavement. While all of Egypt is undergoing this suffering, the Israelites (so we learn in the very next verse) "settled in the land of Egypt, in the region of Goshen; they acquired holdings in it, and increased greatly in numbers."[27]

Joseph well understands the game into which he is thrust. From his side, as from Abraham's or Jacob's, the options are limited and unattractive. The very success which enables him to survive as an alien marks him as a man whom the powers that be can employ to their advantage. Egypt is not a democracy, after all. To serve its master means to exploit the subject population.[28] Not to serve him means, quite simply, to perish, or at best to be expelled, and Joseph could not go home to his brothers or their parched earth. He therefore serves his lord with a vengeance and, it appears, without second thoughts. He is not bound by notions of humanity to strangers in any case. If he could not eat with the Egyptians (43:32), he could surely not rely on them to protect him. Certainly the cupbearer had forgotten him quickly enough. He accepts the situation and masters it. The servant of his Lord in Heaven, and so an alien among those who do not know the Lord God, he acts the faithful servant of his earthly lord, in the belief that all which overtakes him is somehow part of a heavenly design beyond his comprehension. "It was not you who sent me here," he tells his brothers, but God. "And He has made me a father to Pharaoh, lord of all his household, and ruler over the whole land of Egypt" (45:7–8).

The consequences unleashed by Joseph's masterful success in the politics of exile follow in the text at once, at the start of the Book of Exodus. Joseph of course does not live to see them, or his homeland. He changes his name, gains a holding, marries an Egyptian woman, and names his first-born son Menasseh—meaning "God has made me forget completely my hardship and my parental home"—and his second son Ephraim—meaning, "God has made me fertile in the land of my affliction." Home for Joseph is not only innocence and childhood, but also "hardship" and pain. It is not a place to which he can return, but his longing for it continues nonetheless. His final request, ending the Book of Genesis, is to be buried there. Joseph comes home only in death—precisely the condition of the first man of whom Genesis told us, sentenced to wander until he returns to the dust from which he originally came.

Epilogue: "A Sign for the Children"

The book of Genesis finds in these stories of ancient Israelites, a people set apart from the rest of humanity by God's decree, a lesson concerning the estate of humanity as a whole. It is not only that this people, forced to endure the consequences of political exile because of its unique attachment to God, provides a model of the rigors facing all aliens, in every time and place. More important, the homelessness of this people which is never at home, even in its own Promised Land, is meant to instruct those who mistakenly believe they *are* at home upon their earth about the true estate of human beings. The home which Abraham's great-grandchildren are forced to leave behind—neither permanent nor secure—only recalls the Paradise from which Adam and Eve had been uprooted and in which they too had never been at home. In both cases, only the promise of home had been enjoyed, never the reality. It is this taste of home which the exiles carry as each leaves behind his particular point of origin. Home is a place, as yet only glimpsed from afar, toward which they are going, far more than a place from which they have come.

The existential or metaphysical components of homelessness are laid out at the very start of Genesis: expulsion from the childhood garden, alienation from the earth, and estrangement from other human beings—all three elements being united in the scattering or dispersion that is feared, and then incurred, by Babel's tower builders. Most of what we call civilization is a product of that homelessness. Home, by contrast, means rootedness in that soil which is our origin and destination, the *adamah* which is connected to— and so connects us to—the earth (*eretz*) as a whole, and thence to earth's heavenly Creator. Through the soil and its bounty God showers His blessings upon us, just as His wellsprings and rains originally watered the Garden. A fixed bond to the earth, therefore, means a continuing relation to God, in contrast to the sporadic encounters granted the patriarchs, always when they are wandering roads they have not chosen. Canaanites, ironically, are in this respect more blessed than Israelites.[29] The problem is that they do not know it, and in their ignorance attribute their earth's blessings to gods who do not exist. The sexual licentiousness which the text attributes to them is structually parallel to their misplaced gratitude for blessings of the field— an abuse of the other locus of divine blessing, the womb. In order to teach humanity the truth about blessing and ownership, God deprives Israel of a normal, continuing relation to blessing, much as He from time to time closes human wombs. Exiled from home, uprooted from their very own piece of earth, they can learn what has to be learned—the Source from which blessing, like earth, is derived.

In the meantime, there are famines—the most graphic reminder to those "at home" upon the earth that its bounty is not theirs to control. Famines highlight the link between the existential and political dimensions of exile, by collapsing the space in which the patriarchs and their neighbors had managed to live with minimal friction. Famine forces Abraham to descend to Egypt, and to sojourn in Gerar, compelling interactions with non-Israelites caused in other instances only by war or death. Isaac is forced to Gerar by another famine, and yet another—the most severe—sets the stage for Joseph's rise to power in Egypt and Israel's long sojourn there. Famine makes goods and property scarce. It thereby enables God to teach three lessons about the real estate of humanity, the knowledge of which sets the family of the covenant apart from all others.

First: property is as much the gift of God as the rains which make it valuable. What God gives, He can take away. The Canaanites are soon to lose what they seem to own; the Israelites will soon acquire what they do not possess. Rashi's opening midrash on Genesis is right on target.[30]

Second: the retention of property depends on how one uses it, even more than on the business acumen exhibited by Ephron the Hittite. "And they [the Israelites] shall return here in the fourth generation, for the iniquity of the Amorites is not yet complete" (15:16). That iniquity is unspecified, but it is presumably akin to the sins which brought on the Flood and the destruction of Sodom.

Third: property is therefore an improper basis for security. Even rootedness in the *adamah*—and so in the *eretz*—is not enough. One is obliged to live, as well, in covenant with God and in justice with one's fellows. Even Avimelekh of Gerar is made to testify to these truths in pleading his innocence before God. One needs, in other words, the commandments: an order to direct human intercourse with God and the conduct of human society. This too is the meaning of home. Genesis here directs us, once again, to the rest of the Torah.

The book's perception of imperfect human arrangements is acute. One could not ask for a more nuanced or soberly realistic reading of the uses and effects of power, in all its political, economic, and even sexual ramifications. Characteristically, however, it is in this very attention to localized interactions between particular hosts and their aliens that the text most directly reveals the existential concerns that underlie it. For power is ultimately control over others and their chances for life. It means the ability to take women as one pleases, and so to cause new life through them; to store grain and stop up wells—and so to give life or take it away. The granting of life belongs legitimately only to God and His agents, and so a text concerned above all else to drive that lesson home cannot but give attention to the ways in which power is experienced on the earth and distributed. Yet Genesis is far less concerned to delimit legitimate uses of power from abuses or to specify correct arrangements of human society than to describe the relations between relatively powerless Israelites and their Gentile hosts. For Israel will acquire the power to institute its own arrangements—and receive the divine legislation required to do so—only much later in its history and in the Torah. First the Sole Power must reveal Himself as Lord of History to all the world, by drowning Pharaoh and his host in the Red Sea.[31]

In the meantime, the text bespeaks resignation, both to the interim role assigned Israel while it awaits a homeland and to the games which a people in exile must play. It also evinces distinct devaluation of any political realm not guided by divine law. Other biblical texts too will take an interest in the political affairs of nations only insofar as these affect the destiny of Israel. The ups and downs of power are requited by God's raising up empires and causing them to fall; when Israelites appoint a king "like all the nations," they too come to be judged by the iron rule of history that he who does evil in the sight of the Lord will suffer His judgment sooner or later.[32] The only politics which the biblical text ever takes seriously are those directed, or engaged in, by God.

We see this nowhere more clearly than in the quintessential biblical book of exile—Esther, widely believed to date from the fourth century B.C.E. and to have attained its final form some two hundred years later.[33] The story occurs, and so manifests God's providence, outside the Land of Israel. More importantly, it reports, not without humor, on the methods by which Israelites of a later day than those of Genesis negotiate their survival as aliens without power. The hero Mordecai is introduced as one whose family had been "exiled from Jerusalem with the exiles who were exiled with Jekhanyah king of Judah who was exiled by Nebukhadnezzar king of Babylon" (2:6)—by no means accidental repetition in a laconic text. For Shushan is the very type of political exile, a place where one queen is disgraced because she refuses to entertain her drunken husband and his guests and another is crowned because she wins a beauty contest; where Mordecai is rewarded because the king has a sleepless night and Haman is hanged because he is outsmarted by Queen Esther—and his plea for mercy on her couch is mistaken for attempted rape. One day the Jews face extermination, and the next all of Persia is rushing to become Jewish (8:16). "For the fear of the Jews was fallen upon them" (9:4)—and the Jews are not slow to exploit this temporary and aberrant respite from the "Lottery" (the *purim*) to slay as many of their enemies as they can. The eternal foe Amalek, represented in the story by his descendant Haman, has been defeated but not vanquished. This is not the last time that a royal adviser will suggest that (3:8)

> there is a certain people scattered abroad and dispersed among the peoples in all the provinces of thy kingdom; and their laws are diverse from those of every people; neither keep they the king's laws; therefore it profiteth not the king to suffer them.

Nor is the story new: even the Jewish/Israelite queen, desired by the gentile king and brought into his household, has roots which we have examined. That it does not end here is a fact to which all too many subsequent "court Jews," palace intrigues, and persecutions have attested.[34]

The Jews of Shushan survive because of their cleverness and because of a great deal of luck ascribed in the text to the "Somewhere Else" ("Other Place") to which Mordecai would have turned directly if all else failed. Joseph too had had his hidden Protector, and in Egypt too the Lord of History had stood at a great remove from the events befalling Israel, and His intervention, while reliable, had been unpredictable. Genesis closes before the revelation of the Sole Power to all of Egypt, before the inheritance by Israel of its land, and before the giving of commandments intended to rejoin God and humanity in partnership upon God's earth. The rest of the Torah comes as a corrective to the condition of homelessness which Genesis describes. It does so, not by eliminating estrangement entirely, but by containing it within a sacred order—as the Torah contains the Book of Genesis.

We who read this first book in the context of the others know that the conditions it describes are temporary. Homelessness is origin, not destination. It, not home, is the estate Israel leaves behind. Even the four hundred years in Egypt soon pass, recounted by the Book of Exodus in precisely two verses. Canaan and Egypt are not lands on which to dwell. They are rather the history which Israel takes with it, as it leaves those lands behind. The Promised Land awaits them.

Yet the irony of the biblical text is of course that exile is *not* left behind. Shushan is yet to come. Israel's recurrent homelessness is foreshadowed at the conclusion to Deuteronomy, as the end to exile is promised in the final verses of Genesis. With this further widening of the aperture of our lens, we see that the home about to succeed temporary homelessness will soon prove temporary as well, a mere prelude to the continued exile recorded in the commentaries of Rabbi Isaac and countless generations of his successors. They saw in the narratives we have examined a foreshadowing (or even a prophecy) of their own wanderings, in which the people of Israel has spent the overwhelming majority of its years to date. Israel's exemplification of a universal human condition (homelessness) and its articulation of a universal human longing (home) do not end with the Exodus from Egypt. Genesis is more than a prologue to the drama; it is the first statement of all the acts to come. Not-yet-home remains the condition of Israel and the human species. "What occurs to the fathers," said the commentator Nachmanides, "is a sign for the children."

And yet—the final widening of the lens—the Messiah will come. Nachmanides, like his "fathers," could *wait* rather than merely endure because he stood convinced that homelessness too would one day prove temporary. Human beings would in the end of days be at home upon God's earth. The true depiction of the human condition comes not at the beginning, with exile, but at the end, with redemption; not in Genesis, but in Deuteronomy.

II

IMAGINING HOME
DEUTERONOMY

In Deuteronomy the people of Israel prepares to come home. The exile initiated by Joseph's descent into Egypt is about to end; the progress from Paradise to wandering recounted in Genesis will now be reversed, in the move from wilderness to Promised Land. Israel listens to Moses' discourse with its back to wandering, facing home, as from "the other side of the Jordan, in the land of Moab" (1:5), Moses tries to sum up what homecoming means and to differentiate it from mere possession of a piece of earth. Even this sort of home in the deepest sense can now be theirs. Israel has only to cross over the narrow river and walk a path marked out for it by God, and homelessness will come to an end.

The perfection of which Deuteronomy speaks, the unity of purpose which it urges, are expressed in the book's own composition and choice of language. Instead of a series of discrete narratives about a variety of characters, intermixed with reworked myth and genealogy, we have a single, sustained exposition, complete with introduction and conclusion. In place of the varied tones and rhythms of Genesis, Deuteronomy consists of a single narrative voice transmitting the words of only two speakers—God and Moses.[1] The cadences are measured, and the repetitions calculated. When Moses' long discourse finally gives way to poetry and then to silence, we have been prepared; the text has taken care to teach us about the nature and limits of its own language. Its title, after all, is *Devarim*—meaning "words," as well as "things." The unity of language and reality for which the text strives is a principal element in its vision of at-homeness on the earth.

Our analysis of Deuteronomy will follow its own threefold structure.[2] Chapters 1–11 of the book lay out in general terms the "way of *mitzvah*" (commandment) in which Israel is commanded to walk. Chapters 12–26 provide a detailed guideline of that path, tracing through the specifics of law—what must and must not be done—the lines which mark out this direction from all others. The final exhortations of Moses rehearsed in chapters 27–34 tell of the blessing in store for Israel if it keeps to the way— long life upon the land—and the punishment which will surely come if it does not. That curse, of course, is exile, and, the text tells us (31:16), Israel may well soon return to it.[3] Even before the people have crossed the Jordan, here on the far bank, God warns Moses, and so us, that the blessing will be short-lived. The homecoming so carefully prepared for, so long awaited, and so uniquely watched over by God will fail. We who hear these discourses of Moses today stand where the Israelites described in Deuteronomy stood at the original oration—outside the Land, awaiting home. In the final section of this chapter I will probe the implications of this enduring homelessness as they are worked out in other biblical and extra-biblical texts and show how the images of home and exile juxtaposed in Deuteronomy became the basis of all subsequent Jewish reflection upon the meaning of both galut and the Land.

The Way through the Wilderness

What Moses claims to offer Israel, on this "first day of the eleventh month" of their fortieth year since leaving Egypt (1:3), is nothing less than the chance to live a life such as the world has never known. The claim astounds us, and is meant to do so. It is as if Moses were to say: all that the world has known of life until now, all the riches of society and culture that your ancestors experienced in Babylon and you yourselves helped to build in Egypt—all this is as nothing compared with the life of *mitzvah* that you can now bring into being, in the Land awaiting you across the Jordan. Moses wants to strip the Israelites of the dress of culture and the pretense of wisdom, to rush by the settled comforts of their routines, and announce the ultimate facts of existence, heretofore unknown. "Hear now, O Israel," he declares. Listen well: for I'm about to tell you what Life is.

This is the reason for the repetition, here and throughout the book, of the four words *hear, live, mitzvah,* and *Land*. It is also the import of the reminder at the outset (4:3) of "what the Lord did in the matter of Baal Peor." Those who worshipped the idol were destroyed, while those who did not "are all alive today." They too will die—but after truly living. "Has anything as grand as this ever happened, or has its like ever been known?" (4:32) Never had human beings lived in a society of perfect justice, at one with their fellow men and blessed with God's own presence. Yet precisely this is promised to Israel. As real as the death of Baal Peor's worshippers witnessed by all the people, so real and more will be the life of perfection that Israel can come to witness across the river. As near as the site of degradation, so is the blessing that comes to greet them, if only they will leave "the valley near Beth-Peor" (3:29) and all it now stands for behind them.[4]

Already here, in Deuteronomy's opening verses, we are struck by the "wooing and imploring form of address"[5] that characterizes the book as a whole. Moses must persuade his people of the possibility of a life such as the world has never known, and only if Israel acts in the way he prescribes, persuaded by his exhortation, will that life ever come to be.[6] Yet language is the only instrument of persuasion available to Moses. He cannot lead them across into the Land, nor can he conjure up the memory of that new life, as he here conjures up the deaths at Baal Peor and the unheard-of events that have come to pass before Israel's own eyes since leaving Egypt. What has never been cannot be remembered—and neither can it be described. All Moses has available is his language, and yet his words will inevitably fall far short of the task assigned them, because it is impossible to talk convincingly about a state of affairs which no one has ever experienced. What do wholeness and meaning look like? What will it be like to be really, completely, at home? Even when stretched to their furthest limits, the words are inadequate to a life as new as that which Moses promises, and yet the possibility of ever living that life hangs on his ability to persuade his audience that what seems so impossible can come to pass. He will, therefore, "woo" and "implore" and cajole and threaten. Words are all he has.[7]

Like any other poet who seeks to construct a bridge between the known world available to memory and the as yet unknown world which exists in imagination, Moses falls back on simile and metaphor. As real as the deaths at Baal Peor, so the life to come; as wondrous as the victories over Og and Siḥon (2:26–3:16), so the triumphs yet to come in Canaan; as certain as the punishments visited upon you in the wilderness, so the rewards for "keeping the commandments of the Lord your God" in the Land. The new life breaks in on human existence from the outside, but it is neither totally unlike the past (if it were, all description would be useless) nor is it unprepared for. God has, as it were, made sense of the vision which Moses conjures— through His own words, breaking in upon Israel from the outside, in the form of His promises, His commandments, and His actions.

Because what Moses says makes sense only in the context of that divine speech, he recalls its several forms to mind before proceeding (chapter 5). Once and only once, at Sinai, God spoke to the human race "out of the fire," in the hearing of all Israel, and even then "you heard the sound of words but perceived no shape—nothing but a voice" (4:12). It would not happen again. Only by hearing *my* words, Moses insists, now and in the future—repeating them to yourselves, transmitting them to your children (16:4–9)—will God's only direct speech remain present in the world.[8] One hears and speaks the words by obeying them (the Hebrew word is the same: *shama*) just as one preserves the way of *mitzvah* only by observing it (this word too is the same: *shamor*). Israel's response to them, its own acts (*devarim*), continue the conversation begun through God's words (*devarim*) at Sinai. In fact, the primary *davar* which Israel is to speak is that mentioned in 4:32–33: its hearing of the voice of God. *Mitzvah* marks out the way on which such hearing is possible. To the "right and left" of it (cf. 5:29), in the "addition and subtraction" of it (cf. 4:2; 13:1), lie a wealth of experiences which testify that the hope of anything better than life-as-usual is a cruel delusion.

Such are the realities which govern the promise of homecoming. Fail to walk in God's way, consistently forget Moses' warnings, and the way will soon disappear, its traces obliterated like a path among desert sands soon covered by the wind (cf. 8:2–6). Walk the way, remember what Moses here teaches, and the actions which you do will be in perfect harmony with the only words that God has ever spoken.

Deuteronomy insists, however—indeed, this is one of its principal themes—that God speaks in another way than with words, namely through events of Israel's history (and the world's) which, given the proper interpretive tools, can be read as a text.[9] These discourses of Moses provide those tools. He therefore seeks to direct his people's vision by channeling their memory, referring again and again to the acts of God which confirm that the new reality he promises them has become possible. Remember, he urges, "the mountain ablaze with flames to the very skies, dark with densest clouds" (4:11). Remember that while testing you in the wilderness "to learn what was in your hearts," God fed you with manna, "of which you had not known and which your fathers did not know, so that He might make known to you that man cannot live on bread alone" (8:2–3). Note the repeated invocation of the word *know* here, as if to say: know now that you have only begun to know, that you can now know what has never been known before. Remember the little that you do know, so that you can learn more from the events which occur to you. Do not forget!

Israel's failure to remember or trust in the reality breaking in upon them, Moses reminds his audience (1:12, 19–45; 9:11–21), has until now been quite steadfast. The likelihood of future remembrance is no greater, and not merely because a "stiff-necked" people has particular problems in looking back. Daily life, the testimony of "eyes and heart" against which the Israelites are repeatedly warned, is simply too full of witness to the failures of divine intention and human striving. Moses has no choice but to recur to the few scraps of evidence that support his promise, relying for the rest upon injunctions to remembrance that are striking in their pathos (6:10–13; 8:11, 14, 18–19). Much of Moses' introductory speech, in fact, is a reminder of past acts of forgetfulness, designed to elicit an unprecedented sort of collective memory.

His strategy, we might say, is to endow every object and event in Israel's past, present, and future with ultimate meaning. Each is to become a symbolic pointer to the message which he wants Israel to recall. The symbols are all the more powerful because they are real: manna which one puts in the mouth, on which one lives, without which one dies; a way through the wilderness, scouted by God, without which the people are literally and fatally lost. All of Deuteronomy's way of *mitzvah* will attempt to be symbolic in this manner. It will try to impress meaning upon life through realities as tangible as male foreskins and boundary stones. Israel will only have to look about, at the facts it created in accordance with God's word, and the meaning of their lives will be apparent. No more will they need to rely upon mere words or ambiguous events to support their vision of at-homeness on their earth. They will find that vision inscribed on the concrete and specific actualities of who owns what, how justice is administered, what the eye sees and the ear hears. Daily experience will testify to the reality of the promise, and not against it. Theirs will be a poetry of law. Moses, from across the river, tries to draw upon the persuasive power of that poetry by filling the body of his discourse, which begins in chapter 12, with mundane details of how life is to be lived on the other side.

We cannot give more than passing attention to that legal blueprint, but should note several features which clarify its intent. First, the laws must prove faithful to the memories of Egyptian slavery and Sinaitic freedom which are repeatedly invoked to legitimate them. Since all facts are words, and so offer testimony to one vision of things or another, the facts to be arranged by *mitzvah* must testify to the possibility of the new life rather than against it. The existence of unfed widows and orphans, unjust judges, unpunished criminals or unabashed adulterers would in the text's view be more than a reproach to God. It would constitute compelling evidence that He was not present in Israelite society. "Business-as-usual" would prove that, as usual, religious preachments are one thing and the way of the world another. The order of *mitzvah* would demonstrate the opposite, enabling a man "to tell his son," on the basis of what he has seen with his own eyes, that life is serious, and God involved with His creation.

No longer will language chase vainly after perfection. Human beings will not have to "go up to the heavens and get it . . . that we may observe it," or "cross to the other side of the sea and get it . . . that we may observe it." Their own eyes will see it. Meaning will be "very close to you, in your mouth and in your heart, to observe it" (30:11–14). It will be on them, in them. Through them it will be in the world.

In many respects this vision is (in our terms) utopian. Moses never promises absolute perfection: poverty will not disappear, wars will still be fought, injustice will need punishing, false prophets will have to be discerned and resisted. Life will go on, and death interrupt it. Yet the vision presented in Deuteronomy is so far-reaching, the promise that it holds out so extravagant, that it is difficult not to consider Israel's entry into the Land as the start of true human fulfillment. The way through the wilderness had been no mere trek in uncharted ground, but a path of instruction fraught with lasting significance. The crossing of the river, similarly, will be no mere conquest. It will rather usher in the corrected relation of human individuals to God, each other, and the earth which the race had sought in vain since its parents left the Garden. In the Land of Israel God will be present, justice the rule rather than the exception, the harvests bountiful. An unprecedented and ongoing divine intervention in human affairs will guarantee Israel's victories, drive out its enemies, assure that there will be no scarcity of resources, and even raise up new prophets to govern according to the law code provided through Moses. Later messianic visions of Israel's return to the Land will be perfectly justified in modeling themselves on Deuteronomy's account of Israel's original arrival. This is no ordinary homecoming. With its accomplishment, as much of an end to human homelessness as there could be without leaving history and returning to the Garden will be at hand.

If this awesome attempt to alter the human condition is to be attempted, let alone realized, a space is needed in which the way of *mitzvah* can actually serve as the law of the land.[10] This is the purpose of the country now to be occupied, cleansed of previous inhabitants who had not fulfilled the intentions for which God had at one time given the Land to them (2:9–12, 20–23). So Deuteronomy understands possession of the earth. If the Land is witness to events out of keeping with its nature—if, for instance, it is forced to swallow blood shed by a murderer such as Cain—it "vomits out" the inhabitants responsible and makes way for a new set of human partners. So it will be with Israel. This, moreover, is no ordinary land. It is

> a good land, a land with streams and springs and fountains issuing from plain and hill, a land of wheat and barley, of vines, figs and pomegranates, a land of olive trees and honey; a land where you may eat food without stint, where you will lack nothing; a land where rocks are iron and from whose hills you can mine copper (8:7–9).

All this so that "when you have eaten your fill," you will "give thanks to the Lord your God for the good land which He has given you" (v. 10).

The Land's fertility, of course, is of basic importance here. It constitutes and signifies its blessing.[11] Still more important, the Land is so created as to lead one, if directed on the proper path, to bless the God who permitted one to inhabit it. Unlike Egypt, in which "you sowed seed, and watered it with your foot, as a garden of herbs," this land "flowing with milk and honey" in which "you shall drink of the rain of heaven," is one "which the Lord your God cares for always, the eyes of the Lord your God are upon it from the beginning of the year until its close" (11:10–12). Israel will not need to eke out a living through a man-made system of irrigation. Water—which is and symbolizes the possibility for life—will be abundantly supplied by God. This is a fact which has both existential and political implications. In place of an earth which testifies only to the human effort required to work it ceaselessly, in accordance with the curse of Adam, Israel will know an earth in perpetual contact with the divine, visibly blessed. In place of a life necessarily devoted to sheer existence, Israel will enjoy an existence freed for the privilege of Life. Abundant rain shall fall equally on everyone from heaven, rather than streaming through channels made and controlled by the Pharaoh. This is a matter of much more than symbolic importance. Whether one has a more or a less repressive social and political order is determined by the varying sources of life-giving water. Israel, blessed with God's rains, will be *His* servants. The Land's fertility both points to the way of *mitzvah* and makes it possible.

When the text wishes to speak about the intimate relationship between a particular Israelite and his or her land, it uses the more localized word *adamah* rather than the more general *eretz*—a distinction which we encountered in Genesis.[12] Israel shall "inherit the *eretz*" but shall enjoy "long days on the *adamah*" (11:8); it shall observe God's law in the *eretz* it inherits "all the days you live upon the *adamah*" (12:1; and cf. 7:13; 21:1). The very real plot of ground a farmer knows like an intimate friend, in daily interaction, serves to anchor God's promises so forcefully that the man knows himself and his life to be well grounded (cf. 11:13–17).

All of this stands in direct contrast to the depiction of homelessness which we examined in Genesis, and the details of that contrast bear repeating before we proceed to the legal code meant to accomplish it.

1. Most obviously, the punishment of wandering and exile will give way to "rest, settlement, inheritance" (3:20), and the lack of fear (v. 22) which goes with them (see also 12:9–10).

2. The perfect relation to the land disturbed by Adam and Eve and inaccessible to itinerant shepherds will now be restored to a pastoral Israel in its Land. The earth which brought forth food for Adam only with great difficulty, and for Cain and succeeding generations of wanderers not at all, will now bless Israel with its bounty so long as they live as they have been commanded. An ideal reciprocity between human beings and earth will thus replace the opposition incurred by Adam and Eve. Moreover, God will bless the "issue of your womb" as well as the "fertility of your soil." (7:13–14). Even sickness will vanish (v. 15)! The blessing which had set the patriarchs apart from others during their wanderings will now extend to the Land and to all of Israel in it, thereby setting it and them apart from all others.

3. Israel will therefore be able to bring God regular offerings, the first fruits of its harvests, at the site of His presence among them: the Temple. As opposed to the sporadic encounters granted the patriarchs, this contact will be institutionalized and so predictable. Instead of a variety of altars, Israel will now possess a Center, to which its own feet will testify in pilgrimages three times each year. This centralization of the cult is, as scholars have long pointed out, one of the principal innovations of Deuteronomy.[13] It is legitimated through a rhetoric of Israel's chosenness and God's uniqueness that seeks to make it inconceivable that the One God who has chosen this One people *not* be worshipped at one and only one location.[14] The existence of a Center, of course, only makes the contrast with previous wanderings that much more complete. It is Jerusalem: the midpoint on the northeast-to-southwest axis first described in Genesis. To be at home now means to be at or near that Center, and as such to have the security, the lasting name, the contact with Heaven, that the builders of Babel had sought in vain through their Tower.

4. Finally, where Genesis portrays no covenant-community beyond the family association of the clan, Deuteronomy sets in place a sophisticated political order. Israel will be the majority which sets norms of behavior

rather than the alien minority which accommodates to them. It will be able to enforce such norms in the only way that norms are ultimately ever enforced: with force. It will have power, and provision is therefore made to contain that power within the *mitzvah* it is meant to serve; in our terms, to specify the bounds of its authority. Israel's order, like any other, will be perpetuated by culture: commandments collectively observed, and remembrances communally reenacted.[15]

This is the substance of Deuteronomy's vision of home. Freed of the insecurity that is the wages of exile in the best of times, not to mention the slavery or total dependence that plague the victims of less fortunate exiles, Israelites will be able to devote themselves to living the ideal life described in Moses' opening discourse. "Rest from one's enemies round about" (25:19) is the external condition corresponding to security within one's borders and within one's self. The "fear of the nations" with which God will now protect all of Israel, as He once protected Jacob and his sons, leaves the nation completely responsible for the curse or blessing that comes its way. If Israel follows the direction set forth here, "rightness will be ours" (6:25).[16] This is as much a homecoming as humans who have eaten of the tree of good and evil, and for whom the tree of life remains forbidden, can ever know.

The Sacred Order

We cannot do more here than note several of the contours of that at-homeness. Indeed the text itself does not chart the way of *mitzvah* precisely. It only marks it, stakes out its limits, in the series of laws set forth in chapters 12–25. The full nature of the new life awaiting Israel will be fully known only once the people have begun to live it.[17] Logically enough, the first laws enumerated (chapter 12) concern idolatry. All altars found in Canaan must be destroyed immediately. This is the bare minimum required in order to bring the new life into being. The text, however, joins the proscription of idolatry to the prescription of centralized worship unknown to the rest of Torah, thereby seeking added legitimacy for its innovation. The second set of laws (chapter 13) follows naturally on the first, ordering strict punishment of anyone who urges Israelites to worship idols, while the third (chapter 14) prohibits such marks of idol worship as gashes and shaven foreheads, as well as commanding dietary restrictions clearly intended to distinguish those who worship the true God. These are the prerequisites of all that follows.

The tithing commanded next (14:22–29) is a further mark of Israel's service of its God rather than of idols, and also introduces the next set of regulations, which ensure that those without independent means are protected. Exile, the most powerful reality known to the Israelites, is repeatedly invoked in the text to urge justice and even generosity for those who will be defenseless among them.[18] The blessing promised as reward (15:6) is that "you will extend loans to many nations, but require none yourself; you will dominate many nations, but they will not dominate you." The blessing, as always, is tangible and bespeaks awareness, as always, of the political and economic dimensions of exile.

Following the observances of the three pilgrimage festivals,[19] a fourth set of laws deals with the various authorities charged with enforcing the new order: judges, kings, Levites, prophets, and the community as a whole (charged with the punishment by stoning of idol worshippers). Each command enumerated seems both necessary to the workings of the order which Deuteronomy envisions and symbolic of the intention of the whole. It is not hard to understand why a person who moves a neighbor's boundary marker is not only culpable (19:14) but cursed (21:17). Boundaries are the essence of Deuteronomy's enterprise.[20] Nor is it surprising that false witnesses are severely punished (19:16–21) or that witnesses to idolatry must themselves cast the first stones used to execute the idolaters (13:10). The people of Israel are to be God's witnesses on earth, builders of an order which enables human beings not to witness the sort of behavior prevalent heretofore.

The code as a whole, through its direction of political, economic, and sexual relationships, seeks to reverse the conditions which were Israel's lot in exile. Egypt, the archetypical location of that exile, is often explicitly recalled in order to prod Israel to attainment of the opposite experience. Its blessings will be in contrast to the "diseases of Egypt" now to be visited upon Israel's enemies (7:15); strangers will of course be treated differently than they were in Egypt; the land itself is compared favorably to Egypt (11:10–12); the king must not take the people—even physically—on the road which leads there (17:13). Israel is even forbidden to abhor the Egyptian, as opposed to Ammonites and Moabites who refused to help Israel on its march home, "for you were a stranger in his land" (23:4–8). The years of enslavement are not remembered here, only the preceding generations of proper treatment under Pharaohs who did "know Joseph." Again: Israel's collective memory is carefully structured by Deuteronomy, so as to reinforce the new reality it wants to bring into being. That is why the enumeration of the laws to govern Israel's homecoming concludes with the paradoxical commandment to remember to forget the most abject consequence of its former homelessness (25:17–19): "Remember what Amalek did to you on your journey, after you left Egypt." The only way to blot out Amalek's memory, while remembering to do so, is so utterly to transform reality that a world in which the weak are mercilessly cut down becomes a distant memory, as distant as the dream of a world in which the weak are protected now seems from across the Jordan. This is the far point of Deuteronomy's vision, the "inheritance of the land" which it is so careful to distinguish from mere arrival or possession (cf. 6:10–17; 6:18).[21] Until it happens, the Israelites will not really be at home.

Moses concludes this section of his discourse with a description of an Israelite for whom such a complete homecoming has become a reality (26:1–15), the quintessential text, in all the Torah, for the biblical vision of the end to exile. He speaks, in future perfect tense, of what it will be like to have known the perfection which at this moment can barely be imagined. The language used to capture that future realization, like the blessing of the Israelite described, is full to overflowing. He will take his first fruits, go to the Lord's chosen Center, and acknowledge that he has seen God's promise fulfilled. As the priest sets the offering on the altar, the Israelite will recite the whole history of Israel's wandering and homecomings. "My father was a wandering Aramean," he will begin,[22] the word for "wandering," *avod*, recalling countless previous usages in Deuteronomy such as those commanding the "destruction" of pagan altars, or threatening Israel with "loss" and "destruction" as punishment for forgetting God's commandments.[23] This Israelite will remember. His ancestors went down to Egypt, God freed them from oppression, and now God had brought them "to this place and given us this land, a land flowing with milk and honey. Wherefore I now bring the first fruits of the soil which You, O Lord, have given me." Similarly, having set aside the third-year tithe for the Levite, the stranger, the fatherless, and the widow (cf. 14:28–29), the Israelite will be able to declare before God that he has done so. "I have not transgressed your commandments. And I have not forgotten!" Therefore, at one with his land and his fellows, the Israelite can be at home with his God, and pray—for himself, his fellows, and the Land. "Look down from Your holy abode, from heaven, and bless your people Israel and the soil you have given us, a land flowing with milk and honey, as you swore to our fathers." His prayer is that the order continue, not that it be established against all expectation. This is the climax of Deuteronomy's vision, the language of a person who is at home upon the earth.

Images of Curse and Blessing

We learn at once that the vision may not be destined for realization; the measured prose which had intoned the laws, and reached its poetic highpoint in the speech of fulfillment just described, now careens out of control, heaping invective upon hyperbole upon repetition in an attempt to capture the possible consequences of the loss of direction to come. Following a set of curses aimed at individual Israelites who perform particularly disgusting acts in secret (misdirecting the blind, subverting the rights of the stranger, sleeping with one's father's wife, etc.) and so are to be punished as individuals (27:15–26), Moses details the blessings and the curses which Israel as a whole will pronounce upon itself—first in a ritual ceremony on two mountainsides and then through the actual living of their lives (chapter 28).

The fourteen verses of blessing are informed by all the images of home which we have encountered in the Torah thus far. The fifty-four verses of curses draw upon the counter-images of homelessness stored up in Genesis, and, no doubt, upon the people's historical experience. The blessings are overwhelmed by the curses: not only outnumbered but outstripped in the concreteness and vitality of the imagery employed. Deuteronomy's tranquil and reticent prose is utterly routed by the fury with which Moses apparently hopes to cow his listeners into obedience. His blessings must prove adequate to the imagined peace of a daily life in which none is afraid—a hard enough task. His curses, however, must compete with all the terrible history that Israel has known heretofore.[24]

The images of both blessing and curse demand careful attention. Blessing is, first and always, fertility: of oneself, one's flocks, and one's crops. This blessing shall rain upon the Israelites everywhere ("in the city and in the country") and always ("in your comings and in your goings"). It confers, secondly, superiority over enemies who threaten it. Because of God's blessing, by which "all the peoples of the earth shall see that the Lord's name is proclaimed over you," the nations will stand in fear of Israel. God's chosen will be creditor not debtor, head not tail, top not bottom. These are the only two sorts of blessing mentioned. Both amount to the promise of life itself. Fertility and security provide the opportunity to live the new life, superimposed upon biological life, which possession of the Land will make possible. The rewards of that life are not detailed. God provides only the space for the endeavor through a secure and fertile Land. He is the Lord of history and the Lord of nature (the two roles corresponding to the two sorts of blessing) but not, apparently, the master of individual or collective will.

The curses which counter these two aspects of blessedness are lengthily— almost lovingly—elaborated. As opposed to fertility everywhere and always, of womb and of soil, there shall be barrenness (vv. 16–19). As opposed to health, there shall be sickness—a veritable plenitude of diseases, enumerated one by one. As opposed to a land whose rocks are iron and from whose hills one can mine copper (8:9), "the skies above your head shall be copper and the earth under you iron" (v. 23). Rather than "rain for your land" (v. 12) God "will make the rain of your land dust, and sand shall drop on you from the sky, until you are wiped out" (v. 24). The balance of power between Israel and its enemies will be reversed (vv. 25–26, 43–44).[25]

All of this is bad enough, but the text does not stop. It proceeds to a series of images of Israel's situation of loss and wandering and destruction, hammered home by repeated use of the root *avod*. The images are unforgettable, precisely their point. "Your carcasses shall become food for all the birds of the sky and all the beasts of the earth, with none to frighten them off" (v. 26). Four plagues suffered by the Egyptians shall be visited upon Israel: boils (v. 27), darkness (vv. 28–29), locusts (v. 38), and death of children (v. 53), in addition to the pestilence (v. 21) which will have driven them out of their land. Soldiers once exempted from military service because they had built but not dedicated a house, or planted but not reaped from a vineyard, or engaged but not married a woman (cf. 20:5–8), shall now find these curses of nonfulfillment to be their lot (28:30). Israelites who had inherited cities they did not build, cisterns they did not hew, and vineyards they did not plant (cf. 6:10–11) shall now see their crops devoured by insects and by the strangers in their midst (28:38–40, 49–52, 43–44). From homeland Israel shall return to exile (v. 36), from a blessing among the nations to a "proverb and a byword" (v. 37) of the fate every nation has prayed most fervently to avoid. Worse: Israel shall fall so far from its privileged station above other nations that it will be lower than all others. It will degenerate to the status of animals, and even less than animals, for would animals "eat their own issue" (v. 53)? The prose is brutally bitter here, using black comedy to drive its arrows to the heart. The most tender and fastidious of Israelite males shall be too selfish to his own brothers—to share the flesh of his children! The most tender and fastidious of women, so dainty "she would never venture to set a foot on the ground," shall begrudge her own family "the afterbirth that issues from between her legs and the babies she bears" (vv. 54–55). Israel will once more be the "scant few" which were to be recalled, as a distant unpleasant memory, in the credo of the day of fulfillment (26:1).

The curses culminate with one last reminder of their essence: exile, scattering "among all the peoples from one end of the earth to the other"— the curse of Adam and Eve, of Cain, of the tower builders. As if this too were not bad enough, there is a further sentence: return to worship of gods of wood and stone unknown even to Israel's ancestors (v. 64). The punishment of idolatry is idolatry.[26] Israel will have no peace, no rest (v. 67). The litany is not even mitigated by the promise in Leviticus's parallel text (26:14–45) that God despite it all will not abrogate His covenant with Israel or destroy them; a remnant shall return to the Land. Deuteronomy's *tokheḥah* (reproof) closes rather with the stern warning that God Himself will do what had been prohibited so strictly: He will send Israel back to Egypt (v. 68). Because Israel had not believed sufficiently in the possibility of the new life, life itself will come to seem unreal (v. 66).

When these verses are read in the synagogue, they are chanted as quickly and as quietly as possible, in accordance with an age-old Jewish tradition which testifies to their power. Moses, for precisely the same reason, waxes long and loud. His situation is desperate. His language must cease where his feet do, on the Jordan's far side. He can climb the mountains of Moab and peer with extraordinary vision into Canaan, but when he has seen all that the eye of faith can see he must fall silent and be "gathered to his fathers." Hence the final plea: the way of *mitzvah* is not in the heavens, or beyond the sea, but in your hearts, close to you (30:11–14). Why would Israel *not* follow it? Who would not "choose life!" (vv. 15–20). Moses says all he can say, does what he can do, and dies (34:5), perhaps knowing with future readers of Deuteronomy that it has not been enough.

Epilogue: Return to the Wilderness

The verses which transform this threat of renewed homelessness to an awful certainty (30:1, 31:16–18) and then follow that prophecy with the promise of return to the Land (30:2–10) may or may not represent a later strand added to the text in the wake of the Babylonian exile in 586 B.C.E.[27] We can say with some assurance that our text consists of two parts: a seventh-century B.C.E. document which legitimated or perhaps even stimulated the sweeping reforms undertaken by King Josiah and a later "frame" which set the work in place as the keystone of the much larger "Deuteronomistic" history of Israel.[28] However, the blessings and curses which one might attribute to the later strand, as a sort of after-the-fact "prediction" of the Babylonian exile, are now held by some scholars to belong to the original. The whole cleverly follows the form of ancient Near Eastern treaties of vassalage binding earthly servants and their lords,[29] and even the specific curses threatened for violation of the treaty represent a borrowing from a foreign source.[30]

It is not impossible, then, that the original text reasoned from the conditionality of God's promises and the frailty of human nature to the belief that the far-from-perfect people of Israel would fail in its unprecedented endeavor, be punished (as always, with exile), and be graced with the chance to try again. If so, Deuteronomy would not be the only blueprint for an ideal society undermined (and lent added profundity!) by the awareness of its own futility.

Socrates too recognizes that his language is inadequate to the Republic which he seeks to describe, for his audience has "never seen our words come true." He too concedes that "to produce a different type of character, educated for excellence on standards different from those held by public opinion, is not, never has been, and never will be possible." Yet to change public opinion one must "wipe the slate of human society and human habits clean." The most he can maintain, therefore, is that "some chance" or inspiration of "providence" will accomplish what no mere mortal could; that is not an impossible hope. It is reasonable to believe that

> Whether it be in the infinity of past time, or in the future, or even at the present in some foreign country beyond our horizons . . . the society we have described either exists or existed or will exist. . . . No impossibility is involved.[31]

"It is not in the heavens," Deuteronomy insists, "neither is it beyond the sea"—and Deuteronomy, unlike Socrates, can count on direct divine assistance. But, as the text tells us, it does not happen.

For our purposes, the debate over the text's provenance is unimportant. What matters crucially is that when Deuteronomy's promise of destruction and exile came true in 586 B.C.E., its inclusion in the Deuteronomistic history of God's salvation and judgment of Israel provided both explanation and reassurance. What seemed inexplicable—how God could permit and even decree that His temple be reduced to ruins and His people utterly defeated by idolaters—made sense in the context of a punishment preordained for a given crime from the beginning. If God and not Nebuchadnezzar stood behind the Babylonian victory (cf. Jer. 29:1, 4), there was hope for future victory and restoration. "He will bring you together again . . . will gather you, will fetch you" (Deut. 30:1–10). God's promise to restore the people to the Land once occupied by "your fathers" could now be read to refer to the literal fathers recently exiled as well as to the patriarchs.[32] By drawing lessons from the two wanderings of Israel's tribal and national past—that of the patriarchs and that of the desert generation—meaning could be imposed on this latest expulsion from the sacred Center.

All Jewish reflection on homelessness and homecoming from the time of that exile until the modern period, including the rabbinic refinements which we will survey in the following chapter, are confined within the framework of explanation and imagery first erected by Deuteronomy. By establishing a vision of home which countered and developed the "negative" set forth in Genesis, then allowing the promised blessing to be routed by a renewed curse of homelessness consisting both of native and borrowed imagery, and, finally, concluding the whole with a promise of future return, Deuteronomy made its model for society in the Land the indispensable guide for reflection and life outside it. The substance of that legacy needs further attention.

First and most crucially, when the prophets and "Deuteronomistic" authors sought to understand Israel's exile—using the verb galoh and its derived nouns golah and galut, all unknown to the Torah[33]—they without exception associated exile and dispersion with divine displeasure. "What happens to the parents is a sign for the children"; there was a lesson to be learned from Adam and Eve, Cain and the tower builders, and the patriarchs. Especially in works dating from the years of exile and return (Jeremiah, Ezekiel, Deutero-Isaiah, Ezra) the people of Israel was repeatedly told to reason back from the punishment of galut to the crime and prevented from pleading ignorance of the law by reference to God's commandments. Israel knew the path and had strayed from it nonetheless. God had chastised them and would return them to their Land. Jeremiah urged acceptance of the punishment, Ezekiel looked forward to its nullification, Deutero-Isaiah urged that Israel "prepare a way in the wilderness" for its Redeemer, and Ezra described the redemption which had come to pass.

The most obvious comfort of such a reading of history was that exile became more bearable, both because it was meaningful and because it was temporary. The book sent by Jeremiah (29:1) "to the elders of the golah and the priests and the prophets and all the people whom Nebuchadnezzar had exiled from Jerusalem to Babylon" begins with the words of "the Lord of Hosts, the God of Israel, to all the golah which I exiled from Jerusalem to Babylon" (v. 4). The subject of the verb makes all the difference in understanding the meaning of the exile. God could forgive as well as punish. Jeremiah is told that God looks upon Israel as upon the "good figs" which He had shown the prophet in a vision. "I sent them from this place to the land of Kasdim for the good. I have set my eye upon them for good, and I will return them to this land. I will build them, not destroy; plant them, not uproot" (24:4–6).[34] Hope was thus a reasonable option, and waiting bearable.

Less obviously, perhaps, such a vision of return to the Center helped future generations to locate themselves on the periphery and to find meaning there. In spatial terms, they did not stand in chaos if they knew which way to look. By remembering that Israel was not at home, the people could recall its reason for being in the first place, and understand its reason for being where it was—in exile.[35] Israel, sent back into the "wilderness," had not been removed from order altogether, in this Deuteronomic-prophetic reading of its situation. Neither had it been removed from one center to another. It had, rather, been exiled from *the* Center and placed on an outlying periphery still subject to divine supervision.[36]

Moreover, since this *midbar* conjured up, through the very usage of the word, the "memories" of a previous national journey through the wilderness, the current exile was also delimited *temporally*. True, God had often punished Israelite transgressions in the desert, but He had also fed the people with manna, given them His Torah, and led them into the Land. Conflation of this exile from the Center with the wandering that preceded the Center's construction thereby enabled the people to regard its current estate as an interruption which would soon end in renewed blessing. As God's care for Israel in the previous wilderness had demonstrated, He— unlike all other gods—did not cease His activity or lose His power of protection outside the borders of His people's Land. Wilderness became a time and place of trial, a sort of *rite de passage*, a purging through destruction and dispersion.[37]

This led, in turn, to a certain "spiritualization" of Deuteronomy's symbolic yet concrete conceptions of home and homelessness.[38] Exile and its opposite are never equivalent to displacement from or possession of the Land in the Torah. From the very beginning, they represent states of being and states of affairs as well as political relations and conditions. From here it is but one short step to Deutero-Isaiah's usage of the imagery of home and homelessness—thirst, barrenness, wilderness, water, harvest, blessing—to depict a *personal* emptiness or poverty of soul which God could revitalize.[39] Much later, Qumran's sectaries quite logically combined the two usages. They saw the wilderness as the only refuge for those seeking ritual or ethical purity[40] and endowed it with all the symbolic associations stored up by tradition. But they also lived in that very real wilderness and recognized its distance from the Center. Not so Philo, whose Promised Land was entirely a spiritual construction. Abraham's entry into Canaan meant only his initiation into "fruitful wisdom".[41]

A second problem which beset later reliance upon Deuteronomy's schema, more serious than the spiritualization of home and homelessness, was that its vision of the covenant at times seemed to promise too much. The extraordinary attempt to contain every societal institution and historical event within a sacred order of divine significance rendered remaining "cracks" in that edifice all the more threatening. And the vision of a God at work in history, when reality seemed to outstrip Deuteronomy's curses in its brutality, rendered the promise of eventual return inadequate. Less patient souls were driven to apocalypse. We will have more to say of this connection between exile, messianism, and apocalypse. For now we note that Deuteronomy's careful balance of memory and hope, poetry and law, seems for the most part to have "worked." The structure which it designed remained standing; the meaning which it promised, even if inadequate, somehow sufficed. Israel clung to the conviction of its covenant with God, learning to conceive of its estate as a midpoint between origin and destination. The original home in Eden, the first wanderings of the patriarchs, the generation of the desert all lay behind. The final home imagined by Deuteronomy lay far ahead.

So long as Israel possessed the Land during the several centuries of the second commonwealth, then, its relative achievement of rest and security pointed beyond itself toward the absolute fulfillment as yet unattainable. Whatever social, political, and economic orders that Israel constructed were held accountable by some to a standard of perfection—true homecoming—which the nation could not meet, even as the nation's achievements were contrasted favorably with the idolatrous "ways of the Gentiles." And when Israel was sent into exile once more in the year 70, its Temple sacked and its population decimated, the rabbis provided a larger frame for Deuteronomy's message, examined in the chapter which follows. Through this new set of interpretive lenses, collective remembrances, and societal institutions, Moses once more found himself addressing an audience outside its Promised Land. "Just remember well," he reminded them through commentators such as Rashi and Nachmanides, "God stood by your ancestors. He has been present with you in the wilderness. He will one day bring you to the Land. In the meantime sustain yourself on His word, locate yourself on His way, direct yourself towards His center, practice yourself in His command-ments." God's involvement remained indisputable, even if His providence, as always, could not be fathomed. The people would come home one day. In the end, Deuteronomy's vision of order, and not Genesis's depiction of homelessness, would prove the accurate measure of human destiny. In the meantime, Israel would have to be sustained by Deuteronomy's guide to their homecoming, one which contained within itself—and so compre-hended—the bitter reality of their long exile.

III

HOMELESS AT HOME AND ABROAD

AVODAH ZARAH

The mishnaic tractate Avodah Zarah, formulated in the aftermath of the Jews' forcible return to exile,[1] makes no explicit reference to the disorientation and destruction reflected in its pages. It does not announce that the wanderings in Genesis have again become the inevitable lot of the patriarchs' descendants. It does not tell us that all too many of Deuteronomy's curses have once again become inadequate to the facts. It neither mourns nor consoles nor "explains." And yet it does: if we probe the book's attempt to order Jewish interaction with idolaters and their ways—to accommodate, in other words, to a reality which according to Deuteronomy should long ago have been extirpated—we find sustained and serious reflection on the people Israel's new experience of Jewish exile, inside the Land where that exile was meant to end once and for all. In the Gemarra which comments on the tractate—composed over several centuries' further experience of galut, primarily outside the Land—all the pain and doubt buried beneath the surface of the Mishnah are raised to the surface and fully exposed.[2]

Both the pain and the doubt were particularly acute, one suspects, because the renewed exile in which the rabbis found themselves was in three crucial respects without precedent.[3] First, the traditional "explanation" first offered by Deuteronomy and the prophets seemed inapplicable. Even if this galut, like all those recounted in the Bible, was "a punishment for our sins," those sins certainly did not include idolatry this time around, and were not, as in the past, readily apparent. The schema of homecoming-idolatry-exile-return could not be invoked without a major effort at reinterpretation, which was indeed forthcoming.[4] No less important, the extent of the exile in geographic space was without parallel in Jewish history. In the Second Temple period, sizable Jewish communities had arisen and flourished throughout the Mediterranean world and Asia Minor, as well as in some points beyond. With the decimation of Judea as a result of the two revolts against Rome—punishments which, unlike God's, required no effort at interpretation—and the perilous economic conditions of Palestine there-

after, Jewish life was geographically scattered as never before, further removed from the Center in the Promised Land. Finally, the latest exile
threatened to be unique in its duration over time. When the Bar Kokhba
revolt failed in 135 to reverse the conditions created in 70, the analogy to
Israel's first exile failed along with it. This time the Jews would not return
after half a century. In fact, it soon became clear, they would not return
anytime in the foreseeable future, but only with the distant coming of the
Messiah. Exile, therefore, could no longer be seen as a mere interruption of
Israel's divinely assigned homecoming. Rather, it was Israel's brief span
upon the Land which had to be regarded as an interruption—of exile. Home
came to seem a momentary foretaste of fulfillments which would be realized
only when historical time came to an end, or in the next world, beyond space
and time altogether.

This life, in this time, was for waiting. The world was hopelessly out of
joint and history a jumble, or at best a cipher the hidden meaning of which as
yet escaped discernment.[5] Those who should have been punished for their
wickedness reigned triumphant over half the world. Those who proclaimed a
false messiah remained unrebuked by history. Those who served God,
meanwhile, had once again been sent into exile, the Temple in which they
offered Him sacrifice once more reduced to ruin. The city destined to be the
center of His kingdom was desolate of Jewish inhabitants—and He too had
once more been "forced" to abandon it, and the Land, to join the people of
His covenant in exile. Exile, indeed, had become co-extensive with the
world itself, in crucial respects which we shall examine embracing even the
Land of Israel in its stranglehold. This was proof positive, if proof were
needed, that sense could not be made of such a predicament. The rabbis of
course had to try nevertheless, and, even more important, to resist.

The principal strategy which they devised for doing so represented a
change from any undertaken previously in Jewish history, a definition of
Torah at once contracted and enlarged. Mitzvah's sacred order could not be
imposed on the Land under present circumstances, let alone outside it. Yet
the rabbis had to ensure that that order survived the destruction of its own
underpinnings. Their solution was the Mishnah and the way which it marked
in the wilderness that surrounded Jews; a code which, in Jacob Neusner's
words, "responded to the profound disorientation of defeat and destruction"
by the imagination of a world in which the Center held true and firm.[6] That
response is clear in the tractate before us, as it had to be, for in Avodah
Zarah, idol worship, the rabbis confronted head-on the locus of both their
problem and their punishment. They lived in a world given over to idolatry
and the abominations it spawned, and their task was therefore the carving
out of a time and space which—however fragile, however contracted—
would enable Jews to live in the only earth that God had provided. Avodah
Zarah does precisely that in its five chapters of thou shalt's and thou shalt
not's, the rabbinic way in the wilderness. The rabbis could not reconquer
their Land from its foreign invaders. But they could and did discriminate the

pure from the polluted, holy from profane, we from they, to the degree that circumstances permitted. They sought to etch into Jewish minds and the landscape of Israel such borders as could be true and firm in an age when, as Neusner writes, "nothing was more ubiquitous than violated boundaries." They would save what could be saved of the holiness of Israel's Holy Land: its fields and mountains and trees.

The Gemarra of the Babylonian Talmud, like the opening and closing chapters of Deuteronomy, then framed this law code with reflection upon the questions which the rabbis sought through their Mishnah to answer. It thereby rendered explicit the earlier text's unspoken rationale. The Mishnah's reticence, largely carried over in the Palestinian Talmud formulated inside the Land, is utterly exploded in the teachings collected in Babylonia. Doubt is not only articulated but shouted—the better to parry and contain it; pain virtually leaps off the page, amid anger and fury reminiscent of no biblical text so much as the curses of Deuteronomy, here heaped on the nations which had cursed Israel with exile. And inside the frame of this explication, the rabbis continued the strategy pioneered in the Mishnah for coping with the contracted space provided for the orderings of the Torah: namely, the expansion of Torah's domain to every pocket of sacredness, every "small sanctuary," which could be constructed by Jews in their wanderings. If every Israelite could partake of the priesthood and transform every table to an altar, sacred order would be not only possible but widespread. Deuteronomy's project would thus be carried on in a situation far different from the one which it described: not a wilderness on the way to a Center but a Center reduced to wilderness, a "desert" full to overflowing with idolatry and impurity, and as wide as the world. The task of carving out sacred order, moment by moment and inch by precious inch, could not possibly succeed, short of the Messiah for whom the rabbis waited. They could pray only that it did not entirely fail.

The "Reconquest" of Space and Time

The Mishnah begins, logically enough, with demarcations of those moments and inches: the definition of Israelite time and space.[7] It is forbidden to do business with idolaters for three days before their festivals: to lend money or accept payment of debts. The relevant holidays are specified and the proscriptions on trade detailed. If idol worship takes place inside a city, one can do business outside; if the idol worship is on the outside, one can do business inside. If a road leads only to a place of idol worship, a Jew may not set foot anywhere upon it; if the road leads elsewhere as well, the Jew may walk it.[8] If only some shops are decorated for a festival, the Jew can do business in the others—as indeed happened once, the text relates, in Bet Shean (1:1–4).

How does one live as a Jew in a world—indeed, a land of Israel!—

pervaded by that which precludes Jewish life and the elimination of which, in Deuteronomy, is the prerequisite for the order which follows? The answer is by drawing boundaries—by seeking, insofar as possible, to delimit a Jewish time and space into which idol worship and its attendant impurity do not intrude. The attempt can only be partial—and so, to a degree, pathetic. The world is what it is, after all, and Jews must live there. Rabbi Ishmael's suggestion that Jews cannot be parties to trade for three days after idol worship (1:2) is rejected, because, one suspects, it would have prevented Jews from making a living. The point, we remember, is to *live* in this polluted universe. Rules about which roads lead where and how shops are decorated represent a similar adjustment to necessity. Such guidelines are hardly foolproof. They are only the best of the bad alternatives. Compromise, inherent in the very enterprise of demarcation, is evident too in the list of appurtenances to idolatry which Jews may not sell to Gentiles on *any* occasion. White cocks used for sacrifice may not be supplied. But if a white cock is included in a set of other fowl it is permitted (1:5). One might have suspicions about the use to which the cock will be put. These must be ignored; it is pointless to demarcate the Jews out of existence.

At the chapter's close, the logic underlying these regulations, and their pathos, are articulated clearly. Jews are not permitted to join in building the courts of law in which they are sentenced,[9] the platforms from which they are judged, the scaffolds on which they are executed, or the stadiums in which so much that is abhorrent to them occurs. They can construct the relatively innocuous public and private bathhouses which they, like their enemies, frequent. "But when they reach the vaulting [niche] where idols are set up—it is forbidden to [help them] to build" (1:7). A line must be drawn, and this one is certainly much further along than the rabbis would have liked. If God had not permitted His chosen Land of Israel to be conquered, let alone polluted, none of this would have been necessary. As it is, they are forbidden to sell a Gentile "anything attached to the soil" of Israel, lest they acquire still more land and complete the Jews' exile (1:8). And yet—the question inevitably occurs—was the intent of these prohibitions not already defeated before the effort of the Mishnah began? Has the divinely owned land of Israel not been profaned beyond foreseeable repair?[10]

In the tractate's second chapter we find that the rabbis, forced to live surrounded by aliens in their own land, reacted to the outsiders much as their ancestor Abraham had in a similar situation. Cattle may not be left in the inns of Gentiles, lest the latter abuse the cattle sexually.[11] A Jewish woman may not remain alone with Gentiles, for they "are to be suspected of sexual immorality." A man may not remain alone with them, since they "are to be suspected of shedding blood." Israelites may not have their hair cut by Gentiles, except, according to Rabbi Meir, "in public domain," where passers-by would observe any foul play (2:1–2). The parallel to Genesis is precise. Most chilling of all, perhaps, Israelites are forbidden to assist in the propagation of these dangers to their well-being. An Israelite woman "may not assist a gentile woman in childbirth, since she would be helping to bring to birth a child for idolatry" (2:1–2). As modern readers we cringe. That a calm and dispassionate text should come to throb with such raw and awful judgment upon its neighbors enables us to gauge the anguish underlying the Mishnah's patient and seemingly routine delineations of yesses and no's, shalt's and shalt not's.[12]

Chapter Three turns to the nature and realities of idol worship themselves, imparting detailed information which Jews, if all were right with God's world, would never have known or needed to know. Rabbi Meir would prohibit Israelite traffic in all images, since all were worshipped at least once a year; the majority of the sages, however, draw a wider circle. "Only that is forbidden which bears a staff in its hand or a bird or a sphere," and so itself supports the presumption that it is actually used for worship. Fragments of images may be reused by Israelites for other purposes, unless the fragments themselves be objects of worship, in the shape of a hand or foot. If a shard bears the figure of the sun or moon, it must be thrown into the Dead Sea. Rabbi Yosi's suggestion that one shatter the object and scatter it to the winds is rejected, for then some Israelite might unknowingly end up using it for manure (3:1–3).

Again, the problems are obvious. Coins too bore forbidden images, rendering the famous question to Jesus inevitable and provoking the likely rabbinic response: giving unto Caesar what is already his; in other words, using the coins despite their impurity. Moreover, the very hills and trees of Israel had become objects of idolatrous worship. Could Israelites now make no use of their earth itself, the Land given them as a blessing? Lines had to be drawn, compromises resorted to. The hills were permitted, but what was on them was forbidden (3:5). A tree planted especially for worship (called an *asherah*) could not be used by Jews for any purpose. A tree trimmed for use by idolaters could be used, after the fresh sprouts had been pruned. Even the shade of an *asherah* could not be used to help grow vegetables, except in the rainy season when such shade was superfluous. Jews could not sit in that shade or pass under that *asherah*. Such contact rendered the Jew unclean.

Both the logic and the pathos of these details are highlighted by a remarkable story placed in their midst (3:4).

> Proklos the son of Philosophos asked Rabban Gamaliel in Acre while he was bathing in the Bath of Aphrodite, "It is written in your Law, and nothing devoted [to idolatry] shall cleave to your hand. Why [then] do you bathe in the Bath of Aphrodite?" He answered, "One may not answer such questions in the bath." When he came out, Gamaliel said, "I did not come within her limits; she came within mine! People do not say, 'Let us make a bath for Aphrodite,' but 'Let us make an Aphrodite as an adornment for the bath.' Moreover, even if they offered you a great deal of money you would never agree to appear before your goddess naked, or after suffering pollution, nor would you urinate before her! Yet this goddess stands at the mouth of the

gutter and all the people urinate right in front of her! It is written, 'Their gods' only; thus what is treated as a god is forbidden, but what is not treated as a god is permitted."[13]

The explanation is convincing, and yet it is not. True, Aphrodite's presence in the bath is incidental to its purposes, and popular behavior in the bath could hardly be said to be appropriate to her putative divinity. However, such niceties were not evident in Deuteronomy, nor do they mitigate the prohibition of Jews helping to build the very niche in which Aphrodite sits in her splendid irrelevance (recall 1:7). The ruling that "what is not treated as god is permitted" contradicts the previous interdiction on the use of image-bearing pottery, even for manure. Gamaliel's logic carries the day, perhaps, because there is simply no alternative: Israelites must bathe. More importantly, his assertion of Israelite sovereignty over the polluted Land of Israel ("she came within my limits") is essential to Jewish survival.

Chapter Four's listing of the ways in which idols can be neutralized (vv. 5–6) is thus an exercise in wish fulfillment, the details lovingly elaborated in order to provide imaginary satisfactions impossible to achieve fully in reality. "If a Gentile cut off the tip of its ear or the end of its nose or the tip of its finger, or battered it . . . he has desecrated it. . . . If he spit in its face, or made water before it, or dragged it about, or threw filth at it, he has not desecrated it," because the idol can survive, as it were, to fight—and so fight the true God—another day. An idol abandoned in time of peace—wish of wishes!—is permitted for Israelite use; one abandoned in time of war, under duress, is not. One senses the pathos here, as an infinity of idols, their number constantly replenished, mocks the efforts of the One God and his One People to free their Land and His world of pollution. The task simply cannot be accomplished.

Only as the tractate reaches its conclusion (the only remaining concern being traffic in wine, used routinely by Gentiles for libations) is the question underlying all of these many rulings given clear voice, and answered as well as the facts allow (4:7). "They asked the [Jewish] elders in Rome"—the very center of the world out of joint, the anti-center of Jerusalem—"If God has no pleasure in an idol why does He not make an end of it?" The rabbis' response to this most basic of questions is notable for its awareness of God's own predicament. Should God put an end to the sun and the moon, because some people are stupid enough to worship them? "Shall God destroy His world because of fools?" Why not then, the Romans retort, destroy those objects of worship *not* needed by the world? "We should but confirm them that worship them, for they would say 'Know ye that these are [true] gods, for they have not been brought to an end.'" God is once more caught in a web of his own devising.[14] In the desert, He could not destroy Israel lest the nations conclude that He did so because of His inability to save them. Now, He cannot destroy idolatry, without at the same time confirming it, or else destroying His entire—and "very good"—creation.

The Mishnah can only live with the consequences of that divine entrapment. It moves, in a final series of prohibitions, to draw bounds around the use by Israelites of wine which Gentiles might have offered—with a mere flick of the wrist—as a libation to their gods.[15] Variations on the theme are many, and seemingly all of them are rehearsed by the Mishnah (4:8–12, 5:1–6). One stipulation in particular rivets our attention: if libation wine is mixed with water, or libation water with wine, the whole is forbidden only if the forbidden liquid has imparted flavor to the whole (5:8). The parallel to Israel's larger dilemma is precise: how to be "bathed" in gentile "waters," surrounded in its own Land by gentile ways, without acquiring a gentile "flavor" and becoming essentially other. To do so would preclude Israel's very existence as a people consecrated, in purity, to God.

The tractate ends as it had begun: with legal detail rather than outcry or attempted explanation. Gentile utensils must be cleansed before use by Israelites. One must scald those customarily scalded, making "white-hot in the fire" those normally treated in this way. "A spit or gridiron must be made white-hot in the fire; but a knife needs but to be polished and it is then clean." Except for the several moments of self-conscious reflection which we have noted,[16] the tractate bears out Neusner's generalization about the language and the substance of the Mishnah as a whole: "an orderly, repetitious, careful, precise document in both language and message. It is small-minded, picayune, obvious, dull, routine—all the things its age was not."[17] Other texts of its time and place reacted to the chaos of destruction with apocalyptic visions, or cries that men would have done better not to be born rather than witness what their generation of Israelites had been forced to see. Still others took the loss of God's Temple and David's city as a message that a new era for the Jews had arrived, their law supplanted by a surer path to meaning and salvation.[18] The Mishnah proceeded quietly: elaborating "grey areas" and "excluded middles," erecting boundaries and insisting "that there are distinct spatial domains, the reality of which is invoked by the advent of the holy day."[19]

Before proceeding to the further employment of this strategy—and its articulation—in the Gemarra, we should briefly review its four principal elements, all of them evident in the tractate before us. First, and most important, pure would be demarcated from polluted, insofar as this was possible in circumstances of pervasive pollution unaccounted for in Deuteronomy's call to sacred order. Second, the rabbis took for granted and reiterated the imputation of immorality to idolaters encountered in the stories of the patriarchs. Trade with Gentiles would proceed, because it had to. But neither man nor woman nor beast of the congregation of Israel could be left unguarded, even momentarily, in the presence of the gentile host. Third, the rabbis implicitly conceded what Jews knew all too well: that they too would be tainted in and by this world gone mad. The compromises forced upon them were inevitably arbitrary, and always insufficient. Israelite minds meant for other and higher things would be forced to master the intricacies of idolatry, so as to avoid entrapment in the wide net which they cast. Israelites *in extremis* would be driven to extremes of obsessive concern with the tiniest drop of Gentile wine, fearful of the havoc which it could wreak on their fragile order. Finally, the rabbis conceded through their speculations and their silence that the explanations which had hitherto served would no longer suffice. God had not abandoned either Israel or the world, but He had surely absented Himself from Aelia Capitolina, once known as Jerusalem. His voice was still audible in scripture, but it no longer animated prophets of consolation. Indeed, even in the tractate's own pages, the Lord is directly quoted only a mere half dozen times (1:9, 2:5, 3:3, 3:4–6).[20] The rabbis could not give up on history entirely, but they would not expect very much good from it any time in the near future.

The upshot was that Israel stood alone as never before, even if God continued to dwell among them in their wanderings.[21] They had been punished in the traditional manner—with destruction, dispersion, and exile—but without the traditional comforts of explanation. Sacred order would therefore have to be improvised, in both homeland and diaspora, until such time as the situation at the Center was more propitious.

The World Turned Right Side Up

The talmudic tractate Avodah Zarah highlights all that the Mishnah had subdued, releasing the fantasy and fury that the Mishnah had "recollected in tranquility." It does *not* begin with direct commentary on the Mishnah's first pericope. Instead, as a sort of Genesis to the Mishnah's "Torah," or Mosaic prologue to its Deuteronomic code, the Gemarra seizes on the key word of the Mishnah's opening stipulation in order to tell the stories, and ask the questions, around which all its later exposition turns. The questions reduce to one: why has God allowed all of this to happen? The stories imagine the day when it all will end—with the oppressors begging for God's mercy and Israel, along with its Land, restored to glory. By the conclusion of the text—some one hundred fifty pages later—much has been articulated but little resolved. I will not attempt to summarize those pages, even schematically. Rather I will focus on three points at which the rabbis' strategy for orienting Israel in its dispersion is especially pronounced.

Again, we begin at the beginning. The Gemarra's initial reflections are occasioned by the double meaning of the word used by the Mishnah to denote idolatrous festivals. *Ed* with an *ayin* means a "witness"; *ed* with an *aleph* denotes a calamity. When would "the day of their calamity [be] at hand," as prophesied in Deuteronomy 32:35? When would the idolaters be ordered to "bring their witnesses [testimonies] that they may be justified" in their ways before God (Isa. 43:9)? The rabbis imagine the scene. "In times to come" Rome would be called to account and plead before God that all it had done was "only for the sake of Israel, that they might [have leisure] for occupying themselves with the study of the Torah." God, however, would discern the pagans' real motivation and punish them accordingly. "All that you have done, you have done only to satisfy your own desires." Next Persia would step forth, the empire which had redeemed the first exiles from Babylonia and sheltered many of the second from Rome. Yet it too would be punished, offering the same excuse before the judgment seat only to depart, like Rome, "crushed in spirit." So it would be with all nations, leading them to protest collectively that the Judge was unfair, because they had never been offered the Torah which set Israel apart. True, God would reply, but the nations had not even observed the seven precepts of Noah which He *had* given them.[22] How could they have coped with 613? (A.Z. 2b) Had Israel observed the Torah? the nations retort. Yes—as Nimrod, Laban, Potifar's wife (all witnesses to the patriarchs' blessing),[23] and Nebuchadnezzar himself are forced to testify. Finally, the nations would plead for a second chance, and fail miserably when it was granted (3a), thereby provoking the laughter of God. "Said R. Isaac: 'Only on that day is there laughter for the Holy One, blessed be He!'" To which the words of R. Aḥa are later added: God has not laughed since the destruction of His Temple (3b).

A blacker comedy than this could not be imagined. The vision is the very picture of *ressentiment*, climaxed by the powerful image of divine laughter at the discomfiture of Israel's enemies. Jews mired in pathetic powerlessness imagine Romans reduced to pathetic argument, powerless before God's judgment. All the good which gentile nations had performed, and from which Israel had benefited—the building of bridges and roads, markets and baths—is nullified by attribution to desire, lust, which in the Jewish mind rules all that the ruling powers may do. The cultural attainments of gentile civilizations are simply not mentioned. What is more, the very texts of apocalypse so palpably ignored by the Mishnah—principally the Book of Daniel—are drawn on liberally by the Gemarra to anchor in scripture the graphic details of its Inferno.

Woven amid and through this negative image is its "positive," the rabbinic this-worldly Paradiso of Torah. The rabbis attest to the reward which comes of Torah's study (even in a time when such study was punishable by execution)[24] and lovingly resolve apparent contradictions between scriptural passages which, not coincidentally, bear directly on the matter at hand. The Psalms and Ezekiel, for example, speak of God's abundant and glorious power, but Job observes that He does not always exercise it. Isaiah asserts that "Fury is not in Me" while according to Nahum, "The Lord revenges and is furious." God will, the rabbis infer, seek the nations' destruction, *pace* Job, and "visit upon [Israel] all [its] iniquities," as Amos had taught, because "you only have I known from all the families of the earth." God *was* "angry every day," as the Psalmist had written, but "how long does His anger last—a moment. And how long is a moment—one 53848th of an hour is a moment" (4a). It would soon pass.

(The Palestinian Talmud, we might note, takes a somewhat different approach, but to much the same effect. It focuses on the idolatrous excesses of Jeroboam, the rebellious first monarch of the northern kingdom, thereby turning attention to past idolatry by *Israelites*, also committed inside the Land. But the lessons to be learned are the same: first, that just as Jeroboam the idolater had been punished with destruction, his population deported from the Land and scattered, so it would be with the Land's current idolatrous rulers, and how much more so; second, that just as Israel had been forgiven that sin—crime and pardon both recalling the Golden Calf— so this generation too could expect forgiveness—and return.)

Until that occurred, however—until exile gave way once more to home-coming—Israel could take consolation not only in its future revenge against the nations but in the present continuing blessing of the Torah. The opening speculation on the past dynamics of Israelite transgression and divine pun-ishment—(in *both* Talmuds)—offers additional comfort. Finally, in the con-cluding verses of this passage (3b), the text provides perhaps the soundest advice of all for enduring exile. In order to study the words of the Torah, "one must cultivate in oneself the [habit of] the ox for bearing a yoke and of the ass for carrying burdens."[25]

Having constructed the frame in which Israel's present experience of idolatry could be contained, the text proceeds to elaborate on the Mishnah's demarcations of prohibited from permitted. Why *three* days? Suppose for-bidden business has already transpired? What festivals precisely are we talking about (5b–8a)?[26] Succeeding sections alternate between law and their "frame": between commentary upon the Mishnaic code and attempts to answer its underlying questions. Where must the line be drawn? How widely must the net of safeguards be cast? "Said Abbaye: we should be particular not to place a stumbling block before [the blind], but we need not be so particular as to avoid placing it before one who may place it before the blind" (14a; see also 15b).[27] The rabbis distinguish, too, between good Gentiles and bad,[28] permitted and forbidden partners. One should not sell idolaters bars of iron, lest they make weapons out of them. "Why then do we sell it now? Said R. Ashi: [we sell it] to the Persians who protect us" (16a). History was fluid; the boundaries could not be made hard and fast.[29] The parallel issue of where to stop when building a basilica then takes the rabbis (16b) to a lengthy and fascinating exposition of their principal dilemmas in which sex and politics, as in Genesis, are intertwined inextricably. We shall examine it in some detail.

R. Eliezer, we are told, was once arrested for *minut* (heresy, i.e., Chris-tianity) by the Romans and brought to judgment in the local basilica. Speculating on the sin which might have led God to punish him with this double ordeal (arrest by Rome, on suspicion of being a Christian), Eliezer recalls (17a) a conversation with one Jacob of Kefar-Sekaniah—apparently a disciple of Jesus—in which he approved of a teaching offered by Jacob in the name of his master. The scriptural passages at issue are crucial: "Thou shalt not bring the hire of a harlot . . . into the house of the Lord thy God" (Deut.

23:19); "For of the hire of a harlot hath she gathered them and unto the hire of a harlot shall they return" (Mic. 1:7); and "Remove thy way far from her, and come not nigh to the door of her house" (Prov. 5:8). Both heretics and the "ruling powers" are then associated by the rabbis with harlotry, and indeed imagery of sexuality and whores fills the succeeding pages of this Gemarra to overflowing, along with details of atrocities committed by the "ruling powers" against Israel.

I will cite only several examples. Two daughters cry from hell, "Bring, bring!" Who are they? "*Minut* and the government." Next: a warning from scripture that "none who go into [a harlot] return, neither do they attain the path of life" (Prov. 2:19). Then: a tale of R. Eleazar B. Dordia, who "did not leave out any harlot in the world without coming to her." Next: the story of R. Ḥanina and R. Jonathan, out walking one day until they come to a fork in the road. One path leads to a place of idol worship, the other to the door of a harlot. One rabbi proposes that they choose the former because idolatry poses no temptation; the other insists that they defy inclination "and have our reward" for doing so. The harlots withdraw at their approach. This tale is followed at once by an account of the arrest and execution of rabbis Eleazar b. Perata and Ḥanina b. Teradion (17b–18a) which leads back, in turn, to the story of Rabbi Meir's sister-in-law, who apparently had been kidnapped to a brothel. The section concludes (18b) with renewed consideration of Israelite boundaries (could an Israelite enter a stadium?) and sustained commentary (18b–19b) on a single verse of scripture: "Happy is the man who has not walked in the counsel of the wicked nor stood in the way of sinners, nor sat in the seat of the scornful" (Ps. 1:1).

The choice of verse was of course not coincidental; it perfectly articulated the crux of the matter. It is a verse problematic in any age when the righteous suffer and the wicked prosper—in other words, in any age. It must have strained Israelite credulity even more in this one. For this people, so obsessively concerned *not* to walk in the counsel of the wicked, stand in any idolatrous road, or sit still for any contact with false worship, was nonetheless unable—even by stretches of its considerable imagination—to describe its condition as happy. As R. Simeon b. Pazi expounded the verse, "'Happy is the man that has not walked,' i.e., into theaters and circuses of idolaters, 'nor stood in the way of sinners'—that is he who does not attend contests of wild beasts." The rabbis are not without answers to the awesome question of theodicy which they raise here. Homilies of reward and punishment abound: "He who scoffs, affliction will befall him. . . . He who scoffs will fall into Gehannah [hell]" (18b). But no reply is as powerful as the question itself, and the rabbis' only real response, once again, is to extol the delight of meditation on God's Torah, day and night (the following verse of the psalm which they have cited). A long excursus on that verse returns the text (19b) to the original issue: how much of a Roman basilica could a Jew legitimately build, before he had to stop and draw the line.

The tone throughout these pages is matter-of-fact. Even when describing how Ḥanina b. Teradion was wrapped in the Torah and burned at the stake, the narrative is tranquil—like Ḥanina, one infers, who calmly faced, and even converted, his executioner. Yet these are matters concerning which the rabbis were far from dispassionate. The quality of the prose does not so much belie the intensity underlying it as lend further credibility to the portrait of Israel's oppression which the text presents. Talk of the enemy turns—inevitably, as it were—to sex and violence, and to the two together. "At once they sentenced him (Ḥanina) to be burnt, his wife to be slain, and his daughter to be consigned to a brothel" (17b). This imagery reaches its climax outside our tractate, in the horrific report (Gittin 56b) that Titus "took a harlot by the hand and entered the Holy of Holies and spread out a scroll of the Law and committed sin upon it."[30]

The imagery of prostitution is endemic to our text for several reasons. Most obviously, it is the principal prophetic metaphor for idolatry, employed on numerous occasions to excoriate Israel for its "whoring" after false gods. It is also, we recall, the locus of traditional stereotypes of the Gentile. Idolaters, as the Gemarra proceeds to demonstrate, are people in servitude to gods of their own creation, i.e., to their own desires. Devotees of homosexuality, buggery, and adultery, tyrannized by their own passions, are not free to serve the eternal God—and cannot qualify as reliable moral agents. Their conduct is prima facie suspect, despite examples of the righteous Gentile. The only safeguard left Jews, in such society, was retreat into Torah: wrapping themselves in its parchment, as Ḥanina did, even unto death. In its study the satisfactions and confirmation unavailable in the external world were secure. In its commandments lay protection against the animal urges, "the serpent's venom" to which Gentiles not reined in by law were prone.

No less important, the sexual potency of the idolater, highlighted in rabbinic depictions of Roman depravity and prostitution, corresponds to the oppressor's actual power in another domain: the political. The relation between the two is familiar to any attentive reader of Genesis, and goes beyond the sad truth that political domination often translates, sooner rather than later, into rape. Take for example the marvelous story of Raba (65a), who one day found his gentile friend Bar-Sheshek "up to his neck in a bath of rose water while naked harlots were standing before him." "Have you anything like this in the world to come?" he asks Raba. We have something better, the Jew replies: a future world without fear of the ruling power. Bar-Sheshek, protesting that he has no such fear even now, is interrupted by a summons to the king. "May the eye burst that wishes to see evil of you," he salutes Raba on departure—at which his eye promptly bursts. Even a seeming friend could not be trusted, if he were a Gentile—perhaps because he has no fear of the true Ruling Power.[31]

If even Bar Sheshek has good cause to fear the ruling power, how much more so the Jew—and how much less, since in the world to come the Jew will be rewarded by the True Power and Bar-Sheshek will not. The defini-

tion of paradise as a refuge from fear of the empire is searing. Not coincidentally, the tractate ends with a tale of a good king, so good that he ritually
cleans his knife ten times in the soil before using it to slice a citron for a
Jewish visitor. Why did you not do so for me, protests another Jew? " 'Of him
I am certain that he is observant [of the Torah],' the king replies, 'but not of
you.' According to another version he said to him, 'Remember what you did
last night!' " (76b).[32] Here reward for virtue comes even in this world, from
its ruling power, in the form of citron sliced in purity by a king. The
Gemarra closes, then, with a tale belying the reality which necessitates its
entire discussion and is so evident throughout that discussion; a reality, in
other words, where the ruling power is brutal rather than kind and the true
Ruling Power unaccountably absent. The real world was rather one of
prostitution—not of the faithfulness possible only with covenant.

Prostitution is linked thematically to yet another immediate concern of the
rabbis: intermarriage. When one sage suggests that Gentile beer is forbidden "because it might have been left uncovered," another gives the reason
as "because of marriages" (31b), a rationale then taken up in the subsequent
discussion (32b) of why Gentiles' milk, bread, oil, and other products are
prohibited. Various reasons are given, and disagreements on the subject
rehearsed, until it is said (36b) that the prohibitions are intended to reduce
intercourse between Jews and Gentiles. The rabbis had legislated "against
their bread and oil on account of their wine, against their wine on account of
their daughters, against their daughters on account of another matter, and
against this other matter on account of still another matter." Eating with
idolaters would lead to drinking with them; that barrier crossed, Jews would
be more likely to marry them, and whereas the Torah had only prohibited
marriages with the seven Canaanite nations (recall Rebecca's concern about
Jacob marrying a Hittite), the rabbis (like Ezra) had acted to bar all such
liaisons, with ample scriptural precedents now cited. The reasoning is
straightforward: intermarriage would likely involve adoption of the spouse's
gods or at least their presence in the house, and to avoid that possibility the
rabbis draw the line at an "earlier" stage of Jewish-Gentile relations, the
sharing of food and drink.[33] Such precautions, for a people struggling to
maintain itself as a minority, were not illogical; and they were still more
important because of the rabbis' hope of making every Israelite a priest,
every table an altar. Purity would have to be pursued actively, now that it
could not be achieved routinely. Control of sexual liaisons, when they could
lead to marriage and when they could not, was instrumental in that effort.

One matter, however, is still unclear—the nature of the "other matter"
and the "still another matter," and its resolution brings us back to the point
at which we began.

> What is the meaning of the phrase used above? . . . R. Nahum b. Isaac said:
> They decreed in connection with a heathen child that it should cause defile-
> ment by seminal emission so that an Israelite child should not be accustomed
> to sexual relations with him.

Bread and oil led to wine, wine to marriage, marriage to idolatry (the first "other matter") and idolatry to the illicit sexuality which the rabbis believed to be part and parcel of gentile life, and utterly detested. The subject is then discussed matter-of-factly (37a). "From what age does a heathen child cause defilement by seminal emission?" Boys from nine years and one day, girls from three.[34]

It is possible, of course, that yet another factor was operative as well. It could be that the rabbis caught a glimpse of their own lower selves in the actions which they attributed to their oppressors, as Plato says a normal person does when dreaming,[35] and that they recoiled at what they saw. Saul Lieberman has argued convincingly that idolatry offered no temptation to the rabbis;[36] it is unlikely, therefore, that fear of *that* attraction in themselves, or the guilt resulting from it, lay behind the anger directed at those who permitted such desires to be satisfied. This might not have held true of *sexual* desires, however, as the tale of R. Ḥanina and R. Jonathan states explicitly. Still: it seems more reasonable to assume that the rabbis' fear of and repulsion at the Romans had a more direct source. The conquerors had killed huge numbers of Jews, often with great cruelty. They had reduced Jews to slavery and prostitution. If the rabbis proved unequal to their task, the Romans would succeed in killing Jewish faith as well. Small wonder, then, that death and sexual desire—linked since the first crime and punishment, in the Garden—were very much on the rabbis' minds. Small wonder, too, that the first instrument of that punishment, the serpent, is itself an obsession in this section of Avodah Zarah.[37] Nor is it coincidence, finally, that wine—ever linked to sexual licentiousness and idolatry—should be the other overwhelming concern of the tractate. Some forty pages of text (55b–75b), a quarter of the whole, are devoted to exposition of the mishnaic restrictions on libation wine. For a tiny drop, a mere flick of the wrist, could subvert the rabbis' long and painful effort at sanctification of their world. In sum, this cluster of images dominates the pages of Avodah Zarah both because they had always been associated with idolatry in Jewish tradition and because the forces symbolized by them and the anxiety which they engendered dominated the time and space in which the rabbis lived. Unable to control the forces of assault, the rabbis struggled to name them and to build boundaries against them.[38] Imagination is marshaled in these pages— as in the Mishnah and Deuteronomy—in the service of law.

The third discussion which we should note comprises the textual and substantive center of the tractate: idol worship itself and how to cope with it. Much of the commentary on the Mishnah here is routine. Difficult lines are drawn and redrawn and reinforced. The heart of the matter, as in the Mishnah (4:7), is the response given by Jews to Romans who wondered why God put up with such a world if He really despised idolatry—God could not destroy His earth because some of His creatures had utterly corrupted it temporarily. The Gemarra amplifies this response, but proves unable to improve upon it. In fact, its own questions seem to multiply.

Why does stolen wheat, when sown, sprout just the same? If a man has intercourse with his neighbor's wife, why does she conceive? The world pursues its natural course, the rabbis reply, but fools will one day render an account.

Another: Why does God punish the idolaters instead of the offending idols? Response: is it the idols' fault if some people are foolish enough to worship them?

The notion that idolatry is part of the world's "natural course," that justice is not forthcoming, is abhorrent to the rabbis' fundamental convictions. And yet, it seems, so the world turns—upside down. "And as for the fools who act wrongly, they will have to render an account." Someday, but not yet. The rabbis can only understand the postponement of that judgment by recourse to a poignant divine dilemma. Either God would repeatedly interrupt history and nature, suspending both His own laws and human freedom, or idolatry would persist and Israel suffer as a result. The rabbis are aware, I think, that a philosophical resolution to their dilemma will necessarily elude them. Their answers are in the end clever but unavailing. Yet, after all, it was not they who had created the difficulties; and so, it is reasonable for them to conclude, resolution of those difficulties would have to come from "some other Place." They could only resist. To be a Jew was to be other, separate, holy; in short, to be in exile from all the reality there was.

Avodah Zarah is an exercise in facing the abyss, so as to avoid falling in; in constructing a fragile and shifting guardrail, wherever possible, so that Jews could live at the precipice with some impunity. The rabbis could not turn the world right side up. They could not depose Roman rulers, establish the jurisdiction of Jewish courts, or restore the Temple to its glory. All they could do was protect the purity of Israelites who followed their lead by eating, drinking, having sex, and marrying in accord with the rabbis' own comprehensive regulations. For the rest, they relied on imagination to set right, through fantasy, what no amount of demarcations could salvage. Their time and their place—their exile at home and abroad—allowed no more.

Epilogue: Somewhere Else

The rabbinic reconception of galut which we have just examined, no less than the rabbis' reshaping of Jewish life as a whole, remained authoritative—indeed, virtually unchallenged—until Emancipation both loosed Jews from the bonds of their tradition and promised to redeem them from the woes of exile. All subsequent developments occurred within the interpretive framework which the rabbis defined; wandering after banishment after destruction was viewed by later commentators in accordance with the method pioneered in the first several centuries after the destruction of Jerusalem and its Temple. A survey of these developments is impossible here, for it would involve nothing less than a history of Jewish exile itself. I will focus only on several salient features of the medieval and early modern reinterpretation of galut, proceeding in terms of the three principal components of the rabbis' achievement: their recognition that exile consisted of both the interrelated dimensions which we have termed "political" and "metaphysical"; their association of homecoming to the Land with the fulfillment of Torah; and, finally, their pronounced ambivalence concerning the Land's centrality— the fact that memory of and aspiration for the Land paradoxically made possible and meaningful a life lived somewhere else.

Avodah Zarah sustains the tragic sense that we encountered in the opening stories of Genesis and the conclusion of Deuteronomy: the knowledge that home is a place one looks back to and forward to, but never actually inhabits except briefly. God too, in rabbinic texts, is somewhere else, even if He could also be near at hand. His image, contrary to what pagans believed, could not be domesticated, and his recurrent visits—whether to individuals or to peoples—were not without terror. All the truly important questions, the rabbis knew, could never really be answered, but only rehearsed. Jews, as adults long gone from the Garden, might bemoan this state of affairs, and did, but they could not alter it. In another world, perhaps, things would be different.

Yet for the rabbis, as for the Bible, galut was more than this universal *condition humaine*. It was also the political estate of a particular people: their exile in and from a particular piece of earth, their political and sexual subjection to the whims of earthly lords. Each dimension of exile was bound up in the other; indeed, political homelessness was feared, in large measure, because it exposed Jews to the metaphysical exile from which rootedness in a state and its soil offered a degree of protection. The roots of "exile" and "uncovering" are in fact identical in Hebrew—*galoh*—and while this may not be significant etymologically, it does point to the significance of exile as the rabbis understood it.[39] They transmitted this inherited set of meanings by means of the imagery through which it had been passed on to them: harlots and snakes; verbal jousts with Gentile rulers; temptations to be resisted; boundaries to be made firm.

The second element of the rabbinic achievement was likewise a refinement of the biblical legacy: the association of home with sacred order. Homelessness did not stand in opposition to simple possession of the Land of Israel, but to the observance there of Torah. And so long as Jews were homeless, the Torah constituted their principal refuge. Its study is therefore recalled time and again in Avodah Zarah, both as God's treasured gift to Israel and as the people's principal comfort in its times of trial. Torah preserved Israel in the literal, "sociological" sense by surrounding it with safeguards of its distinctiveness in a time and place when assimilation was all too likely. Torah also preserved Israel psychically, providing a sense of order, an orientation, when all else was chaos, and seemed to threaten Jews with nothingness. Finally, Torah provided Israel with a *raison d'être*, a continuing link to God and the promise of future redemption.

But this equation of homecoming with the kingdom of Torah involved as well the third component of the rabbinic strategy for enduring exile: the combination of memory and neglect which made of the Land both a center of aspiration and a periphery to actual existence. Had the rabbis not preserved the memory of the real, physical Land and insisted upon its centrality, they would have been unable to orient Jews in the unbounded time and space of their many dispersions. But by doing so, by identifying homecoming with the sacred order of Torah, they acted to mitigate the Land's centrality; for all intents and purposes they rendered it dispensable. For God could be encountered anywhere; His commandments, or the greater part of them, could be observed everywhere. Exile, therefore, was not only the "cemetary" to which one rabbinic parable compared it: a place of sin and corruption and death.[40] It was a wilderness marked by the way of life: Torah. It afforded a life not lacking in meaning, or atonement, or salvation; a life, as the prayer for the new month would have it, of "fear of heaven, and the fear of sin." The sages, unlike the priests of old, could live in such a cemetary, even if they lacked the intimacy with God available to those who attended on Him, as it were, at home. God, like the Jews, remained somewhere else. But He could be brought near through prayer and through the study and performance of His commandments. In this way Jews brought the Land near as well: recalling its blessings every time they thanked God for their daily bread, and imagining their longed-for redemption, in this world and the next, in terms of return to Eretz Israel.[41]

Such observance as was possible in exile remained but a foretaste of that return. But return meant primarily more complete observance of the Torah which Jews already observed, in large measure, in exile. That Torah, in fact, was not only their portable homeland but God's. "Since the destruction of the Temple the Holy One Blessed be He has only the four cubits of the halakhah" (Berakhot 8a). *That* was the territory which the rabbis marked, explored, and inhabited. It could by no means be limited to or by the borders of Eretz Israel.

In fact, as one scholar has noted, the ten degrees of holiness attributed to the Land by the Mishnah (Kelim 1:6–9) are themselves proportionate to the observance of the Torah mandated at each holy site mentioned. "The land of Israel is holier than any other land" because "from it they may bring [the offerings of the] *omer* [sheaf], the firstfruits, and the two loaves, which they may not bring from any other land." Each of the next nine ascending gradations is likewise ascribed its sanctity by virtue of what can or cannot be done there, in accordance with Torah.[42] Exile outside the Land was "an emaciated life," a cemetery, because huge areas of the Law could not be fulfilled; it was, on the other hand, a life both sacred and redeemed— because it too was a life in accord with Torah.

These were the tensions inherited by future generations of Jews, the sources from which the varying medieval interpretations of *galut* derived. Take, for example, the combination of memory and forgetfulness which continued to mark the Jews' relation to their Land, as indeed it necessarily characterized the whole of their relationship to their tradition. Yehudah Halevi, arguing in the *Kuzari* (ca. 1130) the urgency of return, the sinfulness of resignation to exile, and the intrinsic unique holiness of the Land, drew upon the sources which we have examined no less than Maimonides (1135–1204) who in keeping with the Mishnah I have cited attributed the Land's sanctity to the commandments discharged upon it and was far more accepting of the exile which Jews would endure until God decided to end it. The ideas of exile and Messiah were of course intimately related, witness Yehudah Halevi's longing to be freed from "service of those numerous people whose favor I do not care for, and shall never obtain, though I worked for it all my life." That freedom could only be obtained through the rebuilding of Jerusalem, which in turn would occur only "when Israel yearns for it to such an extent that they embrace her stones and dust."[43]

Few did; in fact, the "spiritualization" that transformed the messianic idea following Sabbatai Sevi's abortive attempt to gather in the exiles, according to Scholem, transformed the concept of galut no less dramatically.[44] Jews' relation to their land could not but become more and more sentimental and idealized as time went on, less and less rooted in the realm of oil and wine and herds. The change was a function of, and perhaps an atonement for, the fact of distance from the Land which the vast majority did nothing to overcome.

That tendency—the triumph of the metaphysical over the political—reached its peak in the kabbalah expounded by Isaac Luria (1539–1572), masterfully explained by Scholem as a response to the Spanish expulsion. God, according to Luria, had contracted His infinite essence at the start of the "cosmic drama," in order to make room for His creation. Even before the Beginning then, there was exile: this first "primordial exile, or self-banishment" of God's withdrawal. Next, the "archtypes of all being" had emerged, including Adam Kadmon, "Primordial Man," the first form taken by creation. But the "lights" of primal energy had burst from Adam Kadmon's ears, mouth, and nose, shattering the vessels of creation intended to receive them. Again there was exile, "the decisive crisis of all divine and created being." As a result, Scholem explains,

> nothing remains in its proper place. Everything is somewhere else. But a being that is not in its proper place is in exile. Thus, since that primordial act, all being has been a being in exile, in need of being led back and redeemed.[45]

This redemption was the task of all humanity, but particularly of the Jews. The work of *tikkun* or restoration, accomplished through performance of God's commandments with full and proper intent, meant nothing less than putting the shards of God's cosmos back together again. Indeed, given the Kabbalists' vision, it meant putting God back together again. For He too was, as it were, in pieces, scattered, lacking unity. He too, as the rabbis had taught (but in a different sense), was in exile.

The vision is awesome, bold. It takes the rabbinic framework on its shoulders and carries it off to a new—a cosmic—foundation. Isaiah had equated return from Babylonia with the end of days. The rabbis had equated restoration of the Land and Jewish sovereignty with the messianic redemption of the world and even resurrection of the dead. Now the Kabbalists equated redemption with the perfecting of God and His cosmos, a process in which the actual Land of Israel itself figured marginally, if at all. Indeed, it was Jewish exile *from* the Land which made "the existence and destiny of Israel, with all their terrible reality . . . fundamentally a symbol of the true state of all being," including God's. "Precisely because the real existence of Israel [was] so completely an experience of exile, it [was] at the same time symbolic and transparent."[46] This is the cognitive comfort which we noted earlier. If the Jews were not where they should be, neither was anything else. Greater "company" for those in "misery" could not be conceived.

There was, it seems, an added consolation: work which needed doing and which only Israel could perform. Exile was not merely a time of waiting, or even of keeping busy while waiting. It was the occasion for performance of a mission. "In the course of its exile, Israel must go everywhere, to every corner of the world, for everywhere a spark of the Shekkinah is waiting to be found, gathered and restored by a religious act."[47] If a particular galut brought Jews nearer to Palestine, as several Spanish exiles noted happily of their own expulsion and resettlement,[48] how much more so could the work of *tikkun* be welcomed. Proximity to the Land of Israel was taken as yet another sign that the end was approaching. But one senses that Luria's conviction of the approaching end was less connected with geography than to the cosmos as a whole. The spiritualization of home and homelessness which we observed in Philo or Qumran, and saw developed in the rabbis' own ambivalent relation to the Land, now reached its fullest flowering. Exile was far more than exile from a particular land. When the end expected by Luria (or Sabbatai Sevi) failed to materialize, therefore, Jews were able to go on in their galut as before. The *tikkun* of the whole world waited. There was work to be done.

But the precisely opposite tendency—political realism—was also evident in medieval reflection, and it too developed dramatically in the wake of the Spanish expulsion. The commentators recognized that not all exiles were alike in causation or dynamics. There were Shapur and Antoninus on the one hand, Titus and Nebuchadnezzar on the other, and indeed the various stories of the patriarchs were viewed as foreshadowing the different sorts of exiles undergone by their descendants. *Tosafot* acts to ease the restrictions on trade with Gentiles imposed by Avodah Zarah, for the economic circumstances had changed, but the need of Jews to make a living had not. No less importantly, the very definition of the Gentile opposite whom Jews lived underwent adjustment. Rabbi Menaḥem Ha-Me'iri's category of the "nations bounded by religion," as Jacob Katz has taught us, represents a supplement to the threefold definition of Jew, idolater, and "child of Noah" formulated by the Talmud.[49] Rashi notes that "he who subverts the right of the stranger, the fatherless and the widow" (Deut. 27:19) deserves to be cursed, for such victims "have no power"—and such elementary political observation finds an echo of utmost sophistication in Abravanel's marvelously insightful reading of the story of Joseph, informed by bitter personal experience. This sort of awareness led, after the Spanish exile which so opened Abravanel's eyes, to political analysis in the modern sense of the term, and to a burst of historical writing best represented by Ibn Verga's Shevet Yehudah (ca. 1520).[50] Jews now probed the social, economic, and political causes of particular exiles, all the while attributing the events to their single ultimate cause, the will of God.

Indeed, argues Haim Hillel Ben Sasson, the writings of Spanish exiles exhibit a deep understanding of the reasons for their expulsion. The exiles could identify both with the insiders and the outsiders. They recognized the Christians to be God-fearing, and believed the rulers of Spain especially grateful to God for the taking of Granada and the resultant unification of Spain. Furthermore, they reasoned that any kingdom must be undergirded by a common religion, the observance of which was rightly imposed by the monarch. Given this logic, perhaps, the Christians had no choice but to expel the Jews from Spain. It was the Jews' bad luck that they had been concentrated in one kingdom, unable to flee to the welcoming embrace of another. But this, like all so-called luck, was of course divine providence and had to be accepted.[51]

Here we reach the limits of the rabbinic framework, in several senses. The beginnings of political and sociological analysis threaten to supplant the simpler cause-and-effect schema of the tradition, even when couched in the traditional form of commentaries to sacred texts. The rabbis had been forced to understand idolatry inside out, in order to defy it; now Jews seemed to comprehend the motives of gentile oppressors in a new way and to identify to an extent with gentile power. It was one thing to deem exile unavoidable because God had ordained it, quite another to see it as the inescapable consequence of political conditions. Jeremiah, we recall, had insisted that it was not Nebuchadnezzar who had exiled the Jews to Babylonia, but God. Political defeat in his view offered neither comfort nor the promise of return. An act of God offered both. For modern Zionists, the truth was exactly opposite. Politics was the only hope. If Ben Sasson is correct, the Spanish exiles prepared the way for such a realization.

Spanish Jewry, finally, also created a phenomenon which exhibits the rabbinic understanding of the link between political and metaphysical homelessness rather precisely: the Marrano. Mishnah and Gemarra Avodah Zarah had been faced with the predicament of an idolatrous land of Israel, an idolatrous world. They had responded with the creation of small pockets of Jewish time and space, maintained precariously and with great effort. Jews had persisted in that enterprise throughout their medieval dispersions. Suppose, however, that even these fragile constructions became unavailable or unavailing? Suppose the rabbinic strategy for coping with exile ceased to work for some? Luria's kabbalah seems a response to that situation, a further step along the path which the rabbis pioneered. Jewish life, like God, could be contracted from a small pocket to a point—a point from which an infinity of possibility could then emerge. Jews hemmed round about by restrictions, both of their own making and of the Gentiles', could stretch the limbs of their imagination as far as they could reach, penetrating even ultimate mysteries. More concretely, Jews unable to bear either the disabilities of Jewishness or the guilt of apostasy could differentiate between life on the "outside," in a time and space entirely gentile, and the true life which they lived on the "inside." Their invisible sanctums of home or soul, unknown to the world, could remain Jewish, even if on the outside they were, to all intents and purposes, Christian. Here too, for the Marranos, a tiny point opened out to infinity.

The Spanish exiles, reports Ben-Sasson, had mixed opinions about the Marranos. Some attributed their public conversion to Christianity to an understandable weariness with the fate of galut. Others saw a simple desire for personal advancement. The important point for us is that all the exiles seemed to understand the Marranos as one more example of the idol worship which was, as Deuteronomy promised, the worst punishment of galut. "We have seen with our own eyes" that Deuteronomy's curses have come true, wrote R. Isaac Ben Moses Arama (1420–1499). Marranism, to many of the exiles, was "the punishment of *galut,* carried to its conclusion."[52]

Jews had become used to schizophrenia. What else does Avodah Zarah's strategy for coping with the world represent? One was allowed to build a bathhouse in which idols were placed routinely, but had to stop building at the niche where the idols would stand. Worse, in the medieval period, Jews were forced to sign oaths not to travel from a certain locality, which they had to leave in order to make a living, so they signed, with the permission of the *halakhah,* while maintaining a *reservatio mentalis* as they did so—an inner reservation that the signature was conditional.[53] From here it was still a large step to being a Marrano, but not an inconceivable one; Marranos, wrote one rabbi, simply worshipped God in their hearts, while serving Avodah Zarah with their hands. One could understand the logic of the act, even if one found it despicable. For the logic was an outgrowth of the rabbinic contraction of Jewish time and space, even if its outcome was far from what the rabbis had intended. In the nineteenth century, as we will see in the next chapter, assimilated Jews carried that logic one step further, and the founders of Zionism rejected it in its entirety.

In the meantime, few Jews actually took up either swords or plowshares in an attempt at the return promised by their prophets. Instead they sought means of adjusting to exile, and even prospering. We will never know exactly how the majority understood their own predicament: what it meant to sit in France, but pray for Zion; to wait for the Messiah, but (by and large) make no overt effort in worldly terms to hasten his coming. We can only infer that the commentators were not alone in deriving meaning and comfort in exile from the tradition's reflection upon it; in fact we are driven to conclude that by the only available measure the rabbinic strategy worked— Jews remained Jews (or at least some did), and (many, at least) came to regard the rabbinic corpus as authoritative. The strategy worked because of rather than despite the ambivalence which we have observed in the rabbis' relation to home and homelessness; because of and not despite their insistence that perfection—home—was not where the Jews were. It lay somewhere else, at the Center, where Jews were not. God, who defined that Center and *was* perfection, was somewhere else as well. The strategy worked until Emancipation promised Jews the opportunity to be at home *without* going somewhere else, and modern Zionists challenged both that latest reconception of galut and the original. They would end galut once and for all, by bringing the Jews home.

Part Two

IV

HOMECOMING
THE REVIVAL OF THE SPIRIT

The complex relationship of modern Zionist thought to the religious tradition just surveyed is nowhere more apparent than in the essay which first set the movement for Jewish return to the Land on its feet: Theodor Herzl's *Der Judenstaat*, published in 1896. Herzl's analysis of the Jewish problem is compelling, his prose crystal-clear, and his plan to bring exile to an end, in his words, "essentially quite simple." The reader's movement from premises that he or she cannot deny to a conclusion remarkable in its audacity—"the world needs the Jewish state; therefore it will arise"—is seemingly inexorable. And yet, Herzl is driven to observe, neither the rational colonization of the Land which he proposed, nor the desire of European anti-Semites to be rid of their Jews, nor the sophisticated organizational apparatus which he hoped to set in motion would be sufficient to effect the homecoming which he urged. "No human being is wealthy or powerful enough to transport a people from one place of residence to another," Herzl declared. For that something more was needed, which Herzl found ready to hand: an idea.

That idea was, of course, the "princely dream" which had sustained Jews "throughout the long night of their history," which Herzl called, in modern translation, the "state idea." For centuries Jews had lived by the refrain "next year in Jerusalem"; now, if that idea were reformulated and the people's minds cleansed of "very old, outworn, muddled, and shortsighted notions," fulfillment would come to pass—if not next year, then surely soon after. "The Jews who will it shall achieve their State," he proclaimed. "We shall live at last as free men on our own soil, and in our own homes peacefully die."[1]

In the following chapter I shall examine Herzl's plan to secure the Jews' salvation and its roots in both Jewish and European thought. Even the few sentences cited here, however, reveal that Herzl had subjected the biblical and rabbinic conceptions of exile and the Land which we have examined to considerable revision. The redemption awaited by Jews for millennia would now be achieved, in Herzl's view, almost at once, by the simple exercise of collective national will. It would perhaps not involve return to the Promised Land of milk and honey: "Jerusalem" could, if necessary, be located in

"Uganda" or Argentina or wherever else the "Society of Jews" and/or "Jewish public opinion" determined.[2] Still more important, all this could and would occur without the agency—or even the blessing!—of God. *His* "return to Zion in mercy," beseeched for centuries, was now irrelevant. It was the people who would return, propelled by the power of their idea. In modern terms: ideology, high finance, and realpolitik would accomplish what God—not even mentioned by Herzl—could or would not. The Jews would go home: led by their own Messiah to a place of their own choosing.

And yet, for all that, the traditional conception of galut reverberates loudly in Herzl's essay. Its continuing power is attested first of all by the imagery and cadences of Herzl's rhetoric, and is further witnessed by Herzl's very emphasis upon the Idea as Zionism's indispensable inspirational force. More than misplaced confidence in scientific progress underlay Herzl's certainty that his messianic project would not fail. More than the weight of "Jewish public opinion," or the disappointments of international diplomacy, would soon bring him home from East Africa and other exotic locales to Palestine. Given the degree to which Herzl's success depended on the "state idea," even in his own estimation, the influence of that idea upon his imagination of the return is not surprising. His followers—many of whom were far more at home in the Jewish past, if not more committed to its beliefs—could not but feel the weight of the tradition even more powerfully.

In rejection and in triumph, therefore, openly or in disguise, the conceptions of homelessness and homecoming which we have examined continued to direct the thinking of cultural Zionists, political Zionists, non-Zionists, and anti-Zionists alike on what it meant for Jews to come home. That homecoming, as some Zionists conceived it, might have been to a place which the rabbis would not have recognized, located in a continent which the Bible could not have known. But it was, nonetheless, a *Jewish* home which such Zionists sought, defined by three thousand years' experience of what it meant to be without one. We cannot understand how this modern homecoming was imagined without recalling the experience of homelessness from which the Zionists hoped to be redeemed.

My aim in Part Two of this study is to provide that link: to describe the influence which the traditional notions of galut examined thus far have exercised upon modern Jewish discourse about homecoming. I will not, of course, attempt to survey the full range of Zionist and non-Zionist thought on the broader set of issues which has preoccupied the movement and its adversaries for nearly a century now. Rather I will again be selective in my analysis, focusing on the handful of thinkers and texts most decisive in setting the terms of contemporary debate about galut and its termination. Our starting point will be the foundation of modern Jewish thought itself. For the two thinkers who first attempted to bring ideas of exile and the Land in line with the religious and political assumptions of the modern world were also the thinkers who set the agenda for *all* Jewish thought in the modern period, religious and political: Benedict Spinoza and Moses Mendelssohn. Their transformation of the conception of galut, we will find, was radical, involving what I shall call the demystification, universalization, and politicization of the tradition. Without that transformation, modern Jewish nationalism could not have arisen, and would certainly not have taken the paradoxical form of Zionism: a largely secular movement of return to a Land rendered sacred by Jewish faith, resulting in a secular Jewish state which the tradition could neither have sanctioned nor conceived. This inherent paradox (not to say contradiction) of Jewish homecoming, we will find, continues to beset Jewish thought even today.

"A Certain Strip of Territory"

Spinoza's *Tractatus Theologico-Politicus*, published in 1670, was concerned only marginally with the Land, and understandably so. His immediate concern, in the work, was whether and how the Jews, along with other religious groups, could fit into the new political and conceptual order which he perceptively saw emerging in the West. His conclusion was that they could *not* fit, except by disappearing or rendering their distinctive faith innocuous. Given Spinoza's concern and his conclusion, it is hardly surprising that the issue of Jewish return to the former Jewish homeland does not arise in the work, except for one brief parenthesis which we shall note presently. Spinoza left the matter of Jewish homecoming to the realm of fantasy and "superstition" where, apparently, he felt it belonged. Instead he focused—though he of course did not use the word—on Jewish life in exile.

The omission of the Land is striking from our perspective, if not from Spinoza's, because at the very moment that he wrote, thousands of Jews in the thrall of the old convictions were staking all they had and knew on the immediate fulfillment of their people's messianic fantasy and preparing to follow Sabbatai Sevi, God's apparent anointed, home to Zion. Not even a hint of their ferment penetrates the *Tractatus*. Spinoza could rest confident, with his usual prescience, that this messianic homecoming, like all the others, would fail, and that following that failure the centers of Jewish political and spiritual concern would lie elsewhere. *Home* would lie elsewhere, in other words, on ground which his *Tractatus* first charted, because exile and not Zion would henceforth be the site of all the redemption which Jews (or anyone else) could hope to achieve. The Land of Israel, as a result, could be consigned to memory, or even oblivion—along with the God who had once chosen it, and indeed the "chosen people" itself.

We cannot enter into the details of Spinoza's argument in the *Tractatus*.[3] Suffice it to say that Spinoza had to undermine the Jews' claim to chosenness, and the authority of their scriptures, in order to establish that "right over matters spiritual lies wholly with the sovereign"—thereby resolving the bitter age-old conflict between church and state.[4] The power of religion, "a tissue of lies and mysteries," in Spinoza's words, would be supplanted by the only two authorities which Spinoza believed the modern world should recognize: human reason (i.e., philosophy) and the state.[5] The point essential to our concerns is that Spinoza's repudiation of Israel's chosenness involved the thorough *demystification* of the idea of the Land. Election referred only to the "social organization and the good fortune" with which the ancient Israelites had "obtained supremacy and kept it so many years." The Promised Land chosen for their inheritance was merely a "certain strip of territory on which they could live peaceably and at their ease"[6]—until some other nation, "chosen" in precisely the same manner (that is, by fate or history) appeared on the scene to displace them. Politics and sociology, not theology, could explain the Jews' conquest of the Land, their expulsion from it, and their survival for two millennia in exile among the nations. Reason could suggest, as well, that "if the foundations of their religion have not emasculated their minds [the Jews] may even, if occasion offers, so changeable are human affairs, raise up their empire afresh, and . . . God may a second time elect them"[7]—a statement not lost upon nonreligious Zionist readers centuries later.

All this followed, as day follows night, from the few axioms concerning humanity, nature, and divinity with which Spinoza began. If "the help of God" could mean only "the fixed and unchangeable order of nature or the chain of natural events,"[8] then prophecy could teach no more than philosophy (and often less), the religion of Israel should give way to a religion of reason, and the Land and people of Israel had lost their claim to uniqueness.

The impact of the *Tractatus* upon subsequent Jewish thought, religious and political, simply cannot be over-estimated. No Jewish thinker who identified himself as such could ignore Spinoza. Subsequent discourse on the Land in particular could not avoid the fact that Spinoza had stripped away the many-layered dress of imagery and significance in which the Land had been draped for centuries. Exile had ceased to be exile; Jerusalem, in Spinoza's view of the world, was no longer the center of Jewish geography in any sense. Spinoza redefined the salvation traditionally centered in the Land, and linked to the coming of God's Messiah, in such a way as to make it accessible to the rational soul in any and every present, everywhere. Jews could achieve redemption wherever and whenever they sought it through political reform and philosophical inquiry—the agencies of reason—rather than through prayer. It is not too much to say that Jewish reflection on galut, in the wake of the *Tractatus*, would never be the same—a transformation essential for the development of modern Zionism some two hundred years later.[9]

Subsequent Jewish theorists, while challenging Spinoza's conclusions on other matters, retained and furthered the demystification of exile and the Land which he had initiated. Moses Mendelssohn, for example, conceded that true religion was both rational and universal. It was available to every human soul and could therefore not be identified with Torah—a unique system of "divine legislation" binding only upon the Jews, which contained as well universal teachings aimed at their reason.[10] Mendelssohn also conceded in his essay *Jerusalem* (1783) that religion in the modern world had no right to exercise coercion upon its adherents, force being a prerogative of the state alone. When pressed to reconcile that view with the clearly opposite opinion of scripture, Mendelssohn made yet another concession, for our purposes the most important of all. The "Mosaic constitution" detailed in the Bible, which had united state and church in ancient Israel—and so employed coercion, legitimately—was no longer applicable.[11] Israel's "theocracy, if you will" was a thing of the past, unique in the annals of history but utterly without relevance in the present. And, Mendelssohn added, "only the Almighty knows among what people and in which century something similar may appear once again."[12]

Mendelssohn's relegation of the "Mosaic constitution" to the distant past is striking enough. The phrase "among what people" (in the sentence just quoted) is little short of astounding. Was Mendelssohn seriously suggesting that God might one day choose another people, as he had once chosen Israel? Did he really believe that the messianic kingdom might be centered elsewhere than in Jerusalem? He did not; his words were rather meant to further the polemical aims which had prompted him to write *Jerusalem* in the first place: refutation of those who had challenged the Jews' right to Emancipation, on the ground that their loyalty to any homeland was suspect so long as they entertained the hope of return, one day, to Zion. An injunction to the Jews to "adopt the mores and constitution" of the country in which they found themselves, while remaining steadfast in upholding their religion, follows the passage at hand almost at once.[13] Mendelssohn retained the traditional faith in eventual messianic return to the Land. But his message in the passage just quoted, and in the essay as a whole, represented a decisive break with all previous formulations of that faith. How much more striking, then, that he should have called this essay seeking the Jews' political and cultural integration into the societies of their dispersion *Jerusalem*.

In one sense Mendelssohn's strategy was far from new. The rabbis too had stressed the centrality of Jerusalem and the Land at the very moment that they severed Jewish faith and practice from dependence on both, as we have seen. They too had invoked the Land's sanctity in order to distance Jews— and Gentiles—from the belief that it, along with God's Temple, would be rebuilt "speedily and in our days." But Mendelssohn took the rabbinic strategy a step further. He effectively located the "heavenly Jerusalem" awaited by the rabbis in an *earthly* "exile" where Jews would enjoy full civic and religious liberty and fully participate in the surrounding culture. This the rabbis could not have conceived. In place of their careful balance between messianic hope for return to the Land and temporal preoccupation with exilic existence in the meantime, Mendelssohn devised a strategy for a more far-reaching adaptation to the gentile order. He may have believed that he was only reiterating the classic principle that "the law of the land is the law," thereby pursuing an age-old Jewish strategy of adjustment to the circumstances of exile. In fact, however, he conferred a legitimacy on that law, a *permanence* to the gentile order, which the rabbis would never have countenanced—all this in an essay which bore the name *Jerusalem*.

Mendelssohn chose the title, writes his biographer Alexander Altmann, in order to indicate "that Jerusalem, though destroyed and bereft of power, was still the symbol of the true worship of God."[14] Precisely the point: a city possessed in the tradition of enormous symbolic power, but a real city nonetheless, in a real land, had become *only* a symbol for "true worship" possible on *this* side of redemption—wherever human beings lived and rationally recognized their Creator. Mendelssohn had profoundly altered the conception of galut bequeathed him by tradition, further *universalizing* (or "spiritualizing") a notion already laden with universal symbolic meaning. In *Jerusalem* the real city of Jerusalem, in the Land of Israel, loses its reality as a place in which, and for which, Jews might actually live. The center of Jewish concern, religious as well as political, the locus of Jewish aspirations, shifts to exile.

Mendelssohn's *universalization* of "Jerusalem," when combined with the *demystification* of the Land first undertaken by Spinoza, left Jews free to regard their present and future estates primarily in *political* terms. Neither the Bible nor the rabbis were unaware of the political dimension to galut, as we have seen. "Antoninus" and "Rabbi" refined games of power and influence played by Pharaoh and Joseph, while in the writings of the Spanish exiles (from whose ranks Spinoza descended) the political perspective was both pronounced and acute. It now became predominant and, more important, taken for granted. The nature and focus of Jewish aspirations moved from return to Zion in the indefinite future by the hand of God, to opportunities which could be seized in the short term in Europe, through real-world instruments of political action. Mendelssohn and Spinoza opened the space for such action—which later, paradoxically, came to focus on the Land—by directing Jewish political energies *away* from the Land. The task for Jewish *religious* thought, as a result, became the imagination of Judaisms compatible with Emancipation in lands where the Jews resided. Those countries would soon not be called *galut* at all—but rather *diaspora*.

The principal nineteenth-century thinkers who pursued these related religious and political objectives followed Mendelssohn and Spinoza in minimizing the importance of Eretz Israel. Emphasis upon Jerusalem (and by extension the Jews) as a symbol, albeit "bereft of power," of the "true worship of God" soon developed into the notion of a Jewish "mission unto the nations" which could be fulfilled only if the Jews dwelled among those nations—that is to say, in exile. This development is by now well known; we need note only that Orthodox thinkers who shared Mendelssohn's conviction that the "divine legislation" was still binding upon the Jews preached the doctrine of a Jewish mission no less than Reform thinkers for whom, in the wake of Kant, religious duty had been reduced to ethical obligation. The Land, in all this literature, is of marginal importance at best.

Samson Raphael Hirsch, for example, the founder of modern Orthodoxy, gave Eretz Israel short shrift in his sacred history of the people Israel, touching briefly on occupation of the Land as a means to the fulfillment of the demands of Torah and devoting the bulk of his *Nineteen Letters on Judaism* to a prolonged peroration on the meaning of exile.[15] Nachman Krochmal, in his *Guide for the Perplexed of the Day (1851)*, divided Jewish history into cycles of youth, maturity, and decline. Neither possession of the Land nor exile from it plays a decisive role in this chronology.[16] In the writings of Abraham Geiger—one of the founding theologians of Reform— the era of Israel's "compact nationality" is seen as a short but necessary prelude to the performance in exile of the Jews' "world-historical mission"[17]; that mission was the centerpiece of Geiger's Judaism.

Only Heinrich Graetz, insisting in *The Structure of Jewish History* (1846) that "the totality of Judaism is discernible only in its history," affirmed that political sovereignty was an integral part of the Jewish past, and so belonged to the essence of Judaism.[18] Even Graetz, however, did not believe that task either urgent or given to success in the foreseeable future; his emphasis, like that of the other thinkers, was rather upon a Jerusalem which could, like William Blake's, rise in England's "green and pleasant land," or anywhere else.

The issue of exile, then, is essentially irrelevant in all four accounts; the Land is simply not important. In fact, with Jewish energy focused else-where, only a mere handful of Jewish thinkers before the 1880s did pay the traditional notions of *galut* and *eretz* much attention. For all practical pur-poses, these few reduce to one—Moses Hess (1812–1875)—and in fact to only one of Hess's works, though by far his finest: the quixotic masterpiece *Rome and Jerusalem* (1862). Alone in his generation, Hess combined a call for pragmatic, rational, *political* efforts at return to the Land with a vision of universal redemption derived from the prophets. The synthesis was unheard of in Hess's day and roundly ignored. But it became of major significance a generation later: the foundation of "cultural," as well as of socialist, Zionism.

The roots of the synthesis seem to lie in biography. Hess was raised in a family which had resisted assimilation and received a solid Jewish education at the hands of his grandfather, a man both pious and learned. The typical move to universalist commitments followed nonetheless: "Jewish patriotic sentiment," Hess later recalled, "had been stifled in my heart by a greater pain which the suffering of the European proletariat evoked in me."[19] Hess turned to the communist Babeuf for leadership and was perhaps responsible, a few years later, for converting Karl Marx to the cause. But Hess's univer-salism of spirit precluded the dogmatic certainty characteristic of Marx, earning him Marx's ridicule in the *Communist Manifesto*. That openness was already evident in his first major work, *The Holy History of Mankind, by a*

Young Spinozist (1837), which, writes Isaiah Berlin, derived a "vague rationality, and belief in the unity of all creation" from its namesake, and for the rest borrowed eclectically from Fichte and Schelling, Hegel and Schleiermacher. Its central thesis was that "in the beginning men lived in an undifferentiated unity of spirit and matter."[20] This primitive communism had later been vitiated by property, and it was the task of modern man, "armed with consciousness of his historic mission," to restore the pristine harmony by bringing property to an end once and for all. The vision of the Hebrew prophets, Hess proclaimed, would thereby be vindicated and fulfilled.

The "Young Spinozist" expressed admiration for the ancient Jewish state as well, for it represented, in his view, a unity of polity and religion (i.e., matter and spirit) which would always be worthy of emulation. Like Hegel, however, Hess asserted that the Jews as a nation had been rendered obsolete by Christianity. "The people chosen by their God must disappear forever, that out of its death might spring a new, more precious life."[21] Not surprisingly, the final chapter of the work, accompanied by a citation from First Corinthians, is titled "Das neue Jerusalem und die letzten Zeiten." Like Spinoza and Mendelssohn, Hess believed that the new order would be built "here, in the heart of Europe."[22]

Twenty years later, Hess published *Rome and Jerusalem*—less a change of heart about human redemption than a significantly different vision of the Jews' role in it. "I am back with my people," he declared, his long "estrangement" at an end.[23] Hess's universalist commitments remained intact. He continued to be one of the principal leaders of the socialist movement in Europe. But, as Hess explained, he had come to see the revival of Jewry and Judaism as a crucial part of the cause for which socialists labored. One stimulus to this new outlook, perhaps, was the disappointment with Emancipation widespread among European Jewry in the 1860s, particularly in Germany, where the hopes of the 1840s had largely come to naught. Hess spoke for many of his generation when he poured scorn upon the universalist pretensions of German philosophers, who, he argued, cared only for the protection of the "pure German race." The Germans would never accept the Jews, because they objected "less to the Jews' peculiar beliefs than to their peculiar noses."[24]

The point is crucial: *Rome and Jerusalem* represents both the first comprehensive statement of modern Zionism and the most systematic analysis of modern anti-Semitism in its day. Hess concluded that anti-Semitism was incurable, because Jews once made outcasts by virtue of their faith would now be excluded from modern societies by virtue of their nationality (i.e., their "noses"). The two aspects of Jewish identity were inseparable, he argued, and not only in the eyes of Gentiles. Pious Jews throughout the ages had always been, above all, Jewish patriots. "The most touching point about [the] Hebrew prayers is that they are really an expression of the collective Jewish spirit." Everything which reminded Hess's grandfather of Palestine, he relates, was "as dear to him as the sacred relics of his ancestral home." Reform Jewish assertions that the Jews were a religious group, and only that, were merely a "false theory of recent German invention" which "need not be taken seriously." Jews were in fact united by powerful national sentiments founded upon the central institution of the family.[25] Not since Yehudah Halevi's *Kuzari* had a work of Jewish thought articulated the *national* character of the Jewish people in exile so forcefully.

These conclusions led Hess to proto-Zionism, rather than to despair, because he saw the nationalist tide on which German anti-Semitism rode as history's appointed vehicle for the inauguration of universal redemption, rather than as the scourge of Jewish hopes for Emancipation. A new age was dawning. France and Italy had already shown the way and would help the Jewish nation to follow in their path. Success was guaranteed, for the Sabbath of all history was at hand. As a nation returned to their ancestral homeland, Jews would receive the acceptance which they had been unable to attain as individuals in the lands of other nations. Universalism and particularism, the heavenly and the earthly Jerusalem, were one. Thus Hess could write, "When I labor for the regeneration of my own nation, I do not thereby renounce my humanistic aspirations." "The thought of my nationality," Hess wrote elsewhere, "was connected with my ancestral heritage, with the Holy Land and the Eternal City," the birthplace not only of the Jews, but of "belief in the divine unity of life and of the hope for the ultimate brotherhood of men."[26]

It is impossible to convey, in such a brief account, the sheer excitement which animates *Rome and Jerusalem,* generated by the author's powerful discovery of the union between the messianic age dawning in his day and the return of the Jews to Zion. Hess could labor, as a Jew, for the same goal which summoned him as a human being. He could help to prove the rabbis and prophets of Israel correct: Jerusalem would be rebuilt. In Hess's secular translation of their vision, of course, the return would occur through political means. But it would occur, and would involve not only the Jews' return to the Land of Israel, but the achievement there of a socialist "sacred order"— justice for all, political as well as economic—and even the renewed flowering of religion. In exile, he wrote, faith had atrophied, suffering at the hands of Reform (which "never learned anything") and Orthodoxy ("which never forgot anything") alike. Once the Jews had been redeemed, the renewal of Judaism would follow as a matter of course, as would the redemption of all humanity.[27]

Galut and the Land, then, were accepted by Hess in the universalized conceptions bequeathed him by Spinoza and Mendelssohn. At the same time, however, those conceptions were reparticularized and concretized. As Buber put it, Hess opposed the "dissolution of the firm and single messianic faith into shadowy abstractions"—a process which dominated Western Jewry in his day. "Jerusalem" *would* be built in the heart of Europe, but only after redemption had been brought closer through the return of the Jewish people to the real Jerusalem and the establishment there of model social institutions.[28] Hess, like the rabbis and the prophets, linked the metaphysical with the political dimension of homelessness. Exile from the Land was inseparable from alienation in and from the world, homecoming from redemption.

In the name of that link between universal and particular Hess derided Israel's alleged mission unto the nations,[29] though his own commitment to socialism seems derived in part from the same reading of Israel's prophets which inspired Geiger and other advocates of Israel's exilic destiny. He even offered his own reformulation: the Jews were called "to be the bearers of civilization to the primitive people of Asia, and the teachers of the European sciences to which [their] race has contributed so much."[30] Mission or no mission, however, exile was exile—and the Jews could not hold up a lamp of progress before the nations without sovereignty in their own homeland. "A common, native soil is the primary condition, if there is to be introduced among the Jews better and more progressive relations between Capital and Labor." The echoes of Marx and Lassalle in this vision of the imminent end-time sound as loudly as those of Isaiah and Deuteronomy, and it was the combination of the two—of "universal and particular"—which generated the special power of Hess's teaching. It would soon do the same for Zionist thought as a whole. At home upon their own soil, Hess wrote, "Jews would participate in the great historical movement of present-day humanity."[31]

Hess's final legacy was the pragmatism which undergirded and lent credibility to his prophetic vision. *Rome and Jerusalem* makes frequent reference to political and scientific developments. Studies proving the feasibility of the Land's reclamation are cited in detail. More importantly, in the ninth of ten appendices to the work, Hess predicts that not all Western Jews will emigrate en masse to Palestine. Even after the Jewish state's establishment, "the majority of the Jews who live at present in the civilized Occidental countries will undoubtedly remain where they are," comfortable in the equal rights which they will have received. Hess then supplies a precedent for this situation of partial exile in an era of redemption, finding it in the "central unity" which had always existed among Jews, in his view, no matter how dispersed they were geographically. Jews had

> maintained a relation with the spiritual center wherever it was. No nation has ever felt as keenly the excitement going on in the spiritual nerve center as have the Jews. Every spiritual sensation spread rapidly from the center to the extreme periphery of the national organism.

Each and every Jew had shared in the "fortunes and misfortunes" of the entire people. Today, with distances reduced by new means of communication, it mattered little "whether more or less of the Jewish race dwells within or without" the borders of the Jewish state. Every nation had large numbers of its people dwelling abroad, and the Jews, at last, would be no exception to the rule.[32]

In the meantime, Hess urged two tasks upon his readers. First, they should work for the political rebirth of the Jewish people, beginning with the founding of Jewish colonies in Palestine. No less important, "the Jews who live in exile" should "strive to obtain naturalization and 'emancipation', though they may by no means abandon the hope of the restoration of the Jewish state."[33] Note the telling punctuation here: the word *emancipation* is enclosed in quotation marks: *exile* is not. This alone sets Hess apart from his contemporaries and makes him the principal forerunner of those who, a generation later, began to found agricultural colonies in Palestine and address the issues of Jewish homelessness and homecoming systematically.

No thinker since Hess has surpassed either the grandeur or the prescience of *Rome and Jerusalem.* Herzl's confidence that the Jewish state would arise because "the world needs it" pales before Hess's magisterial sense of the place of the Jewish return in the renewal of history and the cosmos. Even the sweeping vision of Rabbi Abraham Isaac Kook seems only to recall Hess's own synthesis between the European revolutionary tradition and the promises of Israel's prophets. That synthesis rendered all subsequent thinkers who insisted that political homecoming be linked to metaphysical return Hess's heirs—chief among them the founder and principal theoretician of "spiritual Zionism," Ahad Ha'am. For despite his unrelenting call for the replacement of heady dreams of return with steady and sober realism, Ahad Ha'am could not but assume the mantle of the greatest Jewish "dreamer" of modern times. The "priest-prophet" of the Jewish homecoming to Eretz Israel invoked and transformed Hess's idea of the Spiritual Center, thereby transforming him from a voice crying in the wilderness to the principal forerunner of Jewish nationalism.

"Flesh and Spirit"

Ahad Ha'am (born Asher Zevi Ginzberg, in 1856) continues to engage us, a century after the writing of his first essay and sixty years after his death, because the achievement of the state he believed impossible has rendered his Spiritual Center the single most important concept in Zionist discourse. He has triumphed, in large measure, because he failed. The Zionist movement as a whole refused to be swayed by the clear and direct Hebrew prose style which he fashioned especially to persuade his readers to be patient. His counsels of settling for the attainable fell on deaf ears; his dichotomies of "priest and prophet," "flesh and spirit," were not resolved by the compromise that he invariably proposed but by a more ambitious synthesis between renewal of the Jewish spirit and resurrection of the Jewish body politic. Contrary to Ahad Ha'am's oft-repeated conviction, it was the second which proved the more easily achieved—with the consequence that the first now claims our attention.

Zionist thought both inside and outside the land now focuses on the possible meanings of the Spiritual Center to those who live there as well as to those who live by choice on its periphery. We will find that the concept is far more complicated than is usually assumed, presuming a redefinition of Judaism that is not only problematic but fraught with self-contradiction. Ahad Ha'am demystified, politicized, and drastically revised Jewish tradition in a way that would have horrified the rabbis—all the while remaining remarkably faithful to much of what they intended for their people and their Land. These contradictions cannot be resolved, no matter how clear one's prose; they will likely prove recalcitrant as long as the Jewish state is conceived in the traditional terms of homecoming which Ahad Ha'am both distorted and reaffirmed.

"This is Not the Way," the essay which launched Ahad Ha'am's career as prophet-priest in 1889, argued that too much had already been attempted in the Land, too quickly. The wrong people had gone to Palestine, for the wrong reasons, armed with the wrong assumptions about what was needed if they were to succeed. "The heart of the nation is the foundation on which the land will be rebuilt—and the nation is fragmented and undisciplined." A scattered people could not work successfully on so difficult a task, until its spirit had been transformed and given focus. Private interests, for the same reason, had to be suspended for the sake of the general good.[34] The conviction that the Jewish people needed priests, not heroes—that foot soldiers had to be educated to service of their people, as it were, before they could be enlisted—led Ahad Ha'am to criticize those closest to his heart, the young colonists already at work upon the Land. In "A Friendly Attack" the criticism gave way, briefly, to sober praise: the "general good," he wrote, depended upon the efforts of *Hovevei Zion*.[35] In "Truth from the Land of Israel" (1891 and 1893), however, Ahad Ha'am again warned his readers that much had already been ruined, and little more should be attempted in the short term. The vineyards were withering, the Arabs not about to disappear.[36]

This was demystification in two senses. First, the "truth from Eretz Israel" stripped the Lovers of Zion of their lingering romanticism, laying bare the disappointing facts and figures of what had actually been achieved. Second, as Ahad Ha'am wrote in 1892, little could be done about the Jewish condition as long as the idea of return to Zion was "wrapped in a cloud of phantasies and visions."[37] He himself offered no paeans to the special beauty of Eretz Israel and expressed no longing for its hills or holy places, despite the love for the Land which, he said, had been imbued in him by childhood reading of Judaism's sacred texts. This was not merely a matter of temperament or style. The Land was never more than a vehicle, in his mind, to a more important goal: national regeneration.

The occasion for the first statement of that vision for the Land—its designation as the Spiritual Center of the Jewish people—was an essay eulogizing Leo Pinsker, whose pamphlet "Auto-Emancipation," published ten years before, had brought thousands of Jews to the Zionist cause and led to Pinsker's election as head of the Lovers of Zion movement. Pinsker, Ahad Ha'am conceded at the outset, had at first been indifferent as to the location of the renewed Jewish homeland. "The deep love for the land of our forefathers was foreign to him, love which is unconditional, which we— raised on (*ḥanikhei*) the Bible and the Talmud—feel in our hearts from our earliest childhood."[38] Any land which would remove the Jews from the hands of their enemies was good enough for Pinsker. There was no solution to the Jewish problem except such a homeland, Pinsker believed, because the cause of the Jews' persecution lay in their being a "ghostlike apparition"—a nation, long since dead, which nonetheless lived among and competed with other peoples. So long as the normal xenophobia of any group to the outsiders among it was exacerbated in the Jewish case—because Jews never played host to the guests of other peoples, but were always the guest, eternally alien and dependent—there could be no end to anti-Semitism. Rather than awaiting emancipation by other peoples—or God!—therefore, Jews had to take matters into their own hands: convene a national congress, establish a national institute, and acquire a productive territory for their own resettlement, wherever it might be. "We must not attach ourselves to the place where our political life was once violently interrupted and destroyed. The goal of our present endeavors must be not the 'Holy Land' but a land of our own." Israel's "God-idea" and the Bible had "made our old fatherland the Holy Land, and not Jerusalem of the Jordan," Pinsker continued, though if the Holy Land "again [became] ours—all the better."[39]

By the time of the founding conference of Lovers of Zion in 1884, Pinsker had been converted from his territorialism, as it came to be called—satisfaction with any site for the Jewish homeland—to Zionism: insistence that the work go forward in Palestine.[40] It was this later Pinsker whom Ahad Ha'am praised lavishly in 1891, then and after using him as a foil for criticism of unconverted territorialists, first among them, of course, Theodor Herzl. Pinsker supported Hovevei Zion's efforts to effect the Jewish homecoming in Palestine, according to Ahad Ha'am, even though it could *not* serve the function which he, Pinsker, had originally stipulated: provision of a *miklat batuqh*, a secure refuge, for the Jewish masses. Instead the Land would function as a "national spiritual center," a refuge for *Judaism*, in which the "national spirit" (not the ancestral faith; neither man was religious) would be awakened.

In a passage of remarkable prescience, Ahad Ha'am then relates the following "dream" of a future time when the Jews had become emancipated and happy, but their Judaism (*yahadut*) had languished. The people turns to Palestine in the hope of awakening national sentiment, planting colonies and raising a generation of Hebrew farmers. Jews from around the world come to visit. The Hebrew speakers of Palestine travel abroad, and soon the spirit of the *golah* is transformed. Slowly, Palestine becomes the Spiritual Center of Judaism, a place to which Jews flock in order to see the "model of a man of Israel, in his true aspect." At this point the dreamer wakes—to find his own generation so preoccupied with the troubles of the Jews that it has no time for the decline of Judaism. It was not possible to address both problems simultaneously, Ahad Ha'am insists sternly. The Jews were "still not enough of a people" to aspire to freedom in their own homeland. "Auto-Emancipation" could only develop slowly, out of love for Judaism and the Land.[41]

I will assess the accuracy of this prophecy—at once so much on target and so very wide of the mark—later on. For the moment, let us only note how drastically Ahad Ha'am has reinterpreted the traditional notion of galut, along lines originally set forth by Hess. The Spiritual Center, in his concep-tion, actually *serves* its periphery! This may have been true of Jewish life in the Land during the second commonwealth, and the *idea* of the Land, as we have seen, certainly had sustained the Jews in exile ever since the Temple's destruction. But the rabbis, though perhaps intending precisely such an outcome through their ambivalent conception of exile and the Land, would never have openly avowed or legitimized the subservience of an *existing* Center in the Land to its periphery—even as a temporary expedient. Yet that is precisely what Ahad Ha'am has done—only for the short term perhaps, and *de facto* but not *de jure*, but none the less for all that. The Land, as Spiritual Center, would by definition now be at the *periphery* of the life which the vast majority of the Jewish people lived elsewhere.

The change is related to Ahad Ha'am's more significant departure from the rabbis: his transformation of the meaning of Judaism. What for the rabbis had been a faith—a way of life in service to God—was for Ahad Ha'am a culture, the product and expression of the Jewish people's "national spirit." The object of allegiance had shifted; the "god-term"—the root of one's standard of conduct, the object of one's ultimate loyalty—had become the Jewish people itself. Small wonder that the Land should be in service to the people. All of Judaism, in this secular reconception, is said to serve it as well.

In his introductory essay to the first published collection of his writings, *At the Crossroads* (1895), Ahad Ha'am took his idea of the Spiritual Center one step further. Ridiculing the notion of a Jewish mission—trumpeted in count-less sermons, Ahad Ha'am wrote caustically, but changing people's lives not one iota—he again urged that Jews attend to the "*concentration* of the nation in Zion." Redemption of souls would have to precede full salvation (*ge'ulah*); Hovevei Zion's colonies would not succeed unless the freeing of "the nation's *spirit* from its inner bonds" had been accomplished. Ahad Ha'am then explained that "concentration of the spirit" (note the conjunc-tion of the two words which I have just italicized) was a well-known psycho-logical phenomenon. It consisted in "a particular spiritual matter in the depths of the soul gaining predominance over all other affairs, until it succeeds, imperceptibly, in uniting all of them around itself, in making them subservient to its purpose, and in changing the characters of all in accor-dance with its need." What was possible for one person, he continued, was not impossible for the spirit of a nation. The "concentration of the *people*" in

Zion had to be preceded by "concentration of the nation's *spirit* through Ḥibat Zion"—to which effort he dedicated the volume of his essays.[42]

This is a somewhat different Spiritual Center than the one encountered earlier. Now the Center is, at least initially, the *object* of the spirit's concentration, not its address, let alone the address of significant numbers of the Jewish people. The people focuses *on* Palestine rather than residing there. As individuals could unify fragmented selves by concentrating on a single task or idea, so a people. The spirit does not dwell *in* the Center, or emanate from it, but is concentrated, from outside, *upon* it, and only later comes to be concentrated in the Center itself. Ahad Ha'am has taken Hess's notion of the "spiritual nerve center" quite literally and in a new direction. Periphery is more prominent in relation to Center, exile to homeland, than in Hess's version or Ahad Ha'am's own earlier conception. Actual colonization of the Land, let alone the political means necessary to attain it, are even more effaced. Finally, as Buber noted, Hess's Spiritual Center was defined by a redeemed social and political order. Ahad Ha'am's Center would consist primarily of cultural artifacts that could be created in a variety of political contexts. A state—despite later protestations that he had been misunderstood—was not required.

Small wonder that Ahad Ha'am's many critics were not satisfied with this vision of Jewish homecoming, partial in the extreme. I will turn to the most vehement of his opponents—the political Zionists—in the following chapter. Here I wish to draw out several further implications of the Spiritual Center idea by tracing Ahad Ha'am's debates on the issue with two more sympathetic critics: Micah Joseph Berdiczewski (1865–1921) and Simon Dubnow (1860–1941). Both stood far closer to Ahad Ha'am than the political Zionists, both shared his concern for the renaissance of Jewish culture, and both—from opposite points of view—succeeded in highlighting the many strengths and the essential weakness of Ahad Ha'am's position.

Berdiczewski's critique was twofold. First, there was no unitary Jewish spirit which could be revived, or transformed, or centered, in the Jewish homeland. Second, Ahad Ha'am's personal definition of that spirit was too traditional, too sober, and too prosaic to inspire the renaissance which he sought. Talk of spirit was misdirected. What Israel lacked was matter, life, nature, earth. "Abstract Jews" of the galut had to become "Hebrews"—and this Ahad Ha'am's Spiritual Center would not make them.[43]

The focus of several attacks was Ahad Ha'am's most coherent attempt to delineate the substance of the national spirit: "The National Morality," published in 1899. In rather conventional Idealist terminology, Ahad Ha'am had asserted that each people possessed a distinctive spirit, expressing itself in every aspect of life—literature and language, morality and law—and found inside the heart of every healthy member of the nation. Whereas Western Jews had mistakenly come to believe that their spiritual inheritance consisted only in religion, Eastern Jews understood that the Jewish spirit was "a law for life," and not a "leisure time activity"; it involved fulfillment of "spiritual obligations" which fell on believers and nonbelievers alike. Different elements of culture, to be sure, predominated in the various national spirits. Among Jews, the spirit had taken the form of a unique commitment to moral excellence—a distinctive moral code. In the past, that code had been part and parcel of the Jewish religion, but it had now come to be recognized as independent—the ground of Israel's uniqueness among the nations. Not everyone lived up to or understood its demands: Herzl, for example, had just written a drama in which the Jewish protagonist fought a duel to defend the honor of his people against an anti-Semite. Any real Jew, in whose heart the nation's "moral spirit lived," would have known that the Jewish morality had a different idea of honor, commanding the Jew, in such a situation, to give the Gentile "a quick look of disgust, and go his way." Properly expounded, the natural morality could come to give similar guidance in "all affairs of life" and penetrate to the depths of Jewish hearts.[44]

This formulation of Judaism as national spirit centered on morality was essential to Ahad Ha'am's thinking for two reasons. First, in the wake of Kant, ethics had become the proper task of religion in the minds of many "enlightened" believers, its only continuing relevance. The Reform Jews whom Ahad Ha'am attacked had accepted this premise as the foundation of their faith, and he, as a thoroughgoing rationalist except when it came to romantic belief in the *Volksgeist*, now did the same. Second, if Judaism as a *culture* was to take the place of Jewish *faith* and constitute a vital force for the preservation of Jewish identity, it had, as Ahad Ha'am put it, to constitute a "guide to all the affairs of life." Only morality, among the elements of culture, could exercise such an influence. Art and literature could not, and the law of the Land—another possibility—was not in Jewish hands. That left morality. By establishing it as the modern equivalent of Jewish faith, Ahad Ha'am hoped to make it possible to be a "good atheist Jew," "kosher" in culture and nationality although heretical on matters of belief. Jewish culture—the Jewish nation—could thereby survive the loss of faith.

Herzl, by having his protagonist fight a duel, had only revealed once again that he was *not* such a Jew, imbued to his very core by the national morality. When he proposed consideration of East Africa ("Uganda") as the Jewish national home, therefore, Ahad Ha'am could profess a complete lack of surprise. "Metaphysical" questions about the concept of "place" could be left to others, he wrote in 1901. The Jewish nation recognized its proper place. Those "in whose hearts the national sense still truly lived" knew better than to consider any alternative to Zion. In a similar vein, a year later, he mocked Herzl's fantasy for the Jewish state, *Altneuland*, with a single question: what made it Jewish? Herzl could just as well have been envisioning the return of the Nigerians to Nigeria.[45]

Berdiczewski, however, posed precisely the same query to Ahad Ha'am: what made *his* vision Jewish? Had the national morality, as Ahad Ha'am articulated it, inspired the Israelites to conquer the Land under Joshua? Had it been present at the rabbinic academy of Yavneh in the year 70—or among those who chose to die by the sword inside Jerusalem's walls, rather than exchange political sovereignty for the study of Torah at Yavneh under Roman rule? When had the "national morality" ever existed, let alone predominated? The essence of any true national morality, Berdiczewski countered, was the love of a people for itself, and such love often involved the very use of force ruled out by Ahad Ha'am but without which the national culture which he endeavored to promote was impossible. Jewish morality at any given moment, Berdizcewski wrote, was just one element of Jewish culture among others, and like all the others was the product of specific historical circumstances. It changed with time. "The nation of Israel is an event in process, not an eternal account, fixed and delimited."[46] In short, there could be no unitary conception of the Jewish homeland or the Jewish homecoming. Ahad Ha'am, as it were, had not held up a magnifying glass to the Jewish past, but only a mirror to his own prejudices.

The subjectivity of Ahad Ha'am's vision did not, in and of itself, bother Berdiczewski. As an ardent follower of Nietzsche, he recognized the "perspectival" character of all truth and welcomed it. The issue was rather the character of Ahad Ha'am's Spiritual Center, which, Berdiczewski feared, would be utterly stultifying of subjectivity if Ahad Ha'am carried the day. The latter did not create thoughts, Berdizcewski observed shrewdly, but only judged them as to their moral value or their practicality. He was totally "unwilling to uproot what has been planted." His guiding principle was moderation in all things.[47] But this was a time when caution was destructive and uprooting inescapable. All had become too certain for the Jews, too fixed. "Remove all that's clear," Berdiczewski urged. "Plant doubt!"[48] Ahad Ha'am had accurately described the Jewish people's subservience to its sacred texts, but the measures which he prescribed would only perpetuate that servitude. He had exposed the "inner slavery hidden under external freedom" among Western assimilated Jews, but failed to recognize that "our utter surrender and enslavement to the backwardness of our inheritance is still more pathetic than that." Slavery to others could be overcome, but life in thrall to a distant past was more difficult to alter. Ahad Ha'am sought to usher in the new on the back of the old, to introduce new content to old forms, but it could not be done. The old could not nourish the new; as Nietzsche had taught, nothing could be built except on the ruins of what went before—and yet Israel, alone among the nations, had kept its "broken tablets inside the ark." It was now too late for that, Berdiczewski asserted. The past was now past. The great step forward had been taken. "The clouds of old age are passing, and the dew of childhood is on its way."[49]

This is the message declaimed repeatedly in Berdiczewski's many essays—like Nietzsche's short, crisp, and packed with a dazzling array of allusions and metaphors; unlike Nietzsche's never truly deep or possessed of stunning insight. In large part Berdiczewski's critique of Ahad Ha'am seems to have derived from differences of biography and temperament. He vividly recalled his first experience of the abyss separating the world of "grandfather

Israel" from the "big wide world" of modernity, "life," and "nature." Ahad Ha'am either never suffered such angst or resolved never to speak of it publicly. Moreover, like many others of his generation and the partisans of Jewish Enlightment generally, Berdiczewski experienced Jewish tradition as *personally* suffocating, an obstacle to personal fulfillment as much as national renewal. Where was the individual in Ahad Ha'am's national morality, he demanded. The group, the tradition, were everything.[50]

This difference may in turn have prompted the divergence between the two regarding the *tactics* of Jewish renewal. Ahad Ha'am, convinced that little could be done to alleviate the pain of exile, practiced silence. Berdiczewski by contrast cried out from the anguish of galut with all the poetic power at his command. Ahad Ha'am agreed that exile was harsh, degrading, and oppressive. But he could never permit himself explosions such as Berdiczewski's "How narrow are your tents, O Jacob, your dwelling places, O Israel."[51] Parody was a common device for the expression of Jewish fury at the age-old Jewish predicament,[52] but not one of which Ahad Ha'am could avail himself. He cultivated the restraint of the Mishnah, while Berdiczewski screamed with the fury of the *tokhehah* and argued forcefully that redemption of the spirit was not enough. The soul could not be nursed to health if the body could not stand. "They want to make a spiritual center," he complained, "but they and their thoughts are in exile, their culture is in exile, and their existence is in exile." Jews needed "real ground, tangible life." They had to "build a home again"—not a Spiritual Center.[53]

Ahad Ha'am responded to such outbursts with the patience of a father who understands the impatience of the young. We might recall, in this connection, Freud's recollection of his own anger as a child upon learning that in anti-Semitic Vienna a Gentile had asserted supremacy on the sidewalk by knocking the hat off his father's head. The elder Freud had responded exactly as Ahad Ha'am's national morality would have ordained. He had quietly picked up his hat and walked on.[54] Why cause further trouble, he had reasoned. The son by contrast demanded action, and an outlet for his (partially Oedipal) anger. Berdiczewski, like his father figure in debate, saw no solution to the plight of East European Jewry, but insisted that the Jews could not simply walk, without protest. Ahad Ha'am, like any good father, treated his outbursts with indulgence—which was of course all the more infuriating. Did the young Nietzscheans want a Jewish Superman? They already had one: their *nation*, elevated by its national morality ("Transvaluation of Values," 1898).[55] Did the young radicals want to start all anew? He could understand that feeling, but demanded that it be examined *rationally* ("Torah Out of Zion," 1911: a reply to Y. H. Brenner).[56] It is no wonder that Berdiczewski could not bring himself to affirm, in any sense, either the diaspora or Judaism, both of which Ahad Ha'am wished to transform only gradually.

Berdiczewski's substantive critique of Spiritual Zionism was entirely on the mark. The separation which Ahad Ha'am sought to effect between the moral "content" of Jewish tradition and its religious "garb" is tendentious and unconvincing. Discard the nineteenth-century assumption of a unique national *geist* informing every aspect of culture, and the easy discernment of "Jewish values" becomes problematic in the extreme—a cover for the articulation of Ahad Ha'am's often idiosyncratic judgments. The consequences of this failure for contemporary cultural Zionism (examined in Chapter Six) cannot be overestimated. But Berdiczewski's contrary attempt to sunder the Zionist present from the Jewish past—also not without its heirs among contemporary Israeli thinkers—was even more problematic. He himself conceded that in moments of detachment from the Jewish question he found the dichotomy of past and present untenable. It was only because he stood in the midst of things that he felt compelled to oppose in anger the past which he experienced as "a stone weighing us down." A dispassionate observer, he recognized, would likely have viewed matters differently.[57] In the end, despite or because of his passion, it is Berdiczewski and not Ahad Ha'am who strikes us in many ways as the realist. For he knew what needed to be done and what could not be done. Ahad Ha'am, for all his sobriety, rationality, and caution, relied far too much when all is said and done upon a blind and romantic faith in the will to live of the national Jewish organism and staked Jewish revival on a dubious theory about religion's natural evolution into ethics and culture. The problems in cultural Zionism to which Berdiczewski pointed have since become visible for all to see, as have the grounds for the admiration of Ahad Ha'am evident throughout his critique.

A somewhat different tactical dispute, no less revealing of the problems besetting the idea of the *spiritual center*, divided Ahad Ha'am from his friend Simon Dubnow. The great historian of the Jews contested the feasibility of the concept so as to argue for Jewish cultural and/or regional autonomy in the diaspora. He agreed that the history of modern European Jewry represented a series of tragic errors in need of correction. Emancipation had come at the price of national self-definition. Political Zionism had compounded the mistake by concluding that the solution lay only in emigration to a Jewish homeland. Given a choice between exile and a reborn state, most Jews would remain where they were.[58] Dubnow's dispute with Ahad Ha'am concerned only the best means of preserving the exile. The historian championed "autonomism," a scheme by which Jews would participate in the political and civil life of their host societies but retain freedom of self-determination. Such communities would constitute a worthy and legitimate end in themselves, not a stepping stone on the way to realization of the Spiritual Center, as Ahad Ha'am seemed to regard them. Palestine could not be a Center of the Jewish people in any sense, including the Spiritual. The diaspora was not peripheral.[59]

Dubnow was wrong in his reading of Ahad Ha'am. Normality served the father of spiritual Zionism as Jewish messianism had served many Jews in the past: a consummation devoutly to be wished, a standard by which to measure interim accomplishments, but not a goal, much less a program. Dubnow admitted as much when he went on to note Ahad Ha'am's real objection to his theory: diaspora autonomy was a pipe dream. The nations would not permit it. Jews would not receive minority rights now, when nationalism reigned supreme, and not later. The majority would always win out, hence the need for a place where a small elite of Jews could constitute such a majority and through it revive their national culture. Until the far-off day when more could be attained, he and Dubnow shared a "field of work" in the *golah*. Anyone who repudiated assimilation, Ahad Ha'am wrote, subscribed implicitly to "the entire Torah of Zionism."[60]

When Dubnow countered with the arguments summarized above, and wondered aloud how Ahad Ha'am could be so certain that Palestinian Jewish culture would direct Jewish culture elsewhere, rather than be influenced by it, Ahad Ha'am replied with his only systematic statement on the subject of galut: "Negation of the Diaspora" (1909). All agreed upon the "subjective negation" (i.e., dislike) of exile, Ahad Ha'am wrote. Only "weak-kneed optimists" could possibly embrace the condition of a lamb among wolves as a divine dispensation (i.e., a mission), and even they would gladly follow the Messiah out of exile if he ever came. The issue, therefore, was "objective negation" of the diaspora: the belief that Jews could not long exist in exile now that the loss of *halakhah* had left them defenseless against the "ocean of foreign culture." Assimilationists and political Zionists believed that such diaspora existence was not possible. However, neither had persuaded the Jewish masses, who continued to live there under the guidance of their unconquerable national will to survive. If Herzl were wrong and the diaspora continued, it *had* to be lived in, for all its evils. *Subjective negation*, therefore, had to be combined with *objective affirmation*. On this he agreed with Dubnow.

However, he reiterated, complete national life involved full use of the creative faculties of a people's culture and the opportunity to transmit that culture through education. Political, economic, social, and moral factors were all means to that end—and largely unavailable in the diaspora. The immediate task, then, was establishment of a fixed center in the land of the nation's birth, where, eventually, a full national life could be achieved.[61]

We emerge from the debate more convinced than ever of the weaknesses inherent in Ahad Ha'am's distinction between "subjective" and "objective" negation. The terminology itself provides a clue to the confusion. It is unusually befuddled for the master of crystal-clear prose—and unusually laden with jargon. The two dimensions to galut and its negation cannot be so neatly distinguished, as Ahad Ha'am well knew. The fact that there was no alternative to diaspora existence did not make such existence possible. Ahad Ha'am engaged in fantasy when he pictured a diaspora infused with the culture of its center in Eretz Israel, obeying a national morality "without any foreign admixture" and seemingly immune to the influences of its many and various surroundings. Nor could the religious way of life bound up in the exile which Ahad Ha'am "subjectively negated" be translated so easily into a secular Jewish culture which he could "subjectively affirm." To do so was to smooth over the divide between traditional faith and "enlightened" Jewish culture which loomed so large in the biographies of his generation and the Haskalah generally. On all this Berdiczewski was correct.

Yet what choice did Ahad Ha'am have? He could never "affirm the diaspora," because he saw no hope for its future without a national spiritual revival. He could not "negate the diaspora," because he saw no alternative to its existence: the Messiah was not about to come, and only God could gather in the exiles.[62] Nor could Ahad Ha'am permit himself to scream in desperation. There was therefore no alternative to the gradual upbuilding of a Spiritual Center, whatever its flaws. This was the point at which the "priest-prophet" of the Jewish return reached the limits of legitimate imagining.

Ahad Ha'am, to the end, could honestly not understand the criticism to which those limits were subjected by political Zionists. Would achievement of a Spiritual Center preclude material settlement of the Land? Certainly not: the Center depended upon such settlement and, once established, would strengthen the national consciousness of Jews all over the world. And what more than this was possible? Economic and political life could not possibly radiate from a national Center in the way culture could. This did not mean that he saw no importance in the establishment of factories, trade, and commerce there, Ahad Ha'am emphasized, but only that Warsaw, as he put it, could not possibly be the economic or political center for Poles around the world. Therefore, he argued, once one used the word Center one had become a spiritual Zionist, for no Center could survive without a periphery—a diaspora which had not disappeared—and the diaspora was not about to disappear.[63]

There was, of course, far more to it than that, as the political Zionists well knew. Their dispute with Ahad Ha'am concerned issues of real substance; both the purpose of Jewish homecoming and the best means of accomplishing it were at stake. Ahad Ha'am was right in arguing that he too was a political Zionist, in that he had politicized the traditional ideas of exile and return by embracing rational, human effort as the only method of achieving a national homeland. But it was mere sleight of hand to deny the difference between himself and his critics on the grounds that Zionism in all its forms had "always been essentially political," seeking "absolute independence . . . at some distant date."[64] Herzl was not willing to wait, in part because he, unlike Ahad Ha'am, did not live and breathe the classical Jewish texts of exile. Herzl could surrender to the messianism which in Ahad Ha'am's polemical lexicon functioned only as a term of abuse. The "agnostic rabbi"[65] was not blessed with such saving ignorance. He could not but wait for an ingathering initiated from "some other place"—in this too a faithful son of the tradition, as Berdiczewski discerned. He would wait—and in the meantime do whatever work could be done: "*Gegenwartsarbeit*," the "work of the present," of culture.

That labor proved indispensable, providing—in a modern, somewhat secular form—the traditional link between homecoming's political and metaphysical dimensions. Spiritual Zionism broadened the national movement's sense of its own goals and secured its appeal among Jews who never would have been stirred by a secular "state idea" alone. Homecoming had to go hand in hand with the renewal of Torah in order to be credible to those who would accomplish it. And for all that Ahad Ha'am drastically altered the concept of Torah, substituting the survival of the Jewish people and its culture for a life in service to God, he nevertheless remained faithful to the biblical-rabbinic notion that territory and sovereignty were only a means to higher ends—and made the highest end of Zionism the moral regeneration in exile of the Jews. Had Ahad Ha'am believed this goal as impossible of realization as sovereignty, he would have wanted no part of Zionism, spiritual or political. A "son of Moses" to the end, he would not have seen the point, let alone the legitimacy, of an exodus which did not lead to Sinai—and neither would many of those who followed him home to the Promised Land.

"Hebrew Humanism"

Contemporary Israelis and diaspora Jews alike have been heavily influenced by Ahad Ha'am's complex legacy, thanks in large part to its transmission by two thinkers: A. D. Gordon (1856–1922) and Martin Buber (1878–1965). Both edged closer to the religious tradition that Ahad Ha'am was never able to embrace; both had a keener sense than he of the unique possibilities which life in and on the Land afforded. As a result, Gordon and Buber were able to link spiritual Zionism with greater attention to the political and economic institutions of the Yishuv, a synthesis which, with the addition of socialist ideas going back to Hess, accounts for much in the thought of the Jewish state's founding fathers.

Gordon, who arrived in Palestine rather late in life to work the land, devoted one of his first systematic addresses on the meaning of the Zionist return—occasioned by the proposal for a "Hebrew University"—to a trenchant critique of Ahad Ha'am's Spiritual Center. The Zionists' dispute over matter and spirit, he charged, was but the latest chapter in an age-old quarrel, empty and artificial. Jews did not suffer from too much of either matter or spirit but from the sickness of both, caused by the spirit's exilic detachment from the body, its flight from earth into the heavens. Ahad Ha'am's idea of the Spiritual Center had no content, Gordon complained, and the spiritual revival which he urged had not occurred. Flesh and spirit remained "sick" even inside the Land, in large part because Zionists like Ahad Ha'am, who claimed to favor a synthesis between the two, had concentrated upon Jewish culture rather than upon real physical labor on the Land. Spirit could emerge only from the normal, complete existence of a nation, Gordon argued, and such existence was always founded upon the work of the hands.[66]

Gordon's call for such labor was unrelenting, and his criticism of all Zionists not committed to its centrality untempered. Life not rooted in the soil was a life of barren intellectuality, of the stock exchange—not really life at all. Exile was slavery, sickness, alienation, darkness, estrangement, and death. It was—Gordon's favorite term, repeated on countless occasions—an existence of *parasites*.[67] An abyss separated that existence from national revival, and the divide had not yet been crossed. Halfway measures such as those adopted thus far had only brought parasitism and galut inside the borders of the land. They had created "the life of galut, in a new version, Eretz-Israeli . . . which, as we know, is even worse than the life of galut in other lands. . . . The land of Israel despite all this remains the holy land, but the life within it is largely one of schnorring, of commerce, of rot."[68] Instead of urging work and more work—the only cure for the "plague" of exile—the Yishuv had been misled by the "Satan of *galut*," infected by "*galut* wisdom" and divisiveness.[69]

Meanwhile, outside Israel, the Jews had no life, no relation to nature, no pure air, no independence of thought or activity. The Gentiles "pollute your daughters, judge you all day long, scheme to do you evil," Gordon wrote in 1912 in a "letter not sent at the time" to his "friends in the *golah*." While Jews inside the Land also had their share of problems, their sufferings, unlike those in exile, were not in vain, for the fruit of their dedication remained behind to inspire others.[70]

Gordon's language, like Berdiczewski's, is full to overflowing with allusions to Jewish tradition. His assertion that fulfillment could come only through work upon the *adamah* of the Jews' national *eretz*, work which brought the Jew into contact with nature as a whole, and so with Heaven, comes straight from Deuteronomy. In the absence of such contact with Earth and Heaven, Gordon writes, Jews are "*avud*"—lost, orphans, wanderers, at the mercy of foreigners and their cultures—again a precise echo of Deuteronomy, which had employed precisely the same root, *avod*, for its description of galut. Adopting the rabbinic term for idol worship, *avodah zarah* (literally "foreign work" or "servitude"), Gordon inveighed against the use of Arab labor and the importation of European culture into Jewish national life. Invoking kabbalah, he called for a "shattering of the vessels" which would make way for a new creation. Employing the imagery of Genesis and Exodus, he wrote that a deep abyss separated the state of exile from Eden, galut from renewal and the future—and there were "no eagles' wings to carry us over."[71]

Such traditional language lent enormous power to Gordon's special pleading on behalf of his particular Zionist vision, and helped to "Judaize," as it were, the principal tenets of his thought. For despite his strictures about European imports, those tenets were overwhelmingly borrowed from well-known European inventories. The Tolstoyan origin of Gordon's belief in the redemptive power of labor has long been noted. His perennial opposition of *Gemeinschaft* (organic life rooted in the soil) to *Gesellschaft* (urban cos-

mopolitan society) was no less a mere echo of themes first sounded elsewhere by others. By clothing his eclectic borrowings in Jewish terms,
however, Gordon was able to endow the effort of Jewish national return with
a cosmic importance which no other non-Orthodox Zionist since Hess had
claimed for it. Return to the soil offered renewed community and a restored
connection to the whole of being; it promised, as well, the *tikkun* of the self.
The national *I* which gave birth to language, concepts, religions, and world
views was father to every individual *I*, Gordon explained. It stood, alternately, in the relation of the whole of an organism to its various parts. The
individual Jew, therefore, was dependent upon the nation as a whole for his
or her personal well-being. Only if the people as a whole, currently alienated
from nature, returned to it "to live more, to live nature," to "resurrect the 'I'
of the nation, in nature," could the Jews as a nation or as individuals be
saved.[72] Having returned, they would be saved—yet another messianic
claim for Zionism by one of its principal theoreticians.

For Gordon, immersion in nature was a religious act, and the enterprise of
restoring the Jews to nature a religious activity. Israel's national awakening,
he wrote, might in former times have been called a "*gi'lui shekhinah*"—a
revelation of God's presence.[73] Again, the term is traditional but Gordon's
use of it is not; *vox populi* is never equated by the rabbis with *vox dei*. In
another passage Gordon urged the nation and its individuals to take direction not from the mind or the spirit but from the soul (*nefesh*), from
immediate life, which was natural and vital and should therefore "be our
teacher at all times."[74] One could hardly wander farther from Jewish tradition, which was ever on guard against the urges of the "eyes and heart."
Gordon's view of religion, predictably, was Romantic. One had to distinguish the *feeling* of faith, the "religious relation" which preceded verbal
expression, from the fixed forms of a particular tradition. The feeling was
alive, eternal, in the soul, lodged deeper than morality. The forms were too
often antiquated, if only because groups were less susceptible to change than
individuals. Religious feelings, moreover—like nations, and unlike religious
traditions, or "societies"—were intrinsically connected to nature. They accorded access to the "tree of life" denied those who had eaten of the rational,
technical "fruits" of the "tree of knowledge."[75] This midrash too, while it
might have won the approval of some daring kabbalists, was certainly at odds
with the rabbis. It presumes, quite openly, repudiation of the commandments.

Ahad Ha'am could never have endorsed such romanticism, just as Gordon
could not accept Ahad Ha'am's position on the issues of "spirituality" and
Arab labor. But the two remained very much in the same tradition. "I am not
a student of Ahad Ha'am," Gordon wrote, but "I know his worth."[76] Gordon, too, sought renewal of the "spirit" to restore a sick and parasitic people
to health and depended upon a vanguard in Palestine; he too employed the
metaphor of a national organism to argue that revival of one part of the
Jewish people, through manual labor upon the Land, could save and inspire

the whole. The entire people, he conceded in 1920, could be healthy even if only a minority of its members returned to work the ancestral soil. Once the nation had been led by that elite to self-awareness, other countries would no longer constitute galut for Jews, but merely places where they dwelled as *gerim* or resident aliens. The crucial question was whether Jews outside the Land were an influence upon others or "passive" recipients of foreign cultures.[77] Again the metaphor of the organism proved decisive. Gordon's negation of the diaspora, as a result, was a good deal less than absolute. He had adopted the concept, if not the term, "spiritual center."

That is not to deny the principal difference between the two: Gordon's insistence that attention be paid to the Jewish body first of all, and in particular to its need for work on the Jewish soil. In part this too was a function of Gordon's mystical and romantic proclivities, but in large measure it can be traced to his unusual experience of intimacy with the Land. In his letter to the diaspora Gordon beautifully evokes the landscapes of Israel, the greenery of Galilee, the light which "reveals all in cruel clarity." He summons up the memories of Elijah and Jacob, recalling to mind the lyricism of Yehudah Halevi.[78] Nature was not an abstract idea for Gordon, nor was Eretz Israel the site for fulfillment of the commandments. The Land was more than the precondition of national regeneration. It was, for Gordon, the very real soil though which, in middle age, he had come to know personal fulfillment—a sort of rebirth, and even redemption.

This may account, as well, for Gordon's messianism. How could people live all their lives as if the world were not theirs, he once asked, as if the infinite did not touch them?[79] The image recalls Genesis's verdict upon the human condition rather precisely—in order to repudiate it. Redemption *was* possible, Gordon insisted, and the infinite well within reach. Only in rare moments do we glimpse Gordon's doubts. Was it all perhaps an idle dream, a hallucination, the product of weak nerves? Where were the eagle's wings to carry Israel across the abyss from galut to new life? Gordon usually chased away such thoughts with the self-reminder that his own redemption was beyond dispute. Besides, there was simply no alternative—no other "way to think and feel without despair or self-deception."[80] Like the rabbis in this respect, he worked on faith. He counted on manna, as it were, because he had tasted it and so was unwilling to live like Ahad Ha'am on the bread of rational expectations alone.

It is not difficult to understand the immediate appeal of Gordon's vision to the young pioneers of the Second Aliyah who promptly transformed his life into legend and treated his every word with a seriousness born of veneration. Nor is it surprising that interest in Gordon has revived among Israelis in our own day, principally kibbutznikim who share Gordon's intimacy with the Land and regard it not merely as a near-personal presence in their lives but as a value of the highest importance.[81] They too think of Eretz Israel in such terms because of and not despite their alienation from much of traditional Jewish religion, and like Gordon seek to transform and adapt that tradition to their own purposes. In these respects Gordon has proved extremely influential, and in one more: the use of the tradition to negate a diaspora often far more traditional than its negators.

To an outsider to these affairs of the heart, however, Gordon's failings are far more obvious than his strengths. His constant harping on parasitism rankles. His romantic faith in the redemptive quality of manual labor seems anachronistic and self-serving. The man seems small in his enthusiasms, unconvincing in his eclectic borrowings, and positively dangerous in his claims for the "organic" and the "instinctive," his unbounded faith in the rightness of those once more in touch with the Land.

Not so Buber's very different Ahad Ha'amist synthesis of "body" and "spirit," a vision of homecoming both more sophisticated than Gordon's and far better grounded in Jewish tradition. In the early years of his affiliation with Jewish nationalism, Buber shared many of Gordon's presuppositions and even much of his vocabulary. The series of *Reden über das Judentum* which date from the first decade of the century express a tenuous relationship to Judaism, and articulate a negation of the *golah* which could not be more extreme. Diaspora existence is variously described as poor, distorted, sickly, sterile, sunken, abysmal, fragmented, tortured, tormented, lacking in unity, and characterized by a barren intellectuality.[82] Like Berdiczewski, Buber complains that

> for centuries, we did not hit back when our face was slapped. Instead, inferior in numbers and in strength, we turned aside, feeling tautly superior as 'intellectuals,' and this very intellectuality—out of touch with life, out of balance, inorganic, as it were—fed on the fact that, for millennia, we did not know a healthy, rooted life, determined by the rhythm of nature.[83]

Galut had meant "unspeakable torment," "everlasting torture," the "longest and most painful martyrdom ever suffered by any people on earth."[84] In a second set of essays, dating from 1911–1914, Buber added that the Jews were the very picture of the homeless world. Their need to create "a solid home for the spirit," out of their own soul and on their own soil, would overcome the rationality and alienation from nature affecting all the modern "homeless" world—and so pave the way for universal human fulfillment.[85]

Unlike the depiction of galut as endless suffering and intellectuality—a staple since Graetz's portrait of Jewish life in exile as a mixture of these two characteristics—the elevation of Jewish exile to a symbol for all *modern* humanity represents an innovation. The source, one suspects, was less the Kabbalah's mythology of a world permanently out of joint, symbolized by a scattered Jewish people, than Nietzsche's various and powerful descriptions of the modern world as not at home, cast off, unchained from its sun, now that it had lost God, and with Him the belief in Good and Evil. Whatever its source, however, the idea was a potent one and became even more so when, in Buber's later work, extravagant descriptions of galut were eliminated and the vision of return became far more concrete. Beginning with *I and Thou*

(1923), Buber diagnosed the sickness of modern life as a withering of "I-Thou" relationships of wholeness and trust (i.e., *Gemeinschaft*), and the excessive growth of "I-It" relationships (i.e., *Gesellschaft*)—part and parcel of the technological and bureaucratic world. People unable to relate to each other as "thou's," he explained, not surprisingly found it difficult to relate to the Being who is eternally a Thou—God. The most urgent task facing mankind, then, was the creation of communities and institutions which would facilitate I-Thou relations rather than preclude them. It was in that conceptual context that Buber placed the Jews' return to Zion, and particularly the founding of kibbutzim. The Bible, more than any other book, had articulated God's demand that human beings live in justice and wholeness, and Zionism, by undertaking that task through the building of communities in the Spiritual Center, had provided the Jewish people with the chance once more to prove exemplary.[86]

Return to Israel, then, meant a renewed possibility to achieve personal wholeness impossible in the urban diaspora. More important, it provided the opportunity to live within institutions shaped by Jewish commitments as Buber understood these: that is, responsive to the Bible's demand that human beings live in justice and wholeness. Jews more than any other people had come to know the indivisibility of the national and religious dimension of existence, Buber wrote in his definition of "Hebrew Humanism." This knowledge, in fact, constituted their choseness. The Bible did not urge renunciation of force and realpolitik, he asserted, but it did demand recognition of the compromises forced upon moral actors and the awareness that some compromises were morally unacceptable.[87] Without the responsibility which necessitated retreats from principle, however, Jews could not accomplish the "transforming deed for humanity" of which Buber had written as early as 1917. A concrete homeland was needed in order to direct age-old Jewish wandering toward the eternal goals which Buber identified with "the spirit of Israel."[88] Zion as symbol alone would not do. In *Paths in Utopia* (1958) Buber's thinking became still more precise. After a survey of utopian socialist thought he declared a federation of kibbutzim in Palestine the best way to restore the Jews to proper life in the world. It was, he wrote, the one experiment in human community which had "not yet failed."[89]

Negation of the diaspora is deemphasized in these later writings. The Land is by and large demystified. I qualify the statement because Buber never could entirely abandon the traditional sense that "long life upon the land" was conditional upon Israel's moral conduct. Infidelity to God's covenant would somehow result in the land "spewing forth" the Jewish people—not by magic or special providence, but via a natural order made supremely moral at this one single point of creation. That conviction is articulated forcefully in Buber's most extended meditation on the meaning of the Land—*On Zion* (1944), both a hymn of praise culled from the tradition, ancient and modern, and a critical reading of most of the texts examined in the present study. Buber's interpretations of Genesis 12 and Deuteronomy

26 are masterful, his treatments of the rabbis and Kabbalah far more sympathetic than elsewhere in his work and his comments on Zionist thinkers from Hess to Kook often incisive.[90] It is as if the Land has stretched his own imagination, further testimony of the powers of which he wrote. For all that, however, Eretz Israel in Buber's thought remains primarily a precondition for what can be achieved there, rather than an end in itself or a place of inherent sanctity. It provides an opportunity for wholeness that Jews could not know within alienating modern societies rendered doubly alienating by the fact that they were gentile.

Buber also universalized the concept of the Land, for in a sense, and to a degree, I-Thou relations were possible at any time in any place and facilitated by any true community. Jews could come to know their fellows and their God no matter where they lived, as any mystic could experience the divine regardless of material circumstances. Homeland, Buber wrote, was "unarbitrary life in the face of God."[91] Conversely, when God asked the Hasid "where are you" and he answered "somewhere else," the reply would not have been any different if the Hasid had lived inside rather than outside the Land. In Eretz Israel, too, a man had to wonder "where in the world am I"—meaning that there too exile had not ceased.[92] Not surprisingly, concern with the Land and its upbuilding occupies only a small part of Buber's work, most of which is devoted to a Jewish spirituality and ethics applicable anywhere.

Unlike many others of similar bent, however, Buber found homelands of the spirit insufficient. Modernity, he believed, had set a peculiar trap for spirit, Jewish or gentile, which could be avoided only with the establishment of true I-Thou communities. Jews could create such communities only in Zion, where they had control of political and economic institutions. In the diaspora they were condemned to the practice of Judaism as a mere religion— and religion, Buber wrote, was "the exile of man," which "wills precisely to cease being religion" and to become "all of life." This "will" or "feeling," which was prior to belief, Buber labeled "religiosity" and lauded—in contrast to "religion," which he consistently attacked.[93]

The point here is that Buber's sociological understanding of modernity and his definition of religion as the impulse to unify life and self led him to see ultimate religious meaning in the Jewish return to Zion and to be dissatisfied with life of the spirit in exile. Unlike Gordon, he allowed for a vigorous spiritual life in the diaspora. Unlike the political Zionists, he saw no point in a return not accompanied by the biblical commitments which he titled "Hebrew Humanism." Unlike Ahad Ha'am, finally, he held fast to the belief in a real and personal God who comes forth to encounter human beings in the world. When all is said and done, however, Buber's vision too is essentially that of spiritual Zionism. The Center serves both itself and its periphery. Jews inside and outside the Land owe obedience to a sacred moral and cultural order derived from Jewish tradition. Jews could not, because of that unique service, build a state like other states or become like other peoples ("normalized"). Nor were they likely, short of the Messiah's coming, to pick themselves up from exile and stream home to the kibbutzim of Palestine. They did not need to, so long as the Center for their nation's spirit were properly revived. A measure of wholeness would then be possible for Jews everywhere, just as a degree of moral compromise would remain inevitable even in the Promised Land. This aspect of the Buberian notion of homecoming is consistent with the rabbinic tradition, the politics and metaphysics of exile joined once more, even if Buber was unable to follow the rabbis in other matters. He did not believe in their God of history or obey Him as the author of the commandments, but he too subordinated the Zionist return to "Torah"—and only, as such, supported it.

Conclusion

Buber's stance in a highly ambivalent relation to the Jewish religious tradition was typical of all the spiritual Zionists whom we have examined. Like the rest, he was profoundly shaped by the tradition, devoted his energies to its reinterpretation, and repeatedly turned to it—or, better, to selected elements of it—for reassurance that his path was the right one. Yet like Gordon, Ahad Ha'am, and Hess, Buber was also the product of a very different culture—that of nineteenth-century Europe—which led him to challenge many of Judaism's basic assumptions. Neither assimilation nor Reform were acceptable solutions to these men, and Orthodoxy was out of the question. They formulated spiritual Zionism, in part, as the only solution available—one which gathered up the pieces of their fragmented spirits, even as it promised in the long run to gather in the Jewish people from its exile.

Not surprisingly, the conflict which moved the spiritual Zionists to action also came to inform their visions of its overcoming through Jewish homecoming. They were themselves unable either to affirm the past or to do without it. The decisive break urged by Berdiczewski, and achieved without difficulty by Jews such as Herzl who had never been deeply linked to the Jewish past in the first place, was to them impossible. They had to go home—to return—to a place the Jews had been before, in every sense of the words *home* and *return*. Tradition held them, even as it pushed them home. It told them where and what home was, both through the biblical-rabbinic vision of ingathering and through description of the exile they knew too well from personal experience—description which shaped that experience and helped to constitute it. Outright negation of the diaspora was therefore impossible to spiritual Zionists. It would have meant negation of themselves—of the possibility for survival of all that was meaningful in the reality from which they had come and to which they remained attached even in rebellion. Ahad Ha'am and those who followed him were caught in the middle, pulled from both ends. They had made the decisive break, but could not bring themselves to let go.

The reasons for that break are by now well known—all the more reason to remember that if the spiritual Zionists felt the need to escape from exile, this imperative too came from tradition. For centuries Jews had learned to endure their exile by ascribing it to divine punishment and imagining a divinely initiated redemption. By the late nineteenth century in Eastern Europe, patience had once more begun to wear thin. Secular writers lamented Jewish impotence with bitter parody of the classical sources, excoriating those who found comfort in exile or a purpose in the dispersion. The negative picture which such writers painted of exile came both from the reality all around them and from the tradition itself. The imperative to escape that reality could likewise be traced far back, all the way to Deuteronomy. The spiritual Zionists, then, imagining the Jewish escape from powerlessness, made full use of this picture common to their Eastern European Jewish world. And that iconography of exile was visual no less than verbal. Samuel Hirszenberg's epic painting "Golus" (1904), to which David Roskies directs our attention, depicts a crowded remnant of Jews in gray and black, surrounded by (suspended in, really) white empty space. The refugees have salvaged only a Torah scroll, a prayer shawl, and a tea kettle. All are bent over, resigned, in flight.[94] Such images, in the lexicon of spiritual Zionism, recur and predominate.

The other staples of that lexicon came from the second inheritance passed on to Ahad Ha'am and his followers by previous generations of European Jews: The modern reconception of galut and Eretz Israel inaugurated by Spinoza and Mendelssohn. The Land had been *demystified:* considered now not as the fount of revelation, but in terms of its suitability for large-scale immigration. The idea of return to it had been *politicized:* a matter of calculating financial arrangements and the shifts in the balance of power, rather than a ledger of sin and repentance on which the Messiah's coming would be inscribed. Finally, exile and homecoming had been *universalized:* exile becoming a place where every human being lived until the perfection of life on earth, especially in the homeless modern world; Jerusalem and the Land becoming symbols of the perfection to come.

This last transformation of the tradition was perhaps the most crucial, paradoxically making possible the real return of the Jewish people to the real Land of Israel and Jerusalem. Labor in the fields of Palestine would have seemed pointless to the spiritual Zionists, and even immoral, were they not convinced that through such labor the Jews served all mankind, directly or indirectly. Even Ahad Ha'am, who professed time and again that such efforts were the product of an innate national will to live, and that alone, couched his vision of Jewish homecoming in terms of universal moral purpose. His failure to universalize the significance of the return even more—to make it a foreshadowing, or a paradigm, of the redemption of humanity—was probably the result of his refusal, as an heir to Jewish tradition, to ascribe messianic significance to a homecoming both partial and secular. Had he been more of a believer, or less the "agnostic rabbi," he might have allowed himself more hope and exercised less caution. Buber—not a messianist by any means, but certainly a believer—permitted himself to see the Jewish homecoming as the one experiment in building human community which had not failed, at least not yet. Only as such did it claim his allegiance.

The universalization of the concept of exile also served the interests of the spiritual Zionists. Buber's Hasid spoke for all mankind when he explained that he was always "somewhere else"; that, after all, is why Buber transmitted the teaching. The Jews, who in Lurianic kabbalah were the symbol of universal alienation, now became the symbol of the special estrangement inspired by modernity. Berdiczewski's description of Jews tied strongly to each other but separated into seventy languages and dispersed over the face of the earth reminds us of the parable offered by Kafka in "Investigations of a Dog," one of the epigraphs to the present study. "Dog" stand first of all for "Jew"—but after that for modern humanity as a whole.[95] Once more, the situation of Israel articulates *la condition humaine.* The twentieth century's reduction of millions to the status of homeless refugees has only added to modernity's estrangement of the spirit, thereby making the Jews, at least in their own eyes, even more a symbol in their suffering of the general predicament. One thinks of their forebearer Mendele, the Shtetl Jew who was the narrative persona for author Shalom Jacob Abramowitsch. One day Mendele meets a Pole who, like him, has come to know the debasement of life on the run. Finally, the Jews had something useful to teach the Gentiles, Mendele remarks: the trick of survival in exile. Now they could truly be a "light unto the nations."[96] Modernity had made them such.

Alternatively, they could become Zionists. Nowhere is the power of the complex legacy of Moses Hess and Ahad Ha'am more clearly visible than in the writings of David Ben Gurion, whose hard-headed pragmatism and "political Zionist" credentials were otherwise impeccable. Ben-Gurion began, writes Shlomo Avineri, with two guiding principles: revolt against Jewish tradition and the building of the Yishuv through socialism. Zionism represented nothing less than a "historical transformation" of the Jewish people, Ben-Gurion wrote in 1933. It was in essence a "revolutionary movement," a "revolt against a tradition of many centuries, helplessly longing for redemption."[97] The Zionist revolution, he asserted in 1944, was directed "not only against a system but against destiny, against the unique destiny of a unique people." For galut had meant dependence, its greatest courage that of nonsurrender. Zionism meant Jewish mastery over Jewish fate; independence in every sense—political, economic, moral, cultural, and intellectual.[98]

And yet, when Ben-Gurion came to argue for his revolution, he appealed to his readers to "open the Bible" and recall Jeremiah's lesson to Johanan and Jezaniah, or Joshua's conquest of the Land, or the awful dilemmas confronted by Isaiah. He recalled Israel's belief in its "pioneering mission to all men," its gift to the world of "great and eternal moral truths and commandments." The example of Jewish revolution would one day serve "as a model for the workers' movement of the world." Even "the complete ingathering of the exiles into a socialist Jewish state" was not "our ultimate goal," but rather a "precondition for the fulfillment of the real mission of our people." Once the Jews had become free men on their own soil, they would address themselves to "the great mission of man on this earth—to master the forces of nature and to develop his unique creative genius to the highest degree."[99]

The final image, of course, derives more from the European Enlightenment, and particularly Marx, than from Judaism, but then that is typical of both spiritual Zionism and the socialist Zionism linked to it by the common ancestry of *Rome and Jerusalem*. From Hess onward, appeal to Jewish tradition had been married to a secular messianism couched in terms of both Israel's prophets and Europe's. Zionism was a revolutionary transformation; but Ben-Gurion, like others among its leading thinkers, could neither transform nor revolutionize without the rooting and the mission—the legitimacy, in a word—which the tradition conferred. Indeed, he probably could not have believed in his own secular messianism, lacking as he was the comfort of Hess's mysticism or Marx's materialist science, were it not for the legacy of the religious tradition against which he proclaimed total revolt.

Ahad Ha'am, then, left his mark on the Zionist project, because his synthesis of "priest and prophet," of return to the Land with spiritual revival, proved of enormous appeal to many who followed him home and of essential importance to what they did there. The spiritual Zionist legacy continues to inspire and haunt Israeli thinkers today, as they seek to salvage Ahad Ha'am's reconception of Judaism from the wreckage of his philosophical assumptions and to make the notion of a Spiritual Center relevant to the Jewish state which Ahad Ha'am did not believe would arise either in his lifetime or in our own.

V

HOMECOMING
THE RESURRECTION OF THE
BODY POLITIC

For Herzl, matters were far less complicated; in his own estimation, in fact, "quite simple." What is striking as we read Herzl today, and always was, is the utter confidence with which he put forth his plan for bringing the Jews home after two thousand years of wandering. "I claim no new discoveries," he wrote in *Der Judenstaat*. "Let this be noted at once and throughout this discussion." The success of his scheme rested only on the "propelling force" of the Jews' indisputable plight. If enough of them simultaneously agreed to follow his instructions for easing that plight, achievement of a Jewish state would present "no difficulties worth mentioning." Herzl's second premise was equally simple: the Jews were "a people—one people." Anti-Semitism had survived in the modern world, a "misplaced piece of medievalism," because the nations were reluctant to tolerate large numbers of another nation—the Jews—in their midst. Economic success had only exacerbated this antagonism; assimilation had not ended it; previous attempts to ease it, through emigration to small agricultural colonies, had not worked. Herzl believed that he would succeed where others had failed because he presumed rather than denied the Jews' nationhood. The "state idea" would move Jews to leave their present homes, the "Society of Jews" and the "Jewish Company" would secure them a new one, and the nations where they had lived—overjoyed to be rid of them—would wish them godspeed.[1] The plan was indeed "essentially quite simple," brilliantly so.

Unlike Berdiczewski's prose, or Buber's, or Gordon's, Herzl's is dry, flat, spare. Its rhetorical power lies precisely in the matter-of-fact tone through which Herzl seeks to erase all suspicion that he is indulging in mere fantasy. The authorial voice reminds us constantly of its own realism, presenting its controversial claims as but a series of obvious facts. "Steam is generated by boiling water." The Jews were a nation. Anti-Semites hated them. The rich knew "full well how much can be done for money." "The scientific plan and political policies which the Society of Jews will establish will be carried out by the Jewish company." Palestine was preferable as a homeland, but

Argentina would do. "The world needs the Jewish state; therefore it will arise."[2] Ahad Ha'am had more than met his match, when it came to sobriety, rationality, and clarity. Herzl achieved the upper hand in their contest, however, not because of his superior prose, but because he could offer Jews something which Ahad Ha'am could not give them: the hope of immediate redemption—in a word, the Messiah.

I insist on the word *Messiah* in this connection, though I use it with caution, because one cannot understand either the daring of Herzl's convictions or the dilemmas of contemporary political Zionism without it. But we should not forget that usage of the term is problematic, for several reasons. Not the least of them is the fact that Herzl delivered on his promises. He set in motion the founding of a Jewish state. The desert blooms; exiles have been ingathered. What is more, he accomplished all these wonders—in the persons of those who followed him—without appeal to God. He depended only on the laws of nature and history as he perceived these, and refused to look beyond. Modern technology would achieve what prayer could not; the process would be entirely rational, even mechanical. The end of the story as envisioned by Herzl is no less unusual for a messianic tale; not "universal brotherhood," Herzl declared, nor the dreamlands imagined by "amiable visionaries of all kinds." Conflict was essential to man's highest efforts. Even after their redemption, therefore, "the Jews would always have enemies— just as every other nation."[3]

One hesitates to invoke the hallowed name "Messiah," then, and hesitates even more in the face of Herzl's repugnance at what it implies. Yet he draws the label to himself, renders it virtually inevitable, precisely in the casual utterance that the Jews would always have enemies "just as every other nation." For this was the substance of Herzl's messianism, the appeal which drew the Jewish masses to him like a magnet and continues to inspire Israelis even today. Finally the Jews would be normal. It did not and does not matter that Herzl failed to associate homecoming with universal peace. Deuteronomy too, we recall, had allowed for crime and disease and false prophecy in the perfected realm of Torah which it depicted. The crucial point is that Herzl proclaimed with the calm assurance of prophecy that the Jews would henceforth have a foothold on the earth and the enemies that go along with it. They would be "as every other nation." And "once settled in their own land," they could "never again be scattered all over the world. The diaspora cannot be revived."[4] Not because God would not permit it, but because the Gentiles would never permit it! An ingathering of the exiles, accomplished with the help of anti-Semites and protected by their hatred of the Jews. How marvelous were the ways of history!

And how marvelous the visions of its self-appointed agent. Herzl's translation of traditional hopes for ingathering was made credible as no mere messianic fantasy could be by the language of "boiling water" and anti-Semitism, international finance and realpolitik. And it was lent added power by the age-old longing for normality which stretches back to the twelve tribes' request that Samuel anoint them a king, that they might be "like every other nation." Herzl's double promise has now been fulfilled. The Jews are at home in their land, and they, like every other nation, have enemies. Contrary to his vision, however, the *Judenstaat* finds itself linked irrevocably with a diaspora that refuses either to disappear, as he expected, or to be ingathered. Small wonder then that messianism, religious and secular, is resurgent in the Jewish state, and the value of the state's many achievements constantly called into question. The ambitions set into motion by Herzl were too large. They were rendered even larger by the claim to rationality, the deprecation of mere messianism, that persisted in the generation of Ben-Gurion. The flourish with which Herzl concludes *The Jewish State*—invoking the "cause," the Maccabees, a "wonderous breed of Jews"—succeeds because until that point his prose has been utterly matter-of-fact. Herzl's final sentences sweep us away because they sound all the major notes of the Jewish tradition concerning exile and homecoming with apparent effortlessness and grace: life, home, peace, *adamah*. Death is a return, as in Deuteronomy and the story of the Garden, and life for all its cares is marked by tangible redemption. "We shall live at last as free men on our own soil," Herzl promises, "and in our own homes peacefully die."[5] This *is* messianism, as Herzl's admirers and detractors both realized. The Jews were coming Home.

In part, one suspects, Herzl's ignorance of the details of Jewish tradition, his failure to confront that tradition as an adult, are the secret to the innocent power of his rhetoric. He recalled in an autobiographical sketch in 1898 that as a child he had once been punished for forgetting the details of the Jews' departure from Egypt, while "today, there are scores of teachers who would like to thrash me because I remember the Exodus from Egypt all too well."[6] The reminiscence is telling in its account of Herzl's appeal; so too is the well-known dream as a boy of twelve, recounted shortly before his death, in which "King Messiah came" and "took me in his arms," sweeping him off to a meeting with Moses in the clouds. "It is for this child that I have prayed," the Messiah calls to Moses, and to Herzl he says "Go, declare to the Jews that I shall come soon and perform great wonders and great deeds for my people and for the whole world."[7] Ahad Ha'am could carp at the unreality of Herzl's ambitions, which to him too seemed messianic, and warn of the danger of such flirtation with despair. But he could not compete with them, especially so long as they seemed to be working. When Herzl's fantasy of the reborn Jewish state, *Altneuland*, was published in 1902, Ahad Ha'am ridiculed its simplemindedness, marveled at its utopianism, wondered how the anti-Semites had been made to disappear and the Arabs become so accommodating, and cried out in desperation that there was nothing Jewish about Herzl's state—only to be chastised for his disbelief.[8] It was not only that he criticized the leader of his people. His strictures just could not hold a candle to Herzl's melodrama. Neither he nor his successors in contemporary Israel understood the messianic dynamics at work in political Zionism.

Spiritual Zionists have proved unable either to use those dynamics successfully or to contain them.

Consider the plot of *Altneuland*, a dreamlike voyage by a "cultured and
despairing young man" (i.e., the Jewish people and Herzl himself) "willing
to try one last experiment with his life" after nearly committing suicide.[9]
Frederick journeys to a kingdom beyond the sea—Palestine—escorted by a
kindly Gentile named Kingscourt. "I should be proud as the devil if I were a
Jew," the older man tells his young protégée. All that the pair see in their
initial journey through Palestine, however, serves to weaken Jewish pride
rather than to inspire it. Jaffa is impoverished and shabby; the countryside
lacks greenery and water; the beggars at the Western wall seem "degenerate
exploiters of our national mourning" to whom Frederick feels no connection
whatever. "Nobody can be deader than the Jewish people," he tearfully
concludes. His spirits are revived somewhat by the flourishing agricultural
colonies established by Hovevei Zion. Kingscourt, as they leave for Egypt,
counsels Frederick—and his people—to dream and to plan. Use science and
technology to help yourselves, he urges. Set up a new land on your old soil.
"What have you to lose?"[10]

Twenty years later, when Frederick and Kingscourt return for a second
visit, the land is flourishing. The pair find "All Nations Square" in Haifa full
of traders and a tram going up and down Mount Carmel. A "little begger Jew
boy" has become a prominent leader of the "New Society," a man who could
stand up for himself. Women have equal rights in the New Society, and
Arabs participate freely. There are potash works and railroads, waterworks
and hospitals; theaters, newspapers, sports, even an opera about Sabbatai
Sevi—all because, the beggar-turned-leader explains, the Jews had stopped
waiting for miracles and instead had trusted in their own strength.[11] Most
powerfully, as in Deuteronomy 26, there is a description of what it will be
like to know redemption and look back from a distance to the time when
Jews had been ashamed of themselves. "To be despised, and in the end
despise yourself—that is the fate of exile." The chapter is entitled
"Jerusalem."[12]

Berdiczewski complained, justly, that the problem of securing sovereignty
had been avoided in *Altneuland* and that Herzl had pictured his state in
terms borrowed from the progressives of Europe, when in fact the details of
its development could be known only once the Jews had actually returned to
the Land.[13] But this too, while a fair criticism, is of course beside the point.
Herzl's vision appealed to Jews, one suspects, precisely because it was up-
to-date and just like those of the Gentiles. The jargon of science and
technology in which Herzl couched his vision showed him to be a man who
could make it come to pass: someone at home among Gentiles, a Moses
comfortable in the court of Pharaoh, who could not be cowed by the rulers of
the earth or dismissed for his bad manners at their tables. Israel had to be
less Jewish in order to become like other nations. The trade-off was one
which political Zionists were willing to make. Ahad Ha'am's attack on the

book stirred violent protest because he denied the messianic hope which Herzl had brought down to earth by clothing it in the latest of European fashions. In the name of redemption one could even forgive Herzl the very last lines of *Altneuland*, a Siddhartha-like meditation that all activity was a dream one day and would again turn to dream. For Herzl, the political Messiah, could hardly do less than dream. That was his calling. The message that there were worse things a man could do on earth than dream, that dreams were often not as far from action as people commonly believed, was one that his readers were obviously prepared to hear.[14] "If you will it, it is no dream."

My concern in this study is the current status of Herzl's vision of home-coming, and the focus of our inquiry into political Zionism will therefore be the twofold agenda bequeathed by Herzl to followers for whom, unlike him, return to the Land could never be "quite simple." They had to demonstrate, first, that the dream could become reality: that political ambitions, in other words, were more than a recipe for despair. To that end political Zionists pointed to concrete progress, which was indeed impressive, and—a strategy more relevant to our concerns—engaged in a relentless critique of the diaspora. A political solution would be found, they argued in effect, because one *had* to be found. The conditions of exile, which they subjected to intense scrutiny, simply would not support continued Jewish existence. This re-mains a prominent thrust of Israeli self-justification even today. Second, political Zionists had to show that their *Judenstaat* would be Jewish in more than name or population. Their appeal among the East European masses depended upon convincing them that normalization would not uproot Jews entirely from their past. This too remains a prominent theme of current discussion. The "Jew" and the "Hebrew," in Berdicewski's terms, could be synthesized. Judaism could lend itself to other redefinitions than Ahad Ha'am's, some of them thoroughly compatible with statehood.

I will examine this twofold agenda by looking in some detail at the writings of two of the movement's most thoughtful theorists: Jacob Klatzkin, an author and editor who provided political Zionists with a negation of the diaspora unmatched in its totality; and Yehezkel Kaufmann, whose *Golah Ve-Nekhar* (1929–1930) remains the finest historical sociology of Jewish exile. Klatzkin's vision of Jewish homecoming continues to influence con-temporary Zionist thinkers, while Kaufmann's work remains unparalleled in both its insights into the experience of *galut* and its impact on subsequent reflection upon our concerns.

In the second section of the chapter I turn to those who opposed Zionism of whatever sort because they believed it to be *inherently* political, and as such inconsistent with the status of Jewry and the mission of Judaism. The nineteenth- and early twentieth-century critique of Zionism by Reform Jews is well known; so too is that of Orthodox Jews galvanized by their horror at secular homecoming to form the movement known as Agudat Israel. I have therefore chosen a very different focus: an anti-Zionist thinker of great depth who elaborated a more subtle notion of Israel's eternal role on earth and who has exercised great influence on contemporary American Jewish thought on our subject as on others: Franz Rosenzweig.

I turn in the third section of the chapter to the only coherent attempt at synthesis between political Zionism, including both its messianism and its negation of the diaspora, and the Jewish religious tradition, including its conviction of Israel's unique mission and chosenness. Religious Zionism, because of its marriage of Orthodoxy and messianism, could reconcile what other schools of thought could not: statehood with Torah; return to the Land through secular means with the divine ingathering of the exiles. It alone could politicize the concepts of exile and the land without universalizing or demystifying them. The movement has had several prominent spokesmen in our century, but none so influential or profound as Rabbi Abraham Isaac Kook. After analysis of Kook's writings we will be in a position to assess how all three streams of thought—political Zionist, anti-Zionist, and religious Zionist—drew on the traditions examined earlier as well as rejected them, remembering and forgetting with immeasurable consequences for the current state of Jewish homecoming.

The Pathology of Exile

In Klatzkin's essay *Tehumim* (1925), the reason for negation of the diaspora is straightforward: the *golah* simply could not exist much longer. If Jews were to live, as Jews, they would have to do so somewhere else. Pious Jews had been able to endure life in exile for centuries because of their conviction that God watched over them there and would one day bring the Messiah. Modern Jews, informed by sociological understanding, knew that without such faith there was no way for the Jewish people to preserve their distinctiveness among the nations, except for persecutions which strengthened the Jewish "spirit" (i.e., identity) while destroying the body—hardly a good bargain. And religion was on the wane, with nothing to take its place. Judaism as culture could not preserve the people in the way religion had done for centuries, with rewards and sanctions which culture alone could not match. [15]

Ahad Ha'am had been mistaken, then, in both of his two most critical assumptions. Judaism, first, could not be secularized into Jewish culture and go on performing the same functions as before. *Within* a Jewish state, Jewish tradition could evolve freely without threat to the nation, because whatever emerged inside that state would presumably be Jewish, by definition. What else could it be? *Outside* a Jewish state, however, Jewish culture would be overwhelmed by the cultures in which Jews lived (a point made, of course, by both Dubnow and Berdiczewski). The nation would disappear. But the Spiritual Center (the second key assumption) could not *be* a center if there were no Jews on its periphery. "Our sages said it well," wrote

Klatzkin. "The nations of the world, even when exiled, are not really in galut, but Israel, who eat of the nations' bread and drink of their wine, *their* exile is galut." Western Jews had now begun to eat of the nations' bread, to drink of their wine, and—the next step in the rabbinic litany to which Klatzkin alluded—to marry their daughters. Ahad Ha'am's diaspora could not be affirmed, then, even "objectively"—i.e., on the assumption that it would continue to exist.[16]

Here we see a new twist in Jewish reflection upon *galut*. Contrary to the rabbinic assumption of a single age, "this time," extending from the destruction of the Temple to the coming of the Messiah, Klatzkin posits that not all exiles are alike. What is more, those before Emancipation had been less galut-like than those afterwards—a reversal, this time, not of the rabbis but of those who had rejected them in the name of Emancipation or modernity. The possession (or promise) of civil rights had in fact weakened the Jewish people, Klatzkin argues, by weakening the capacity of modern Jews to maintain a separate culture. In rabbinic terms, Emancipation had compromised the Jews' distinctive time and space. Jews had become utterly dependent on outsiders, body *and* soul—a situation unprecedented in Jewish history.[17] This utterly negative evaluation of Emancipation has since become a staple of Zionist historiography.[18]

Even if such a galut could endure, therefore, it should not be allowed to do so because it distorted the national Jewish character. Modern exile had made Jewry a shadow of its former self and had perverted the character of individual Jews as well, making them wanderers between two worlds. "If it survives, its individuals will survive torn and broken . . . exhausted by a war without end." Klatzkin's midrash on the mark of Cain was precise. Furthermore, he continued, the co-existence of galut and national homeland would divide the energies of an already weakened people.[19] Exile, therefore, should be understood as a "passageway" (*prozdor*) to renewal of the people in its homeland (as the rabbis had understood this world as a "passageway" to the next). As such and only as such, it should be preserved for the time being. "Without negation of the diaspora, there is no point to its affirmation." The *golah* would serve the rebuilding of the Land and then disappear—exactly the reverse of Ahad Ha'am's idea of the "spiritual center." Galut could not enjoy a long life as the kingdom of the Jewish spirit, for Jewish culture could not take the place of faith. As Klatzkin put it succinctly, "God has no heir."[20] Because He also had no future in Klatzkin's view—faith was on the wane—there was only one option for survival available to the Jewish people: homecoming to the Land. With the eventual disappearance of the diaspora, the boundaries of Israel would come to mark the limits of Judaism as well. "As long as our nation has no fixed abode," Klatzkin wrote in another play on the rabbis, "the *shekhinah* is exiled with them. As soon as it establishes a fixed residence, the *shekhinah* will cause its spirit to dwell there: the spirit of the nation will depart from galut and contract itself into its own portion."[21]

That claim echoes the rabbinic dictum that when a Jew resides outside the Land it is as if he lives without God. Klatzkin's midrashic skills here as elsewhere are considerable. But he is also indebted to the tradition in a more profound way. The sources which Klatzkin cites or parodies enable him to conflate his sociological judgment of the *golah* with a decidedly normative critique. The diaspora not only *cannot* exist, it does not deserve to exist. It has no *right* to exist. In part the ground for this claim is moral: Jewish dignity and authenticity are compromised in exile. But the real ground of Klatzkin's indictment of galut is his rather precise rendition of the *tokheḥah* from Deuteronomy 28. Exile, he reminds us, is punishment, destruction, and defeat. It means the loss of blessing, of fertility both cultural and biological. It means, finally, *avodah zarah:* the worship of strange gods, subservience to non-Jewish cultures. Like the author of Deuteronomy's unsurpassable curses, Klatzkin seeks to convince us that *galut* is literally a fate worse than death. The logic of that judgment lies primarily in the text which his reproof of Israel calls to mind.

In one crucial respect, however, Klatzkin departed from the tradition and cleaved to Herzl: the understanding which he evinced for gentile hatred of the Jews. Emancipation, he reminds his readers, had been offered Jews on the condition that they assimilate. Only as full Germans or Frenchmen could Jews demand equal rights. Non-believing Jews, moreover, could hardly claim to be Germans or Frenchmen of the "Mosaic persuasion." No one could demand to share power in another's house. Every nation distrusted strangers, particularly those who seemed to emasculate the host culture and to threaten its national uniqueness with cosmopolitanism. Assimilated Jews were like a "scab" on the nations of the world (an allusion to a well-known rabbinic epithet for converts). In fact—here Klatzkin's source seems to be Nietzsche—"it is a good sign for the cultures of the goyim, if assimilating Jews arouse in them feelings of hatred and disgust."[22]

One winces at this appropriation of anti-Semitic stereotypes, with its explicit justification of "Jew-hatred." But the theme neither began with Klatzkin nor ended with him. Pinsker and Herzl too had sought to depict anti-Semitism as an inevitable, almost natural development, the better to argue that Jews had no alternative to sovereignty. They in turn inherited the theme from the Haskalah's critique of the Jews as a people, corrupted by its ignorance and its persecutors. *"Tout comprendre, c'est tout pardonner,"* and the "pardon" of anti-Semitism, like the attempt to understand it, has remained a feature of secular political Zionism to this day. How else convince Western Jews to perform *teshuvah* (return or repentance—Klatzkin's term for Jewish homecoming)[23] if not by arguing that their souls had been "damaged" irreparably by assimilation, and their bodies would not long be spared the fate of their brothers in the Ukraine. How else convince Jews in the Land that their sufferings were not in vain? The only alternative persuasion was Herzl's promise of redemption through rational planning. The true realists among his disciples eschewed this line of argument in the name of realism—particularly once the hardships and failings of actual life in the Jewish home had made it untenable. The inevitability of anti-Semitism, by contrast, was a claim made more cogent with every passing year.

Klatzkin's position was stated somewhat more subtly, and with significantly more documentation, in Yehezkel Kaufmann's monumental study *Golah Ve-Nekhar (Exile and Estrangement,* 1929). The work is still little known, except among specialists, in part because its density, length, and loquaciousness have made translation difficult, in part because its allusions to other Zionist figures and schools of thought render it opaque even to the Hebrew reader. That is unfortunate, given Kaufmann's comprehensive and probing analysis of exile, and doubly so given Kaufmann's unparalleled statement of themes which continue to dominate Zionist debate even today.[24]

Kaufmann begins the work with a discussion of methodological assumptions which need not detain us, except for several crucial definitions of terms. *Exile,* as Kaufmann understands it, is a set of interrelated processes that includes *ḥurban* (destruction of the Temple and, by extension, of the Jewish community), subjugation, wandering, confinement to ghettoes, and (the most recent development) assimilation. *Estrangement (nekhar)* is defined as the essence of the Jewish experience of galut, its subjective correlate and consequence.[25] *Nations* are seen as groups united on the basis of blood, language, land, character, mores, law, religion, history, the consciousness of unity, and the will to preserve it. Kaufmann denies that any one factor is decisive, but soon accords primacy to language, observing that tribes or ethnic groups come into being only with the development of a distinct language. A people's language is the external sign of the feeling of special kinship which is the essence of its national identity. Ethnicity exists only by virtue of language.[26] Land, by contrast, is not a determining factor. The residents of North America are ultimately members of the same nation as those of Great Britain, though separated by an ocean. A homeland's true borders, Kaufmann summarizes, are marked by the limits of its national language.[27]

Kaufmann then turns to a second cultural boundary of great historical importance: *religion,* which he defines as "the sphere of practical relationship between man and the hidden aspect of being." From the beginning, human beings had postulated the existence of purposive will behind nature's regularities: god(s). Mythical religions had subjugated divinity to the laws of nature. Israelite religion, in a remarkable transformation, came to see nature as subject to the will of a sole, transcendent God. In both cases, Kaufmann writes, the "source" of individual religious life was concern for the soul in the next world (and not, presumably, wonder at the force behind nature). Because of that concern, religion had sanctions at its disposal by which it could impose and transmit values and obligations among its adherents, and thereby came to play a uniquely important role in the identity of nations.[28]

With these definitions in place—all of them controversial and vital to

Kaufmann's later argument—he comes to the Jews, the "only exilic nation in the world."[29] As such, the Jews—or rather their survival in exile—posed a riddle for the historian which Kaufmann states through a second series of controversial assumptions. Unlike the Gypsies, for example, the Jews had generally *not* been separated from their surroundings by culture, economy, or pattern of settlement. All three factors, Kaufmann argues, had in fact served to link Jews with their host societies. Neither had the Jews spoken a separate language, but only dialects which, Kaufmann claims later on, were a means to assimilation rather than the reverse. How then could we account for the persistence of the Jews as a separate nation, despite unparalleled scattering throughout the globe and a persistent effort to assimilate culturally? Anti-Semitism could not provide the answer, for hatred of the Jews had developed, in the Roman world, as a *reaction* to Jewish exclusivity. A national will to live, as postulated by Ahad Ha'am, simply did not exist.[30] There could only have been one source of Israel's preservation, Kaufmann concludes: its unique religion. "There is no doubt that we should seek the secret of Israel's distinctive historical path in this distinctive factor." Israel was a "holy people" (cf. Ex. 19:6). Only as such had it survived. Even when faith in the strict sense had attenuated, Kaufmann adds, religion in its "wide meaning, the religious factor in all the scope of its social functioning," had kept the Jews a "people apart."[31]

This is the most important claim of Kaufmann's book, and I will examine its several implications one by one. Note first that in Kaufmann's view neither land nor language had contributed to the Jews' survival. He takes great pains to show (without success, I believe) that Jewish dialects such as Ladino or Yiddish represented efforts at acculturation to the surrounding societies rather than reinforcement of Jewish identity. His contempt for Yiddish, which he refers to as the "jargon" (a common epithet of derision) is complete. The Jews' neglect of their true language, Hebrew, is for Kaufmann the sign that their ethnic identity was on the way to utter destruction.[32] Only Jewish faith prevented them from crossing the line entirely.

Culture, Kaufmann emphasizes, played no part in the maintenance of Jewish distinctiveness—and it is here that we first glimpse the polemic against Ahad Ha'am waged throughout *Golah Ve-Nekhar*. Jewish cultural creativity in exile was virtually nil, Kaufmann charges. In fact, the Jews were not really an ethnic group at all much of the time, but rather a "pseudo-ethnic" group which barely clung to its own identity.[33] Culture alone had never managed to preserve any group. Where are all the magnificent cultures in which the Jews had found themselves in the course of their wanderings? Why had they all disappeared?[34] Only Israel had survived, Kaufmann argues, because its faith conferred ultimate meaning and wielded ultimate sanctions which culture could not match. "And you who cleave to the Lord your God are all alive this day" (Deut. 4:4).

The obvious problem with this explanation is that most, if not all, the cultures in which Jews lived were also religious; faith had been no less important a force in these societies than among the Jews themselves. Where were those religions now—particularly if, as Kaufmann maintains, religion is an independent element in culture, apart from all others and *sui generis*, a mover of society rather than a product of social or economic forces. Why had other faiths not managed to preserve other societies as Judaism had saved the Jews? Kaufmann's argument makes no sense without an underlying assumption which he rarely voices explicitly. Faith as such does not have the ability to resist decline and disappearance, but the unique monotheistic faith of Israel did and does. It alone has the power which he ascribes to religion as such. The social scientific generalizations in *Golah Ve-Nekhar* mask the belief articulated most forcefully by Krochmal's *Guide for the Perplexed of the Day*. Israel had survived for three millennia because its faith constituted truth of a different order, better grounded in the absolutes of existence. It is not enough to argue that "religion differs from secular cultures." Kaufmann must make the further argument that "religious creativity embodied itself in Israel in a unique form that has no parallel in all the world." Only so can there be "no doubt that we should seek the secret of Israel's unique historical path in this unique factor."[35]

It is a major claim of Kaufmann's book—though not, I think, essential to his argument—that the faith of Israel is in its essence universalist: suitable, that is, for all human beings, regardless of their nationality. Judaism was not inherently particularist, i.e., the culture of a specific national group. Christian claims to the contrary throughout the ages were wrong, and so was Ahad Ha'am's assertion that the Jewish people had developed its faith through an act of collective national will as a bulwark against assimilation. Kaufmann insists that Israel's essentially universalist faith had remained the Jewish people's own "peculiar treasure" only because the historical circumstances of exile had rendered it unattractive in that form to other peoples, or because efforts at proselytization had been strictly forbidden by the ruling powers. Why would anyone voluntarily join a persecuted people by taking on its faith, Kaufmann asks rhetorically, when he or she could acquire the very same faith and at the same time join the ruling power—becoming a Muslim or a Christian? Historical accident had restricted the Jewish faith to the Jewish people, then—and by doing so had made it the instrument of Jewish survival in exile.[36]

And yet, Kaufmann argues, the faith of Judaism had spread to all the world, in the form of its "daughter religions," Christianity and Islam, which were essentially identical to the original.[37] His recourse to the familiar distinction between form and essence, given the obvious and substantial differences among the three Western faiths, is fraught with difficulties. Jesus's messiahship, for example—the cause of his rejection by Israel— becomes in Kaufmann's view a dispute over symbolism, a matter of the "forms of divine revelation." Had Israel accepted the crucified Christ as their savior, Kaufmann writes, "this would not have constituted a fundamental change in their religion." Similarly, neither miracle working, nor the exorcism of devils, nor revival of the dead were concerned with "substantive and moral beliefs."[38] The essence, apparently, consisted only of God's oneness and his morality. Christianity and Judaism, therefore, were in essence one and the same, meaning that nothing essential would have been lost for Jews—except two thousand years of misery—had they exchanged one form of monotheism for the other. In fact, Christianity's victory over Israel in the world represented a victory for Israel's universal faith.[39]

The source of these problematic claims seems to lie in Kaufmann's un-feigned wonder at the grandeur of the monotheistic idea, which he regarded as an unparalleled leap forward in the development of humanity. Kauf-mann's *History of Israelite Religion* (1937–1957) pays eloquent testimony to his conviction that the origins of Mosaic monotheism remain a mystery. Israel's faith did not develop over time but sprang forth, as it were, in full flower. By the time of the Babylonian exile, Israel's new religious idea had begun its "unique and unifying activity." Subsequent developments, within and outside Judaism, paled in importance by comparison.[40]

Kaufmann stands on shaky ground here. The verdict that Christianity's apparent victory over Israel in fact represented the triumph of Jewish faith recalls Nietzsche's verdict in *The Genealogy of Morals*. The related claim that Judaism "desired" to burst its national bonds (i.e., to shed its particular-ist form) but could not do so because of exile[41] is only one of many in which not only an essence but a will is attributed to Judaism. Israel's faith is often made the subject of sentences and followed by active verbs. Judaism creates, protects, transforms.[42] One reification—Ahad Ha'am's "national organ-ism"—has been replaced by another.

The intent underlying these difficulties is clear. Kaufmann wishes to defend Judaism against Christian charges that it is insular and narrow. To that end he emphasizes that Jewish exclusivity was the result and not the cause of anti-Semitism; his assertion that more unites the monotheistic religions than divides them, against the background of the world's other faiths, is of course not without merit. More important, however, Kaufmann desires to undermine Ahad Ha'am's assumption that Jewish culture had perserved the Jewish people in the past and could do so again in the future. If Ahad Ha'am were correct, diaspora existence could continue, the periph-ery to a Spiritual Center in the Land. But if he were wrong, nothing less than sovereignty—redemption from exile and estrangement—could suffice.

Kaufmann believed firmly that Ahad Ha'am *was* wrong, if only because Jewish existence in exile was threatened by another enemy: anti-Semitism. His analysis of the harsh treatment accorded the Jews over the centuries at times runs counter to his assertion that Judaism had failed to become the religion of all the world only because no one wished to take on the faith of a despised and persecuted people.[43] There was, he reports, another factor at work: had the nations of the Roman world accepted Judaism, they would have been obliged to work for fulfillment of its messianic goals—the return of the Jews to political sovereignty in the Land. "For the faith of Israel promised the nation the revival of its kingdom as well."[44] Israelite religion, in other words, was inseparable from Israelite nationality, meaning that the Jews would never have been permitted to assimilate freely even had they wanted to. More than the desiccated culture and "jargon" of a "pseudo-ethnic group" divided them from the nations, then, more even than the particularist rituals of a universalist faith. The Jews were *a separate nation.* So they regarded themselves and so they were regarded; consequently, regardless of the legal status enjoyed by Jews in any particular society, popular perception of them as aliens was universal. In fact, Kaufmann continues, the prevailing situation of the Jews throughout their wanderings was one of "war" conducted "by an alien people in a foreign land."[45] In order to survive that conflict, the Jews had to rely more than once on the protection of the authorities whom they served, against the populace which, by serving those authorities, the Jews had helped to exploit.[46] The story of Joseph was never-ending.

It is in this context that Kaufmann places belief in the Messiah. The hope for his coming was directed primarily at an end to gentile rule. It expressed the people's fervent wish to leave galut and return home. The Messiah symbolized national identity and national will. It testified to an awareness of estrangement so deep that even citizenship in the modern world could not uproot it, though until their Emancipation Jews had done nothing to end their exile but had rather endured it passively, inside the quasi-homeland of the ghetto.[47]

Like Klatzkin, Kaufmann finds nothing extraordinary in gentile persecution of the Jews, given the exclusivity at first demanded by the religion of Israel. Anti-Semitism was given further impetus by the Jewish view that Gentiles were in essence idolaters and, as such, worthy of death. Islam and Christianity shared this view of heathens and invoked it to slaughter idolaters when given the chance. The Jews, who had no such opportunity, could only hate, and this *ressentiment* was "undoubtedly one of the sources of the nations' great hatred of Israel."[48] Finally, Kaufmann writes, no nation can open all its gates to a group that remains culturally and socially distinct. How could one expect any group to integrate a people who regarded its country of residence as a temporary dwelling, a misfortune, and prayed daily for deliverance to another land, *the* Land?[49] The causal chain was unbreakable: monotheism in a pagan world demanded exclusivity, exclusivity provoked enmity, the essential universalism of Jewish faith was prevented from following its natural course, and Israel's religion thereby came to be the guarantor of its distinctiveness—which led, of course, only to further hatred. Only the departure from exile could break the cycle and bring redemption. Once again, as in Klatzkin, anti-Semitism has been viewed with understanding, in order to serve the promotion of political Zionism.

Kaufmann's second volume traces the origins of the Jewish problem's solution. Zionists were not the first to see the inevitability of the cycle. Partisans of assimilation had realized it before them and attempted to escape it through the Jews' absorption into their host societies. Kaufmann calls this ambition messianic;[50] had it succeeded, we infer, there would have been no need for his own "messianic" proposal: political Zionism. The same is true of the attempt to create autonomous Jewish communities without leaving exile—a doctrine of assimilation, Kaufmann charges, in a new guise.[51] This too Kaufmann would gladly have supported, had it been practicable. But it was not, he writes, because the Jews were unique—the only modern minority group whose achievement of civil rights was conditional upon repudiation of its national identity. Once again, the vestiges of Jewish identity were symbolized by the religion of Israel: even Reform Judaism had been sufficient to keep Jews from surrender and to prevent the nations of Europe from accepting them. Even if only a name, a fossil, a minimal reminder, religion remained the *kelipah* (husk) which protected Jewish distinctiveness—a "shadow of their ancient identification" under which Jews would live as long as Judaism survived.[52] It would survive, even in the modern secular world, because man was essentially a religious being. Therefore, as Zionists had realized at the end of the nineteenth century, the "defect of exile" could be corrected only by taking Jewish ethnicity to its logical conclusion—nationhood.[53]

Spiritual Zionism could not further that goal for two reasons. First, it denied that redemption was possible. Only Herzl sought to remove the Jews from galut; Ahad Ha'am felt compelled to leave the suffering masses where they were for the time being, while raising up an elite which would revive the Jewish spirit from its Center. There was no time for that. The diaspora was in acute danger, and Ahad Ha'am threatened to distract Jewish energies from the immediate task of saving Jewish lives.[54] In this prognosis, of course, Kaufmann was proved correct, despite the tendentiousness of his history of modern Jewry (Emancipation doomed to failure; pogroms, if not Holocaust, inevitable) and his reiteration of anti-Semitic stereotypes. At the late date of 1929, almost thirty years after the furor over Herzl's proposal of a homeland in "Uganda," Kaufmann remained pessimistic about the chances of gaining sovereignty over the Land of Israel and therefore continued to urge investigation of other possibilities.[55] The question raised by his contemporary disciples is whether the post-Holocaust diaspora is also doomed to disappear, through a combination of assimilation and anti-Semitism, or whether, thanks to the Spiritual Center, it can survive—thereby fulfilling the original promise of the Emancipation.

Kaufmann's conviction that it could not rested on a second criticism of Ahad Ha'am's plan: "culture" could never replace religion.[56] The Jewish "national morality" did not exist, witness less than lofty Jewish ethics in the area of commerce;[57] only faith had the meaning and the sanctions to compel continued Jewish distinctiveness. Unlike some other critics of Ahad Ha'am, however, Kaufmann recognized the problem posed by this conclusion to Jewish survival inside the Land as well. Berdiczewski was anachronistic in his call for the destruction of Judaism, Kaufmann asserted. For its end had already come.[58] "Our situation is indeed tragic," he wrote in an earlier essay. "It is hard to reconcile ourselves to the idea that our nationalism derives from a faith that no longer exists in our hearts." Kaufmann came much closer, in that essay, to the position of the spiritual Zionists. He even titled it "The National Will to Survive"—an explicit echo of Ahad Ha'am—and concluded that negation of the rebirth of the diaspora meant negation of Jewish redemption itself, since the "affirmation of redemption is inconceivable without affirming the renascence of the Diaspora."[59] By 1929, he had concluded that no such spiritual creativity could be promised.[60]

Here again Kaufmann anticipated the contemporary Zionist agenda. No single question looms as large in current Israeli discussion of the meaning of homecoming as the sense in which statehood *is* homecoming or return—a Jewish state in substance as well as population. What would be the content of Jewish culture, Kaufmann wondered, if spiritual creativity rested on a faith attenuated by the forces of modernity and secularization? What would be the ultimate point of Jewish survival, beyond survival itself? Would it rest only on Kaufmann's conviction—denied by many other political Zionists, Klatzkin among them—that assimilation would always be impossible, and so on the fact that for the Jew survival as a Jew would necessarily remain equivalent to survival as such? But what would make that survival possible? Could political Zionism alone, bereft of the larger purpose conferred by "faith" or "culture," provide the content necessary to mobilize the nation's energies and integrate its various groupings and interests?

At the end of the two long volumes of *Golah Ve-Nekhar*, Kaufmann has no answers, only the knowledge that there is no alternative. Given the opportunity to escape galut, the jews could hardly refuse. Redemption from exile and estrangement was redemption enough. Jewish bodies needed to be saved. Life had to be chosen over death. Spirit would wait. The metaphysical dimension of homecoming would have to be left to another, a better, time.[61]

Eternal People, Eternal Exile

For many Jews, both inside and outside the Zionist camp, these arguments between political and spiritual Zionists were too subtle to be of interest. Many of those who supported Jewish homecoming regarded it simply as a philanthropic effort to relieve Jews from persecution and to restore the morale of the Jewish people. Those who opposed it by and large found homecoming as such to be objectionable, regardless of its shape. Leaders of the Reform movement assailed the return as a threat to the rights which Jews had received in the West and a betrayal of the Jewish mission among the nations.[62] Kaufmann Kohler, for example—the leader of the movement in America at the turn of the century—assailed Dubnow along with Ahad Ha'am "and the rest of the nationalists" for underrating "the religious power of the Jew's soul" and threatening to reduce the "religious mission of Israel" to mere nationalism. Jerusalem symbolized the "messianic goal" of "One holy God and one, undivided humanity" and only that.[63] Distinctions among those who wavered from this goal were unimportant. They were no more relevant to Orthodox thinkers who attacked the Zionist movement on remarkably similar grounds. Return to the Land, they argued, could come only with God's Messiah; a secular homecoming was not only a betrayal of Torah, but a reneging on Israel's pledge to endure the burdens of exile patiently without attempting to "hasten the end." The founding conference of Agudat Israel called in 1912 to counter the Zionists declared that "the Jewish people stands outside the framework of the political peoples of the world and differs essentially from them; the Sovereign of the Jewish people is the Almighty; the Torah is the law that governs them, and the Holy Land has been at all times destined for the Jewish people."[64] It would remain their destiny, and not a homeland among others, until an authority greater than either Ahad Ha'am or Herzl decided otherwise.

These positions are familiar and require no elaboration here; the latter, though not the former, can be heard to this day, inside as well as outside the borders of the Land. I shall focus instead on Franz Rosenzweig (1886–1929), one of the most influential Jewish thinkers of the century, whose approach to Jewish nationalism adumbrated and influenced much contemporary argument, Zionist and non-Zionist alike. Rosenzweig's faith in Israel's unique destiny was tempered by the realization that the nationalists' attempt to save world Jewry was of vital importance. "There are better Jews among the Zionists than among us—regardless of theory," he wrote.[65] Rosenzweig took particular exception to the writings of Klatzkin, but added that Zionism, like other movements, should be judged not by its theory but by its earthbound practical activity—and that activity in the case of Zionism should be supported, powerful theoretical objections notwithstanding. "According to the words of a philosopher whom I regard as an authority even greater than Hermann Cohen, what is not to come save in eternity will not come in all eternity."[66]

All of that having been noted, one is struck nonetheless by the illegitimacy of the Zionist project according to Rosenzweig's own theoretical masterpiece, *The Star of Redemption*. A Jewish state is simply inconceivable according to the view of God, world, and humanity set forth in the work. The "eternal people," unlike all others, had forsaken attachment to the "night of earth"— that is, to homelands inevitably "watered by the blood of their sons." Only by virtue of that renunciation had Israel remained eternal, trusting in its community of blood and maintaining the self-awareness of a stranger and a sojourner never permitted to "while away time in any home."[67] The Jews also lacked the native language possessed by every other people, for language too, like all things mortal, would in time disappear. Finally, Jews lacked an "outwardly visible life" such as all other nations lived "in accordance with their own customs and laws."[68] Nature, culture, and the state had all been forsaken, as in the biblical departures from Eden, Babel, and Egypt; land, language, and sovereignty—the three pillars of Zionist renewal—are thus declared inconsistent with Israel's status as the eternal people.

What is more, they are impossible of attainment given the divine order which had fixed that status. Israel already stood, in Rosenzweig's conception, at the goal which all other peoples strove restlessly to achieve—unity of faith and life. It was "the fire" at the core of the Star.

> But just because it has that unity, the Jewish people is bound to be outside the world that does not yet have it. Through living in a state of eternal peace, it is outside of time agitated by wars . . . therefore the true eternity of the eternal people must always be alien and vexing to the state, and to the history of the world.[69]

Eternity is the object of Rosenzweig's quest in *The Star*, the most precious of all gifts stored up in the truths of Jewish faith and the cycle of the Jewish year. "Blessed art Thou . . . who hast planted eternal life in our midst." The fire *is* "eternal life." Time "rolls past" Israel's "life everlasting." How could Jews possibly abandon this ultimate blessing for the dubious advantage of normality? Why would they "sink their roots into the night of earth, lifeless in itself but the spender of life"?[70] Land and landlessness, in this magisterial survey of the human condition *sub specie aeternitatis*, are symbolic of a larger order, the ultimate order of death and life.

Had Rosenzweig lived to see the actual Land of Israel reclaimed and the actual state of Israel reborn to fight repeated wars, he might have declared both land and state aberrations from the cosmic order engraved (so he believed) on a six-pointed star.[71] Or, more likely, he would have abandoned theory and gravitated back to earth, recalling that "if a symbol is to be more than an arbitrary appendage, then it must somewhere and somehow exist as an entirely asymbolical reality."[72] A Zionism more modest in its aspirations than either Herzl's or Ahad Ha'am's might have satisfied him: a state which promised only a more secure way station for the Jews than was otherwise available at present. So long as the ingathering remained incomplete and Jewish faith resisted translation into secular culture, Rosenzweig would probably have been content. But he might also have found such a *modus vivendi* inherently impossible—and thus been driven to regard Jewish homecoming of any sort as a tragic if necessary mistake. We shall of course never know. *The Star*, along with private correspondence, remains Rosenzweig's definitive word on the subject. He did not live long enough to change his mind.[73]

We are left, therefore, with his refusal to accept any politicization of the concept of the Land and his utter universalization of Jerusalem, which in his view was only a heavenly city—in fact, one might say, a Star. Demystification of the Land was out of the question. Rosenzweig insisted on remystifying the people of Israel to a degree unparalleled in non-Orthodox thought since Spinoza. The Jews were God's eternal people. Galut, therefore, was the normative Jewish condition. Life at the center of the Star would have been impossible had the Jews lived, in the normal sense, anywhere on earth; they could never be at home in this world to any degree, in any numbers, whether in body or in spirit, at the periphery or at the center. Jewish homecoming would mean relinquishing the Jewish people's eternal mission, and to sacrifice all that made the life of the individual Jew ultimately meaningful. This Rosenzweig could not permit.

His opposition to Zionism in principle, whatever his qualified support for the movement in practice, is of immense importance in understanding the revolutionary nature of the Zionist homecoming. For Rosenzweig was no narrow ideologue, blind to all but his own few ideas. His proposed motto for the adult education institute which he founded was "nothing Jewish is alien to me." Zionism could not be entirely alien to Rosenzweig, for it sought to save the Jews and derived from longings and even convictions which he shared. Yet neither could Rosenzweig bring himself to endorse the movement, because it *was* alien to a large degree. It demystified, universalized in a very different sense than he, and politicized. It was a secular, national movement, born with other isms of its ilk from the breeding ground of nineteenth-century Europe, whereas he believed the Jews an eternal people and the essence of Judaism eternal truth. Zionism sought to do what in Rosenzweig's traditional scheme of things was impossible: to end Jewish exile without the help of God's Messiah. This decision in turn concealed the deeper resolution to dispense with the Jewish God,[74] and to proceed with the redefinition of His chosen people as a nation like any other. The political Zionists embraced both fateful choices, while Ahad Ha'am tried to formulate a Zionism which bridged the gap—and in the process disguised the extent to which even his modest spiritual center represented a dramatic break with the Jewish past. Rosenzweig uttered a resounding "no" to both schools, on principle. He pronounced in effect "a plague on both your houses," in the name of the eternal House of Israel and its God.

Only the religious Zionists, convinced that redemption was on the way or even at hand and that the Zionist movement was God's unknowing instrument, could affirm Israel's unique status on earth and nonetheless say "yes" to the project of return. They alone could even attempt to combine politicization of the idea of Eretz Israel, and belief in the universal significance of the Zionist effort, with a mythic conception of the Land's unique character and a fervent trust in the coming of God's Messiah. Religious Zionists differed on the imminence of his arrival, but not on the supreme importance of rejoining God's chosen people to His chosen Land—with the ultimate aim of establishing a kingdom of Torah.[75] The great majority of Orthodox Jews, doubtful that a secular movement would ever embrace that goal and opposed in principle to "hastening the end," refused to support the Zionist homecoming. For those who believed that homecoming a giant step toward the final redemption, however, involvement in it was not only permissible but a religious obligation of the first order. The Yishuv, no matter how secular its character and its leadership, represented the "beginning of the flowering of our redemption."[76]

The claim, of course, is awesome and fraught with dangers all too evident on the contemporary Israeli landscape. But we should note at the outset that nothing less than such a claim could have rejoined Jewish peoplehood with Jewish faith, the political and the mythic conceptions of the Land. In no other way could the breach effected by the modern world, and first discerned by Spinoza, be healed. Rabbi Abraham Isaac Kook, the principal theorist of religious Zionism, could bring together in himself and in his philosophy what Herzl and Ahad Ha'am, Klatzkin and Rosenzweig could not, only because he believed that the Messiah was actually on his way— sent not by history, let alone a Congress, but by God.[77]

"The Beginning of the Flowering of Our Redemption"

"Rav" Kook's thought did not emerge *ex nihilo*. Already in the mid-nineteenth century, two contemporaries of Moses Hess, Rabbis Yehudah Alakalai and Zvi Hirsch Kalisher, had insisted that return to the Land on a small scale did not represent an infringement on divine prerogatives but rather a first step toward the divine ingathering of the exiles. The purchase of parcels of the Holy Land from the Turks constituted a double "redemption" (the traditional term), for it would also permit fulfillment of commandments dependent upon its possession. This call, of course, fell on deaf ears. Moreover, despite the two rabbis' prescient call for organized funding and settlement, their concept of the Land remained unpoliticized. No demystification is evident in their thought, and the symbols associated with the Land in their tracts are strictly traditional. The prerequisites of Zionism, in other words, were not present.[78]

This pattern changed somewhat with the rise of the religious Zionist movement known as Mizrachi in 1902, under the leadership of Rabbi Yitzḥak Ya'akov Reines.[79] Its organizational meeting was prompted by the resolution of the Fifth Zionist Congress in 1901 to promote Jewish culture as well as the upbuilding of the Land—a substantive challenge to Orthodoxy in a way that a merely instrumental Zionism was not. The movement formulated the slogan "the Land of Israel for the people of Israel according to the Torah of Israel," thereby countering the visions of homecoming propounded by political and cultural Zionists alike. It also articulated the crucial contention that the Torah in the *golah* "can no longer exist in its fullness, nor can the observance of the precepts." Return to the Land was therefore not merely permissible but absolutely necessary. Orthodox Zionists would cooperate with the movement as a whole in attaining the Land, in order that the commandments dependent upon its possession might be observed. With regard to spiritual matters they would remain at odds with secular counterparts—and postpone the final reckoning to a later date.[80]

This synthesis of a traditional, mythic conception of the Land as the unique fount of God's blessing with modern symbols and a political effort at return received full expression only in the copious writings of Kook (1865–1935) several years later. The chief rabbi's perception of all history and nature as a single unified process, moving toward redemption, enabled him to reconcile elements far more disparate than the views of Theodor Herzl and Rabbi Akiba. Modern atheists, he wrote, were unknowing purifiers of the faith who served to cleanse religion of harmful superstition and rigidity.[81] Secular Zionists, in his kabbalistic view, concealed holy "sparks" in their modern, profane "husks" (*kelipot*). Violators of the Sabbath, professors of disbelief, they were nonetheless the agents of God.[82] Such was the cunning of Spirit. Those who discerned it were capable of syntheses inconceivable to other minds.

Kook's own magisterial synthesis is immediately evident in his remarkably fluid and lyrical language. Exile is described as bitter, hard, dark, the sleep of death, sick, a time of neglect for the body and deracination of the spirit[83]—stock images in a vocabulary shared by Klatzkin and Gordon, Buber and Ahad Ha'am. However, Kook even more than Gordon invokes another vocabulary, largely kabbalist, which renders common critique of exile and praise of the Land infinitely sharper and more compelling. Return to the Land, for example, assumes added significance when joined explicitly to the concept of *teshuvah* (return or repentance). Failure to seize the opportunity of return is a more serious offense when it is called *hilul hashem:* "profanation of the Name"—of Israel![84] Even flourishes such as these are superfluous, however, given Kook's reliance on another theme, reiterated on countless occasions, to motivate and legitimate the Zionist renewal—the Land's unique and transcendent holiness.

Eretz Israel, Kook wrote, was the spatial center of holiness in the world, radiating holiness vertically to the Jews who lived upon the Land as well as horizontally to other portions and peoples of the earth. The spirit of the Land was entirely pure and clean, while spirit elsewhere was mired in *kelipot* of impurity.[85] The air of the Land really did "make one wise," as the rabbis had said. In a typical elevation of sociology to theology, Kook argued that the Jewish imagination outside the Land had become stunted and even deformed. The cause was not merely assimilation to gentile cultures possessed of far less light and holiness than Israel. In addition, the Jews had depleted over two millennia the store of creativity carried away with them into exile. During their absence, the flow of spirit had ceased. Its gradual diminishing was responsible for the character of galut life. Realizing these facts, at last, the Jews had now grasped the urgency of return.[86] Moreover, since the entire world was poor in holiness and sunk in wickedness, all humanity was utterly dependent upon the Jews for a renewal of light and spirit. Israel's return to the Land would thus mark the end of a worldwide era of darkness and initiate the redemption of all humanity.[87]

It is astounding to read such claims in a twentieth-century work; indeed, it is difficult to cite any Jewish source since the *Kuzari* of Yehudah Halevi which more directly recapitulates Deuteronomy's far-reaching hymn of praise to a land blessed with rains and fountains and springs, a land in which no good thing would be lacking. Kook, instead of engaging in apologetics for the grandiosity of such claims, merely notes that the unique qualities of the Holy Land cannot be comprehended by human reason. "Eretz Israel is . . . no mere national possession, serving as a means of unifying our people and buttressing its material, or even its spiritual, survival. Eretz Israel is part of the very essence of our nationhood; it is bound organically to its very life and inner being." What the Land meant to Jews could be "felt only through the Spirit of the Lord which is in our people as a whole, through the spiritual cast of the Jewish soul, which radiates its characteristic influence to every healthy emotion."[88] Once such assumptions have been granted, they legitimate a powerful critique of galut life and galut Judaism, in which the full force of Jewish life, according to Kook, had been stunted. These convictions also enable Kook to sanctify political activities and conceptions that would otherwise have been unacceptable to a person of his commitments.

We have already noted, for example, Kook's belief that the Jewish spirit meant to guide the rest of creation had sunk in exile to imitation of "uncircumcised" Gentiles. The Jewish body, sorely neglected, had suffered a comparable impoverishment. The full and varied character of Jewish life could not achieve expression, given oppression and exposure to foreign winds.[89] For Kook, this low estate explained a phenomenon which, rightly understood, was a contradiction in terms: Jewish atheism. Many Jews of thoughtful and moral character had cast off their inherited faith, he wrote, because Judaism had degenerated to the point where superstition passed for true belief, and Jewish practice had become frozen in old forms. However, the people of Israel was inseparable in its very essence from God. Many Jewish souls had expressed their rebellion, therefore, precisely by returning to the Land of Israel where God's spirit most reposed—thereby releasing the light trapped in exilic husks and facilitating the renewal of Jewish religion. Both thought and practice would return to their original purity once the nation had returned to full life upon its holy soil. Atheism and rejection of the "yoke of the commandments" would gradually disappear.[90]

Note Kook's orchestration of the various themes sounded by God's non-Orthodox Zionist "instruments" of redemption. Like Berdiczewski and Klatzkin, Kook called for attention to the body. Flesh was no less holy than spirit, he declared.[91] Like Ahad Ha'am and Berdiczewski, Buber and Gordon, he railed against religious observance grown oppressive and superstition masquerading as faith. Kook comprehended souls such as Ahad Ha'am, affirming that one 'could be a good atheist Jew—to a degree, and in a special sense, which Kook took great pains to elaborate. He also echoed Gordon's call for a return to nature, lamenting that, in exile, the Jews' original link to and appreciation of nature had been disrupted.[92] Most important of all, Kook agreed that the secular enterprise of return constituted an authentic (if

sinful) expression of Jewish commitments, an activity of the sparks of redemption. Assimilation, and even stultified Orthodoxy, on the other hand,
represented a triumph for the *kelipot*.

Kook had no illusions about the essentially secular character of the Zionist
project. His qualms about the movement, and the public disregard of
mitzvot in the Yishuv, were overcome by the confidence that in God's good
time, soon to be upon us, such deviance would be seen as the "arrogance"
that tradition had said would accompany the first footsteps of the Messiah.[93]
Kook criticized departures from *halakhah*, but at the same time asserted that
"every labor and activity, spiritual or material, that contributes directly or
indirectly to the ingathering of our exiles and the return of our people to our
land is embraced by me with an affection of soul that knows no bounds."[94]
No less important, Kook could explain away the clear inapplicability of
halakhah as it had taken shape over two millennia of exile to the actual
conditions of the land and society which he wished that *halakhah* to govern.
The law's insufficiencies were the result of exilic darkness and needed
correction. The profane indecencies of the Yishuv were a necessary stage to
be endured and transcended. Thesis and antithesis would give way to
synthesis; so worked the God of spirit.[95]

In our terms: politicization and universalization could be harmonized with
a nondemystified tradition, as part of a larger cosmic order, a more inclusive
divine plan. Kook's confidence that he lived in an advanced state of the
continuing process of redemption was unbounded. "Redemption continues—and advances."[96] Homecoming to the Land anticipated the end of the
process and hastened it. When Jews fulfilled the commandments of *terumah*
and tithing, "even when the concrete foundations of these are lacking," the
vision of God's Holy Temple stood before them, and "we long for the
fulfillment of older times."[97] One cannot read Kook's splendid prose and
escape the conviction that that fulfillment would not be long in arriving.

Nowhere is the power of Kook's synthesis more evident, or more relevant to
contemporary events, than in Kook's linkage of holiness to *gevurah* or "heroism," in kabbalistic language an attribute or emanation of God's being associated with justice, sterness, and rigor—the opposite of its paired attribute of
hesed.[98] "In the heroic strength of Israel, holiness grows strong."[99] A measure
of "material *gevurah*" was required in order to obtain spiritual greatness;
courage and "inner *gevurah*" would be enhanced by external splendor and
glory in the *shlemut* or fulfillment of statehood.[100] Doing battle for the Lord is
a common religious metaphor, of course, and Kook may have used it in that
sense in the passage just cited, as well as when he wrote that Israel had to be
called by its rabbis to *teshuvah* (return and repentance) "to do valiantly for
God, to return again to the supreme heroism."[101] We should not forget the
saying in *Ethics of the Fathers* that the true *gibor* is the person who conquers
his own evil inclination. Consider however another passage, in which the
connection between holiness and heroism seems to go beyond mere metaphor:

And the spirit of revival, when it has reached the gates of Jerusalem, will know its own portion. It will recognize that its turn has come to stand on its feet, at the ready; its hour has arrived to shake off, in one blow, together, the forgetfulness of God and lassitude *(rashlanut)*, and to return and receive the two good gifts joined one to the other: holiness and heroism, linked, the splendor of holiness and heroic valor.

Kook adds that

Holiness and strength will fill our hearts, together, with all that is bound up in the name of the City of God, where they will serve as a shield against the sufferings attendant on the twin illnesses caused us by departure of the light of majestic holiness and the light of heroic valor.[102]

It is hard to know exactly what Kook had in mind here, because poetic flights of language such as these—typical of Kook's lyric prose—lend themselves to more than one interpretation. Israeli debate on the matter remains fierce. I suspect, however, that his son Zevi Yehudah Kook, whose writings we shall examine in the following chapter, was not wrong to take the linkage of holiness and power in these passages quite literally. The elder Kook was after all a political Zionist, who supported the return to the Land and the establishment of Jewish sovereignty there as the redemptive will of God, knowing full well that these ends could not be attained without the application, to some degree, of coercion. He did so, I think, for two reasons. First, Jewish bodies needed to be saved. Kook wrote during the First World War that despite his saying "a thousand times" that the spiritual Zionists were right and the political Zionists wrong, those words held true only for "normal" times (when, presumably, the *character* of the Spiritual Center was of utmost importance). However, at a time when the "ship of the nation" was tossing in a "stormy political sea," leadership at the helm was essential, and the rabbis were obligated to strengthen it, along with the resolve of the people as a whole, and raise both to holiness.[103]

But Kook's support for the Yishuv and its political leadership went deeper, I believe. The Zionists were not only trying to save human lives. They were trying to save Jews—a people bound indissolubly to God—and thereby to usher in the redemption. Kook's was a messianic time; hence, he believed, its awful upheaval. *Vox populi*, in such a time, and in the case of the Jews, was *vox dei*. "The spirit of the Lord and the spirit of Israel are one."[104] Herzl, then, had been wrong in arguing that Zionism had nothing to do with religion. It had everything to do with religion—and religion, therefore, had to do everything to support (and purify) it. The movement's fundamental principle, as taught by Mizrachi, was "the rebirth of the nation through the Torah on its Land."[105] Kook well knew that this could only be accomplished through force, and yet he did not flinch from its support, confident that those who wielded force in the effort at return—at first the British, and then the Jews themselves—were really brandishing the sword of God. Israel's holi-

ness was tied to its heroism in the most concrete, least metaphorical, sense
possible.

Others, of course, were not sure. They remained unconvinced that the
Messiah was at work and were unable to reconcile the contradictions which
Kook had brought together. The Orthodox Jews who treated the Yishuv as
one more galut among others and regarded it as a usurper of divine prerogatives have offered an alternative and no less convincing reading of Jewish
tradition and Jewish history. The majority of Orthodox Jews who endorsed
the political realm once sovereignty was secure have chosen to act out in
practice a course which in theory is difficult to sanction or explain. This
strategy too continues in the present, and I shall return to it in the following
chapters.

Here we should only emphasize, once again, how much of a break with
rabbinic tradition Kook's messianism permitted him to make, in the name of
the Jewish messianic tradition which had always been in tension, to some
degree, with the outlook of the rabbis. [106] Galut, Kook believed, was about to
end. The people's rebirth in its Land signified God's forgiveness of its sins.
Its rabbis could now "offer comfort to Israel, telling it that it had already
been punished twice over by the hand of God for all its transgressions, and
that its sin had been pardoned." Kook recognized that this was generally
regarded as "a very dangerous step" to take, a sort of flattery of the nation
which could embolden the arrogant to transgress. [107] But he took it anyway,
convinced more strongly than Berdiczewski ever could be that a new sort of
Jew was about to be born, more confident even than Herzl that the Jews
would never again live in galut. He pronounced the dawn of the new age,
sanctified the political efforts to achieve it, and urged all Jews to join in the
Zionists' bold attempt to bring their people home.

Conclusion

Kaufmann's two grave doubts about the Zionist homecoming's chances for
success remain at the center of the political Zionist agenda. Could world
Jewry survive the pressures of anti-Semitism and assimilation long enough to
carry out its ingathering in the Land? And, with the loss of faith—the Jewish
people's raison d'être for centuries—would there be any point to that
survival beyond survival itself, anything to unify the nation and mobilize its
energies? [108] Perhaps A. I. Kook was correct when he wrote that "without an
eternal and independent ideal purpose" which raises all involved to a higher
level, "no movement is at all important nor can any be long-lasting." [109] Both
of these problems raised by Kaufmann are inherent in the political Zionism
which he espoused. They result from the movement's relationship to the
tradition of Jewish reflection on galut—a tradition which political Zionists
sought to end, by ending exile.

On the one hand, Herzl's heirs bore the classical sources a great debt.

Much of Kaufmann and Klatzkin, as we have seen, can be read as a virtual midrash on the Bible. The depiction of Jewish history as nothing but suffering and persecution, a staple of political Zionism to this day, derives from a whole range of biblical and rabbinic sources lamenting the sad estate of galut, as well as from the depressing accounts of nineteenth-century historians such as Graetz. The Zionists' repeated bemoaning of Jewish impotence and degradation likewise continues a tradition going back to the wife-sister stories and the rape of Dinah, accented in prophetic and rabbinic depictions of Israel in exile and handed down to their own generation via the writers of the Jewish enlightenment. Even the frenetic round of "shuttle diplomacy" and intercession on which Herzl embarked owed its origins to a long tradition of galut politics carried on by "court Jews" and other *shtadlanim* who, since Joseph, had negotiated with the lords of the earth on behalf of the Lord's chosen people—all this among Zionists who demanded a clear break with the Jewish past and in some cases proclaimed that they had achieved it.

In part, of course, they had. Political Zionism does represent a radical departure from the rabbinic tradition, both in its secularism and in its activism. Berdiczewski was not alone in associating galut with the plight of Eastern European Jewry, and the rabbis with galut. The rich panoply of two millennia, which had included the Golden Age of Spain and in which Jews had frequently known prosperity along with cultural achievement, understandably became reduced in the popular mind to the Pale of Settlement. Exile came to mean an oppressive Czar, rabbis with side curls in long black coats, a prison outside which life teemed with experience—all that the Zionists wanted desparately to leave behind. In need of a usable past, they turned to the romantic and heroic sagas of the Bible, so much admired by Nietzsche: to conquest, and nature, and love. They turned against the tradition associated with exile. It did not matter that the lens through which they viewed their own experience of galut was itself a legacy from the past. The new reality which they hoped to build demanded new lenses, a culture more suited to the very different facts which that reality would hold up to view.

For this political Zionism paid a price. Its disdain for the rabbinic tradition and its lack of connection to the convenantal theme in the Bible made it unable to see any point to Jewish exile. But if life *in* exile had no transcendent meaning, neither did return from exile. No sense of higher purpose could be provided the Zionist project, beyond physical survival itself—and even this, as Herzl admitted from the start, could not be guaranteed.

Such an outcome was unacceptable to cultural Zionists, religious Zionists and religious anti-Zionists alike. Moreover, it threatened the very possibility of homecoming. Chaim Weizmann therefore sought a synthesis between the two masters—Ahad Ha'am and Herzl. Ben-Gurion constantly hearkened back to the heroes and prophets of ancient Israel. Once statehood had been declared, he sought to undergird the new national identity with myths and symbols from the Jewish past, disregarding those Israelis (known as "Canaanites") who urged an immediate declaration of total independence from the Jewish past as well as from the contemporary diaspora. But Ben-Gurion could not entirely disavow the political Zionist heritage which his own policy of "statism" logically extended.[110] He too was caught in a dilemma inherited from Herzl, forced to seek a purpose for the state which the founders of political Zionism had been unable to provide.

He and they together provided something far more important, of course: the state for which purpose could be sought. More, they gave the current generation of Israelis a compelling interpretation of Jewish history, and a sociology of exile which predicted the diaspora's imminent demise—a powerful legitimation for their homecoming, whatever its character. The internal Israeli conversation over the larger purposes of homecoming which we shall examine in the following chapter stems directly from the questions raised by Herzl, Klatzkin, and Kaufmann and answered with radical confidence by Kook. So too does the more acrimonious debate (analyzed in Chapter Seven) between the homeland, which claims to be the Jewish people's present center and only future, and the American diaspora, which denies both claims and aspires to be a home in its own right. As we shall see, the two debates only rehearse the logic of the more venerable distinction introduced at the very beginning between political and metaphysical homecoming. Jewish tradition continues to dominate the discourse of those who crave the meaning and legitimation which it alone can confer.

VI

BETWEEN HOMECOMING AND REDEMPTION

The two events which have dictated the terms of Jewish existence in our generation—Holocaust and Statehood—have had an especially profound effect upon recent Israeli reflection concerning the meaning of Jewish homelessness and homecoming. The reason is not far to seek. Exiles had been destroyed—and ingathered. Jewish communities by the hundreds had been reduced to dust—and Jerusalem had risen from the dust. Countless prayers had been ignored, and others—uttered for two millennia—had been answered. Jewish history, in short, had taken on a mythic dimension which, some forty years later, is still difficult if not impossible to assimilate. Its impact upon Israeli discussion of galut and the Land was immediate. Before turning to the current debate on these issues, then, we need to look at how its basic terms were transformed in the immediate aftermath of the awesome events of the day.

Most obviously, the Holocaust fundamentally altered the facts of Jewish geography, and did so in a way that was deeply confirming of the tenets of political Zionism. The surviving Jewish communities in the West were small, in some cases pathetically so. More important, the East European galut against which the Zionists had railed was now a Jewish problem beyond all solution. The images of shtetl and yeshivah which had exercised the Zionist imagination, and come to represent the bleakness and the impotence of exile, now joined a past destroyed. Both the disappearance of this *golah* and the manner of its disappearance seemed illustrations from a text written by Herzl and his disciples. Mythic description seemed inevitable. The curses visited by the Nazis upon Jewish bodies were far worse than those ever imagined by Jewish minds; the blessings which came to fruition in the Land immediately thereafter were among the most far-reaching ever dared by Hebrew prophecy. The kingdom of death linked to exile and dispersion from the very beginnings of Jewish reflection had been established for all to see in the heart of twentieth-century Europe, enrolling almost every Jew among its subjects. Only those who had refused to wait there for God's Messiah were "all alive this day" to tell the tale. Only they—many of them nonbelievers, and by virtue of that nonbelief Zionists—had tasted liberally of redemption.

The tale they told was passed on to their children through the civil religion fashioned by Ben-Gurion in the early years of statehood.[1] He assembled a treasury of myths and symbols that left little room for the postbiblical Judaism associated in his mind and that of his generation with exile, passivity, and powerlessness. Israelis would exemplify other virtues: dignity, courage, perseverance, self-reliance. They would be Maccabees, repelling the foreign invader in the name of authentic Jewish culture; they would resemble the Israelites who of old had conquered the Land under Joshua. Heroes and events which had been peripheral to the rabbinic tradition now took center stage, while the character ideals promoted by the rabbis were displaced and even mocked. Two thousand years of history were skipped over. Israel's legitimacy would derive from its biblical past, never forgotten in two millennia of exilic longing. Its spiritual undergirding would come from Isaiah's vision of a "light unto the nations," and not from rabbinic Judaism or its commandments. Indeed, God's marginal role in the modern Jewish state was adumbrated in the passing and ambiguous reference made in Israel's Declaration of Independence to continued reliance upon the "Rock of Israel." Ben-Gurion's generation had no need to be reminded of the fruits of *that* dependence. History's lesson was all too clear. They would wait for no Messiah, having already experienced the personal redemption of return to the Land and looking forward with the rest of humanity to the ultimate redemption of universal brotherhood and peace which, Ben-Gurion said, he knew would never come.[2]

The consequence of this break with the exilic tradition and its God, effected in order to overcome the fateful pattern of all past Jewish history, was a certain denigration of Jews outside the Land. The latter could make no hard and fast distinction between themselves and the Jewish past. Living in the *golah*, they could not but represent the continuation of Jewish history, no matter how attenuated their ties to the tradition might have become in other respects, and regardless of whether they referred to their *golah* as "exile" or only "diaspora." To Israelis, the only relevant point was where these Jews of the West "sat": by the waters of Babylon, as it were, and not in Zion; or, in the words of Ahad Ha'am, in the situation of slavery in the guise of freedom. The fact sheet on their case was often rehearsed. Western Jews had been unable to prevent the Holocaust or to mount operations of rescue. They had barely raised their voices in protest while the slaughter proceeded. And now, when offered the chance to trade in powerlessness for self-determination, they had demurred—often in the name of the same "mission to the nations," or a variant thereof, mocked by all the Zionist founders. The need for a break with them and their galut was therefore as imperative as the need to step aside from the course of Jewish destiny in exile.

Ben-Gurion sought to dramatize the split by denying the title "Zionist" to any Jew who declined to come on *aliyah* (literally "ascent") to live in the

Land. "I have no part" in any such "pseudo-Zionism," he declared at a conference of Jewish leaders assembled in Jerusalem in 1958. Only a person who saw his own future or that of his children in Israel and regarded the state as the only possibility for "the secure and normal existence of a free Jewish people" qualified for the honorific which Ben-Gurion felt entitled to define. Golda Meir added that a Zionist who did not "pack his bags and come to Israel" was no more "important" than a Jew who sat in exile bewailing the destruction of the Temple. Both leaders emphasized that they intended no denigration of diaspora Jews, but only of their choice to remain in exile. But this separation of the Jew from his or her Jewish commitment was of course disingenuous. Ben-Gurion admitted as much when he told the Jerusalem gathering that he respected the "great moral courage" revealed by Jews over the centuries in the face of enemies who "despised and oppressed and murdered" them. "But the galut in which Jews lived, in which they still live, is in my eyes pitiful, poor, wretched, tenuous—and nothing to be proud of. On the contrary: we must negate it absolutely."[3]

Ben-Gurion was not unaware of the American diaspora's achievements. Its population was growing, he conceded, its cultural resources and political influence on the rise. But he declared that it too was part of the galut, on the ground that it stood on the verge of assimilation, a danger disguised by its achievements.[4] The point was crucial to Zionist self-understanding. With the destruction of Central European Jewry, the relatively meager resources of West European Jewry, the bondage of Soviet Jews, and the dismantling soon after statehood of North African and Asian Jewish communities transplanted virtually overnight to Israel, only American Jews boasted the political and cultural resources needed to challenge Ben-Gurion's political Zionist ideology. Only American Jewry could credibly deny Israeli centrality in Jewish life or the wholesale negation of the diaspora. That denial, as we will see, came both explicitly—through polemic against Israeli contentions—and implicitly, through the very existence and vitality of the community as well as the fact that its contribution to the existence of the state was immense. The Center was in debt to its own periphery—dependent on the very communities it was meant to supplant. As the years went by, that dependence increased, as did the self-confidence of American Jewry.

The challenge demanded a response, and so the American *golah* assumed the role in Zionist thought which the Pale of Settlement had played in Herzl's generation and the Holocaust in Ben-Gurion's. America was now the typecase of galut, the immediate reality of exile against which Zionist thinkers defined the virtues of Jewish homecoming. America was the test of Zionist convictions. "Fleshpots" and assimilation replaced shtetl and pogroms as shibboleths of Zionist ideology. The freedom apparently enjoyed by American Jews had to be shown up as illusory, the Judaism practiced in America as inauthentic, the community's self-confidence as self-deception. As always in Jewish and Zionist thought, *home* was defined first of all by what it was not. The novelty was the use of Ahad Ha'am's rallying cry of "slavery under freedom" to set the Center against the periphery it was meant to serve, in the name not of Judaism but of the survival of the Jewish people.

But then came an acknowledged turning point for the perceptions of both Israelis and diaspora Jews: the danger and triumph of 1967, followed all too quickly by the Yom Kippur War of 1973.[5] These events directly set the stage for the discussion which we shall examine in two senses.

First, they reinforced the links between Center and diaspora, the Israeli present and the exilic past, that Ben-Gurion had sought to weaken. "We are one," the slogan of diaspora fund raisers, now rang true for many Israelis. Their history seemed continuous with the Jewish past after all, despite the dividing lines of Holocaust and statehood. The isolation experienced in the two wars is generally cited as a principal cause of this shift. If diaspora Jews and they alone could be counted on to stand by Israel in time of need, Israel really was both "one people" and "a nation dwelling alone." And if all the old anti-Semitic stereotypes had again been pressed into service as part of an all-out effort to liquidate the Jewish people, the Holocaust could no longer be regarded as the consummation of exile, left safely behind by the establishment of Jewish sovereignty. It represented a present danger which had to be confronted and comprehended, so as to be resisted, and in fact became a central myth of the "new civil religion" promoted in these years, particularly by Menachem Begin.[6] Twenty years after the event, the Holocaust could finally be faced head-on, as it was in America at the same time, for many of the same reasons. Israelis were now back within the Pale of Jewish history. Negation of those who had left it could no longer be unequivocal.

Israelis were also thrown back—not without resistance in some quarters—into the embrace of the Jewish religious tradition. The societal "return to Judaism" in these years is symbolized (but not exhausted) by the much-touted movement of *hozrim b'teshuvah* who have forsaken the secular Israeli life-style for study in yeshivot established especially to serve them.[7] In part the renewed interest in Judaism represented the usual need of a second generation for the transcendent meaning supplied to their parents by the project of nation building itself. Jewish sources, never entirely absent from Zionist self-understanding, constituted the depository of meaning closest to hand. Nor should we discount the traumatic effect upon Israeli society of the two wars: exhilarating victory and near-total defeat turned to a resolution far more sober, all within the short space of seven years. Whatever the cause of this shift, we should neither overestimate the dimensions of the Orthodox return within it nor underestimate the challenge to received interpretations of homecoming which the turn to Judaism as a whole involves. The *hozrim b'teshuvah* who now celebrate Israeli Independence Day with denunciations of the state as a trespass of God's commandments are once again a symbol of the larger dilemma. Defining Jewish homecoming in terms of the Jewish tradition lends unequaled sanctity and significance to the Zionist project. But the fledgling state cannot but be eclipsed by a three-thousand-year tradition of obligation. The dimensions of the Zionist revolution are greatly diminished. To the degree that Israelis "return to Judaism," they run the risk of seeing their state through the eyes of a tradition fashioned—and still observed—in exile.

I do not mean to exaggerate the convergence between Israeli and diaspora self-understanding wrought by the new civil religion. On the contrary: the following chapters will make clear that the themes and assumptions of Israeli Judaism remain profoundly different from those of diaspora thinkers. Kook and Gordon and the Buber of *On Zion* resonate loudly in contemporary Israel. They are virtually unknown, or at least rarely heard, in America, where Rosenzweig and S. R. Hirsch and the Buber of *I and Thou* hold sway. The Land and its sanctity, central to the first discussion, are virtually irrelevant to the other.[8] Nevertheless: to the degree that homecoming is interpreted by Israelis with reference to the Jewish religious tradition and regarded as dependent on authentic continuation of that tradition, the connection with diaspora Jews and Judaism cannot but be strengthened. This in turn means the weakening of Herzl's legacy and the renewed empowering of Ahad Ha'am's rival vision. In the Israel of the 1980s, the definition of Jewish homecoming seems a contest between the Spiritual Center of Ahad Ha'am and the Religious Center of A. I. Kook. Political Zionism, to the delight of the diaspora, is well-nigh dormant.

I will analyze and comment upon this debate from the point at which the Center and its diaspora turned decisively toward one another, about twenty years ago. The questions at issue within and between the two communities reduce to two: Is Israel home? Is America exile? I will take up the first in this chapter, the second in the chapter which follows. As always, my focus will be selective. Matters which are germane but not central to the two issues at hand have been omitted from consideration, as have Orthodox thinkers who deny that the state in which they live represents a legitimate Jewish home-coming in any sense. I begin with those whom they most frequently attack— the Orthodox Zionists—because it is among them that the relationship between state and homecoming is most difficult. Orthodox Zionists are asking today, as they must, whether God really intended and supervises the imperfect apparatus which Israelis have erected; asking, too, whether the days of the Messiah are truly now upon us.

Reading the Text of History

Rav Kook the elder, while answering these questions in the affirmative and rejoicing in the answer, was nevertheless able to equivocate somewhat concerning the consequences of what he affirmed. For he lived before the state had arisen: before Orthodox Jews had the power to legislate messianic theory into practice. Kook could put off until tomorrow decisions which today are expressed in one form or another as policy. The difference is crucial to contemporary Orthodox Zionist debate.

I am not speaking here of the modus vivendi with those outside Orthodoxy at which the Mizrachi movement arrived at its inception. That set of compromises, to a large degree, still holds, even if it is weakened now and again by attempts to erode the status quo in the direction of principle. Orthodox Zionists sit in Israeli governments as they once cooperated with Chaim Weizmann; as they reserved the right at the outset to differ in matters of substance or "culture," they now maintain a separate network of schools and institutions dedicated to their own worldly and transcendent ends. My concern here is not this divide between the Orthodox and secular camps but the related and deeper split inherent within Orthodox Zionism itself. Cooperation with the state means postponement of the governance of Israel in accord with the Torah—the end for which, according to its founding slogan, the Mizrachi was established. Acquiescence in the status quo—any status quo—means immersion in the real world of politics, economy, war, and social welfare—a world already shattered, albeit invisibly, if God has really reentered human history in order to bring it to an end. What does it mean to describe the present as "the beginning of the flowering of our redemption" if one goes on with business as usual? And how can one justify a long-term strategy of accommodation with secularism and its manifestations if one's real intent is to institute God's sovereignty in the Land of Israel through the rule of halakhah?

Isaiah Leibowitz (b. 1903)—philosopher, scientist, and for the past two decades a sort of societal gadfly—has answered the second question unequivocally. A state of Torah is a contradiction in terms. In an essay written thirty years ago, but still debated, Leibowitz argued cogently that according to Jewish tradition faith may never be a means to any end outside itself, for example undergirding a society's moral standards. Given that belief, could the state of Israel have any religious significance whatever? One tendency within Jewish tradition, he reported, held religion to be independent of the socio-political situation of Jewish believers. Another, represented most notably by Maimonides, believed perfection of the social and political orders a divine demand, and therefore an essential part of Jewish religious life. But even the latter sources put forward no specific political program for an *actual* Jewish state. In fact, Maimonides knew only the state of the distant past, ruled by the kings of Israel, and the state of "King Messiah" which would be established in the far-distant future. Nowhere in Jewish tradition do we find mention of a state created without direct divine intervention in the interval between destruction of the Temple and the Messiah. Leibowitz's conclusion was unequivocal: religious Zionists were seeking legitimacy from a tradition which did not and could not consider the possibility of their state's existence.[9]

What is more, Jewish law presumed from start to finish a social reality utterly at odds with that of a sovereign Jewish state. The Jews who appear in its pages, bound by its commandments, either live in exile among the nations (recall the talmudic tractate Avodah Zarah) or are subordinate to gentile authority within Eretz Israel (as in the Mishnah). In both cases, Leibowitz wrote pointedly, the Jew required to say the Shema each morning could rest confident that a gentile police force and gentile firemen and gentile water workers, etc., had been on the job all night to make his fulfillment of that commandment possible. Orthodox Jews in the state of Israel, however, had to rely on other Jews, obligated like them to obey the law. At the very moment that they demanded that the Jewish state be governed according to the letter of halakhah, the Orthodox acquiesced in an arrangement whereby they remained a sect within a larger state and depended on that state for the preconditions of their own religious observance. The Sabbath could be a day of rest only because Jewish policemen, in violation of the law, elected not to rest. This, Leibowitz charged, was hypocrisy pure and simple.[10]

The immediate upshot of this argument, emphasized time and again in Leibowitz's early essays, was the need for halakhic reform. Kook too had believed such change inevitable. Jewish policemen, say, had to be able to work on the Sabbath without violating God's commandments. But the issue goes deeper, to the heart of religious Zionism. Leibowitz put the case well. Either the Torah's legislation was intended a priori and so comprised a model to which any Jewish state had to conform—in which case the Orthodox anti-Zionists known as Neturei Karta, "Guardians of the City," were correct. The state was illegitimate, the Zionists were heinous sinners. In our terms: the politicization and universalization of the tradition were incompatible with Judaism. Or, the Torah's legislation was enacted after the fact in accord with particular circumstances prevailing once but no longer. If that were the case, a review of halakhah commensurate with the revision of Jewish history accomplished by Zionism was permissible and even necessary. The conflict between halakhah and the conditions of sovereignty was not proof of the latter's illegitimacy. Zionism's revolution in Jewish life could be rendered "kosher" in the accepted terms of halakhah—if Orthodox Zionists had the courage to make it so.[11]

The Zionist terms in which this call is couched are by now familiar to us. Leibowitz's claim that halakhic life had been stunted in the *golah* echoes Kook rather precisely. It constitutes a variation on the general theme of exilic narrowness and inauthenticity sounded by Gordon and Buber.[12] The positive valuation of dignity, autonomy, and responsibility points to the marriage in Leibowitz's thought of prominent Zionist norms ("auto-emancipation") with the pervasive influence of Immanuel Kant.[13] Not without reason has Leibowitz been forced time and again to defend himself against the charge that his revision of halakhah would undermine the law's authority, his "Zionism" in other words running counter to his Judaism. In response he has appealed to both traditions. "We who destroyed the galut and established the state and accomplished the greatest turnabout in the reality of Israel did not do this according to traditional authorities, and [so] have already undermined them."[14] Abbaye and Rabba, leading figures in the

Babylonian Talmud, were "Jews just like us."[15] Change in the law was mandated by the essential continuity of poststate Judaism with the exilic tradition and not the reverse.

But for all that he appeals to both authorities, Judaism and Zionism, in fact *because* of his commitment to both, Leibowitz has urged their institutional separation. In his later writings this theme is predominant and the call for halakhic reform muted. State and religion must be disjoined. The struggle between Judaism and "the secularism of the State—of any possible state—is eternal."[16] The latter could have no conceivable interest in the former except its exploitation for utilitarian ends such as societal morale and legitimation or, worse, partisan political ambition. Authentically understood, Judaism could lead only to a *Kulturkampf* between religious and secular Israelis. Leibowitz has welcomed that battle in the belief that it would lead to the purification of both Judaism and the Jewish state.[17]

This would seem to mean the end of religious Zionism as understood until now—or, if one wishes, the extension to its logical conclusion of the Mizrachi's original distinction between instrumental and substantive cooperation. Leibowitz, as usual, is uncompromising. Israel was not and never would be the utopian society of which thinkers such as Buber dreamed. It had certainly not become the "secure refuge" sought by Herzl. Normalization was unattainable. The greatest Jewsih creativity in the past had come not in the Land but in exile. No Jewish values could possibly be fulfilled through the establishment of the state, an apparatus of bureaucracy and coercion. But why then have a Jewish state? For one reason only: "because we are fed up with being ruled by the goyim."[18] A religious Zionist could hardly have strayed farther from the original Mizrachi slogan of "a state for the people of Israel, in the Land of Israel, according to the Torah of Israel." Leibowitz's Jewish state guarantees, at best, the space in which halakhic observance can proceed free of outside interference, an arena in which Orthodox Jews can conduct the struggle for Jewish hearts and minds which Herzl portrayed (unsympathetically, of course) in *Altneuland*. Like Herzl, Leibowitz expects that for the forseeable future the secularists will come out on top.

Other religious Zionists have sought to articulate a stance which leaves the Mizrachi's sense of homecoming intact. Their reconciliation of state with halakhah generally follows the lines laid down clearly twenty years ago in an essay by Aharon Lichtenstein, the American-born head of the prestigious yeshivah at Alon Shvut. Lichtenstein's assumptions diverge as much from Leibowitz's as his conclusions. Society, in his reading of Judaism, attains its proper end as a "vehicle for, and a manifestation of, personal and collective beatitude." God, though transcendent, provides us with "indirect expression of His will as manifested in nature and in history," revealing Himself as well through "direct communication with man and through an ongoing dialectical encounter with him." Israel, by entering into covenant with God, had "assumed a unique position in history . . . invested with a special character and unique responsibilities."[19]

Leibowitz would characterize Lichtenstein's stipulation of societal beatitude as a messianic hope and justifiably demand clarification of the terms *indirect expression, direct communication,* and *ongoing dialectical encounter.* The claim to a "special character" is to his mind a destructive current in Jewish thought running from Korah (cf. Numbers 16) through Yehudah Halevi to A. I. Kook.

Lichtenstein agrees that no single political theory is dictated by the fundamental principles enunciated above. But they are not irrelevant to contemporary politics, nor can the utter separation of religion and society be countenanced. The relevant question is therefore the optimum relation between Judaism and the Jewish state at any given moment, that which "will best enable the community to attain its collective spiritual ends." The details of Lichtenstein's persuasive argument need not detain us here. My point is only that religious Zionism must make an argument of this sort—affirming the search for "societal beatitude" if not its actual attainment—in order to fend off challenges from Leibowitz on the one side and the messianists on the other. Such a position is likely to disturb secular and Orthodox Zionists alike. The former will be outraged at Lichtenstein's insistence that Jewry is "in its essence . . . a religious community," and so must take some step "down [the] Platonic road" to religious coercion. The state must encourage or even compel action required to maintain the religious community's ideals and character. But Lichtenstein is no less aware than Leibowitz of the danger which such a step poses to authentic faith: "spiritual pride writ large," the transformation of the rabbinate into an officialdom of mere functionaries, a loss of religious liberty which "diminishes man's spiritual stature" and "fractures the *tzelem elohim,* the 'human face divine' within us."[20] Orthodox Jews may well prefer to sacrifice some personal religious liberty on the altar of "societal beatitude." Like Lichtenstein, however, and unlike Leibowitz, most religious Zionists have sought to put off that day of reckoning. They have supported the "status quo" relation of compromise with the secular state and proceed cautiously in the matter of halakhic change, if at all.

Their failure to heed Leibowitz's warnings is linked to disagreement with him on the other question crucial to the meaning of Orthodox Zionism; the messianic status of contemporary Israel history. Here too Leibowitz put the question unequivocally. It was because Jews like himself had not "penetrated the *pargod*" (divine curtain) and so could not know for certain that their state represented the "beginning of the flowering of our redemption" that they were obliged to undertake halakhic reform. They had to "decide for themselves regarding new religious problems which we ourselves have called forth." God would not solve the problem, and neither would a Messiah.[21] As the influence of the messianists within religious Zionism has grown more pronounced since 1967, Leibowitz's rhetoric has grown more strident. In the wake of the religious exultation following the reconquest of Old Jerusalem, he contrasted the Maccabean revolt, sparked by a martyr who had died rather than eat pork, with the city's conquest by kibbutznikim who not only ate pork but raised pigs for a living. The latter could be more aptly compared to the idolatrous king Jeroboam or the evil king Yannai, both of whom had also enlarged the territory of the Land.[22] His critique reached its climax in the Swiftian proposal, barely a month after the war, that a discotheque be erected near the Western Wall (known in Hebrew as "the kotel," i.e., "the wall"). It would be called *Discotheque Ha'shekhinah*, the Discotheque of God's Presence, or for short the "Diskotel." Religious and secular Israelis would celebrate there together, the latter as they always did in discotheques, the former because this one would bear God's name—just like the conquest itself and the state.[23]

Underneath the sarcasm lies a theological point of utmost seriousness for the meaning of Jewish history—and therefore of Jewish homecoming. In contending that God neither works miracles which interrupt the course of nature nor interferes in the affairs of nations,[24] Leibowitz is carrying on the part of the rabbis in the age-old struggle of the legal tradition against the threat of radical innovation posed by messianism.[25] In contemporary Israel too the stakes are high. Religious law and public policy hang in the balance. On the one side stand those who argue that there can be no homecoming without God's Messiah. Since the Messiah has not come, the Zionist return is a delusion and a crime. On the other side stand those who agree that homecoming short of the Messiah is not possible and conclude that since the Zionist return is a fact the hidden presence of God's hand must be presumed. Closest to Leibowitz, in the middle, are those who ritually affirm the messianic character of the return but deny that its fulfillment is in any way imminent. Their hesitation about halakhic reform is joined with unwillingness either to declare or deny unequivocally that "the flowering of our redemption" has begun. Both they and the "hard messianists" demand our attention.

The latter derive indirect inspiration and authority from Rabbi Zevi Yehudah Kook (1891–1972), who in turn claimed with much justice to teach in the name of his revered father. It is hard to judge the accuracy of that claim precisely, because the difficulty of projecting the stance of any thinkers into conditions which he or she did not live to see is here compounded by the fact that Zevi Yehudah faced the task of translating his father's highly dialectical and often abstruse teachings into practical applications of policy. The general thrust of the two is identical; there can be no doubt that the son's discernment of "divine approval of Zionism" in the events of the decade following the elder Kook's death—further ingathering of the exiles, continued settlement and cultivation of the Land, growing faith in God's providence—was thoroughly in line with the legacy which he inherited.[26] Such certainty is not available to us regarding particular pronouncements of policy or more detailed readings of the text of contemporary history.[27] In 1947, for example, Z. Y. Kook denounced the Partition of Palestine—accepted by Ben-Gurion and the Zionist leadership—as the unacceptable continuation of the exilic tendency to seek accommodation with Amalek, Israel's eternal enemy.[28] In the years immediately following statehood he quoted the Mishnaic saying that "a man who owns no land is not a man" and applied it to the individuals and the nation of Israel. "As galut meant the destruction of national life, by cutting it off from its (proper) place, this redemption, the cancellation of galut, is the raising up of the nation's life, its revival as of old, in its connection to its place."[29] The real Israel, he wrote, was now identical with the tangible Israel which "has been redeemed: the state of Israel and the army of Israel"—and not with the exiled diaspora.[30] The ideological implications of this stance were entirely consonant with Ben-Gurion's position: the diaspora was negated and the state sanctified—a convergence of decisive importance for Israeli politics in the eighties.

Sociologists Charles Liebman and Eliezer Don-Yehiya, citing this last passage, compare the elder Kook's attempt to "expose and activate the elements of sanctity within the nation and to impose sanctity upon the Zionist enterprise" with Zevi Yehudah's vision of the state's very existence and achievements as "manifestations of the revelation of holiness."[31] The point is well taken. I believe, however, that the disagreement may once more be a matter of timing as much as of principle. Zevi Yehudah lived to witness events which his father could only imagine, as it were, from across the Jordan. The lyricism of the vision from afar gives way, up close, to declamation.

Once Israel had stretched its borders to the West Bank of the Jordan in 1967, Zevi Yehudah's confidence in his reading of the signposts of history permitted him to declaim with immense authority. He declared that any government which dared to return the conquered territories, or even hindered Jewish settlement therein, would thereby pronounce itself illegitimate, by violating the commandments to settle and conquer the Land. Jews were duty bound to obey the halakhah—and disobey the government.[32] They could defy political reality, and not merely the elected leaders of Israel, because the end-time was near. The rabbinic saying that redemption would come gradually rather than suddenly referred only to the final redemption that awaited Jewish repentance. Present reality, however, indicated that repentance was well under way. Even Maimonides, who had discouraged "calculation of the end-time," had not questioned the "clear and decisive words of the sages" that "no end time could be more apparent" than that signaled by the renewed fruitfulness of the Land. And behold, the Land was again fruitful. Hence Zevi Yehudah's conviction, voiced before 1967 and repeated since, that "this is already the middle of redemption. . . . We are in the *traklin* (drawing room) and not the *prozdor* (the hallway)."[33] Whether the elder Kook would have been so undialectical in his verdict upon the present age, had he lived to see it, is open to conjecture.

The political messianism carried on in the name of the Kooks, father and son, has been the subject of considerable scholarly attention of late and need not be described in this study in any detail.[34] One aspect of the movement, however, is central to our concern: its insistence upon homecoming with a vengeance. The end of political exile, the assumption of political power, is the instrument for bringing metaphysical exile to an end as well; the fact that the former has occurred is taken as proof positive that the second is also in process—for the two dimensions are inseparable throughout Jewish tradition. History is reentered, with the Zionists, in order to be transcended, messianically.

> The Zionism of redemption, the great forerunner and expounder of which was Rav Kook, of blessed memory, did not come to solve the Jewish question through the establishment of a Jewish state. Rather it served as a tool in the hands of divine providence to prepare Israel for its redemption. Its innermost goal is not normalization of the Jewish people, to be a nation like all others, but to be a holy people, a people of the living God, whose center is Jerusalem with the Temple at its midst.[35]

Thus Rabbi Yehuda Amital, of the Gush Etzion Yeshivah, in 1974. As Zevi Yehudah Kook had written thirty years before, "not for nothing did God gather in the exiles, give life to a barren land, renew the holy tongue, influence kings and sway the policies of nations, bring to nought plans to harm Israel, fill the remnant of his chosen ones with heroism and dedication, and bring the bearers of Torah to their proper place."[36] The truth of homecoming was too good to be merely true. "Not for nothing" had it occurred, meaning that it had to be of ultimate significance, signaling redemption. It therefore mandated the free mingling of the vocabularies of religion and politics kept separate during the centuries of exile.

Others, even among the messianists, are more cautious, relying to a greater degree on Maimonides' rationalist and gradualist approach to the Messiah's coming rather than upon the mystical assurance that characterizes Nachmanides and the two Kooks. Shlomo Goren, a former chief rabbi, enunciated the various identifying elements of redemption scattered throughout Jewish tradition and then declared, on the authority of Maimonides, that there could be an independent Jewish state *before* the start of the process of redemption. "We are in an intermediate period" between destruction and redemption, charged with the tasks of conquering the Land, ingathering the exiles, and making barren soil flower. The fourth task, rebuilding of the Temple, was as yet far off. Whether the present state proved to be a part of the messianic process or a false start depended on the conduct of its citizens.[37]

The volume from which these words are taken was issued in 1964, before the events which galvanized Israeli political messianism to action. Uriel Tal's exhaustive survey of the post-1967 literature,[38] like my own more limited reading in these sources, suggests that debate is now couched in Zevi Yehudah's urgent and mystical terms, abandoning the caution which Goren derived from Maimonides. Only in the former terms, for example, to which Maimonides is subsumed, can we comprehend the debate over the Jewish terrorist underground recently conducted in the pages of *Nekudah*, a journal of Gush Emunim settlements. They account for the opinion that the appropriate response to Jewish terrorism is still more settlement, in all the Land of Israel. For "Eretz Israel confers, according to our faith, moral values and greater qualities of character on all who dwell within it."³⁹ The elder Kook had affirmed precisely this rabbinic dictum on the very first pages of his meditation upon the Land.⁴⁰

Leibowitz has argued that this stance is the inevitable consequence of a religious Zionism which inserted into all Orthodox prayer books used in Israel a plea for God's blessing upon "the beginning of the flowering of our redemption," for His aid in the victory of the state's defenders, and for His speedy ingathering of those Jews remaining in the diaspora. Others are more cautious. Ephraim Urbach for example—an elder statesman among religious Zionists and a scholar of rabbinic Judaism—has generally refused either to affirm or deny that we live in an advanced state of redemption. The sources on the matter permit more than one inference. He has condemned the translation of prophets and sages to "everyday language"; the price, as Scholem had warned, was too high. He has criticized the "tone of messianism in many religious circles," some of whom claimed to know even the "stage of redemption we are now in." He has opposed the "unfortunate pairing of religion and politics."⁴¹ But he has also refused to rule out messianic terminology entirely. One could use the term *ge'ulah* (redemption) loosely and call our age the "start of redemption." It *was* a time of *ge'ulah*, according to a certain concept. Though he did not like the expression "the beginning of the flowering of our redemption," one could not avoid seeing the present as a "great achievement" which might lead to a future greater still.⁴²

Others are less equivocal, seemingly renouncing messianism altogether. David Hartman (b. 1931), like Lichtenstein American-born and like Leibowitz a student and teacher of Maimonides, is wary of both the messianists and of those who, like Leibowitz, would deny history any divine presence whatever. One need not claim to know the meaning of a historical moment in order to respond to God "via a living connection to events." The present "mediates" the living God of Israel. If we focus exclusively on God's action in history, He will appear a liberator one day, an enemy the next. But neither can we adopt the traditional halakhic orientation and empty present-day history of all religious significance. In short, we cannot know how contemporary Israel is related to the end of days, but we can and do know its relation to Israel's eternal covenant with God.⁴³

Hartman argues that the Zionist homecoming has led to renewed commitment to that covenant. More, it was in keeping with the "normative orientation of Judaism," the "halakhic concern with details," the tradition's blend of universalism and particularism. Homecoming conferred the potential for a religious Jewish society even if the reality still fell far short. In this limited sense, Hartman can claim that "in making contact with the Land of Israel, one is led to make contact with the God of Israel." Jewish homecoming had "enabled Judaism to become once again a live option."[44]

The modesty of these claims is striking, as is their ambiguity. Is Hartman reducing God's presence in recent Jewish history to the "living connection to events" experienced by Israelis? Or is he making the stronger claim of an actual divine incursion, immanent or transcendent—in which case Leibowitz's strictures apply? (The former, I believe.) Is the parallel between halakhic concern for details and the "nitty-gritty" character of Israeli life experienced by the American *oleh* mere sentimentality or symbolic of the standard religious Zionist aspiration to enlarged public scope for the halakhah? (Again, it seems, the former, though if the latter is intended, Leibowitz's qualms are relevant once more.) Finally, in saying that the state's failure to renew Judaism and the Jewish community thus far is no proof that it will not do so in the future, is Hartman expressing a hope for what will be or—more typical of religious Zionism—stating an outcome distant or impending, awaited confidently in faith? Again, I suspect, the former: messianism in Hartman's Zionism is thus minimized or even eliminated.

The ultimate meaning of Jewish homecoming is at stake in these distinctions; alternately put, the degree to which Israelis too live in exile. Religious Zionists find themselves in a space which the rabbinic tradition could not imagine: between political and metaphysical homecoming. Even the former has been limited by the state's inability to secure the condition stipulated by Maimonides as indicative of the messianic era's final stages: peace from Israel's enemies. Metaphysical homecoming, or the nearest approximation Maimonides allows, the reign of Torah, seems to the nonmessianists as distant in our generation as it ever was in exile. As a result, the rabbinic picture of exile inside the Land—of Jewish time and space carved out from an Eretz Israel dominated by idolatry (in this case, secularism)—threatens to seem as applicable to present circumstances as the rabbis'countervision of a redemption appearing "little by little." Deuteronomy's depiction of wholeness and perfection similarly seems far less relevant than its description of a condition between conquering the land and actually coming "to inherit" it—in other words, between homecoming and redemption. The text of present-day history allows of more than one reading.

Contemporary religious Zionists, if unable to join the ranks of the messianists, face a problem very similar to that which confronted Moses from across the Jordan. How does one describe, through language, a reality which has never existed—and so motivate the children of Israel to bring it into being? How does one prepare for the perfect life of Torah, despite the tragic knowledge that this attempt may well fail? Three thousand years after the original homecoming, in the wake of numerous exiles and wanderings, in the immediate shadow of near-total destruction, the problem is more acute than ever. Religious Zionism is hard pressed to summon the commitment needed for the monumental task of religious nation building without the promise of fulfillment which the rabbis Kook, unlike Deuteronomy, are willing to supply. Part of the required force is generated negatively: in the reasons which Leibowitz need not even state for being "fed up with living under the goyim," or the claim which Hartman need not argue that the state "creates possibilities for a renewal of Judaism not present in galut,"[45] or Z. Y. Kook's extravagant rhetorical contrast between Jewish existence inside and outside Eretz Israel. But the essential momentum for the religious Zionist enterprise—required, as it were, for the long jump over the inherent contradictions pointed to by Leibowitz—can come only from the positive promise that this Jewish state will not fail like its predecessors. This homecoming will be the last. As Hartman puts it: the covenantal memory of Sinai alone may not provide the strength which this generation needs in order to persevere. The redemptive memory of Exodus may be required[46]—and this he cannot summon. The messianists need not rest content with such "passionate sobriety." Their cup of salvation is full.

Thinkers such as Hartman walk a narrow tightrope indeed and balance on it at the price of no little ambiguity. Those who prefer the messianic jump to the other side run even bolder risks, while Leibowitz's leap to safety involves the abandonment of religious Zionist expectations. It also denies much that is most powerful and most precious in the definition of Jewish statehood as Jewish homecoming.

"Normalization" versus "Grandfather Israel"

For some non-Orthodox Israelis, even the most modest claims of religious Zionism go too far, though these thinkers too are unable to imagine a Jewish state not linked in some substantive way to the Jewish exilic past. The inspiration for their approach is of course Ahad Ha'am, transmitted in the somewhat more religious key first sounded by Martin Buber and A. D. Gordon. Ahad Ha'am has assumed a pivotal role among contemporary non-Orthodox Zionists largely by default. There simply are no other persuasive live options. Yehezkel Kaufmann, we recall, pointed to the problem half a century ago: with the achievement of statehood, secular political Zionism would reach the fulfillment of its program, and so the limit of its ability to generate commitment. The dream which had motivated generations of Jews to sacrifice, once realized, would not offer sufficient meaning to their children. The vacuum created by the loss of religion—traditionally the bulwark of Jewish identity—would then be obvious to all. Kaufmann was convinced that Jews could not remain Jews without a living connection to their tradition, even with the state. But he also believed that religion was everywhere on the decline and that substitutions such as Ahad Ha'am's "Judaism" of culture would not do. Hence the pessimism which pervades Kaufmann's *Golah Ve-nekhar*. Ahad Ha'am's solution to the Jewish problem would soon

prove necessary—but would be doomed to failure. Only the latter contention seems in dispute in contemporary Israeli literature on the subject.
Overt rejection of Judaism and the Jewish past is now rare.

The need for the grounding which Ahad Ha'am first proposed has been
aided and abetted by the sterility of socialist Zionism in the years since
statehood. Before 1948, socialism dominated political Zionist ideology, along
with Jabotinsky's revisionism; in the years after 1948, socialism was subordinated by Ben Gurion to the ideology of "statism" that we have examined
briefly.[47] Today's kibbutz generation finds itself marginal to contemporary
Israeli society, in contrast to the centrality of its parents before and after the
state's founding. The decline in vitality of Western socialism generally has
dictated that the kibbutznik's search for meaning be conducted elsewhere.
Judaism is the obvious repository. Few secular voices on the left, as a result,
now fail to advocate some sort of Ahad Ha'amist alternative. Those who do
opt for secular political Zionism are uncertain and defensive.

A recent secularist manifesto, for example, proclaims that the basis of the
New Zionism, "social Zionism," will lie in the sovereignty of the individual
above all else—his or her freedom from religious and political coercion. The
program declares that Judaism is "open" for the free choice of every individual, that the diaspora exists and should be strengthened rather than negated,
that citizenship must confer equal rights on everyone living within Israel's
borders, that peace with Arab neighbors is essential to the realization of
Zionism, and that society must be viewed as the field of creativity and
responsibility of the individual.[48] In its language the manifesto combines
Western liberalism and social democracy. Its program is largely platitudi-
nous. Most relevant here, its description of Judaism as a storehouse of
cultural resources, a usable past to be drawn upon by each individual as he
or she sees fit, is far from the call for renewal of a binding tradition urged by
Ahad Ha'am. It rather rehearses Berdiczewski's experience of religion as a
coercive burden to be cast off. Whatever its merits, I think it fair to say that
this is hardly the stuff of which the meaning of Jewish homecoming will be
fashioned some forty years after statehood.

Other secular political Zionist efforts are no more promising. The novelist
and essayist A. B. Yehoshua (b. 1936) centers his own vision of homecoming
on a negation of exile which we shall examine in the following chapter. He
urgently calls for normalization. Jewish exceptionalism must be abandoned.
Jewish existence must be adapted to the demands of the world. Exile had
answered the need to be a unique and chosen people, but homecoming must
mean the end of that self-destructive quest. Jews should henceforth be
defined as those who regard Israel as their state or land, a shift in self-
understanding which Yehoshua allows might take a century to accomplish.[49]
In a more thoughtful work, the jurist and politician Amnon Rubinstein (b.
1931) traces the history of Zionism's various ideals in an attempt to comprehend and to counter the rise of Gush Emunim. Messianism is the foil for the
normalization which Rubinstein advocates. He calls the book's final chapter

"Without Exclamation Points," a typical thrust in recent secularist writings. If normalization fails, Rubinstein avers, so will the state. Yet he observes at the same time that Israel has not eliminated anti-Semitism, but only given it a new twist, and that a "subconscious wish to be different" continues to play a role in the making of policy. Rubinstein finds Orthodoxy intolerable on religious and political grounds and derides non-Orthodox streams of Judaism in Israel as inauthentic. There was but one option: a return to Herzlian Zionism, through which Israel could exist as a Jewish state, remain the leader of world Jewry, and become an independent people dwelling securely in its homeland.[50] The heady dose of Herzlian utopianism invoked here compensates for the lack of content in Herzl's Zionist vision and in Rubinstein's. He seems to desire no such content; it is precisely the free play of conflicting forces, political and religious, which "normalizes" the Jewish state and staves off the twin dangers of messianism and religious authority.

The most coherent secularist statement of recent years is that of the novelist Amos Oz (b. 1939), whose starting point is the explicit rejection of Ahad Ha'amism. "I am a Zionist Jew. I do not lean on religion in saying this; I have not learned to concoct verbal compromises like 'the spirit of Grand-father Israel' or 'the values of Jewish tradition.'" For both the values and the tradition "stem directly from principles of faith that I cannot accept." Only a fool could deny the religious underpinnings of the drive for Jewish independence in the hearts of those who had worked for statehood. But the Jewish state they created was not the model kingdom of David, or the second commonwealth with its Temple, or the East European shtetl "transported on the wings of Chagall to the hills of Canaan."[51] Secularists had of late become defensive about their stance. They stuttered before the Orthodox that "you are of course more Jewish but we're also okay, aren't we, even though not at your level." The secularist creed needed reassertion. Israel was not a "new interpretation of an old civilization, as the disciples of Ahad Ha'am claimed and celebrated." To Oz, Judaism was rather a cultural legacy from which he could choose at will, assigning its treasures to the living room or the attic as he saw fit. He would do so "as one of the legitimate heirs: not as a stepson, or a disloyal and defiant son, or a bastard, but as a lawful heir."[52]

The vehemence of the defense betrays the power of the attack. Oz's resentment pours forth openly against those who claim that only their Judaism is authentic and regard secularists such as himself as mere rootless bohemians. He is especially critical of the messianists, for three reasons. First, they had appropriated to themselves not only Judaism but Zionism, settling West Bank hilltops like the kibbutz soldiers of old and "stealing the hearts of some of our spiritual mentors, as if here were the heirs of the pioneering spark that had dimmed." Worse, they had robbed the original pioneers of "spiritual autonomy" by regarding them as misled individuals who "thought they were acting from an idealistic world view but were really no more than an instrument of God." Finally, the messianists were dangerous. Their moral insensitivity, their use of Judaism to underwrite their own chauvinist ambitions, would, if unchecked, bring disaster. Zionism had begun with and remained conditional upon the surrender of messianic hopes. "Israel, trust in the Lord" was a non-Zionist, perhaps an anti-Zionist, slogan.[53]

Oz's positive vision is that of the Jewish socialists and includes their commitment to internationalism. Jews had been forced to adopt a state because they had for too long been the only people without one and had suffered as a result. But Oz cannot take pride in the trappings of nationalism.[54] Nor does he express attachment as a Jew to the Land of Israel. Indeed, Jews had built their state there for the simple reason that "the Jews would not have come to any other place to renew their independence and become a nation again."[55] Oz unabashedly embraces the Western ideals of humanism, social democracy, and pluralism rejected by many among the Orthodox. When he articulates the outlines of his utopia it is in these terms. Jewish tradition, even the prophecies of Isaiah, are absent.[56]

The result, he concedes, is a certain fissure in his Zionism, a marked incompleteness. His defense, like Rubinstein's, turns to high rhetoric. "Here I stand. In the life of society, in love, standing over against the other, and over against death. We, human beings who are not religious, are fated to experience contradictions and fissures. Would that it were so in Zionism as well."[57] Again, hardly the stuff of which the significance of Jewish homecoming will be fashioned, and hardly in keeping with Oz's own repeated call for sober realism: "Patience, I say. There is no shortcut."[58]

Only in one respect do Oz and his fellow secularists agree with both the Orthodox and the Ahad Ha'amians: in their negation of the diaspora. When Oz rushes to attack the conviction that Israel is fated to be "a people that dwells apart," unable to trust the nations of the world, he writes that perhaps the combination of whining and self-righteousness which he finds in Israel of late is the identifying mark of *galut*. The exilic Jew could not look a Gentile in the eye, but either squinted from below in self-abasement or looked down from above in superiority. To claim that "all the world is against us" was to leave Zionism for galut. To abandon socialist self-sacrifice for lavish "weddings and holidays, for petty-bourgeois life"—all the "old neuroses"—was likewise to return to galut in all its "delightful ugliness."[59] Here Oz brandishes the ultimate Zionist insult, exile, and hurls it at his adversaries. His homecoming, like theirs, can only be defined in terms of the past they have claimed to leave behind.

All contemporary Israeli Zionists, as we will see in the following chapter, are more or less agreed on such negation of the diaspora, and the negation tends to be all the more strident the less a positive definition of Jewish homecoming is available. "The family," as Oz calls the many varieties of Jewish homecoming, is defined in the last resort by who is outside it. On other matters, however, the secularists are divided among themselves, most obviously on the importance of the Land. What for Oz, Rubinstein, and

Yehoshua (whose politics are left of center) is an instrument of normalization—the only "plank at which Jews could grasp," in Oz's metaphor, to keep from drowning in the sea of nations—is for secular adherents of Gush Emunim an absolute value which brooks no questioning. The Land is the one weapon in the ideological arsenal of political Zionism which still commands the field. In fact, the demand that all the Land be settled and the short-term consequences be damned gives political Zionism a new lease on life, postponing the reckoning which Kaufmann foresaw. So long as parts of the Land remain unpopulated by Jews, the original political Zionist vision remains relevant. Oz's pluralist social democratic internationalism is hard pressed to compete with the symbolic power of the Land for Jewish or Zionist loyalties, as recent events have demonstrated. So is Rubinstein's Herzlian liberalism. The future may be another matter. When the borders are finalized, whether at the Jordan or farther to the west, the problem of meaning beyond political Zionism will surface once more, even on the political "right." In all likelihood it will carry remaining secular Zionists to the address at which most non-Orthodox thinkers can already be found in our day: a renewed and somewhat religious Ahad Ha'amism.

Attempts at Religio-Cultural Synthesis

I describe this Ahad Ha'amism as "somewhat religious" because while recent cultural Zionists have steered a course midway between normalization and Orthodoxy, they have also replaced the militant agnosticism of the master with some sort of return to Jewish faith. Personal religious commitments of the thinkers concerned have no doubt played a part in this shift. But it has also come as a result of their common recognition that the idea of the Spiritual Center lacks credibility unless the Center visibly reclaims and revitalizes Jewish tradition. Precisely how it could or should do so is rarely spelled out in their thought, prompting the sort of cynicism about the Ahad Ha'amist program evinced by Oz. A non-Orthodox Israeli Jewish culture, we can safely say, will either be a very long time in the making or eventually prove impossible. Ahad Ha'amists are all too aware of the difficulties.

The philosopher Nathan Rotenstreich (b. 1914), for example, points to two. It was reasonable in the late nineteenth century to assume that the Center would be linked to its periphery by language. Diaspora Jews in our day, however, were largely illiterate in the language of the Center. Israel's ability to transmit culture to them was severely compromised.[60] More important, Ahad Ha'am had not fully understood the corrosive effect of modernity upon historical tradition as such. He himself had described and assisted in the erosion of religious consciousness, and the Jewish state, by providing a wealth of experiences not encompassed by traditional concepts, had further weakened the ability of past commitments to obligate the present generation of Israelis. But the decisive factor had been modernity itself.

In ways which Ahad Ha'am could not have foreseen, the very notion of tradition on which he based all his hopes was now at risk.[61]

As a result of these difficulties, Rotenstreich concedes, Israel at present consituted a Spiritual Center more by virtue of the problems which it incarnated than of the cultural resources which it created or transmitted. The state had supplied the diaspora with a new image of the Jew: active and sovereign rather than passive and dependent. It now served as the principal symbol and prop of Jewish identity. It had given Jews a foothold in the world of nations and paid the price for that role by becoming the focus of anti-Semitism. In short, the "messianic" normalization sought by Herzl was mocked by Israel's notorious insecurity, while the role of "spiritual center" to which Israel should aspire made "continuing abnormality" inevitable. The problem of supplying positive Jewish meaning to the Center, and so the periphery, was more intractable than Israel's social and economic woes. For the present only an eclectic collection of fragmentary responses seemed possible.[62]

Rotenstreich, typically for the the the Ahad Ha'amists, proposes only the most general of religio-cultural Zionist paths: gradual renewal of the halakhah, through return to the fundamental ideas to which the law gave expression. By the latter, he intends primarily the idea of man as subject to divine judgment before his Creator. The modern Jew could be won back to Judaism only if he or she believed it to contain "valuable ideas to which he can subscribe." Were these suitably reformulated (Rotenstreich seems to have Hermann Cohen and Martin Buber in mind), "even a secular Jew would not find it unreasonable to mold his life increasingly in accordance" with them. Rotenstreich recognizes that institutions as well as norms are required if the Spiritual Center was to be Jewish in any substantive sense, but he urges Israelis to resist attempts at coercing religious observance through state legislation.[63]

Eliezer Schweid (b. 1929), a scholar of medieval and modern Jewish thought, tends to derive his vision of the marriage between "humanism" and Judaism from Gordon and Kook rather than Buber and Cohen. Yet the basic dilemma, and the upshot of his deliberations upon it, remain the same. How can a modern Israeli define "a concept of Jewish culture as set forth by Ahad Ha'am and [Chaim Nachman] Bialik?"[64] A recent work attempts to promote a synthesis between Zionism and Jewish tradition by tracing the theme of the Land from biblical to contemporary sources. Rabbinic Judaism, exiled from the Land, had idealized and romanticized it. It had made Eretz Israel a "land of promise" exclusively, no longer the true home it was to the Bible. Modern Zionism, conversely, had restored the latter dimension to the Land but eliminated the former. The desired synthesis, which demanded knowledge of Jewish sources pertaining to the Land as a prerequisite, could arise only from "ways of life, forms of culture, created in the Land." These of necessity would involve incorporation of the "religious meaning originating in the Biblical concept of the promised land"—a far-reaching change in "the

world view and paths of realization of secular Zionism." A "direct confrontation" with the tradition's values was essential.[65] Schweid argues in a recent
essay ("Humanistic Secularism and Religious Content in Israel," 1981), that
without such "content" neither secularism nor the state could hope to
inspire commitment. The attempt by Ahad Ha'am and Bialik to translate the
tradition into secular terms by separating moral or aesthetic or national
attributes from their religious "garb" had solved nothing. When all was said
and done, the only vitality in the secularized tradition lay in the religious
content that it had incorporated and transmitted.[66]

Schweid's program for succeeding where the founders had failed seems
beset by the same realities as Rotenstreich's. The essay just cited, for
example, seeks to break down secular opposition to religion by confuting the
conventional wisdom that faith is something that either "happens to one" as
the result of forces beyond the self's control or does not. Schweid urges
Israelis to take responsibility for their belief and to remain open to the
possibility of faith. They need not become religious in the "established
sense," by "returning in *teshuvah*," Schweid writes, or give up the positive
elements of secular culture. Traditional Judaism itself had accepted pluralism, as long as Torah remained the behavioral norm. But Israelis did have to
understand that religiosity required a social framework of collective institutions to express and sustain it. This above all other groundings for Jewish
tradition was lacking at present in their society. There was no shared
parhesia or public space. Schweid therefore expresses the hope that a
religious-humanist synthesis, combined with innovation within the halakhah, will eventually lead to some form of halakhic state, established by
popular consent and so not undemocratic. In the meantime, he endorses the
Orthodox call for *mishpat ivri* (Hebrew law): derivation of civil legislation,
wherever possible, from Jewish rather than non-Jewish precedents.[67]

The flaws in this vision are all too obvious; Schweid too seems aware of
them. Halakhic reform has so far not been forthcoming. A halakhic state,
even if ratified by a majority, would hardly be democratic. If there is a
Jewish tradition of pluralism, it is at best limited and utterly marginal.
Schweid tends to understate the conflict between secularism and belief, the
better to argue the possibility of synthesis;[68] Rotenstreich's pessimism on
this score seems better grounded. Finally, there is the problem of theology.
Students of Ahad Ha'am who reject the master's agnosticism are obliged to
clarify the beliefs which they unlike him affirm—revelation first of all. Only
then can they ask others to adopt or "remain open to" the "tradition"; only
then do we know what we are adopting, and to what we remain open. In the
absence of such clarification, Israeli thinkers join diaspora counterparts in
exploiting a lingering symbolic attachment to the tradition, and the meaning
conferred by reading its texts and enacting its rituals, but can hardly lay
claim to a normative Jewish culture. The feature of Jewish tradition which
Schweid embraces wholeheartedly in this fashion is the Land, which stands
forth as a real and personal presence in his thought, as it does in Deuteron-

omy and Gordon and Kook but not in Ahad Ha'am or Oz or Rotenstreich. Here too, however, one wants to know just what religious significance is claimed for the Land, in the absence of the various beliefs which Deuteronomy and Gordon and Kook take for granted. The quotation marks which Schweid places around the word "religious," in urging a return to the biblical notion of the Land, are revealing.[69]

The most penetrating account of these dilemmas to date is informed through and through by awareness of the limited options available to contemporary Jewish religious thought. Gershom Scholem (1897–1982) was never sanguine about solving the theological problems which he addressed. "All I can propose," he wrote in 1974, "are reflections. I have no answer—ours is a generation of crisis."[70] He confessed the following year to anxiety that "the threat of death, oblivion" hung over "the processes unfolding here."[71] Elsewhere he compared Israeli society, indeed contemporary Jewry as a whole, to life on top of a volcano. "Let us face it: the experience of the German murder of the Jews, and of the apathy and hardheartedness of the world, has also been followed by a profound exhaustion."[72] Not a small part of the contemporary Jewish dilemma lay in the problem of Jewish belief. "When the collective to which Revelation addresses its pronouncements is itself the source from which they emerge, as in Ahad Ha'am," legitimation of any particular revelation was problematic. "The yardstick for what should be considered 'Jewish' becomes questionable, and credentials uncertain."[73]

Scholem himself worked all his life to widen the "accepted yardstick" of Jewishness through his investigations into the "underground" tradition of Jewish mysticism. But he was also driven by the need for authentic Jewish credentials. As a result, he defined himself as a "former follower of Ahad Ha'am."[74] After a certain point, the master's atheism could not be countenanced. In an interview given the kibbutz journal *Shdemot* in 1975, Scholem described himself as one who at the beginning of his Zionist commitment "took the Biblical passage, 'And you shall be unto me a kingdom of priests and a holy nation' (Exodus 19:6) as the definition of Zionism." He added that "although I have since learned a great deal, I cannot say that there is nothing to this passage." The careful formulation is typical of Scholem: religious content, in a way he will not define here, was fundamental to his Zionism. He had remained an Ahad Ha'amist nonetheless because of his opposition to the goal of normalization—"an Ahad Ha'amist but more religious than Ahad Ha'am."[75] Additional testimony to that orientation came in an address upon Israel and the diaspora delivered in 1969. We are first and foremost Jews, he declared "without hesitation." We are Israelis "as a manifestation of our Judaism." The state was meant to serve the Jewish people. Deprived of this goal, it "loses its meaning and will not prevail long in the stormy course of these times."[76] Elsewhere Scholem defined his Zionism in quintessential Ahad Ha'amian language. The movement represented a "return to ourselves," to renewed integration in the historical centrality of Israel, and to responsibility "for our lives on every level as Jews and Jews alone."[77]

The problem was of course how to accomplish that return: a problem complicated not only by secularization ("the barbarization of the so-called new culture") but by the Holocaust—a "trauma" of the Jewish collective consciousness "that no analysis will ever resolve."[78] Scholem recognized that this dilemma was built into the contradictory aims of the Zionist project itself. Was Zionism "a revolution in the life of the Jewish people, a rebellion against the latter's existence in galut?" Or was it to be understood "from the perspective of an awareness of historical continuity?" The question had never been clearly resolved, "for the good reason that no unequivocal answer to it was possible." Unresolvable or not, however, it remained of crucial importance. Could the "two tendencies—the conservative, indeed reactionary one, and the revolutionary, indeed utopia-oriented one—reach an understanding or at least a common ground on which they could meet without mutually annulling and negating each other?"[79]

Attentive students of Scholem's scholarship cannot but hear an echo in this formulation of the two conflicting tendencies which Scholem had discerned in Jewish messianism.[80] There were the conservative forces directed "toward the preservation of that which exists and which, in the historical environment of Judaism, was always in danger"—the world of halakhah. And there was the utopian urge to realize an ideal future which "will in fact be nothing other than the restoration of what is ancient." The messianic idea which crystallized in rabbinic Judaism "deeply intertwined these factors" in a "dialectically-linked tension."[81] I believe that we should regard Scholem's own messianism as "dialectically linked" to his Zionism in similar fashion. Investigation along these lines indicates the way in which Scholem believed that the Jewish state could and could not, should and should not, be a homecoming.

We might begin by noting that Scholem omitted from his account of Zionism the third tendency which he found in messianism: the "restorative." Along with other Zionists, he regarded this ambition as purely mythic. No Zionist thinker has seriously proposed a return to the pristine state of the Garden or the Davidic monarchy; Kook too had depicted a new age unlike the days of old. The struggle within Zionism as a whole, then, and within Orthodoxy in particular, was between the very real forces of "conservatism" and "utopianism"—between rootedness in the tradition and radical uprooting from it. Scholem's account of his personal conversion to Zionism, like his well-known essays on "the myth of the German-Jewish dialogue," leaves no doubt as to his conviction that a break with the exilic past was unavoidable.[82] Orthodoxy had counseled passivity before the political forces assailing Jews. Waiting for the Messiah had condemned Jews to a "life lived in deferment, in which nothing can be done definitively."[83] Liberal Judaism, even worse, had used the messianic idea "to forbid the Jews to live their lives on the historical level"[84] (an explicit critique of Hermann Cohen), celebrating an exilic Jewish reality which "seemed alive, flourishing" but in truth was "rotten," as the Zionists charged.[85]

On the other hand, Zionism could neither sever its ties with Jewish tradition entirely nor utterly reverse the tide of Jewish destiny. "Zionism is a process—a most legitimate process," but not a messianic movement. "And that is its secret. Because as a messianic movement it is doomed in advance to failure."[86] Or again: "the greatness of the Zionist movement was that it . . . accepted historical responsibility," that it "understood tasks and accepted responsibility for our actions, without any messianic pretensions."[87] In short, messianic hope had provided the energy for, but not the goal of, the Zionist return. It had provided two further elements as well, alluded to earlier, which demand closer attention.

First, it had returned the Jews decisively to history. Scholem's view of the Jewish past—shared by Rotenstreich and Schweid, indeed standard in Zionist thought—assumed that Jews since the destruction of the Temple had been somehow outside history: its objects rather than its subjects; acted upon far more than acting. There are at least two normative judgments at work in this pronouncement: one inherent in the definition of activity and passivity, the second in the positive evaluation given the former but not the latter. Scholem, from whom one expects more subtlety in this regard, spared no hyperbole in his portrait of traditional Jewish existence. He deprecated exilic life as "Jewish so-called Existenz," and described it in an unflattering sexual metaphor as a "tension that never finds true release . . . never burns itself out"—for it constantly awaits fulfillment which does not arrive.[88] A diaspora historian, Ismar Schorsch, has taken issue with this notion of what consitutes history—common to both Zionists and opponents of Jewish nationalism such as Rosenzweig. He points out that even political history cannot be denied the Jews in their millennia of exile. For political history is a function not of land but of legal status and group cohesiveness, and the Jews had developed in exile both major institutions of self-government and sophisticated strategies of dealing with the forces of their environment. "To depoliticize Jewish history is to make survival either mystifying or fortuitous."[89] Scholem of course knew all this very well, yet persisted in the image of inactive suffrance of the environment, a foil for the initiative and risk taking of the Zionists. A related bias was the sympathy which he demonstrated for Sabbati Sevi, a point on which he was taken to task by his critics.[90] One suspects that the reason for both failings—obvious flaws, after all, in the work of a master—is that "the overtones of messianism have accompanied the modern Jewish readiness for irrevocable action in the concrete realm . . . a readiness which no longer allows itself to be fed on hopes." Messianic movements of the past could not be dismissed out of hand, lest Zionism suffer a similar fate.[91] They had to be understood from within, in order to fathom the wellsprings of the Jewish return.

The second important contribution of the messianic idea to modern Jewish nationalism, in Scholem's view, lay in the shattering of traditional Jewish molds which aroused expectation of the end has always involved. Scholem was not unaware of the dangers posed by such a break. The Jewish people, he stressed, wrestled with the consequences of the Sabbatean fiasco for centuries. More to the point,

> the discrepancy recognized, though perverted, by [Hermann] Cohen between the real history of the Jews, even in its re-entry into contemporary history, and the messianic drive accompanying this history at the same time as it weakens it, represents a genuine problem which any Jewish theology in our time will find inescapable.[92]

Unpacking this difficult statement, we note that messianism weakens Jewish history at the same time as it propels it forward. It demands that Jews stake all on a gamble which may prove ill-advised, and undermines the "conservative forces" which, until this subversion, had invested Jewish life—even Jewish waiting—with ultimate significance.

"Real history" is determined, in the end, not by the messianic forces themselves (and certainly not by the "conservative forces" happily outside history) but by the peace at which the two opposing tendencies arrive. Scholem is firm in his belief that the Jewish future does not lie "in the traditional Orthodox framework." Rosenzweig's direction too was "very far from what is happening in Israel in the area of Jewish renewal." Secularism made it difficult to discern "any seed of future, any fructifying seed. But who knows? Maybe there is no other way of undergoing crises. Degeneration for the purpose of regeneration."[93] Here Scholem paraphrases a well-known slogan of Jewish mysticism, employed to particular effect by the Sabbateans: "descent for the purpose of ascent." From what would the contemporary ascent derive? The present landscape offered no evidence of the breakthrough which he sought; on the contrary, it was rife with features that precluded an outpouring analogous to that of kabbalah. All we could learn from the present, then, was where *not* to seek salvation: mainly in secularism and religion as presently constituted, or (one infers) in any combination of the two. Israelis had to return to the variety of sources within Judaism, in the hope that with God's help something new and unforeseen might arise in the new circumstances to which life in the Land would give rise. Scholem stressed that variety again and again, lest we conclude that present options exhaust future possibility—and despair. Judaism, returned to the Jewish homeland, was once again "an open, living and undefined organism." As in the past, so now too, it was subject to "historical change." One had to be aware of the transient character of all past metamorphoses, the better to "hearken to the voice that might be forming and seeking articulation—that voice in which if we believe in God as I do, we might recognize the continuity of the voice that we call the voice from Sinai."[94] For the moment, however, Scholem, no less than the exilic Jews whom he described, had to practice the patience of deferment. The meaning for which he waited was not at hand.

This is as far as the present generation of Ahad Ha'amists has gone in its attempt to imagine a substantively Jewish homecoming. It is probably as far as they can go. For all assume, correctly, that "conservative" or "utopian" tendencies if left unchecked by the other would destroy the project of return. The "dialectical linkage" between the two has escaped these thinkers because it is plagued by difficulties which Scholem too could only identify, but not resolve—even for himself. Moreover, as he recognized, the greatest problem of all was the contradiction within the enterprise of homecoming itself. Scholem sought what no Jew has ever found: a nonmessianic but authentically religious revitalization of Jewish tradition, made possible by the Jewish people's restoration to its homeland and to history. He was too much the Zionist—and the Jew—to rest content with less. He was too much the realist not to despair of the attainment of such a vision any time soon. Hence the essential pessimism of his religio-cultural Zionist vision, for the short term at least, and his reliance upon religious Jewish faith to sustain hope for the future. One thinks once more of Deuteronomy. The Jordan had to be crossed, though the attempt might fail; the twentieth century's great wilderness had offered the Jewish people no other choice.

Conclusion: A Home for the Diaspora

The defensiveness evident among secular political Zionists of late is well-founded. They are ideologically outnumbered and outgunned. The inner logic of Jewish homecoming, aided and abetted by contemporary history, has rendered the ideal of normalization to which they cling untenable. Israel is not and cannot be a nation like all other nations. This hope is the first and inevitable casualty of political Zionism's success in achieving a Jewish state, the mark too of its failure.

Some in Israel would argue that this verdict is premature. I disagree. It is not normal for a people to return to a land which it had been forced to abandon as a people centuries before. It is not normal for that people to seek the radical refashioning of the life which it had lived in exile, at the same time as it seeks continuity with the exilic past and legitimacy from it. Nor is it normal to regard the state as the center of a worldwide people which continues and will continue to live in large numbers outside the state. The Jewish state, like the Jewish people, cannot but be exceptional in these regards. Orthodox and religio-cultural Zionists are therefore correct in contending that normalization is not a credible goal in foreseeable circumstances, much less an accurate description of present realities. It could become convincing only in the event that the diaspora were entirely ingathered and the "Canaanites" came to set policy: that the state of Israel, in other words, divorced itself entirely from the religion of Israel and the God of Israel and "became" the people of Israel. This is of course unlikely. One therefore need not invoke the traditional notion of Israel's chosenness in order to refute the claim to normalization. Contemporary Jewish history is sufficient.

Israeli thinkers who argue the opposite betray a singular inattention to history in general and Jewish history in particular on three counts. They dogmatically affirm, first, an outdated theory of anti-Semitism which held that once the Jewish "nation within a nation" had become a nation among the nations, antagonism to it would disappear. Yet some of the same thinkers argue (correctly) that anti-Zionism is to a large degree the heir of anti-Semitism. It continues the age-old effort to deny the Jewish people a place on God's earth. Such Israeli thinkers cannot have it both ways, and increasingly do not try, witness the emphasis in the "new civil religion" of the Begin years upon the continuing isolation of the Jews. According to this exaggerated doctrine, "a nation dwelling alone" replaces the political Zionist ideal of "a nation among the nations" as the self-definition of the Jewish State.[95]

It is no less a denial of history to hold that the Jewish people had no history between the years 70 and 1948 (or between 135, the Bar Kokhba revolt, and the start of modern Zionism in the 1880s). The rich fabric of Jewish life in exile, personal and collective, is deemed something less than real history because it lacked what only a Jewish state can provide Jews: sovereignty; a measure of control over their destiny. This is the position argued forcefully by Yudka in Haim Hazaz's famous story "The Sermon" (1942). "I want to state . . . that I am opposed to Jewish history," Yudka declares. His audience laughs—rightfully so. For what is the sense in opposing that which has transpired and cannot be changed? But when Yudka reformulates his conviction, his comrades listen carefully. "I have no respect for Jewish history." Or: "we have no history at all," having endured oppression, defamation, persecution, and martyrdom but not having made the real history of power and initiative.[96] Israeli thinkers still make the point regularly in an effort to delegitimize what cannot be changed. They seek to purchase normalization by dissociating the present from the overwhelming abnormality of the Jewish past. It cannot be done.

There is, finally, a third refusal to look history in the eye; the prediction of the American diaspora's imminent demise, common to virtually all the thinkers examined in this chapter. This conviction is joined with the certainty that the long-term existence of the Jewish state is not in doubt. Yudka, at the end, is more honest. What if survival in exile is possible, he asks, but survival in the Land is doubtful? "What if they're right?"[97] Why are diaspora communities subject to the rule of anti-Semitism and assimilation set forth brilliantly by Kaufmann, but the state immune to the laws of politics and power demonstrated even more dramatically in the history of the previous two Jewish commonwealths? The claim to normalization cannot survive such analysis. Numerous diaspora communities have endured far longer than the two previous Jewish states. One can always hope for the destruction of the *golah,* if one is so inclined. But that is another matter, reserved for the following chapter.

The attempt to come home, then—not merely to achieve liberation from a colonialist oppressor, not merely to regain lands conquered by a neighboring state, but to come home, in a sense defined by three thousand years of reflection—precludes essential likeness to other developing nations. Israelis are rather demanding, in effect, that the world accept them on their own exceptional terms, understanding that these terms will be defined largely from within, dictated by the abnormal dynamics of Jewish history. Israel will differ significantly from those other nations. Its demand for acceptance also differs, therefore—precisely as the traditional Jewish demand for acceptance differed from that of Christians or Moslems. So long as the state defines itself as a Jewish state and/or is perceived as such by others, the continuity between Zionism and Judaism—two abnormal phenomena, statistically and substantively—will be a fact with which Israelis must live. To think otherwise, as Herzl did, is to engage in messianism. Ingathering of the exiles, Ahad Ha'am repeated time and again, is a messianic project. So too, Kaufmann taught, is the attempt to cast off the legacy which had always marked Jews as Jews and yet be a Jewish state.

If this analysis is correct, classical political Zionism is now irrelevant. Its most important objective, the state, has been achieved, and the "Jewishness" of that state has always been left undefined in political Zionist writings, from *Altneuland* to Rubinstein. Other interpretations of Jewish homecoming will have to provide it: classical Ahol Ha'amism, Orthodox Zionism, or what I have termed religio-cultural Zionism. The first, however, seems to share the fate of political Zionism. Ahad Ha'am's key presuppositions of a Jewish *Geist* different from all others and an organic national will to live are untenable. More important, his program of developing a secular Israeli culture out of the sources of an always-religious tradition has thus far proved a failure. One wishes to beware of premature verdicts of defeat. The state is young, and cultures do not flower overnight. At present, however, secular expression in the arts flourishes but secular cultural Zionism as a candidate for Israeli self-understanding does not. Those who might have been Ahad Ha'am's disciples have either rejected the sources on which he wished Israelis to draw—recall Amos Oz's strictures concerning Jewish tradition— or, like Scholem and Schweid, have been drawn to those sources existentially in a way which Ahad Ha'am was not. At present religio-cultural Zionists share dominance of the Israeli ideological agenda with Orthodox Zionists who would subordinate all that Israelis do and believe to the yoke of the Torah.

Neither school has an easy task. The religious Ahad Ha'amists must solve the theological issues besetting all contemporary religious thought in the West. As if that were not enough, they must overcome the social divisions between "religious" and "secular" which run deep in Israeli society. What is more, they must face directly the overriding Zionist dilemma which partisans of normalization had hoped to avoid: the fact that homecoming is at once a return and a revolution. Zionism is an unprecedented movement in

Jewish history, in search of precedent from Jewish history that might justify and make larger sense of it.

Scholem was far more alert to this dilemma than most. He seems to me the wisest student by far of his generation's situation, for all that he caricatured the *golah*. Indeed, he was wisest precisely when he resigned himself to the "waiting" and "deferment" which in his mind were characteristic of exile. The ultimate meaning of homecoming—if such a thing exists—is not to be written in a book or set by ideology. Societal consensus is not achieved in such an arbitrary fashion, but from the give and take of world views such as those we have examined. What the Zionist return comes to mean to those who participate in it will depend on the concepts and institutional forms developed by future generations of Israelis. Scholem's faith in the possibilities of that future, his willingness to envision a plurality of meanings for Jewish homecoming, recall the confidence of Moses Hess that the new Jewish state would bring with it new varieties of Judaism, heretofore untried and unimagined. Scholem's broodings, however, remind one of Yudka's rumination that Zionism was above all "uprooting and destruction"[98]—again a classical description not of homecoming but of galut. It seems fatuous to minimize these difficulties, or to try to resolve them by a return to the crude exploitation of selected elements of the past for purposes of national mobilization. This too has been tried again of late.[99] One cannot but regard the attempt cynically.

Orthodox Zionists, on the face of it, have an easier time. They must assume some divine involvement in the founding of their state. The manifold blessings of return, ingathering, fertility, and survival against great odds cannot but be taken as a sign of divine acceptance. But their own acceptance of the state will continue to be burdened with compromise, unless they sweep away the tension between actual homecoming and the return linked for centuries with redemption by identifying the former with the latter. This messianic stance, as we learn from Zevi Yehudah Kook, carries along with it a whole new set of problems.

Even the more cautious Orthodox Zionist stance retains a degree of messanism if it presumes, in faith, that the present homecoming to the Land will not be reversed. It will lead to redemption. That is a messianic confidence, however long the ultimate resolution is postponed. The Jews who espouse it, however, are willing to live with much less than a state of Torah for the indefinite future. If so, the homecoming witnessed by their generation falls far short of the homecoming awaited for two millennia. One is led to conclude, in fact, that many religious Zionists utter the words about "the beginning of our redemption" which they inserted in the prayerbook as a prayer only and not as a statement of fact. The state may well become "the beginning of the flowering" of their redemption, but they are far from claiming that this is necessarily so. Their unwillingness to amend halakhah substantially is still further evidence of the immense distance to be traveled before reaching true homecoming. Leibowitz is correct: the lack of resolution in amending exilic law to suit the circumstances of sovereignty is a hedging of bets, a gesture of obeisance to the Orthodox who deny the legitimacy of the homecoming to which religious Zionists aspire. This would seem to place the present state of affairs squarely inside what the tradition would call galut. Orthodox Zionists will have to respond with a conceptual innovation: a religious category between the two poles of exile and redemption, based upon but in contradiction to the available sources.

The messianists, for their part, read and reread the sources examined in Part One of this study and take them most to heart. They refuse to believe that the mythic rebirth of the Jewish people in its homeland so soon after the climax of exilic death and destruction in the Holocaust is merely another way station on their people's wanderings through history. But it is hard to avoid the conclusion that the messianic tradition of Judaism figures far less in their thought and their behavior than that of exile and the Land. Only a small number actively prepare for the resumption of sacrifices, and still fewer for an age so different from our own that a rabbi of old was led to pray that the Messiah come, but not in *his* time.[100] What messianists seem to do, as messianists, is settle and work the Land of Israel, in the hope that fulfillment of these commandments will *eventually* change the course of history. They also stretch the limits of conventional political thinking in a way not unknown to the heroes of political Zionism. Homecoming to the Land, even for them, is one thing; return to the Garden, or the Davidic dynasty, quite another. That is a distinction upon which logic insists but which the tradition does not admit. Even messianists are drawn to it because reality, as always, proves the most powerful teacher. What one does with the parting of the ways between the sources and history depends on the larger question— Scholem's, once again—of how one understands tradition in the first place.

In conclusion, we should observe that the facts of Jewish existence, combined with a large measure of agreement concerning the fate awaiting Jews in the diaspora, have somewhat worn down the ideological lines which divided the Zionist founders. Ben-Gurion's civil religion, in its day, married Herzlian and Ahad Ha'amist assumptions rather neatly. In contemporary discussion, talk of a Spiritual Center is often followed in the same breath by the prediction that the periphery will soon disappear. Messianists and atheists work hand in hand for the Greater Land of Israel, and against it. God is sought for and cited by repentant secularists. And all agree that the secure refuge is superfluous if there are other havens, equally secure; that the Spiritual Center is no center if the periphery is or can be Jewishly independent; that the Land cannot be of ultimate importance if diaspora Jews possess equal legitimacy in the eyes of God or history. Some "party" uniforms, at least, seem to have faded.

The most visible evidence of this new Zionist consensus, cutting across almost all the positions which we have surveyed, comes not in a book but a building—the Diaspora Museum in Tel Aviv. Its significance begins with its name: in Hebrew, Bet Ha-tefutzot: the House of the Diaspora.[101] Not "exile," we note, but "diaspora"—a more neutral term, ostensibly free of opprobrium, as befits the new pragmatic approach to relations between homeland and *golah* which some reject in the name of clarity and honesty. The shift from Herzlian to a more Ahad Ha'amist world view is still more evident in the museum's exhibits, a colorful celebration of the Jewish past. Gone is the depiction of exile as mere suffering and degradation. Instead we are treated to the rich and varied cultural achievement of the *golah*—a source of pride to the contemporary Israeli, perhaps even of inspiration.

Yet the reason for the change is less a shift in world view, or even increased sensitivity to diaspora sensibilities, than the fact that today's Israelis possess what Herzl and Jabotinsky, Klatzkin and Kaufmann, did not: a state; in other words, a home for the diaspora. As Berdiczewski observed, one can view the past far more dispassionately once one feels liberated from it. Israelis, having emerged from the trials of that liberation, now seek a renewed connection to what they have cast off. Galut no longer represents so much of a threat. It is rather the raw material out of which they and they alone will build the Jewish future. And so they have built a museum to honor the past and contain it.

Where else but in a museum, after all, can one move from Alexandria and Rome to Baghdad and Pumbedita, and on to Cordova, Worms, Vilna, and Fez, with no sense of dislocation whatever, utterly confident that the past is past and we who visit it at our leisure are not? In the Diaspora Museum one descends the stairs from these reminders of Jewish exile, leaves relative darkness for the light, and returns to the living story of modern Zion—the consummation of all one has seen. Outside, past the postcards and the cafeteria, the light is bright, as only reality can be.

"Remember where you stand," the museum advises. "Only the Land around you, and the sea in the near distance, are real. The rest is not. If you come from a diaspora of the present, know that, sooner than you think, your community too will be a part of our past, a room in our museum." Israeli Jews, of whatever commitment, can agree with and even rejoice in such a message. Diaspora Jews, if they are aware of what the house built for their heritage conveys, can either acknowledge its truth and feel a twinge of anxiety for their future or ascribe it to the ideological *ḥutzpah* essential to Israel's survival as a young and embattled nation. Either way, they will have entered the debate begun by the very existence of the museum (and the state!) over the meaning of their continued life in the *golah*, a debate—as acrimonious as it is important—to which we now turn.

VII

BETWEEN HOMELAND
AND DIASPORA

Nathan Rotenstreich could have been speaking for all the Israeli thinkers just examined when he complained a decade ago of the complacency besetting diaspora Jews, the lack of serious self-scrutiny, the pervasiveness of bad faith. As evidence of the claim, he cited the lack of a document parallel to Buber's indictment of German Jewry at the turn of the century—the *Drei Reden* analyzed in Chapter Four.[1] Scholem's condemnation of the contemporary *golah* was equally severe. The American Jewish situation was one of exile, "though an exile denied by those who inhabit it. . . . The fact of its hiddenness is hidden from them, and perhaps the Hasidic preacher was right when he said that this is the most severe hiddenness of all."[2] Neither the frustration nor the certitude evinced by Scholem here is exceptional among Israeli thinkers on the subject. That diaspora Jews are self-deceived, particularly in America, seems not in dispute among their counterparts in the Land. Negation of the diaspora, including America, stands at the very center of contemporary Zionist reflection. The conception of homecoming continues to depend upon the depiction and delegitimation of Jewish homelessness.

Jewish thinkers in America have portrayed both their own lingering homelessness and the Zionist homecoming in different terms altogether. Indeed, examination of their reflection on exile and return provokes one to wonder about a different lacuna than the absence of a parallel to Buber's *Drei Reden*. Why have there not been more overt attacks upon the "spiritual center" such as the one mounted by the Reform thinker Jakob Petuchowski in 1966? It is hardly surprising that Jews committed to living in a place rather than to leaving it should fail to "negate" their own existence as "distorted, sickly, sterile, sunken, fragmented, tortured and tormented"—but a few of Buber's adjectives for exile, all rehearsed in our day by Israelis. By contrast, *Zion Reconsidered* seems to have a point in its argument that logic and self-interest alike militate against the acceptance by American Jews of the Zionist vision of return. Both "history and theology" should lead to repudiation of the claim that Israel constitutes a Spiritual Center for all Jews, including those in America—a home, to their continued exile.[3] Yet that argument has been voiced as rarely as Buber's. Neither the rejection of Zionist claims nor the self-critique bound up in those claims has been forthcoming.

The reason, I think, is that American Jews have never conceived of the return to the Land as a homecoming, or of America as a province of the age-old exile. Home, they reasoned from Jewish tradition, means one of two things: a place where one lives with dignity, accepted by one's neighbors— as in America; or personal fulfillment, "societal beatitude," the cessation of war, etc.—desiderata so far attained neither in Israel nor in America. Exile in the political sense was a concept inapplicable to their reality; homecoming in the metaphysical sense was a messianic fantasy, inapplicable to every reality. Zionist argument, thereby neutralized, does not need to be rejected outright.

Ben Halpern's unsurpassable Zionist analysis of the American Jew (1956) still stands alone in negating the diaspora unequivocally and insisting that exile embraces even American Jewry.[4] He remains the exception to a rule articulated in this as in other aspects of American Judaism by Mordecai Kaplan, whose "New Zionism," defined in 1955, has become the effective creed of American Zionist thought. American Jews have used Kaplan's approach to parry Israeli secularists and Ahad Ha'amists alike in the name of an authority with whom neither can compete: God.[5]

That is not to say that Israel is without religious significance for American Jews. The Land matters, and matters a great deal.[6] In American synagogues too the prayer for God's blessing upon the "beginning of the flowering of our redemption" is recited weekly. More crucially, the wonder of Israel's rebirth out of the very ashes of the Holocaust seems of incalculable importance to the faith of American Jews no less than of Israelis. The sociological literature stressing the state's role in the maintenance of diaspora Jewish identity barely limns the depths in which the Land's real meaning lies concealed. But the prayer for Israel is preceded or followed in the American *siddur* by the traditional prayer for the leaders of America. It is surrounded by the traditional pleas for an "ingathering of the exiles." American Jews must either ignore those pleas or regard them as inapplicable to themselves. The Land's *existence* is accorded significance, then, but not its historical or physical *reality*. Holiness of space means little. The dispute between halakhists and messianists need not preoccupy Jews for whom it remains theoretical. Debate over God's presence in history centers on the Holocaust, which American Jewry escaped, rather than on the state, to which it has chosen not to emigrate. We might say, with only a measure of oversimplification that Israel's existence, once it has rendered America less of an exile and more of a home and once it has enabled American Jews to "choose life" despite the Holocaust, ceases to matter decisively. As a result, the gap between the religious thought of the two communities inside and outside the Land, as between their varying perceptions of homelessness and homecoming, has of late become immense.

I will begin this survey of the debate over the meaning of contemporary

exile with the Israelis, turning first to moderate and then to extreme nega-
tions of the *golah* and/or the Jews who live in it. American attitudes will then
be canvassed, in the context of a schematic history of American Zionist
reflection on galut and homecoming. In the chapter's third section I will
show the relation between American Jewish thought on our subject and
American Jewish religious thought as a whole by analyzing the significance
accorded return to the Land by rabbis Joseph Dov Soloveitchik, Abraham
Joshua Heschel, and Emil Fackenheim. The division between Israel and
diaspora, we will find, runs far deeper than polemics over "negation" and
"centrality." It reaches to fundamentally different understandings of the
Jewish condition between exile and at-homeness—different visions, we
might say, of what is most important and most profound in Judaism itself.

Good Faith and Bad

Those who negate the diaspora only moderately (e.g., Leibowitz, Hartman, Rotenstreich, Scholem) can be distinguished from more aggressive
colleagues (e.g., Schweid and Z. Y. Kook) on two grounds. First, they
concede the basic insecurity of Israeli existence at present when compared
with that of the American diaspora. The "secure refuge" sought by political
Zionists remains at best a possibility for the future. "Normalization" is
precluded by Israel's estate: singled out as much as Jews had ever been in
exile. Leibowitz writes caustically that Jews are safer today outside Israel,[7]
while Rotenstreich describes the original Zionist ambition to overcome anti-
Semitism through a Jewish state as "messianic."[8] Scholem emphasizes the
metaphysical insecurity—wedded to the political now as ever in Jewish
history—shared by Israeli and diaspora Jews in the wake of the Holocaust.[9]

The second point of contention among the negators concerns the possibility for authentic Jewish life outside the Land. Is the superiority of Israel
in this regard absolute or only relative? Leibowitz argues the greater dignity
and comprehensiveness of halakhic observance in Israel, but he can hardly
deny the possibility of serving God—and so achieving the highest worth
available to a human being—where Jews had lived piously for two thousand
years. Hartman speaks persuasively of the support lent Jewish memory and
belief by life inside the borders of the Jewish land and language. But he too
cannot deny outright either the validity or the viability of diaspora Judaism.
Lichtenstein is on firm Zionist ground in the claim that the search for
"societal beatitude," essential to Jewish faith, is greatly enhanced by the
existence of a Jewish society in which to pursue it.[10] Again, however, Jewish
communities have existed without such a framework for centuries. In short:
the tradition precludes identification of Judaism with Israeli Judaism.

Even Zevi Yehudah Kook, who was far more caustic in his criticism of
diaspora Jewry, was in the end reined in by the Orthodoxy which he shared
with halakhic Jews outside the Land. We have already noted his scorn for

those who failed to recognize or join in Israel's redemption. Not only were they guilty of failure to observe the positive commands to conquer and settle the Land. They were also unable to share in the most profound religious experience known to contemporary Jews, standing outside the history which Kook identifies as that of "true Israel."[11] Nonetheless, Kook and his followers are indissolubly linked to Jews in the diaspora, even as they articulate a faith and an educational philosophy explicitly opposed to all that they deride as "galut Judaism."[12] Orthodoxy can distance itself from diaspora piety only up to a point. For "God is everywhere" and can be contacted everywhere with equal ease or difficulty. More important, His involvement over the past two millennia in the life of His covenant people had invested that life, wherever it is led, with both ultimate meaning and ultimate reward.

Orthodox Zionists are therefore thrown back on the argument first advanced by Klatzkin and Kaufmann and now standard in the Zionist repertoire: that whereas the pre-Emancipation *golah* had provided Jews a semi-autonomous community within which authentic Jewish life could be led, the post-Emancipation diaspora was sheltered by no such wall of resistance to surrounding cultures. Modern Jews, as a result, had by and large abandoned the faith of their ancestors. Hence Leibowitz's stipulation that the process of *ibud* continues apace in the diaspora, among nonreligious Jews.[13] The word is Deuteronomy's term for exile, connoting wandering, loss, destruction, and disappearance. The analysis is Kaufmann's. Jews unprotected by either the borders of the Land or the borders of their faith could not but succumb to the natural process of assimilation. Zionism, like halakhah, provided the freedom within which nature could be overcome.

Rotenstreich offers a similar argument when he disputes the claim that "America is different"—an exception to the general rule of Emancipation. In America too advancement for the Jewish individual was paid for by the dissolution of the Jewish community. Of the three possible levels on which a Jew could relate to Judaism—solidarity with the Jewish people and its traditions, the living of a life substantively shaped by the tradition, participation in Jewish communal institutions—the first was severely attenuated in America, the second nonexistent, and the third by and large limited to a small elite. Even American Jewish self-deception on the subject bore witness to continuity with post-Emancipation, pre-Holocaust Europe. "Slavery under freedom" continued. Only "auto-emancipation" could cure the disease of exile and its accompanying blindness.[14]

Scholem, we recall, concurred. American Jews were blind to the facts of their own situation and bereft of real creativity. After 1967 he became somewhat more optimistic, believing that the isolation experienced by Jews at the time of the war had prompted recognition of the need for closer relations with the state. The diaspora had "absorbed the reciprocity between itself and Israel into its life as a determining force," seeing itself as part of a whole that had to accomplish "more than merely religious tasks."[15] Nonetheless, Scholem asserted in 1974 that he saw no productive forces outside Israel that would "manifest anything Jewish that will endure, anything of enduring value."[16]

Strong as this attack on the integrity of American Judaism may seem, it pales before the assaults mounted by unqualified negators of the diaspora, whether religious, Ahad Ha'amist, or secular. Schweid, for example, combines Scholem's critique of the pre-Holocaust galut, East and West, with a much sharper attack on the post-Holocaust exile of America. In *The Lonely Jew and Judaism* he divides Jewish history into periods of "revelation of the Countenance" and "hiding of the Countenance." The time of grace is identified with "full national life on the Land," that of hiding with exilic history determined by the fate of other nations: a rabbinic conception transmitted to Schweid via Gordon. Jewish history in exile was confined to "Torah literature" and the life directed by it. "In every other sense the Jewish people had no history in its exile—and this in fact is the significance of exile."[17] Schweid's most far-reaching statement of negation came in a speech before Israeli high-school students in 1980 in which he affirmed the lessons of the Holocaust taught by Ben Gurion's civil religion. In a word: galut existence was at an end. Jews could no longer live in exile—a fact evident to some from the onset of Emancipation and hammered home by Hitler, but still not clear to all. The Holocaust had occurred. It could happen again. Jews had to be prepared—and there was no means of collective defense outside a sovereign Jewish state. True, Israel had become the focus of anti-Semitic attack; but the state, unlike the diaspora, had the power to protect itself. "Choose life," Schweid urged the students.[18] The implication that they could make no other rational choice was unequivocal.

The echoes of Klatzkin are pronounced in this oration. Diaspora Jews were fatally self-deceived and had to be roused forcefully from their slumber. Sweetening the taste of diaspora poison would not help but kill them. What is more, the illusion that Jews had a future outside Israel threatened Israelis as well. For it "damages our fortitude and dissipates our strength."[19] We would not be wrong in ascribing to Schweid the conclusion reached by Klatzkin from this train of argument. Diaspora Jews had no right to be where they were. They were wrong to remain there. For their blindness reduced the ability of those who saw more clearly to defend the Jewish people against its enemies. In a related essay, Schweid reiterates Klatzkin's warning that diaspora existence could not hold out against assimilation in the long run. Zionists should therefore return to the classical Zionist demand that "the Jew see in his Judaism a full human content for life, a complete human existence, and in this fashion make his contribution, large or small, to human culture."[20]

Schweid's own restatement of the Zionist consensus emphasizes that Jews outside Israel must be considered to be in galut for several reasons. They lack a national field of labor in which their endeavors can be unified, collective responsibility for Jewish survival, an independent Jewish culture, a clear Jewish identity, and the ability to protect themselves as a people. Schweid emphasizes that he is not rejecting Jewish tradition along with galut, the mistake of thinkers such as Brenner and Berdiczewski. Rather, like his mentors Gordon, Ahad Ha'am, and Bialik, Schweid believes exile untenable but wishes to revive Jewish tradition in the Spiritual Center.[21] He need not mitigate the negation carried out by those mentors because he believes that the diaspora of today is not essentially different than it was before the Holocaust. Jews remained uprooted from the Land, scattered among the nations, a cultural and moral minority in their host countries, poor in economic, social, and political power. Though "rich in the spirituality of others," they were "barren [of] and uprooted from Jewish creativity." Once the majority of Jews had settled in Israel, the state could achieve economic independence and, in time, good relations with its neighbors. And so long as there was a Jewish state, another Holocaust could not occur.[22]

Israeli and diaspora thinkers alike have challenged Schweid's unduly dim view of American Jewish creativity and his overly gloomy forecast of speedy assimilation.[23] I find two other weaknesses in his argument more glaring. First, it is premised on the classical Zionist either/or of diaspora or homeland. But whatever else one may say of the validity of Klatzkin's theories, they are in this respect irrelevant. Unless Schweid wishes to argue that Israel's long-term security is not in doubt, while that of the diaspora even in the short term is uncertain, the choice today lies between residence in the Land alongside an existing diaspora or Jewish life outside the Land which enjoys the indirect protection afforded by the Jewish state. Diaspora Jews rarely question Israel's leading role in ensuring Jewish survival and generally concede the advantages of the Center for the free development of Jewish culture. They assume that Israel will continue to exist, and their diaspora along with it. Schweid by contrast assumes the disappearance of the galut and/or its absorption into Israel. The asymmetry of his argument hinders debate; more important, it is unjustified. The diaspora is not about to disappear.

Second, Schweid's demand that Judaism be "a full human content for life, a complete human existence," is a norm in search of an authority. On what ground of obligation does Schweid say this? Is his authority "the Jewish people" as such? But the Jewish people is not a moral end in and of itself, unless one makes one of three claims. Ahad Ha'am argued from nature: that peoples, like individuals, are endowed with a will to preservation which, given by nature itself, is a good. The biological assumptions for this theory, common in the late nineteenth century, are scarcely credible in our day. Alternatively, one could argue that "it is right and good that each people develop to the full extent of its ability, and it is therefore incumbent upon each individual member of the group to help it do so." This claim would extend the Kantian norm of full development from the individual to the group. But the criticism leveled at Kant applies even more forcefully to this collectivist variation. Why should the full development of a people (if such a thing exists) be an end in itself? Why should it command our allegiance? Schweid seems on stronger ground in invoking a third source of obligation—on which I think his argument in fact rests. Life itself is a good, for an individual and for a people. "Choose life"—particularly when death has claimed so many of one's fellow Jews so recently, and particularly since the Jewish people is the bearer of values and teachings and a culture of immense importance. One's duty begins with those nearest at hand—members of the extended family, one's people, and that obligation increases the more the survival of other Jews is threatened. In our day it is threatened acutely. But this is precisely the nub of Schweid's dispute with American Jews. The latter escape the net of obligation he casts by arguing that the diaspora is *not* in danger and that the support they render the state *from* the diaspora has been instrumental in its survival as well as their own. They, like Schweid, are prepared to recognize such a duty to their fellow Jews, even if they, like him, no longer accept the authority of Sinai. But whereas he insists that "help" must at present translate to *aliyah*, they hold philanthropy to be a fulfillment of their obligation.

Schweid does have one final normative authority: authenticity; the belief that self-deception runs counter to truth, a good in itself. But this argument is so easily contested by diaspora Jews, as we will see, as to be bootless in debate. The norm itself, I believe, is extremely problematic.

Scholem's verdict on this score seems correct. The state of Israel cannot perform the function of arousing awareness of exile in the *golah* "so long as it has surrendered the religious and metaphysical beliefs [concerning galut and homecoming] which alone can give strength" to such claims.[24] American Jews do not lack such a norm—the Jewish religious tradition, which in their minds answers Schweid's quasi-religious Ahad Ha'amism convincingly. They can and do argue that Schweid, no less than they, lives a partial Jewish life carved out of non-Jewish time and space. In this they and he both resemble the sages of the Mishnah and the Talmud. Diaspora Jews defer until God's own time the fulfillment which Schweid seems to claim for his own, in Israel. So long as the marriage of faith and secularism for which he calls has not occurred, therefore—and it is barely even imagined in his thought, for good reason—Schweid's negation of the contemporary galut remains less than compelling, his identification of it with the old galut less than convincing.

The "extreme" positions which Schweid criticizes differ from his primarily in their more bombastic style and lesser sophistication. They differ substantively in only one regard: their rejection of the Ahad Ha'amist premise that the Jewish state must be the authentic heir and transmitter of the Jewish past. Thus, where Schweid denies that the Holocaust was a "necessary or unpreventable" conclusion to Jewish exile, A. B. Yehoshua compares the Jew who bemoans the Holocaust to a man who walks down the middle of a busy highway and then blames the drivers who hit him for not swerving to the right or left. The Holocaust was not only the "final and absolute proof of the failure of golah," but a tragedy which "we forced upon ourselves . . . responsibility for our people's awful fate in this century is its own." Jews had failed to face up to the inevitable. They had not come home to Zion. Galut, before and after the Holocaust, was a "neurotic solution" to the Jewish problem. Health lay only in normality: bringing that problem to an end.[25]

Blaming the victims of the Holocaust for their fate is of course problematic. Another serious problem with this Klatzkin-like negation of the diaspora is that it has so very little to affirm about homecoming. Hillel Halkin, articulating the same position far more eloquently in his *Letters to an American Jewish Friend* (1977), concedes that at present Israel constitutes neither a secure refuge nor an "organic society" nor a Spiritual Center—the home of an authentic Jewish culture. It could perhaps not boast a "real culture" at all, but only a "debased ethnic tradition" characterized by "petrified religious Orthodoxy," "rootless secularism," and aping of the West. (This is exactly how Kaufmann had described the galut of the modern West!). Israel represented only a "community of faith," a "set of beliefs that we have about ourselves and what we are doing here"; allegiance, in other words, to the classical Zionist convictions that a Jew committed to Jewishness would naturally seek to perpetuate Jewish life in himself and his people and that Jewish life outside Israel was doomed. The Land constituted the only option. "Jewish and Israeli history are two converging lines that are ultimately bound to meet." If a Jew wished to be part of one, he or she had to be part of the other.[26] Yet Halkin admits to doubts concerning the state's viability. "I can find no convincing reason to believe that Israel cannot perish too." Nevertheless, "land and language are everything." When all else fails, Halkin invokes Ahad Ha'am's argument that a people, "as everything organic, strives in this world to become or remain its own self." A koala bear wishes only to be a koala bear. Becoming "like all the nations," far from a reproach, was the most worthy goal for Jewish endeavor—the only worthy goal in fact. If Israelis come to have "as much true culture as Albanians or Finns," Halkin would say *dayyenu*. "It would be enough for us."[27]

The pathos of the political Zionist negation of the *golah*, stripped down to the bare bones of life itself, with even that in doubt, is striking. If Halkin is correct, there is little sense in choosing Jewish life in either Israel or America. Should one elect for Israel because "a young state is taking over the burden of Jewish history from an old diaspora"? Because rabbinic Judaism was a lovers' quarrel between "an aging people and its aging God"?[28] This rhetoric too is anachronistic (recall its use by Berdiczewski) and self-serving. The denunciation of all non-Orthodox forms of religiosity, the better to lop off the remaining challenger as authentic but impotent,[29] likewise seems a relic of arguments past. This is a Zionism shrunk to the conviction that all other options for Jewish existence are doomed to failure, sooner rather than later. Life in Israel, no more absurd or less dangerous than any other, offers only the succor of authenticity.

The lack of positive reason for and meaning in the state makes such negation of the *golah* all the more difficult, and all the more necessary. Conversely, as we have noted, Israelis who want their state to be a "return" or "homecoming" cannot entirely negate the present existence of those who, like them, claim to be the inheritors of the Jewish past. They cannot, unless Orthodox, speak of exile as divine punishment; nor can they, unless they are messianists, describe the return in Deuteronomic images of fulfillment. The terms of debate, as a result, remain on the classical Zionist ground common to Herzl and Ahad Ha'am, Klatzkin and Gordon: the charge that the *golah* cannot survive the twin onslaughts of anti-Semitism and assimilation and the question of whether authentic Jewish life is possible outside the Jewish homeland. But while Schweid, Yehoshua, and Halkin press the first issue, less extreme negators of the diaspora emphasize the second. Their Zionist "case" now rests primarily on the rabbinic concern for the survival of Judaism amid *avodah zarah:* "foreign service," the worship of strange gods. Exile is a battleground of cultures.

Diaspora Jews, responding to the second challenge, address the first as well. By establishing the *golah's* Jewish credentials, they make a strong case for its prospects. And while prospects are always debatable, credentials derived from the same Jewish tradition to which Orthodox and Ahad Ha'a- mist Israelis swear allegiance constitute a formidable asset indeed. Not surprisingly, they have been the principal element in the American dias- pora's self-defense.

The Center Affirmed and Denied

That defense has a history; it is, in fact, as old as American Zionism itself, an integral part of the movement's ideology. Contemporary thinkers need not map new paths. They have inherited a tradition of reflection on the meaning of Zionist homecoming which from the outset has modified the claims made by the Zionist founders rather significantly. In this respect, neither the horror of the Holocaust nor the saving reality of statehood has made an essential difference in the American Jewish approach. The two events have rather reinforced a vision of exile and homecoming in place since the beginning of the century.

We might sketch it schematically as follows, focusing on the two men who translated the political and cultural Zionist creeds for American Jews and Gentiles: Louis Brandeis (1856–1941) and Solomon Schechter (1847–1915). The former believed himself a faithful disciple of the Zionist gospel accord- ing to Herzl, was seen as such by his own follower Horace Kallen,[30] and was remembered as such years later by Mordecai Kaplan.[31] Yet the terms in which he described the aspiration for a Jewish homeland were utterly American, variations on the causes which he championed as a Progressive. Equal opportunity for individuals translated into equal opportunity for every people; individual rights became minority rights. Brandeis's political Zionism omitted the crucial Herzlian either/or of assimilation and anti-Semitism in the *golah*, or statehood and fulfillment in Eretz Israel. Rather, as Melvin Urofsky notes in his history of the Zionist movement in America, Brandeis consciously or unconsciously used the words *Jewish* and *Zionist* interchangeably.[32] He described the Jewish spirit as "essentially modern and essentially American" and so arrived at the logical conclusion that "loyalty to America demands . . . that each American Jew become a Zionist." There is no negation of the diaspora here. The Jewish homeland was meant only for Jews who, unlike Americans, had no other home. By attempting to secure such a home for his persecuted brethren overseas, the American Zionist became "a better man and a better American."[33]

Schechter, for his part, began his remarkable endorsement of Zionism in 1906[34] with the observation that Zionism was "an ideal, and as such undefinable." All Zionists agreed only on "recovery of the land of our fathers" and formation in it of a home for "at least a portion of the Jews" who would lead an "independent national life" on its soil. After paying homage to the age-old ideas of Zion and Jerusalem, Schechter proceeded to the principal plank in his own Zionist platform: its role as a "great bulwark against assimilation." By this he did not mean Americanization, but the loss of Jewish identity in *galut*. Exile signified to him "the despair and helplessness felt in the presence of a great tragedy." Thousands of Jews lost by attrition. Sacred institutions destroyed. Hebrew forced out of the synagogue and doomed to oblivion. "I am not accusing anybody. I am only stating facts. . . . We are helpless spectators in the face of great tragedies, in other words . . . we are in Galut . . . the Galut of Judaism." It could be countered only by the work of national regeneration.[35]

Ahad Ha'am could not have chosen a better American spokesman, an expert witness as it were to the reality of "slavery under freedom." But while the master expected Zionists in the West to worry about the problem of the Jews and leave the plight of Judaism to the East, where Jews still knew what authentic Judaism was, here was an Eastern Jew, transplanted to the West, who worried about Judaism—and because he did, regarded Ahad Ha'amist Zionism as only a stepping-stone to its rejuvenation. Despite the ringing condemnation of American galut absent from most later Zionist writings in America, or perhaps because of it, Schechter envisaged a spiritual center in service not only to the people of Israel but to the religion of Israel. "Judaism" was a faith, not a culture; the latter was a means to the revival of the former.[36] The diaspora therefore could not be negated either "subjectively" or "objectively," except in criticism of a situation which Zionism itself would help to remedy.

Brandeis offered a political Zionism shorn of strident nationalism, bereft of negation of the diaspora, and qualified by the usual American claim of exceptionalism to the general rule of assimilation and anti-Semitism. Schechter offered a version of cultural Zionism made palatable to American ears by its emphasis on age-old longing, its clear subordination of peoplehood to faith, and its avowed assumption that the success of the Zionist enterprise, far from undermining American Jewish life, would in fact make it possible. These changes were interrelated. Once cultural Zionism had become religious, the Center could not claim the centrality granted it by Ahad Ha'am. Zion could nourish the mind and stir the heart, but it could not claim the greater part of the Jew's allegiance, because it would not provide the principal content for his or her Jewish existence. In other words: Jewish culture could not be created in exile, at least not yet, and would probably never be equal to that of the Jewish homeland. But God was another matter. He could be encountered anywhere, including America. The Center would lose its advantage over the periphery the moment the Jewish spirit in the diaspora had been restored to faith.

This understanding of Zionism well suited the American Jewish community's emerging self-definition, and both achieved their quintessential formulation in the writings of Mordecai M. Kaplan (1881–1983), whose debt to Schechter was profound.[37] The details of Kaplan's Zionist and Jewish visions need not detain us here, but it is worth noting the development undergone by his ideas from *Judaism as a Civilization* (1934) through *Future of the American Jew* (1948) to *A New Zionism* (1955), for it is a telling expression of the direction taken by American Zionism as a whole. The earlier work, aimed at winning adherents to a Reconstructionist program that included the upbuilding of Palestine, stressed the centrality of the Land in Jewish tradition. Kaplan went so far as to call the people Israel's relation to Eretz Israel the "principal motif" in the Torah. He stated unequivocally that "a land of its own" was "the only medium through which adequate expression is possible to any civilization." Not all Jews would have to live there, of course, but those who did not would never lead a "normal life" in an integrated community—what Kaplan called Judaism as a "primary civilization." Instead they would "live Judaism" only as a "coordinate civilization," if granted the cultural autonomy sought by Simon Dubnow, or as a "subordinate civilization" in countries such as America.[38]

Fourteen years later, with statehood barely achieved, Kaplan retained his Ahad Ha'amist vision of the Spiritual Center, but took still more pains to disavow Herzl's aim of a comprehensive *kibbutz galuyot*. He explained what homecoming meant to Jews through the words of the poet Robert Frost. "Home is the place where, when you go there, they have to take you in." American Jews, he made it clear, would not and should not be going in large numbers. Nor could they permit "isolationists," negators of the diaspora, to "de-Judaize, demoralize and degrade" American Jewry by deprecating the possibilities for Jewish life in the United States. Preparing Jews for a hasty departure to Palestine was "not likely to inspire our neighbors with confidence in the Jews, or with respect for Judaism." It only provided Jews with an excuse for evading the urgent task of rendering Judaism viable in America. Not only was "long-distance building of Eretz Israel . . . no less important than building it on the spot," it also "cannot serve as a substitute for

Jewish life here." The two Jewish problems, diaspora and Eretz-Israeli, were one.[39]

This is the message hammered home time and again in *A New Zionism*, which begins with an attack on negation of the diaspora and can be summarized in Kaplan's declaration—the credo of American Zionism, perhaps—that "Zionism has to be redefined so as to assure a permanent place for Diaspora Judaism."[40] In place of an emphasis on the Land's centrality, we find that the traditional view of the Land's sanctity should be understood as "merely a way of expressing the Jew's own profound attachment to his People." Similarly, while calling upon Zionists to "have the moral courage to present their movement as messianic," Kaplan redefines belief in the Messiah as "the reawakening of the Jewish people to a sense of destiny and the resumption of Jewish nationhood in the land of its origin and development." The state's future direction should be "based on the desire to provide the setting in which the Jewish People could become a fit instrument of this-worldly salvation for every Jew, wherever he resides."[41]

Two corollary assumptions should be noted in conclusion. First, America was a more secure place for Jews than Israel. The latter could exist only so long as American democracy was strong. Second, galut had relevance in our day only as a spiritual category. It connoted the "universally disordered, disoriented and alienated condition of human life." Exile in this sense would end only when ethical nationhood had been attained by the Jews and every other people. In every other sense, it already had ended.[42] Both points can be found in the writings of thinkers who disagreed with Kaplan on the definition of both Judaism and Zionism, for example Abba Hillel Silver.[43] Kaplan stated the Zionist creed with which, and for which, American Jews were prepared to live.

Few challenges to Kaplan's formulation have been forthcoming, whether before 1967 or since. Simon Rawidowicz's *Babylon and Jerusalem* (1957) lent it the authority of a leading scholar of Jewish philosophy. There had been two foci to Jewish life since the destruction of the First Temple: the Land and the communities outside it. "He who denies either denies all. . . . Every Jew worthy of the name is rooted in both." Some Jews mistakenly regarded life outside the Land as "a mere interlude." Others saw no point to Jewish sovereignty. Still others hedged their bets, playing the odds "in favor of Jerusalem" but putting a "small wager now and then on Babylon." Jewish history declared their error. Homeland and diaspora were both required for the wholeness of Jewish life. Jewish creativity had flourished in both, though Rawidowicz made no prediction as to what might be expected from American Jewry. In place of the metaphor of the circle with its center, then, Rawidowicz proposed the two foci of an ellipse.[44]

We find the same position upheld by the majority of the participants in a symposium on the idea of galut published in the magazine *Midstream* in 1963. The editors asked that the concept be understood broadly, as a "distinct Jewish definition of a unique kind of colonial existence that is not to be solved merely by the acquisition of civil or political rights but also affects the social, psychological, and cultural aspects of Jewish relations with their environment and their neighbors." Perhaps because this phrasing was so awkward and opaque, the majority of participants simply denied that America was galut in the political sense or that Israel was home in the metaphysical sense and proceeded to the formulations popularized by Kaplan. Rabbi Jacob Agus spoke for most when he wrote that America made possible "as viable and creative a Jewish religious civilization as we could possibly want." Like Kaplan, he urged that "the impetus of the tradition itself" not be used to "disparage the faith and culture of Diaspora Jewry." The Jewish state was "but one of many institutions" in the service of Jewish idealism, the American dream, and the cause of humanity. Jews could further such noble ends wherever they lived. "All of us are in galut," he concluded. "Those are most in galut who think that they are already at home.[45] Scholem's criticism is here turned on its head.[46] Several of the contributors, most of whom were secular intellectuals rather than religious leaders, demurred somewhat from Agus's exuberant optimism, citing Jewish marginality or the fact that cultural pluralism had yet to be translated from theory to practice.[47] The consensus, however, was Kaplan's.

Only two thinkers challenged this view substantially: Jakob Petuchowski, in his *Zion Reconsidered* (1966) and Ben Halpern, most notably in *The American Jew: A Zionist Analysis* (1956). Halpern (b. 1912) is a secular Labor Zionist and scholar of modern Jewish history whose position not surprisingly derives largely from Yehezkel Kaufmann. Anti-Semitism and assimilation would continue to undermine Jewish life outside the Jewish state. Authentic life in the diaspora would remain impossible for all but a few. Religion, the guarantor of Jewish distinctiveness and authenticity in the past, was at best attenuated in contemporary America, at worst a facade erected to secure acceptance by the larger society. Even so, it remained enough of a force to prevent Jews from assimilating altogether and to keep Gentiles from accepting them. In short, "America *was* different," not in the unique conditions it offered to Jewish life but because the community had never been forced to undergo the trial of Emancipation and was only now, after the Holocaust, coming to understand the facts of its own situation. Honest encounter with those facts, Halpern argued, could yield but one conclusion: America too was exile.[48]

Halpern, like other political Zionists, emphasized that anti-Semitism was endemic to America, as to the West as a whole. The cultural pluralism offered as proof that America was different could never come to exist. For the root of Jewish difference was "too serious for orchestration." Indeed, while Jews were free to worship in the synagogue, true freedom of religion included the freedom "to have one's own idea of what religion really is." In America that definition was Protestant through and through. Jews consciously and unconsciously adapted to the prevailing pattern by minimizing or denying their distinctiveness and in general craving acceptance. This was galut, American style: presentation of "the essentials of Judaism in such a selection and emphasis as will underscore the Judeo-Christian consensus." Only occasionally did the community awake to "a meaning of Jewish fate and a sense of Jewish destiny that are of the highest and most exigent seriousness."[49]

Petuchowski (b. 1925) countered, in effect, that precisely this sense of Jewish destiny had been forgotten by the Zionists. History, it seemed, had triumphed over the vision of a Jewish mission to the nations. Jewish policemen in Tel Aviv had apparently become more concrete symbols of Jewish reality than rabbis who participated in the inauguration of American presidents. But how soon after the event were history's lessons discernible? Had the proposition that Jews "are no longer a nation but a religious community" really been disproved?[50] Petuchowski submitted that it had not, disputing Israel's claims to be either a secure refuge (the argument here is obvious) or a Spiritual Center. The state might develop into the latter, but so might other Jewish communities. Mutual acceptance was required; not centrality, but parity.[51] Yet Petuchowski's own rhetoric is at times untempered. While Zionists longed to return to the "cradle of our faith," American Jews had "already learned that the days of childhood will never return." Israelis who argued that they were not in exile should be met with increduilty "born of a deeper understanding." The Messiah had not come. Nation had not ceased to lift up sword against nation. The "eclipse of God" continued.[52]

One wonders whether this sort of critique would have been written a year later. Jacob Neusner (b. 1932) has called the Six Days War and its aftermath a "moment of powerful and salvific weight" for American Jews. The renewed peril to Jewish existence, followed by dramatic deliverance, "pressed into a fresh perspective everything that had happened from the beginning to the present"—particularly the era's two most awesome events. The murder of the six million became the Holocaust, "the purest statement of evil in all human history," while the rebirth of the Jewish state became "the first appearance of our redemption."[53] Neusner's perceptive analysis is borne out by the sources to which we shall turn momentarily. Yet the effect of the "moment of stark epiphany" which he describes upon American discussion of *galut* and homecoming was paradoxically to rule out severe criticism of either the state or the diaspora. It was as if the existence and vitality of both were no longer open to question, though Jewish thinkers could and did continue to explode the pretensions of each to fulfillment or self-sufficiency. Halpern and Petuchowski were both out of bounds. Holocaust and statehood, grasped in the aftermath of renewed threat and salvation, reinforced the vision of American diaspora and Israeli homecoming articulated by Schechter and Kaplan.

I will not document this claim through a survey of the relatively infrequent discussions of the subject that one finds in the sermons, periodicals, and rabbinical assembly proceedings of American Jewry. Suffice it to say that, except for occasions on which Israelis participate in the discussion and choose substance over politeness, the record consists in large part of a bland rehearsal of the Kaplanian consensus already described. America is not home, yet neither is Israel. The latter *is* the Center and is certainly not exile, but neither can the former be compared to any previous diaspora. "America is different." Nor should its rich Jewish resources be underestimated. The two communities were interdependent.[54]

The variations on this position were few, all the more reason that we examine them in more detail. The first is easy to identify: the adoption by many of the community's leading thinkers (scholars and theologians, usually, rather than pulpit rabbis) of the critique of American Jewry which Halpern voiced in the fifties. The charge of "bad faith" which he leveled at the "public facade of American Judaism" has become standard. His assertion that only a Judaism which went against the American mainstream could be taken seriously is now a commonplace. Arthur Hertzberg (b. 1921), agreed in 1963 that the West was not only prone to the virus of anti-Semitism but endemically ill with the disease. He also endorsed Halpern's view that the American state was not neutral when it came to religion because the majority culture of America was Christian. "America was different" only because it represented the "last best hope of the Jew" to fulfill the "most deep and messianic need to become a normal part of surrounding society."[55] A related essay the following year was titled simply "America is Galut."[56] Neusner, in his *Stranger at Home* (1981), concurred. America was galut in two senses: sociologically, because American Jews comprise a minority not much admired or emulated; and religiously, because American Judaism is a "detached and noncathetic way of living in the world." Neusner compared it to a spectator sport, all eyes being focused on the vicarious experiences of Holocaust and statehood. Jewish history could probably offer no example of a community more ethnocentric or less religiously concerned.[57]

What then of the other crucial proposition in our discussion? Is Israel home? Hertzberg almost says as much in reasoning that Judaism could survive in America only by emphasizing its own uniqueness but was unable to supply it because "apartness must have content" and "for such content we can only wait." Modernity had intervened. Or, Hertzberg concludes, "we can tire of waiting and of its quiet dangers to our own Jewish identities, and start thinking seriously, for the first time since adolescence, of aliyah; at very least, the aliyah of our children."[58] Neusner too edges up to this conclusion. "We are marginal in our situation," he writes in a recent essay. "Israelis are at home."[59] The latter were free to regard themselves as human beings, pure and simple. They could accept or reject elements of their tradition without fear of destroying the heritage of centuries. Yet Neusner can neither be at home in Israel himself nor accept it as the home of the Jewish people. Ultimate metaphysical significance could not be attributed to a political achievement. Galut could not be escaped by crossing the ocean. He celebrates the advantages of the diaspora: the long perspective, openness to the experience of non-Jews.[60] And yet: "In a measure we are aliens; they

[Israelis] are never strangers."[61] And yet a still more recent collection proclaims as its only message to Israelis that "in 1973 they became Jews like us again."[62]

The ambivalence is telling. In the end, of course, both thinkers have chosen to work for the enrichment of Judaism in America, the "content of apartness," rather than to make their home in the Land. Hertzburg's analysis echoes Halpern and Kaufmann, even to the point of suggesting *aliyah*. Neusner too seems willing to concede at times that while he would perforce remain a stranger in Israel should he move there, his children would be at home—albeit not in the metaphysical sense claimed only by propagandists. Elsewhere, however, he seems to argue that the facts of Israeli life preclude the free development of Judaism and the religious fulfillment of the individual Jew.[63] Provinciality and intolerance also exact a price from the soul. Neunser wavers between what I have called the Kaplanian consensus and Halpern's Zionist deviation.[64]

Halpern "deviates" where Hertzberg and Neusner do not, even when they are closest to his position, primarily because he is a secularist. Authenticity is available to him, given his view of Jewish possibility, only through *aliyah*. His assumptions are Kaufmann's. Judaism does not differ from other faiths essentially, in the content and substantive norms of the value system. But its style and symbolism were unique, meaning that Jews would remain isolated in the world by virtue of their tradition even if its symbols had for many of them lost much of their meaning. Israelis could meet the resultant challenge to authenticity simply by being what they were. American Jews tended to slip into a "vague, pervasive malaise" which led them to try to overcome their isolation by inauthentic "symbolic reconciliation with the Gentile."[65]

Religious Jews have a third option, however: substantive Jewish commitment at the price of a degree of alienation from America. Hertzberg and Neusner concede their own *galut*, metaphysical and political, as well as the Israelis' political homecoming. But they refuse to conflate the sociological and religious dimensions of homecoming as Halpern does, and as religious Israelis tend to do for different reasons, examined earlier. Hertzberg and Neusner are concerned, in other words, with the damage done to Jewish religious life in America by conscious or unconscious adaptation to a Christian environment. Perform the thought experiment of removing that particular alienation, imagine a Jewish religious life which thrives in America as it had once in Vilna or Cordova, and the superiority of the Land disappears. That superiority is entirely sociological. It confers the authenticity of a Jewish culture and the clear advantages of confronting modernity from within a Jewish calendar and language. But modernity cannot be overcome even in Israel, nor can true redemption be attained. The Land, therefore, is accorded no positive religious significance. American Judaism, if authentic, is held equal *by definition* to the Judaism of any time or place.

This crucial difference between American and Israeli reflection on homecoming remains even when American thinkers most nearly approach their counterparts in the Land. And the American discussion as a whole is utterly devoid of such angst. Israel's religious significance is not a principal theme. When the subject does arise—most often, in the past decades, in the aftermath of the crises of 1967 and 1973—it is Israel's *existence* which matters decisively, providing rescue from the despair of the Holocaust and indispensable reassurance for the worth of Jewish life and faith. But this inspiration conveys no imperative to live in the Land rather than gaze reverently from afar; more important, it does not take in the actuality of the Land or the state. The revolutionary character of modern Zionism is in effect denied. In short: Israel is a homecoming, but not a home. America may be somewhat less a home than Israel, but is far from exile. Israel does not challenge American Jewish life but rather undergird it—precisely as Kaplan had hoped it would.

The reason for this stance goes deeper than mere self-serving ideology, the explanation most often volunteered by Israelis. Nor should we attribute it entirely to the obvious need of American rabbis and lay leaders to address an audience uninterested in emigration and disinclined (despite a penchant for doomsayers of anti-Semitism and assimilation) to listen to disparagement of its future in America. The cause is rather to be found in the separation between the sociological and religious domains to which I have already pointed, and the loss by both these traditional dimensions to the concepts *galut* and *Eretz Israel* of much of the force endowed them by Jewish tradition. The Land cannot matter ultimately, in the metaphysical or existential sense, to Jews who do not live there. Even exile in the political sense can easily be discounted by American Jews convinced that America *is* different and that Israel will never achieve the true security of a nation among the nations. The admission of a certain marginality in America does not alter the fundamental conviction that all the world is exile in the sense which matters most. In short: American Jews define their Judaism not by the generation of Israelis who have returned to the Land, but by the tens of generations who did not. That they define their faith and their community in relation to the Land at all is of course but one more fundamental continuity between this galut and all its predecessors.

Answering the "Lover's Knock" in America

The ambivalence so pronounced in Hertzberg's and Neusner's writings only deepens when the meaning of the Land is taken up in the context of the larger question of Jewish faith in the modern world. Israel is said to matter ultimately—but we soon learn that it does not. Its rebirth is said to alter the terms of Jewish existence in our time—yet American Jewish existence proceeds as it would have done in any case. Whether we turn to Joseph Dov Soloveitchik (b. 1903), Abraham Joshua Heschel (1907–1972), or Emil Fackenheim (b. 1916)—thinkers associated with the Orthodox, Conservative, and Reform movements respectively—the dynamic of approach and withdrawal is similar. The Land lies outside the central perimeter of their thought, as they remain outside the Land. Affirmations routine to the Israelis are either absent or problematic in the extreme.

The first thing we should note about Soloveitchik's treatment of our subject is that it is seemingly marginal to his published thought. In the twin essays for which he is best known—"Halakhic Man" (1944) and "The Lonely Man of Faith" (1965)—the matter of the Land does not arise. Soloveitchik's aim is rather a modern phenomenology of Jewish commitment. "Whatever I am about to say is to be seen only as a modest attempt on the part of a man of faith to interpret his spiritual perceptions and emotions in modern theologico-philosophical categories."[66] The effort is of the utmost seriousness and evinces Soloveitchik's immense learning. Kierkegaard, Otto, and, above all, Kant are invoked alongside the sages to explain how "halakhic man" reconciles in himself the polar types of "rational" and "religious man";[67] how Jewish faith embraces both the "world of majesty" in which we seek livelihood, dignity, and control of our surroundings and the world of "convenantal community" through which we find purpose, love, and a relationship to our Creator.[68] In this depiction of the ideal Jewish life, the Land is not so much as mentioned, though American Judaism is criticized.[69] The man of halakhah, the man of faith, is a Jew defined by commitments and ideas which took shape in the centuries of exile and reached fruition in the East European exile of Soloveitchik's immediate forebearers.

Only in one major essay does Soloveitchik break with this pattern: "Kol Dodi Dofek" ("The Sound of My Lover Knocking"), written in 1956. The starting point is a general meditation on the two possible human responses to incomprehensible suffering in the world. One can seek philosophic understanding—in vain, Soloveitchik avers. It is not to be had. Or one can contribute to the correction of what is wrong, as commanded by the *halakhah*. "Suffering is the last warning that divine providence provides humanity. . . . It is forbidden not to seize the time." The immediate occasion for this reflection is of course the Holocaust: "a night of gas chambers and ovens, a night of complete *hester panim* (hiding of God's countenance), a night when doubt and destruction rule." And on this very night "comes the lover" as in the Song of Songs (5:2), read traditionally by Soloveitchik as a parable of God's relationship to Israel. "The hiding God" suddenly appeared "and began to knock on the door of the beloved . . . as a result of these knocks . . . the State of Israel was born."[70]

Soloveitchik's interpretation of recent Jewish history as a text is precise: six different "knocks" are enumerated. One, the political recognition of the new state by the nations, an event "almost supernatural." The United Nations was perhaps created for this very purpose. More than the human hand of the assembly's chairman had presided over its meetings. Two, Israel's victory in the field of battle. "The many were delivered into the hands of the few," as Jews read in the prayer celebrating the miracles of Purim and Hanukkah. "The Holy One, Blessed be He" hardened the heart of "Ishmael"—the rabbinic eponym for Arab peoples—just as He had hardened Pharaoh's. Three, "perhaps the most powerful knock of all," Christian theology holding that the Jews would be eternally homeless until they accepted Jesus as the Christ now stood refuted. Fourth, assimilating Jewish youth had been called back to their people. At the very least, "the process of flight has been slowed." Five, "for the first time in the history of our exile, divine providence surprised those who hate us with the thunderous discovery that Jewish blood is not free for the taking (hefker)." Soloveitchik affirms the rabbinic interpretation of "an eye for an eye" as monetary rather than corporal compensation, but declares that "the time has come to fulfill the command . . . literally." The final knock was the opening of the gates of the Land. Jews could now find refuge in the Land of their ancestors. In sum, "the hour of hester panim has ended. . . . Let the matter not be a small thing (kal) in our eyes. Hark! My lover knocks!"[71]

The response demanded of the American reader is apparently aliyah, though the word is never used. Soloveitchik chides American Jews, particularly the Orthodox, for not doing more to speed the settlement of the Land. Eretz Israel had remained faithful to the Jewish people. Had it been densely settled and fruitful before the arrival of the Zionists, "our rights to it would have been null and void." Now that Jews could return, Orthodox Jews should help to perform the important commandment of the Land's upbuilding.[72] Soloveitchik then links such activity to the existential alternatives described at the outset of the essay and proceeds to his principal conceptual innovation. Jews were bound to each other by two covenants: that of "fate" or "Egypt," imposed on the individual like it or not, and the covenant of "destiny" or "Sinai"—freely chosen: "all God has spoken we will do" (Ex. 19:8). American Jews had not fulfilled their responsibilities during the Holocaust. "Now Providence is testing us again in the crisis afflicting the Land of Israel." The state was doing battle with Amalek, in the persons of Nasser and the Mufti, as surely as Hitler had been the previous incarnation of Israel's eternal enemy. Let no Jew forsake either covenant. American Jews were tied by fate and destiny to Israel. Israelis, contrary to some political Zionists, had neither weakened anti-Semitism nor created a "new type of Jew." Both covenants were in force. "All of us are obliged to heed the sound of the lover knocking."[73]

"Kol Dodi Dofek" is remarkable in several respects. Rarely in modern Jewish thought do we find such unequivocal testimony to the divine hand in history. The God of Israel hardens hearts and supervises battle. He sways national policy and refutes mistaken interpretations of His will. There are passages in the essay which read as if written by A. I. Kook. Only Zevi Yehudah Kook could have been more confident in his reading of the text of history, though Soloveitchik is careful to insist that history's future course is not fixed. It depends on how Jews fulfill their obligations under the two covenants.

Those obligations in particular and the essay as a whole illumine the relation between Soloveitchik's picture of human existence and his outlook on the Land and state of Israel.[74] The expansion in scope for halakhah celebrated by A. I. Kook and the Mizrachi dovetails nicely with Soloveit- chik's notion of a "world of majesty" that the "man of faith" must bring into life with God's will, expressed in halakhah. Jews who share only in the covenant of fate can share in the upbuilding of the Land, the advancement of its technology and culture. But unless they embrace the covenant of destiny and join the "prophetic/prayer community" composed of "men of faith," they cannot participate in the setting of goals for the Jewish state. Nor will they have a part in the ultimate achievement of homecoming. Orthodox Jews who stand aside from the enterprise lest their faith be sullied by contact with secular reality can also play no part in that achievement. For they too have failed to embrace the dialectic of religion and reason, majesty and faith, fate and destiny, which Soloveitchik typologically expounds.

What is implicit in "Kol Dodi Dofek" becomes explicit in a series of addresses before conventions of the Mizrachi movement, not without a loss of subtlety. Soloveitchik draws midrashically on many of the biblical texts which we analyzed in Part One of this study: Abraham's entry into the Land, his purchase of Makhpelah, the patriarchs' interaction with the Philistines, Joseph's triumph in his exile, the fulfillment promised in Deuteronomy 26. His point is always to defend the Mizrachi's commitment to Orthodox Zionism against opponents to the "left" and "right." The latter, Orthodox anti-Zionists, are compared to the brothers of Joseph who drove him out of their midst because of his dreams. They were too shortsighted to see him as builder of a new framework for the preservation of Jewish existence. Just as his palpable blessing proved them wrong and only His dreams saved them from destruction, so the state offered refuge to the remnant which survived the Holocaust.[75] Soloveitchik invokes the same authority—history—when explaining his own gradual conversion to the Zionist cause. "If I now identify with the Mizrachi, against my family tradition, it is only because . . . I feel that Divine Providence ruled like 'Joseph' and against his brothers; that He employs secular Jews as instruments to bring to fruition His great plans regarding the Land of Israel."[76] Soloveitchik's second point in the addresses is to deny those "instruments" any ultimate role in setting the destiny of the state which they have done so much to build. He compares secular Israelis to Esau, to the heretic Elisha ben Abuya, to the Hittite from whom Abraham bought the cave of Makhpelah—unflattering comparisons to say the least.[77] Most telling of all is the comparison to the "lads" who accompany Abraham on the road to the mountain where he will bind Isaac (Genesis 22). When the moment comes to ascend they are told to "remain here with the donkey." The midrash is explicit. "To build a State of Israel, we march together with all the parties, because we believe that the State of Israel is the road that leads to Mount Moriah, and it is clear to us that we cannot succeed in this journey alone." But when it comes to "matters that relate to Mount Moriah" there is a parting of the ways. Secular Jews remain behind "with the donkey."[78]

Once more, the split between religious and secular Zionists—a "culture war" which "has already been raging for a long time"[79]—points only to the split within the religious Jew, captured in the division between Soloveit-chik's "man of majesty" and his "man of faith." We see the division clearly in another meditation lent its title from the Song of Songs (5:9), "Ma Dodekh Mi-Dod" (How is Your Lover Different From all Others?). Soloveitchik eulogizes his uncle, Isaac Ze'ev Halevi Soloveitchik (1886–1959) as "the most authentic halakhic man of all"—and explains why the Jewish state "did not find an important place in his halakhic way of thinking or his halakhic scale of values." Sometimes the discrepancy between the ideal world of the law and the imperfections of the actual world was too much for the man who loved the former deeply to bear. Consequently, reluctantly, he withdrew. Soloveitchik's uncle had not been able to "translate the idea of secular political sovereignty to halakhic details and values" and so had stepped aside from "the most important event in modern Jewish history." The state did have a place "prepared for it in the halakhic world view," Soloveitchik emphasizes, on condition that its leaders directed the state's course toward eventual acceptance of halakhic authority. Instead they declared time and again that theirs was a state of secular law and not of halakhah. Isaac Ze'ev, rather than delude himself with "lovely dreams and pleasant hopes," looked reality in the face and drew away. Yet he loved the Land, prayed for its inhabitants, and insisted that his children live there. Was his love for the Land any less than that of American Jewish authors (professed Zionists, apparently) busy "dialoguing" with Israelis?[80]

Soloveitchik, the "man of faith," the "man of halakhah," cannot but have reservations concerning more than ephemeral participation in a secular world resistant to the dictates of his halakhic idea. Hence the declaration that he is not in favor of "Zionism plus religion" or even of "religious Zionism" but only of "Torah," inseparable from the Land which it sancti-fies.[81] Hence too the following statement in an essay professing his support for Israel's religious parties, in which he asserted that "the holiness of the Land and that of the State are completely identical." Soloveitchik wrote,

> I understand the greatness, value and importance of the State, the wonder of its establishment and preservation, only from the point of view of the uniqueness of the people of Israel and its relation to the God of Israel. As a secular-historical entity that is not animated by any covenantal goal, the State does not excite me. . . . And I cannot imagine any tie between the Jews of the diaspora and a state insofar as it is secular.[82]

As one astute student of Soloveitchik writes, the man of halakhah, like the philosopher of Plato's Republic, "invites reality to answer to his message, but is obligated if reality does not accept his truth to withdraw—lest he find himself in surrender to it."[83] The Soloveitchik quoted immediately above is far more sober than the author of "Kol Dodi Dofek." He testifies to no direct divine incursion into Israel's history. He describes the holiness of the Land as "the fruit of the divine inspiration which has rested on the people in its connection to the Creator."[84] This Soloveitchik is truer to the rabbinic warning—derived from a third passage in the Song of Songs (2:7)—not to "awaken nor stir up love, until it please" by seeking to hasten the Messiah's coming. The difference between "Kol Dodi Dofek" and "Ma Dodekh Mi-Dod" marks the dividing line between much of Israeli and diaspora Jewish thought in our day. Soloveitchik, the greatest living Jewish thinker, is clearly torn—and that is perhaps the most telling feature of his reflection on the Land.

The very same tension is evident in the work of Abraham Joshua Heschel, for many years professor of mysticism and ethics at the Jewish Theological Seminary. Heschel's work, like Soloveitchik's, is dominated by other concerns than Israel: in his case the attempt to evoke for less observant or believing Jews than himself the experience of faith and tradition. In his best-known books—*Man is Not Alone* (1951) and *God in Search of Man* (1955)—Heschel attempted to move his readers from wonder at the cosmos, to acceptance of God as the answer to the questions provoked by that wonder, to *mitzvot* as a way of life responsive to the demand posed by encounter with God's presence in the world. In *The Sabbath* (1951) he tried to capture and convey the meaning of Jewish observance; in *The Prophets* (1962) he sought to enter inside the experience of bearing God's demand; in *The Earth is the Lord's* (1950) Heschel sought to conjure in loving memory the Eastern European Jewish world which the Nazis had destroyed. More technical works probed the possible meanings of divine revelation, the symbolic nature of prayer, and the thought of Maimonides. Only one work treated the religious significance of the state: *Israel, an Echo of Eternity* (1967).

My point in this enumeration is twofold. First, I wish to show that Heschel devoted the bulk of his efforts to ministering to the needs of his flock where he found them, rather than deepening their relation to a place where they were not. Second, I want to emphasize the substantive tension between focus on the Land and the burden of Heschel's teaching. The latter is nicely summarized at the start of *The Earth is the Lord's:* Jews "appreciate things displayed in space," but know that what is "genuinely precious" is encountered "not in space but in time."[85] Only thus could Judaism have lent meaning to the wanderings of exile which Heschel eulogized. In *The Sabbath* this theme is expanded. Technical civilization was devoted to the conquest of space, Judaism to the sanctification of time. Jewish tradition represented a radical departure from "accustomed religious thinking" that

God created and was served at holy *places*. Jews were not permitted to flee space, however. Their task was to "work with things of space," even as they remained "in love with eternity." But time alone had "independent ultimate significance."[86] The experiences of God which Heschel seeks to evoke for his readers can occur anywhere. The *Mitzvot* to which he wants to attract Jews are portable. Hence the entire thrust of Heschel's work, and not only the modest place assigned Israel, serves to mitigate the religious significance of the Zionist return. *Israel* itself does the same.

The book's first chapter is a hymn to Jerusalem, the "charismatic city." Heschel summarizes its role in Jewish faith over the centuries. The second surveys the Jewish people's "covenant of engagement" to the Land. "We live by covenants. We could not betray our pledge or discard the promise. When Israel was driven into exile, the pledge became a prayer, the prayer a dream; the dream a passion, a duty, a dedication." Israel's rebirth, a "miracle in disguise," concealed a "radical surprise" and bore witness to the fact that "history is intertwined with the mystery."[87] In Chapter Three, "Between Hope and Resistance," Heschel relates the Jews' devotion to the Land throughout their exile, a hope of return which enabled them to survive persecution, and then places the rebirth of the state in the context of the Holocaust. "Is the State of Israel God's humble answer to Auschwitz? A sign of God's repentance for men's crime of Auschwitz?" Heschel's intent, belied by this formulation, is conveyed soon thereafter. "There is no answer to Auschwitz." But "Israel enables us to bear the agony of Auschwitz without radical despair, to sense a ray of God's radiance in the jungles of history."[88]

Here, when considering the question which forms the heart of the book (and the subject of its fourth chapter)—"Israel and meaning in history"— Heschel is most precise. History is lent meaning by "the promise of the future," a "memory of moments" that make it more than "a flimsy course of disconnected happenings devoid of duration." Time is a "palace of meaning" rather than an "empty dimension" if "we know how to build it with precious deeds." Note the transition between Heschel's usual injunction to sanctify time and the sanctification of place demanded by return to the Land.

> Our imperishable homeland is in God's time. We enter God's time through the gate of sacred deeds. The deeds, acts of sanctifying time, are the old ancestral ground where we meet Him again and again. The great sacred deed for us today is to build the land of Israel.[89]

"Homeland," at first a metaphor (like "ancestral ground"), refers by the end of the passage to the real Land of Israel. The transition repeats the movement from Israel as symbol to actual place of the book as a whole—the same movement accomplished by the Jewish people since the start of modern Zionism.

Only such sacred deeds as building the Land sanctify history. God does not do so directly. Heschel's ambiguous declaration that "the Spirit of God speaks intermittently through the events of history, and our life is a continual wrestling with the Spirit" is at once interpreted unequivocally.

> The presence of God in history is never conceived to mean His penetration of history. God's will does not dominate the affairs of men. God's presence in history is sensed in the correspondence between promise and the events in the relation to God's promise that testify to His presence. Sacred history is the collecting of the threads of His promise.[90]

The formulation is precise. Heschel, a "man of faith" and halakhah, a student of Maimonides, has banished the messianist from the arena. Even the voice of "the spirit of God" is explained to mean our sense of "the correspondence between promise and . . . events" and that alone. In Israel's birth, so soon after Auschwitz, we "sense a ray of God's radiance." Or again: "To the eyes of the heart, it is clear that returning to the Land is an event in accord with the hidden Presence in Jewish history."[91] Heschel does not foreclose the possibility that God might be present in a more direct way, as Soloveitchik or A. I. Kook would have it. But "of that of which he cannot speak," Heschel remains silent—as he did with regard to the Holocaust itself. "History is the realm of divine meaning" *if* human deeds and discernment are equal to the promises of God's prophets. In this context Heschel can aver without danger of misunderstanding that "the State of Israel having been born out of our soul is itself a state of our soul, a reality within us."[92]

This is a far more eloquent formulation of Israel's religious significance than Kaplan's, and the "mystery" that one misses in Kaplan is evident in Heschel in abundance. However, the substantive difference between the two views is small. The state's rebirth was occasion for wonder and celebration, a confirmation of the meaning of history. It was not a clear and present demand for *aliyah* or even the ground for superior experience or awareness of God's presence. "The State of Israel . . . is itself a state of our soul" in the diaspora. Heschel chastised American Jewry for taking the state for granted "until the recent events" (of 1967). They had treated Israel as "a footnote to one's existence enjoyed as a fringe benefit, a nice addendum, a side dish, a source of self-congratulation and pride." The criticism recalls Soloveitchik's. But Heschel demanded only that Israel be taken as "a challenge . . . an urging for spiritual renewal, for moral re-examination."[93]

He adopted the same stance before the Conservative rabbinical assembly when asked to address it in 1958 on the subject of "Israel: People, Land and State." Jewish life after the Holocaust could have been dreadful without Israel, he said. Jews today, thanks to the state, stood at a climax of Jewish history. But the relevant question was not how to make the state meaningful to American Jews but how to make it worthy of two thousand years of waiting. Were American Jews in galut? Yes: "Miami Beach is galut. Some Bar Mitzvah affairs are galut. Our timidity and resistance to take a stand on behalf of the Negros [sic] are galut." Exile was more than a political or geographic condition. It existed wherever the sense of the holy was replaced by "spiritual obtuseness." Not only were all of us in galut—"galut is in us."[94]

Here too Heschel's spiritualization of exile is no less extreme than that of Kaplan. After confessing that "one feels abashed at the thought of being a distant spectator" while others built the Land—"we have the fleshpots, they watch the borders"—Heschel made his diaspora orientation explicit. The only answer "in a sense" to embarrassment at Israel was to bring about an "inner spiritual and cultural aliyah on the soil of America."[95] And the remainder of Heschel's address on "the people, land and state" of Israel—by far its greater portion—was devoted to renewing the faith of American Jews, in America.[96] Heschel pleads guilty to the Zionist charge of clinging to the fleshpots and seeks to discharge his guilt by heeding the call which obligates Jews everywhere: the *aliyah* of the spirit. The logic is telling indeed.

One can argue that Heschel was only meeting the immediate needs of those he addressed. But that is precisely my point. The Zionist goal of "self-fulfillment" through return to the Land does not arise in the American context. Revival of the Hebrew language can proceed only among a small elite. Even recognition of Israel's overwhelming centrality in contemporary Jewish history and the development of contemporary Jewish culture is too demoralizing to be accented. The relative paucity of Jewish cultural resources in America is taken as proof that work remains to be done there rather than that Israel is the only option. As Kaplan put it, negation of the diaspora would merely rationalize evasion of American Jewish responsibilities. What is more, Jewish faith would always be more important than Jewish culture. Space was but a means in the sanctification of time—and time was the dimension of the diaspora. The language of the discussion is far from that of Zionists in the Land, for whom the "sanctification of space" has assumed immense importance, and "aliyah of the spirit" is an expression of simple bad faith.

Only Emil Fackenheim has crossed the line from such Kaplanian formulations and left the diaspora bodily for literal *aliyah*. The Zionist affirmations at which he arrived since 1967 are out of step with his earliest essays, collected in *Quest for Past and Future* (1968) and *Encounters between Judaism and Modern Philosophy* (1973). In these pieces Fackenheim's task was to reestablish the tenets of traditional faith, and principally divine revelation, as living philosophical possibilities in the modern age.[97] The bridge to his later concern with the meaning of Israel was his first head-on confrontation with the Holocaust: *God's Presence in History* (1967). Fackenheim distinguished between "root experiences"—historical events in which Jewish faith originated—and "epoch-making events" which made a "new claim upon Jewish faith," testing it in the light of new historical experience. Two such root experiences are named, the implication being that the list is exhaustive: the experience of "God's saving presence at the Red Sea" and of His "commanding presence" at Sinai. Epoch-making events had been more numerous: the destruction of the first and second Temples, the Maccabean revolt, the expulsion from Spain. Auschwitz, of course, was another in the series. It had rendered belief in God's presence in history uniquely problematic.[98] Fackenheim argues that all we can do is pursue the strategy of "midrashic stubbornness" pioneered by the rabbis, holding fast to God and the world despite the dearth of answers to our perplexity. The "614th commandment" which issues from the Holocaust forbids Jews "to hand Hitler posthumous victories." Secular Jews must not abandon their people or religious Jews their faith. Indeed, the Jewish people now resisted Hitler by its very existence, and particularly by the existence of its state. Even secular Israelis knew that "after the death camps, we are left only one supreme value: existence."[99]

This is the ground—and the limit—of Fackenheim's Zionism. Israel's existence, because of the Holocaust, was sacred in and of itself. Support for the state, he declared in *The Jewish Return into History* (1978) was "the heart of every authentic response to the Holocaust, religious and secularist, Jewish and non-Jewish."[100] The specifics of the claim to God's presence in history are nowhere presented. We are told unequivocally that "the eclipse of God . . . ended and He appeared to us"—not in 1948 but in 1967![101] Did God reenter history only insofar as "He appeared to us?" I think this is not Fackenheim's intent. How then are we to understand previous and subsequent events? Nor does Fackenheim wrestle with the problem posed to the continuity of Jewish belief by the claim that Auschwitz constitutes an absolute disjunction. It is hardly enough to say that "no anti-Orthodox implication is intended by the "614th commandment," "as though the 613 commandments stood necessarily in need of change." But "we must face the fact that something radically new has happened."[102] There is a further problem. We read that to talk of "two Jewish centers—or three, five, or none at all" is to miss the significance of the Holocaust.[103] Yet we are apparently obligated only to a "commitment to the autonomy and security of Israel,"[104] not a lot to ask from the Zionist viewpoint and hardly commensurate with the dimensions of the "commanding voice." Was Ben-Gurion right when he said that "a full Jewish existence is possible nowhere outside Israel?" Time alone would tell, Fackenheim replies[105] the standard diaspora response.

Most disturbing of all is the statement that the rise of the first Jewish state in two thousand years, from the ashes of the Holocaust, meant that the future contained but two alternatives. One was "true peace for the State of Israel—the final defeat of Hitler." The other was the destruction of the state—meaning the end of the Jewish people.[106] If "the future" limned here is the end of days, well and good. But if Fackenheim has this generation and those to come in mind, the apocalyptic cast of his thought aligns him with Zevi Yehudah Kook's millenarianism. This is hardly a "return into history," far more an attempt to jump over its refusal to be as we would want it.

In *To Mend the World*, Fackenheim's most recent work, he meditates further on these dilemmas without resolving them. Israel is again called the principal Jewish response to the Holocaust (along with *aliyah* activism in the

Soviet Union). It is the "orienting reality for all Jewish and indeed all future Jewish thought." Jewish life in our day was "in advance of Jewish thought," a response in the grip of epoch-making events. Support for the state was a moral imperative and an act of faith.[107] Galut Judaism ("if most assuredly not the galut") had come to a violent end. "Jewish anti-Zionism of every kind . . . is of all phenomena in contemporary Jewish life the one most clearly anachronistic."[108] The post-Holocaust world could only be lived in, and even "mended," because during the Holocaust its repair or *tikkun* was "already actual . . . [a] simple but enormous, nay, world-historical truth, the rock on which rests any authentic Jewish future." Christian and Jewish resistance to evil and despair during the Holocaust was "the ultimate ground of our own resistance afterwards.[109] And the principal element of the continuing *tikkun* was Israel. Zionism was a "secular teshuvah," a "prayer in acts rather than words." Christians after the Holocaust "must be Zionists . . . on behalf of themselves and the whole post-Holocaust world."[110]

This tells us a great deal about the substance of Fackenheim's Zionism, of course: the meaning of the state which Christians too, after the Holocaust, are obliged to recognize. He comes to Israel, presumably, in order to share in the "abiding astonishment" of a Land and people reborn. The significance of the state, as for the diaspora thinkers he leaves behind, lies on this mythic level of rebirth rather than the substantive level of what the state is or does, so crucial to Scholem and Rotenstreich, Hartman and Schweid. Fackenheim cites the usual diaspora litany of Zionist achievements, an enumeration firmly rooted in traditional religious expectations of the return: deserts blooming, exiles ingathered, "a City rebuilt," and above all life after death.[111] Whether Israel is more of a halakhic state or less; whether its legislation is derived from *mishpat ivri* or British precedent; whether its Zionist orientation is cultural or political; whether its border is the Jordan or the "green line" further west—these crucial matters of Israeli self-definition, with which Jewish religious thought in the Land must be preoccupied, do not figure in Fackenheim's schema of Israel's religious significance. His homecoming means something very different.

He and they are worlds apart; Fackenheim expresses the meaning of Israel for Judaism as he, a diaspora Jew, conceives that meaning. Not being in the Land; not being party to the moral conundra probed by Oz and Leibowitz, Schweid and Scholem; shaped by a tradition of "galut Judaism" and the non-Jewish philosophies to which it responded, Fackenheim cannot but imagine homecoming as it appears from afar. For all that he admits the Land's centrality and declares it the rock on which future Jewish faith must rest, he cannot escape definition of the Land in terms of what it has accomplished for the Jewish people and the Jewish faith everywhere—which is to say, primarily *elsewhere*. One waits to see whether Fackenheim's thought will shift now that he has come to sit in Jerusalem; whether in this case too "thought will go to school with life,"[112] as he puts it, and carry home lessons it could learn nowhere else.

Conclusion

The dynamics of the relationship we have just examined are complex; the division between the two communities and the Jewish thought in which they engage is deep. The first thing we might do in the effort to make sense of this relationship, then, is to discard the two metaphors most often invoked to describe it. "Center and periphery," the model favored by Israelis, fails to do justice either to the mutuality of the interaction or to the vaunted American exceptionalism to the general rule of contemporary *golah* communities. The "two foci of an ellipse" popular with the Americans seems less than honest in its statement of late-twentieth-century Jewish realities. There *is* a focus to the Jewish world and Jewish history some forty years after Holocaust and statehood, and that center of gravity is not America. Perhaps we should follow in the train of this last metaphor and turn from geometry to physics. Fields of force attract even as they repel, thereby holding distant objects in steady equilibrium. Planets circle a life-giving sun, yet turn on their own individual axes. But such metaphors, too, strain the complexities they are meant to capture. Better, it seems, to abandon the search for a controlling metaphor altogether and turn directly to the several matters at issue between Israel and American Jewry. I will do so, as always, in terms of the venerable metaphors of homelessness and homecoming in which Jews have considered their exile and their Land for two millennia.

One notices at once that the claims of each side in the dispute reinforce as well as delegitimate the arguments offered by the other. Israelis demand that the diaspora grant the unprecedented character of a homecoming between *galut* and *ge'ulah*, exile and redemption. The inherited categories, they maintain, no longer suffice. Yet they are loathe to concede the analogous claim by the American diaspora that its situation too is unprecedented: that "at-homeness," even if not a homecoming, inhabits the same novel space between *galut* and *ge'ulah*. There is much truth in both claims to novelty. Neither condition finds a precise precedent in the Jewish past. Israelis refuse to grant the diaspora's claim, however. It threatens the revolutionary character of their return. If exile is legitimate, home is much less a home. American Jewish thinkers, for their part, fear that if the Zionist homecoming really is the ingathering for which they and their ancestors have prayed, failure to join it is not only foolish but a supreme tragedy. If home really is home, exile is a terrible place indeed. Hence the tendency on both sides to employ the traditional categories as weapons of attack rather than instruments of analysis, to cry "exile" or "false messiah" rather than determine to what degree the classical sources are and are not relevant and draw the appropriate conclusions. Even a cursory acquaintance with the sources, I believe, suggests that they are so relevant as to call into question the stances of both sides to the debate. The key is to distinguish political from metaphysical homecoming, to allow for gradations within each, and to insist on the inseverable bond between the two. Unwarranted pretensions on both sides then stand clearly exposed to view.

Let us begin with the political dimension to exile and return. Why would anyone doubt, were the need to do so not so powerful, that the American Jewish community is significantly different from the German, or the Polish, or (in many ways a closer analogy) the Spanish in the Golden Age? That is not to say that its fate will *necessarily* be different from that of Vilna's Jewish community or Vienna's, but only that at present ideology alone—and not objective weighing of the evidence—suggests that it will not be. America *is* different, in crucial political, legal, economic, cultural, and demographic respects. These cannot be discounted. Nor can it be seriously denied that Israel too represents a fundamental change in the Jewish situation, a far greater change even than America! Analogies to the period of the Second Temple have suddenly become more apt than those to the first half of our own century. Moral dilemmas and political choices which Jews have not confronted for two thousand years are once again before them. A nation rooted in its own land, speaking its own language, enacting its own laws, and defending its own borders is not by any stretch of the imagination the exilic people caricatured by Franz Rosenzweig in *The Star of Redemption*. Home is home, in a way which no diaspora community can be. America is not home in the same sense, even if it threatens Jews with benevolence rather than oppression—and so is a wholly other state of being than traditional exile. Distinctions among exiles—an effort begun seriously by Yehezkel Kaufmann—seem essential if use of the term is to serve any constructive purpose. The same holds true of distinctions among homecomings.

The American Jewish community cannot convincingly be described by the epithets Buber scathingly applied to German Jewry of his youth. It is not "sickly, sterile, sunken, tortured and tormented." It *is* "distorted" if and only if one carefully makes the case for such a conclusion along lines set forth by Halpern: namely, that at the deepest level of self-conception as well as more surface levels of behavior, the expression given Judaism in America is shaped by what gentile Americans prefer and permit. The determinants of Jewish life would ultimately resolve, if so, into a matter of relative political power. The community could be called "fragmented" in the sense that about half of its members are unaffiliated with any formal Jewish organization and many more are affiliated only loosely. It is fragmented, too, in that very few American Jews actually get to see the community whole. They know only their small part of it: a synagogue, a chapter or region of "Hadassah," a local Jewish newspaper. For the rest they must presume and imagine what they cannot see. Israelis need only go out to the street, ride the buses, or turn on the television. This feature of diaspora life too is ultimately rooted in the relative political weakness of the Jewish community.

Yet Israel too is a Jewish community deeply fragmented and, some would say, significantly distorted. My point here is not to enter into sociological description of the two communities, which lies beyond the bounds of this study. I only wish to note that such description and it alone can lend credence to the claims which Israelis and American Jews wield with utter confidence. Objectivity is hard to come by in present circumstances because the enterprises of sociology and ideology are so hard to separate. Israelis regularly discount reports of vitality issued by Americans, while American "sociology of knowledge" can account for that Israeli disbelief quite readily. Intelligent discourse on the state of the Jewish people has suffered as a result.

Scholem's attribution of bad faith to American Jews[113] seems cavalier. If one judges by the person in the street he is perhaps correct, though I have found American Jews more alert to the disabilities of their situation than Israelis are to the disadvantages of homecoming, perhaps because a long tradition of reflection on galut has preceded them. Scholem's accusation is utterly unfounded if it includes the political and intellectual leadership of American Jewry, witness the sources which we have examined. Rotenstreich seems on firmer ground when he argues that solidarity with the Jewish people and its traditions comes more easily to Israelis.[114] How could it not? But the living of a life substantively shaped by tradition is hardly "non-existent" in America, as he charges, nor is participation in communal institutions limited to a small elite. His critique is on target. There is self-deception, attenuation of commitment, impoverishment of learning. But his verdict, like most of those which issue from Zion, is exaggerated. The case is similar with Schweid.[115] American Jews do lack an independent Jewish culture, a clear Jewish identity, and the ability to protect themselves physically as a group. But one wonders, for all that Israel's advantages in these respects are obvious, what it means for a Jewish culture to be independent, whether that is possible anywhere, even in Israel—and whether it is entirely desirable. Can a culture take in nothing from the outside, be as Ahad Ha'am put it "without any foreign admixture" (this while he leaned heavily on Spencer and Mill)? Should it try? Or is it rather a matter of the proper balance between generation from within and importation from without—a balance which Israel has done much to set right for modern Jews? Moreover, how *do* Jews protect themselves as a people? Does the army of the sovereign Jewish state really secure Jewish survival in the world more than the economic, social, and political power of the Jewish diaspora, which Schweid believes is negligible?

I put these questions rhetorically not because their answers are clear but because those answers would take us far afield. I believe that responses adequate to the complexities involved would serve the interests of neither unqualified apologists for the diaspora nor untempered negators. Jewish life now as ever is a series of trade-offs: political and metaphysical and both together. Yoḥanan Ben Zakkai only made the most dramatic bargain of many when he surrendered the hope for political independence from Rome in return for the freedom to teach Torah. He agreed to serve the lords of the earth the better to serve the Lord of Heaven and Earth—and in so doing secured the survival of his people. It is difficult to accept A. B. Yehoshua's harsh judgment of the hundreds of trade-offs made by Jews in the intervening two millennia, even if history teaches us that many proved disastrous. It is also difficult to accept the oft-voiced rationale of contemporary American Jews for ignoring the call to *aliyah:* namely, that they have made a similar calculation regarding the worldly and otherworldly welfare of the Jews. But their behavior is for all that no less defensible on political grounds than that of past generations of exilic Jews. They exhibit an implicit political awareness that is explicit in the strategies of communal defense pursued by their leaders. It is perhaps undignified to flatter kings and cajole ministers. But this is the price a tiny people pays for the chance to exist as a distinct people in the world. Two thousand years' reflection on *galut* have clarified that price, in body and soul, and made its payment all the more difficult. Israelis do no less, however, to secure the survival of their tiny nation-state. The bargaining will end only with the Messiah.

If so, we must reject the attempt by many Israelis to raise the discourse of homecoming too quickly from the political to the metaphysical key. Zionism has wrought a revolution in Jewish life. It has returned a large percentage of the Jewish people to the Land of Israel and secured their sovereignty with real-world instruments of defense. But the Messiah has not come. Israelis are neither back in the Garden nor any closer to it. The fundamental state of Jewish being in the world is therefore as it always was. There is no assurance that this homecoming will be the last, any more than American Jews can count on avoiding the fate ultimately met by Babylonian or Spanish Jewry. The Zionist claim to have reentered history, if it means anything, means that Jews have made peace with the fact that change is inexorable in history— precisely the lesson taught vividly by the wanderings of exile. To turn about and claim that the Zionist revolution is permanent—that the present homecoming cannot be reversed—is to make a political claim in a metaphysical key. One can say as much in prayer. One can use such rhetoric to summon morale. But in dispassionate political reflection it seems imperative to recognize that short of the Messiah there is no permanence in human affairs. The Americans are right, therefore, to remind the Israelis that that is exactly where Jews remain, wherever they live: short of the Messiah's coming. The Jewish people has come home. It has not come Home. The tradition of reflection on galut calls us back to this simple statement of the obvious, even as ideological use made of that tradition tends to conceal it—and confuse us with the either/or of punishment or redemption, persecution or Messiah, exile or a return from which there can be no turning back.

The tradition also points us, however, to the comparable mistake of diaspora thinkers for whom the two realms, political and metaphysical, are entirely separable. It is perhaps true that the meaning derived from Judaism can be experienced anywhere with equal authenticity, that God can be served and encountered anywhere that His Torah can be heard. But this is true in theory only. In practice, Jews like everyone else hear only what they are able to hear, what they are prepared to hear. The thrust of the critique of American Judaism offered by Halpern, Hertzberg, and Neusner is therefore on the mark, though its details, again, require careful study. To the degree that American Jews are estranged from traditional sources and the language in which those sources are written; construct Jewish time and space only with difficulty; are surrounded by a culture hostile or indifferent to their commitments; and are defined in part by that culture's definition of what religion is and should be—to that degree the Judaism of American Jews is filtered through a medium that compromises the clarity of transmission and therefore its authenticity. Israeli Jews too do not receive their Judaism unmediated by disturbing circumstances. Judaism can hardly develop freely there, as Scholem or Lichtenstein might wish, under the internal constraints of an established Orthodoxy. The impact of modernity is pervasive. However, Americans more than Israelis fail to recognize that the political achievements of land, language, and law—in short, of Jewish time and space—are intimately connected to the metaphysical experience of Jewishness. Biblical and rabbinic sources, which always discussed the one in the context of the other, knew better.

Heschel precludes such a recognition, despite his implicit call for it, when he asks "What is the Meaning of the State of Israel?" and responds, "Its sheer being is the message."[116] Like Schechter and Kaplan before him, he at first submits evidence for the prosecution of American Judaism ("Miami Beach is galut," etc.), but then stops short and all too quickly passes over to the defense. Israel too is in exile, and besides, there is work to be done in America. I do not indict Heschel, as the Israelis would, for failing to preach *aliyah* of the flesh and not the spirit. No community has ever transplanted itself voluntarily from a land of plenty to an unknown place of danger. More importantly, no serious or successful body of religious thought has ever addressed itself in terms applicable and comprehensible *only elsewhere.*

But this prompts the recognition that neither side wishes to admit: that Judaism after statehood and the Holocaust ineluctably bears an adjective—"diaspora" or "Israeli." To the degree that it addresses its adherents where they sit, politically and metaphysically, it will differ from other Judaisms which do the same for Jews who sit elsewhere. Soloveitchik cannot be A. I. Kook. Fackenheim cannot be Scholem. These divergences can be obviated only by ignoring the fundamental differences of place and condition which are most demanding of religion's response. Even if diaspora and Israeli thinkers step into the other's shoes, therefore, and consider the facts of exile and homecoming from a perspective other than their own, they will be unable to *be* the other, or even be more like the other. That task awaits the ingathering which, as Ahad Ha'am pointed out, remains beyond the capacity of human beings alone. Without it, however, the relations between Center and periphery which he charted will likely never be without the tension and recrimination that have marked their debate thus far.

All that one can hope to do, then, is facilitate that debate and attempt to make it fruitful. My own suggestion for doing so is that we see the inherited conceptions of exile and homecoming whole rather than in the fragments usually invoked by one side or the other, Center or diaspora, to justify its particular outlook. Jewish tradition and Jewish history are what Israel and American Jewry have in common. This past cannot be used to arbitrate the disputes of the present unprecedented situation, for selection from it to suit particular needs and interpret particular conditions will continue. But the past provides a shared vocabulary unparalleled in its usefulness, so long as we remain responsive to the complexities and doubts which it comprehends. The "not yet home" of the patriarchal narratives qualifies and complicates the blessings of at-homeness sung by Deuteronomy—blessings of which Israelis have liberally tasted. The difficulties of building Jewish time and space inside Eretz Israel, articulated by Mishnah Avodah Zarah, are seen differently in their native context of the Gemarra, which describes the more difficult project of constructing such time and space outside the Land. It is the interplay among these various elements of the tradition that is most helpful in understanding the present situation of Jews: between exile and homecoming, or between homecoming and redemption. The traditional polarities have been narrowed and confused but by no means overcome. For better and for worse, therefore, Rabban Gamaliel in his bath with Aphrodite and Bar Sheshek in his bath of rosewater surrounded by harlots still have a great deal to teach us.

CONCLUSION
"K," "PARIAH," ZIONIST, JEW

It is perhaps one of the greatest ironies of modern Jewish history that the Jewish state established in order to make the Jewish people "like any other nation" is now preoccupied far more than any other nation with defining ideas of its own existence. Other nationalisms past and present have of course had their "missions" to perform and their dreams of eternal glory. The host nation to the world's largest Jewish diaspora, America, arguably united its many ethnic and regional groupings on the strength of a uniquely powerful idea: democracy. But Israel is to an extraordinary degree the sum of the ideas put forth concerning what it is and should become. The discourse of its culture, high and low, is dominated by the concepts of land and exile, return and fulfillment, which we have charted. Those ideas brought Jews to resettle their land and found their state; the conflicts among them are now the fault lines on which the state seems in danger of dividing. Take away their visions of what Israel is and should be, and Israelis of varying commitments would be hard pressed to recognize the Jewish state in which they live.

All of this is of course nothing new for the Jewish people, which began with an idea of itself and in three thousand years was never without it. The people was conceived in order to become a "kingdom of priests and holy nation"; in other words, to transform the world in accordance with a revolutionary idea of God and of God's intention for humanity. Joshua, like Abraham before him, crosses a river which divides far more than adjacent territories, in order to accomplish far more than getting to the other side. The river marks the limit of present reality, the starting point of future realization. Israel is crossing over to a place "which I shall show you." It does not exist, except in the mind of God. The people, with the help of God's Torah, must fashion it.

The fateful step in the modern return to the Land was taken when the founders of Zionism described their own homecoming, however secular, in similar terms. Ideas of exile and the Land would henceforth be as determinative of Jewish politics as they had been of Jewish faith. Hess, first prophet of this holy nationalism, transcribed Isaiah in a socialist key, linking reclamation of the Land to the inauguration of historical, even cosmic, redemption. Herzl declared that only the "state idea"—his reworked version of the ancient cry "next year in Jerusalem"—had the power to move Jews to cross oceans infinitely wider than the Jordan and leave behind the entire known Jewish world. He offered in return the messianic promise of normality: being just like every other nation. Ahad Ha'am too, though he insisted that Jews settle for far less, held out hope for the rejuvenation of a tattered people—no mean ambition—and planned rationally, without a whiff of fantasy, for the establishment in the Land of a Spiritual Center that would raise all Jews to the high moral plane demanded by their God at Sinai. Sovereignty alone, in his view, was unworthy of their efforts. So Gordon believed, and Buber; so too Ben-Gurion, when he set the permanent course for his new state by choosing a name charged with age-old longings and unparalleled ambitions: Israel—"he who wrestles with God," the alter ego of Jacob, who survives in an unredeemed world by keeping his wits and his God about him; the father of Joseph, master practitioner of the politics of exile. Ben-Gurion stamped the covenant upon his state in the name he gave it, all the while declaring total independence.

The legacy, like the name, was not to be shrugged off easily. The Zionist revolution would perforce remain incomplete. And so the current genera-tion of Israelis, and the diaspora Jews who must make separate sense of the state's existence, have been drawn to confrontation with the sources that held the Zionist founders even in rebellion, as they had anchored Jews for centuries in exile. It has not been enough for them, as it would have been for Klatzkin, to reclaim a land, revive a language, and become the "ruling power" within their own borders. Orthodox Israelis look forward to a home-coming crowned in the near or distant future with redemption. The Jewish state will not be home for them unless it is governed, sooner or later, by *halakhah*. Religio-cultural Zionists such as Scholem and Schweid cannot endorse this vision. But they too are not content with less than a state substantively Jewish in ways still difficult to describe. Homecoming must at the least mean revitalization of Jewish tradition—for how else is the Land home? Secularists such as Oz and Rubinstein see in this approach, as in Orthodoxy, a betrayal of the Zionist revolution and its watchword, "normal-ization." But even they put forward secular variants of the messianic idea similar to Herzl's. Only Halkin, in bitter polemic with the diaspora, declares that "land and language are everything," professing contentment with achievements comparable to those of any other nation, no matter how modest.[1]

The Israelis thinkers whom we have examined want more, and know too well the partial character of such homecoming as has been achieved. Hence the preoccupation with the Other—the American diaspora. The path not taken beckons still; the past that Zionism was meant to overcome lives on, and seemingly prospers. If the essence of homecoming is the insurance of Jewish survival, the American diaspora seems in no immediate danger. If the essence is authenticity, American Jews make a strong case that not all they do is bad culture or bad faith. It is axiomatic in Zionist as in Jewish thought that one cannot be both at home and in exile. Nor is there more than one way, one place, in which a Jew can be at home. Israelis are therefore driven to ask, with Buber's Hasid, "Where in the world am I?" American Jews have an advantage in this respect. They are familiar with the question and know how to answer it. Like Jews for the past two millennia, they can orient themselves in relation to the Center where they are not.

I have tried to suggest several ways in which contemporary Jewish reflection on exile and homecoming might be deepened by serious encounter with the concepts and images stored up in Jewish tradition. Three lessons in particular seem relevant. All emerge clearly from the three texts analyzed in Part One of this study.

First—a lesson directed particularly at partisans of the diaspora—the sexual politics of homelessness are always demanding, and at times devastating. The rape or near-rape of the matriarchs and their daughter Dinah are emblematic of the larger set of compromises and violations to which the Jewish people stands exposed as a stranger in strange lands. Politics, the art of the possible, must be played and played well with limited resources, despite the knowledge that it is not ultimately serious. Powers that be must be served, appeased, cajoled—or fled. Security such as that sought by the builders of Babel's tower is not to be had. The human lot of famine and sojournings does not permit it. What is worse, personal integrity can rarely survive these pressures intact. Simeon and Levi perhaps murder needlessly. But Joseph's hands are far from clean, his father Jacob is a thief—and Abraham is forced to become a liar. There can be happiness in galut, then, and a measure of fulfillment. There can be faith. But only by virtue of that faith, and the intermittent contact with God that it makes possible, is galut existence made either bearable or meaningful. Only the promise of going home someday enables one to live so long so far from home. The covenant stipulates all the redemption a person still in exile could imagine: a fertile land on which to be at home with one's fellows and to visit with one's God. One can survive in the meantime, somewhere else, and one can even thrive. But one is not home.

Deuteronomy offers the second lesson—directed at partisans of normalization and diaspora alike. It spells out the promise of Genesis in a poetry of law. Fulfillment takes shape in specific injunctions regarding indentured servants and misplaced boundary stones. It takes the utterly real and tangible form of bread which one eats—or fails to eat and starves; of paths through the wilderness which, if one fails to walk them continually, are quickly covered over by the sand. Deuteronomy insists that law and justice are the only way to homecoming. Morality is made more serious for being social as well as personal. Religion is made more serious—and more dangerous—by being linked inextricably to politics. One cannot transcend the political world, then, but only sanctify it. This effort too will almost certainly fail; one makes it nonetheless because one knows it to be the choice for life. Through the direction of *mitzvah* one comes to experience some of the future perfection known to the Israelite imagined in Chapter 26. Only so do we "hear" and "remember" true *devarim*. All the rest—that which much of the world hears and remembers much of the time—just is not serious, and threatens us in its triviality.

Because of its promise of homecoming and the certainties of its sacred order, Deuteronomy strains modern credibility in a way which Genesis does not. (Hence perhaps the attractiveness of normalization and diaspora, both of which ease the strain.) Deuteronomy knows failure, to be sure, but it knows much more as well—far more than we can credit. It knows the truth. It distinguishes good laws from bad, true prophets from false, and does not shrink from coercion in pursuit of its ends. Our failures by contrast seem to fill the world, our certainties are all suspect and our authorities untrue. If Deuteronomy nonetheless continues to demand a hearing among contemporary Jews, religious and secular, as it compelled Moses Hess and Ahad Ha-am, the reason may well lie in the rabbinic reformulation of its promise and its reproof. The rabbis translated Deuteronomy's vision of homecoming to a homelessness, political and metaphysical, beyond even Deuteronomy's capacity to describe. We recognize our world in the pages of Avodah Zarah as we do not in Moses's oration at the Jordan. We can listen to the rabbis as we cannot to the greatest of all prophets. We are willing at least to entertain the interim solution which they propose, on the way to an ultimate homecoming which taxes our faith severely.

That solution constitutes the third lesson which I wish to highlight here, one directed at Israel and the diaspora alike. For the rabbis' conception of galut comprehends both. The world of Avodah Zarah is the world of Genesis, and of Kafka. Snakes and prostitutes, twin symbols of corruption, are everywhere. Orders of meaning erected patiently over centuries can be demolished in a second by what a pagan holding a drop of wine does with a flick of the wrist. Highest rabbinic authority must bathe in waters supervised by Aphrodite—and complain feebly that she came into its territory, not it into hers. Good Jews must wink at profit from the sale of hens clearly intended for idolatrous sacrifice. They must make a living, as they must bathe; cleanliness suffers on both accounts. We who inhabit the twentieth century's last decades cannot but recognize our world in this depiction. We cannot but be shaken by Raba's observation to Bar Sheshek that the world to come offers reward even greater than baths in rose water surrounded by naked harlots: the absence of all need to fear the ruling power. Faith after the Holocaust strains at nothing so much as belief in a world where the way of the true Ruling Power is both decisive and direct. For the rabbis too such faith did not come easily.

The conditions thus described pertain as much after as before the achievement of Jewish statehood, as much inside as outside the borders of the Land. For even in the Land the sway of the local Jewish power is extremely limited. Faith in the highest Ruling Power—which many Zionists before the Holocaust and many Israelis after understandably felt obliged to do without—seems no more laughable today, if no more credible, than the secular faith in humanity or science adopted in its place by Herzl or Ben-Gurion. It now seems impossible to trust that the far from simple expedient of removing the Jews from exile and gathering them in a sovereign state protected by force of its own arms can remake either the Jewish spirit or Jewish destiny. The old dreams and nightmares have not gone to rest. Zionism, in short, has significantly altered the facts but not the nature of Jewish existence. It has dealt the Jewish people a far better political hand. But the deck remains the same. The metaphysical condition of the Jews remains as it has always been. And so, inevitably, do the odds on Jewish faith and Jewish survival.

It is this recognition, I think, which has driven Jewish political and religious thought in our day to stand apart from the universal discourse on these subjects once so intergral to thinkers such as Hess and Buber. One finds little reference to that wider reflection in contemporary Jewish conversation over exile and homecoming. Indeed, one might well listen to it with care and reach the erroneous conclusion that this conversation has no analogue in Europe or America, no root in the larger culture with which modern Jewry and modern Judaism are fatefully intertwined. I would like in conclusion to dispel this error by briefly sketching the larger context and its impact upon contemporary Jewish debate. We might usefully begin with the reasons for that debate's self-imposed isolation.

The Zionists, we recall, taught the lesson that Emancipation had been an utter failure for Jews. Ahad Ha'am called Jewish existence in the West "slavery in the guise of freedom." Kaufmann declared the hope for Emancipation and acceptance "messianic," convinced that it was doomed from the start to fail. The vitality of American Jewry has challenged but not shaken this axiom of Zionist analysis, and the shock of the world's perceived indifference to Israel's fate in 1967 and 1973 only furnished added confirmation. Israelis predisposed by the Holocaust to place no stock either in the promises of the great powers or the moral seriousness of their cultures now found new reason to turn inward. European political thought seemed mired in a crisis of authority and confidence in any event. Israelis would look to themselves.

But there is a second reason for this isolation: the rejection of modernity now overtaking every traditional faith. The threat posed to religious belief and community by the forces of modernization and secularization is now widely recognized, and Jews like other believers have reacted with varying strategies of defense and various degrees of withdrawal. History and authenticity seem to allow them no alternative. Emancipation has not been the utter failure which some Zionists claim, but it has hardly been an unqualified success. The demystification of the Land and of Jewish tradition as a whole undertaken by Spinoza has had to be halted in order to preserve the remnants of Jewish faith. The politicization indispensable both to sovereignty in Israel and to Emancipation in the West has come at the cost of Jewish community. As a result, the universalization of the tradition underwritten by pioneers of modern Judaism such as Moses Mendelssohn and pioneers of modern Zionism such as Moses Hess is now widely regarded as a move necessary when they made it but in need of correction through renewed particularism—religious or nationalist or both.

There are of course degrees of particularism. American Jewish thinkers, as we have seen, are well aware of the dangers posed to Jewish commitment by the openness of American society to Jewish participation. They increasingly express concern as well about the prevailing morals and mores of their culture. Only the extreme Orthodox, however, have withdrawn physically into voluntary "ghettoes" such as one finds in Brooklyn. In Israel the situation is different on two accounts. First, Orthodoxy enjoys an official monopoly on the definition of Judaism, one in which many secular Israelis acquiesce. More open stances toward modernity are therefore less prominent than they might be otherwise. Second, religious isolation and political isolation are mutually reinforcing. The newspapers provide the data which religion readily "explains," and this explanation then nudges national policy and opinion further in the direction in which it had been moving in any event. Israel is "a people dwelling alone," the rabbis remind their countrymen. The conclusion is well-nigh inescapable: to be a Jew, now as always, is to be in exile from the world.

Soloveitchik, an Orthodox Jew who would also be modern, an Eastern European Jew who has chosen America as his preferred exile, has articulated these dilemmas brilliantly. His type of the "lonely man of faith," we recall, oscillates between the "world of majesty" and the "world of covenant," at home in neither and yet driven to live in both. He is particularly estranged from America, where majesty is counted everything and covenant virtually ignored. But neither can Soloveitchik settle in Israel, for the state cannot live up to the idea which he has of it. Soloveitchik wants the state transformed in accordance with the halakhah. And so he is left with exile. Jacob is drawn to reunion with his brother Esau, in Soloveitchik's telling midrash. He approaches his brother's embrace eagerly. But at the last moment he always withdraws.[2] Esau stands in this midrash for American secularism, as he had symbolized Roman paganism to the rabbis of the Talmud. Esau also stands, we recall, for the secular Israeli who refuses to bow before the demands of halakhah. Ben-Gurion might have found a worthy model for his new state in Jacob's worldly aspect of cunning and prudence. But for Soloveitchik there is no such option. Israel must be Israel, or it is Esau. And in a world ruled by Esau, those who wait for Israel must dwell alone.

The immediate upshot of this act of self-distancing from the West is that one finds little trace in recent Jewish conversation over exile and homecoming—or in contemporary Jewish thought generally—of the larger human discourse in which it is bound up. Jews are not alone in pondering the meaning of homelessness and homecoming at a time of surplus populations, massive voluntary and involuntary uprootings, new and fragile national identities and nostalgia for simpler times past. More important, I think, the question of whether Israel is home and America exile—a variation on age-old Jewish themes—is a particularist formulation of two issues of paramount concern throughout the contemporary world: the legitimacy and ultimate worth of the political order and the possibility of metaphysical affirmation. The first has become particularly central in political thought since Weber, his questions driven home by the rise of communism and fascism and the loss of self-confidence among Western democracies; the second question is of course at the center of twentieth-century philosophy and its quarrel with religion. Jews, then, are far from alone in conceiving exile and homecoming in terms of their political and metaphysical dimensions. Much of current Jewish debate, in fact, can only be fully understood if seen in terms of the larger context which many Jews—Soloveitchik among them—feel compelled both to take seriously and to resist.

I cannot do more than point to that larger context here; rather than attempt to define the dilemmas of political legitimacy and metaphysical affirmation more precisely, I will suggest them through several insights garnered from the ruminations of Kafka and Weber on the Jewish and modern conditions and their interrelation. In conclusion I will argue that these reflections lead to the recognition that certain definitions of Jewishness long put forward by both Jews and Gentiles, like certain expectations of humanity, are after statehood and the Holocaust no longer viable or credible. Homecoming is still before us and exile not entirely behind us, but the facts with which definition of the two must come to grips have been altered in our century. Those facts demand inclusion in our reckonings.

I begin with an apparent digression: the riddle, often put to me as a boy by my father, which has haunted me throughout this study. It involved the logical proof that we are not where we think we are, "Are you in Los Angeles?" my father would ask. "No," I answered readily. "Are you in Chicago?" "No," I had to agree once more. "Are you in New York?" Again no—by now an impatient concession. "But if you're not in Los Angeles, and you're not in New York, and you're not in Chicago, you must be somewhere else. And if you're somewhere else you can't be here!" I was not here. I was not where Moses and Abraham were when they expressed willingness to do God's bidding in the single word *hineni.* I was instead where Buber's Hasid stood when God asked him, "Where in the world are you?" I was somewhere else. "*Etre ailleurs,*" wrote Charles Peguy, "the great vice of this race, the great secret virtue, the great vocation of this people."[3]

Kafka, perhaps more than any other, has transmitted this knowledge of where we stand to the twentieth century. "Kafka knew," writes George Steiner, "As no other speaker or scribe after the prophets, Kafka knew." In his work one finds "an inextricable intimacy between the imagined and the foreseen."[4] He knew just how far we had fallen, how total was our exile. His vocation was to call us to that knowledge, to name it, to force us to see it.

Yet the question must be asked—and it is crucial to Steiner's relation to the Jewish state, as to the Jewish people's relation to modernity and modernism—just what did Kafka know? And here it seems urgent that we follow the judgment of Walter Benjamin, who with Scholem has been faulted by Steiner for failing to see in Kafka the "urgent conundrum of the prophetic."[5] Benjamin is insistent on the point. Kafka did not know the "prehistoric forces that dominated [his] creativeness [and] . . . may justifiably be regarded as belonging to our world as well." He "failed to get his bearings among them." He knew only the guilty and unredeemed morass he found about him, and that only thanks to the "mystical tradition" which named it for him. Kafka's "experience was based solely on the tradition to which he surrendered; there was no farsightedness or 'prophetic vision'. Kafka listened to tradition, and he who listens hard does not see."[6]

This judgment too stands in need of minor correction. He who listens to tradition fails to see only when the *devarim* or words which he hears find no counterpart in the *devarim* or reality all about him, because human beings have neglected to renew the correspondence or have obliterated all its traces. But the burden of Benjamin's assessment stands—and teaches us that we are not to regard Kafka's various narrative personae as representations of the human condition *sub specie aeternitatis*. They do not describe the whole of the political world which we inhabit and cannot escape; nor do they mark the limits of metaphysical affirmation as Kafka understood these, but only the narrower borders of what he himself found possible. The difference, for Jewish as well as non-Jewish discourse on exile and homecoming, is crucial.

We can clarify it by looking briefly at three texts often cited by Kafka's critics in connection with "the Jewish question," first among them of course *The Castle* (1920). "K" seems a character from Genesis, deprived of even the intermittent contact with God that makes its world of exile livable; a figure, too, who steps out of the pages of Avodah Zarah, awash in daily terrors and easy surrenders and confused by the twists and turns which make getting from here to there infinitely difficult. His options are narrowly circumscribed. He can "become a village worker with a distinctive *but merely apparent connection* with the Castle" (my emphasis) or "an ostensible village worker whose real occupation was determined *through the medium of Barnabas*"—a messenger of ambiguous authority (again my emphasis).[7] K, no wise man by any means, opts to be a "fellow-citizen" of the villagers, "if not exactly [a] friend." He supposes that if he becomes indistinguishable from the others "all kinds of paths would be thrown open."[8] The choice, in the terms of modern Jewish history, is not between assimilation and Orthodoxy but between an assimilation in no way possible and a tradition debased and discredited. "This humming and singing transmitted by our telephones is the only real and reliable thing you'll hear," the Mayor tells K. "Everything else is deceptive."[9] In short, K's *political* galut is all too real. "You were discourteous to the Mayor," they charge. "My existence was at stake," he replies.[10] The dialogue is all too familiar; Jews have rehearsed it many times in their long history. But K's *metaphysical* galut is beyond the tradition's most reckless curses. Lacking the dignity conferred by Torah even in exile, he is the caricature of all the faults of *galut* pointed to by the tradition and the Zionists. He is self-deceived, exploitative, calculating, self-pitying, and a liar. He cannot love. What then can he do? How can he escape?

Kafka can take neither the religious path to renewed Jewish meaning proposed in his generation by Buber and Rosenzweig (i.e., renewed metaphysical affirmation) nor the political course to Jewish identity urged by the Zionists (i.e., the granting of political legitimacy and worth to a Jewish state). The modernist course—contentment with the search for meaning, knowing all the while that all meaning is self-imposed—is to him intolerable. At certain points in "The Great Wall of China" (1917) it seems that Kafka's narrator still enjoys the partial protection of the tradition. He knows enough to ridicule a scholar who "proves" scientifically that the Tower of Babel "failed to reach its goal, not because of the reasons universally advanced" but simply "because of the weakness of the foundation."[11] Traditional faith is beautifully articulated. But this Deuteronomic language of fulfillment is untrue to Kafka's situation. It soon gives way to talk of a "high command" that no longer represents either God or legitimate political authority, but only the distant incomprehensible organizational apparatus which is the hallmark of Kafka's world. The narrator's inquiry must be "purely historical." His trust in the wisdom of the wall is long gone. He must "seek for an explanation of the system of piecemeal construction which goes farther than the one that contented people then."[12] Of course there is none.

Yet the story concludes—not without irony, but not without a certain seriousness—that only "a certain feebleness of faith and imaginative power on the part of the people . . . prevents them from raising the empire out of its stagnation." Their weakness unites the people and constitutes the "very ground on which we live." The narrator refuses to undermine them. "And for that reason I shall not proceed any further at this stage with my inquiry into these questions."[13] Kafka could help rebuild neither the wall of faith nor the alternative wall of political homecoming, behind which would-be believers such as Yehezkel Kaufmann preferred to face the larger terrors to which Kafka directed their gaze.

At certain points in "Investigations of a Dog" (1922)—written, reports Marthe Robert, at the time of Kafka's nearest approach to Zionism[14]—the critique of galut existence seems a precise translation into parable of Kaufmann's *Golah Ve-Nekhar*. The investigator, like Kaufmann, is still close enough to his tradition to be shocked at dogs who "uncover their nakedness" and at other dogs who casually condone such sin.[15] But he stands too far from traditional faith to uncover the secret to dogdom's survival. Kafka is concerned with more than the Jews here. Ordinary life had become awesomely difficult for everyone. Galut, as the rabbis and Kabbalists taught, had come to include all the world. Others besides the Jews had failed in their search for an escape because they "prize freedom higher than anything else. Freedom! Certainly such freedom as is permissible today is a wretched business. But nevertheless freedom, nevertheless a possession."[16] Political authority had been corrupted, and Kafka sees no metaphysical authority worthy of the sacrifice of his freedom. And so the saving commitment eludes him. Exile is complete, and Kafka dies in it.

Weber urged a different course. He concludes the second of his two essays on the possibility of political legitimacy and metaphysical affirmation, "Politics as a Vocation" and "Science as a Vocation" (1918), with the warning that the situation of the West "is the same as resounds in the beautiful Edomite watchman's song of the period of exile that has been included among Isaiah's oracles [21:11]: 'He calleth to me out of Seir. Watchman, what of the night? The watchman said, The morning cometh, and also the night: if ye will enquire, enquire ye: return, come.' "[17] One could "inquire," like Kafka's canine investigator and his historian of China's Great Wall. But such inquiry leads nowhere; indeed, it is made more poignant by Weber's argument in "Science as a Vocation" that the worth of scientific inquiry is beyond objective proof. Science, and the process of "rationalization" of which it is the "most important fraction," place in doubt the ultimate value of all that falls under their disenchanting lens—including the value of science itself. What does the word *vocation* mean, Weber wonders, when the sense of calling is entirely subjective? How can one call a "vocation" the very pursuit which deprives every end of ultimate meaning and denies that ultimate truth is objectively available? The way to the good state—political legitimacy—leads through knowledge of the good, and that metaphysical affirmation, like all others, is now impossible. Hence the temptation to "inquire"—which Weber rejects. "The people to whom this was said has enquired and tarried for more than two millennia, and we are shaken when we realize its fate. From this we want to draw the lesson that nothing is gained by yearning and tarrying alone, and we shall act differently."[18]

The characterization of Jewish exile which Weber offers here and elsewhere in his work suffers from the same caricature that we found in Scholem and Klatzkin. Jews did far more in two millennia than "yearn" and "tarry." Weber's conceptualization of the Jews as a "pariah people" burning with *ressentiment* has justifiably drawn sharp criticism.[19] But the essentials of his description are not wrong. Jews did lack "autonomous political organization," suffer "political and social disprivilege," and exhibit a "far-reaching distinctiveness in economic functions."[20] No less important, one can and one should beware of Weber's conclusion that to "set to work and meet the 'demands of the day' in human relations as well as in our vocation . . . is plain and simple, if each finds and obeys the demon who holds the fiber of his very life."[21] Weber knows better. No serious moral decision is plain and simple if "different gods struggle with one another, now and for all times to come."[22] And how can such an advocate of sober ethical responsibility fall back in the last resort on appeal to an inner "demon" and its direction? Again, however, the message is no less clear for all that—particularly to Jews—and no less valid. If one wants to inquire, inquire. Far better to "return, come," even if the political and metaphysical ground for that return are imperfectly prepared.

The "ethic of responsibility" which Weber teaches in "Politics as a Vocation" demands that one take responsibility for the political realm even if moral certainty is lacking, and even if other ethics, just as values, are compromised in the process. Such sacrifices are the essence of the pursuit of politics, and politics must be pursued, though its "decisive means . . . is violence."[23] It is for all that a vocation—and I believe we do not distort Weber's intent overmuch if we interpret the Jewish people's return to the vocation of politics after two thousand years as a response befitting the injunction to "return, come."

Jews have done so, for the most part, in full awareness of the dilemmas to which Weber and Kafka point. Hence their unwillingness to call their return a homecoming, pure and simple. Bereft of the guidance which alone makes for a true vocation, no activity in the political world can be a perfect homecoming. The historical context of disenchantment brought on by modernity and deepened by the Holocaust precludes deception in this regard, as do the traditional texts which we have examined. Only the messianists, reading both history and scripture as a cipher, can march right past Weber's question and Kafka's, oblivious to their century. Other Israelis, and the Americans who share responsibility for their fate, cannot. If Herzl and Ben Gurion vainly regarded the Jewish state as an attempt "to eradicate the deeper truth of unhousedness, of an at-homeness in the word,"[24] that is no longer true of most Israelis, as we have seen. The secularists among them seek only the incomplete protecting walls of a Jewish army, land, and language. They have difficulty believing their state a homecoming precisely because it too is in part an apparatus of bureaucracy and coercion. Its officialdom too is a trial, its legitimacy somewhat suspect. Jews have come too late to nationalism to enjoy its trappings innocently. They have a new nation but an old conscience. Religious Israelis seek to augment this limited realm of protection with the recovery of the "forces of tradition" which enabled Kafka to name the debased *devarim* of the century so accurately. Their confidence is sometimes excessive, but one can with some confidence trust the tradition to temper it. That tradition is after all the source of Weber's warning, and of Kafka's. It knows that we live "somewhere else."

From this I draw two conclusions regarding present debate over Jewish exile and homecoming. First, certain options for solution to the Jewish version of what we now know to be more universal dilemmas are now closed. Certain definitions of what Judaism should be, and related assumptions concerning the nature of humanity, are firmly behind us. It is inconceivable to me that a contemporary Jew could invoke the authority of Kafka's awful knowledge in order to make the case that, in George Steiner's words, "our homeland" is still "the text." "How can a thinking man, a native of the word, be anything but the most wary and provisional of patriots? . . . The locus of truth is always extraterritorial." Steiner approvingly cites the "Orthodox answer to Zionism." The "imperilled, brutalized condition of the present State of Israel, the failure of Israel to be Zion, prove the spurious, the purely expedient temporality of its re-establishment in 1948." He concedes that he has no right to this answer, for he stands outside its faith assumptions. "But its intuitive and evidential strength can be felt to be real."25

No. The answer comes too late. Kafka has taught the West, and particularly its Jews, too much. What we fail to learn from his stories is supplied by the deaths of his sisters in the camps. The Orthodox who deny the legitimacy of what Zionism has wrought are still bound by the laws of the Torah, the sanctity of the Land, and responsibility for their fellow Jews. Steiner is obligated by none of these. Even American Jews who question the state's centrality and assert the legitimacy of exile, choosing coexistence with the state because they have different ideas of it and of themselves, would never revert after statehood and the Holocaust to Rosenzweig's definition of their eternal essence, much less to its hollowed-out Steinerian rescension. Choices have already been made and are binding. It is madness to ask Jews to choose galut over the admitted moral compromise and cultural provinciality of political homecoming on the grounds that the homeland of the text had "concentrated within Judaic sensibility unique strengths and purities of disinterested purpose."26 Scholem's words on the subject are conclusive. "No benefit redounded to the Jews of Germany" for their status as "classic representatives of the phenomenon of man's estrangement or alienation from society." Exile and alienation constituted rather a "powerful accusation."27 Nor can one blithely propose to Jews that they accept Kafka's vision of the world as normative and seek meaning within it as best they can. That is not possible for them, as it was not possible for him. "To do justice to the figure of Kafka in its purity and its peculiar beauty," Benjamin concludes, "one must never lose sight of one thing: it is the purity and beauty of a failure. . . . There is nothing more memorable than the fervor with which Kafka emphasized his failure."28 Jews are commanded rather to choose life.

Because Jews have made this choice, for the most part, in full awareness of the political and metaphysical dilemmas which I have outlined, their conversation over exile and homecoming cannot but be both anxious and unresolved. Jews have opted for a state at a time when political legitimacy is suspect as never before, and have reached for metaphysical affirmation at a time of unprecedented secularization. This isolates them as seriously as the climate of world opinion or their own withdrawal. It seems at times to give Israelis something of the character in the eyes of the world that the messianists have assumed within the Jewish state. To attempt true homecoming is to command attention, and no little suspicion, for reasons of which Jews at home in their history and their tradition are well aware.

All the more remarkable, then, that the sense of homecoming is as secure as it seems and the debate with the doubting diaspora generally civil rather than shrill. Israelis can boast achievements far surpassing Weber's tragic vision, not to mention Kafka's. The desert has bloomed, Hebrew has been revived, a Spiritual Center to world Jewry has been established, and steps have been taken in the difficult direction of an authentic Israeli Jewish culture. This would be no small achievement in any age, and how much less so in ours when Israelis must struggle against the double burden of an era which knows exile intimately but speaks of home only nostalgically and a tradition which teaches Jews how to live in exile, counsels against self-deception in the matter of homecoming, but must be adapted to the unprecedented reality of a state somewhere else, between the two.

Time will tell whether this enormous adjustment is possible, or whether impatience or despair will intervene and force Israelis to settle for a lesser homecoming, a greater exile. Here "inquiry" *is* no longer possible. As Scholem said, we can only wait.

NOTES

Introduction

1. Czeslaw Milosz, "The Nobel Lecture, 1980," *New York Review of Books* 28:3 (March 5, 1981): 11–15.

2. Yehezkel Kaufmann, *Golah-Ve-Nekhar* (Exile and estrangement), 2 vols. (Tel Aviv: Dvir, 1962).

3. For an introduction to the literature on messianism see Gershom Scholem, *The Messianic Idea in Judaism* (New York: Schocken Books, 1971). On Zionism see most recently David Vital, *The Origins of Zionism* (Oxford: Clarendon Press, 1975). On *ḥurban*—destruction or catastrophe—see the fine recent studies by Alan Mintz, *Ḥurban: Responses to Catastrophe in Hebrew Literature* (New York: Columbia University Press, 1984), and David G. Roskies, *Against the Apocalypse: Responses to Catastrophe in Modern Jewish Culture* (Cambridge: Harvard University Press, 1984). The final conceptualization of this study is greatly indebted to both works. Finally, on the idea of the Land of Israel, see W. D. Davies, *The Gospel and the Land: Early Christianity and Jewish Territorial Doctrine* (Berkeley: University of California Press, 1974) and *The Territorial Dimension of Judaism* (Berkeley: University of California Press, 1982); Lawrence Hoffman, ed., *The Idea of the Land of Israel* (South Bend: Notre Dame University Press, 1986); and Eliezer Schweid, *Moledet Ve-eretz Ye'udah* (Homeland and a land of promise) (Tel Aviv: Am Oved Publishers, 1979).

4. New York: Schocken Books, 1977. Baer focuses on medieval and early modern sources treated in the present study only in passing.

5. Ari Elon, *"Higi'u Shamayyim ad Nefesh"* (loosely translatable as "As much heaven as one could stand"). *Shdemot* (Sivan 1980), 11.

6. Eliezer Schweid, *Judaism and the Solitary Jew* (Hebrew; Tel Aviv: Am Oved Publishers, 1975), 79.

7. See most notably the *Pentateuch with . . . Rashi's Commentary*, tr. M. Rosenbaum and A. M. Silbermann, 5 vols., (London: Shapiro, Vallentine and Company, 1930); and *Ramban: Commentary on the Torah*, tr. Charles B. Chavel, 5 vols. (New York: Shilo, 1971).

8. The salient exceptions to this generalization are the works of Jacob Neusner and Gershom Scholem, both of whom figure in the contemporary debate examined in chapters 6 and 7. I cite both frequently throughout, particularly in Chapter 3.

9. E. A. Speiser, "The Wife-Sister Motif in the Patriarchal Narratives" in *Biblical and Other Studies*, ed. Alexander Altmann (Cambridge: Harvard University Press, 1963), 15–28. See also Speiser's commentary to Genesis in the Anchor Bible series (Garden City: Doubleday, 1964) at relevant verses.

10. Michael C. Astour, "Political and Cosmic Symbolism in Genesis 14 and in its Babylonian Sources" in *Biblical Motifs: Origins and Transformations*, ed. Alexander Altmann (Cambridge: Harvard University Press, 1966), 65–112.

11. My methodology in this respect is similar to that enunciated by W. D. Davies in his related study of the idea of homeland in classical Judaism. Davies writes of that idea that "Not the mode of its origin matters, but its operation as a formative dynamic, a seminal force in the history of Israel. The legend of the promise entered so deeply into the experience of the Jews that it acquired its own reality." Davies, *Territorial Dimension*, 8. The substance and methodology of the present work are

also indebted to a mirror image of this study by a leading Israeli thinker engaged in the Zionist enterprise of "negation of the diaspora." See Schweid, *Homeland*, 9–13.

I. Not Yet Home: Genesis

1. Compare W. D. Davies, *Gospel*, 25–27. See also Moshe Greenberg's comments on Ramban's usage of the midrash. Moshe Greenberg, "The Relation between the Jewish People and Its Land in the Bible," in *On the Bible and Judaism* (Hebrew, Tel Aviv: Am Oved Publishers, 1984), 110–24.

2. I have used the translation of the Jewish Publication Society (Philadelphia: 1962) throughout, except where a more literal reading better serves the purpose of this analysis. Here JPS translates "to till and tend it."

3. On the distinction between *eretz* and *adamah*, see Davies, *Gospel*, 15–16 and 87, n. 26. See also Gerhard Von Rad, *Old Testament Theology*, vol. 1, translated by D. M. G. Stalker (New York: Harper and Row, 1962), 159.

4. Speiser attributes both of these stories—indeed the bulk of Genesis from 2:4b to Chapter 25—to the J source, though other scholars take exception to that generalization. See Speiser, 28–29.

5. Alternatively, "more cursed than the ground." Compare Rashi with Ramban here.

6. Rashi on *na va-nad:* "you have no permission to dwell in any one place." On the land of Nod: "In a land in which all exiles wander." Ramban observes that Cain must "eternally be an exile, for the punishment of murderers is exile." He relates Cain's total alienation from the soil to the covering of its bloodstain that sowing and planting would have afforded. Martin Buber suggests that Cain's wandering only mirrors his inner lack of direction, a reading supported by the text's injunction that "sin is the demon at the door, whose urge is toward you, yet you can be his master." See Martin Buber, *Good and Evil* (New York: Charles Scribner's Sons, 1952), 81–89. On Cain's pollution of the earth with the blood of his murdered brother, see Tikve Frymer Kensky, "The Atrahasis Epic and Its Significance for Our Understanding of Genesis 1–9," *Biblical Archeologist* 40:4 (December 1977): 153–54.

7. Abarbanel comments that just as Adam was not satisfied with nature as God set it before him, but rather followed his lusts for more, so the tower builders were dissatisfied with their lot and sought to be city dwellers (*medina'im*) rather than farmers (*b'nei sadeh*). They mistakenly believed that the highest human good lay in urban society, with all its honor, possessions, violence, theft, and bloodshed— unknown in peaceful agricultural settings, where man lives separately from his neighbours. For more on the possible anti-urban thrust of these narratives see Shmaryahu Talmon, "The 'Desert Mofit' in the Bible and Qumran Literature" in Altmann, *Biblical Motifs*, 31–37.

8. Thereby continuing, according to Rashi, the extended wandering which brought him there. Abraham "would wander and go from nation to nation, from one kingdom to another, until he came to the land of Canaan and God said to him: 'To your seed I will give . . .'" Ramban sees in this wandering—indeed, in all the patriarchs' adventures—a foreshadowing of the destiny of their descendants. "All that happened to the fathers is a sign for the children." See his commentary to 12:6.

9. On the wife-sister narratives, see Samuel Greengus, "Sisterhood, Adoption at Nuzi and the 'Wife-Sister' in Genesis," *Hebrew Union College Annual*, 46 (1975): 5–32: see especially p. 26. For an older view see the works by Speiser cited in note 3 to the Introduction.

10. The meeting takes place, significantly, in Egypt—the furthest point on the northeast-to-southwest axis that has linked all of Genesis's narratives, from Nod, to Eden, to Babel, to Haran, and finally to Canaan.

11. For a typical defense of Abraham by the medieval Jewish commentators, see the interpretation of the passage by Ramban.

12. Ramban believes, in fact, that it was Abraham's custom to practice this deception in all his wanderings, not because host populations were wont to prey on alien women but because such women were often brought to the local king, who would then kill their husbands. Avimelekh, in his view, was a "good and honest man" who would never have done such a thing. Abraham, however, had only his experience with the Pharaoh—and possibly others—to rely on. Speiser attributes the first and third occurrence of the story to the J source, and this one, the second, to P.

13. He even casts part of the blame on God, who "made me wander"—or "err"—from "my father's house." Ibn Ezra: the meaning is that he was traveling from place to place, not knowing where he was going. Ramban: "God exiled me from my place . . . and thus it is said (Deut. 26:5), 'A wandering Aramean was my father'—because he was exiled from there."

14. Lest we should think the text unaware of the repetition, we are told explicitly (26:1) that the famine which impelled Isaac's journey southwest was "distinct from the first famine which occurred in the days of Abraham." Moreover, God tells Isaac not to continue all the way to Egypt, but to stay in the land which He will point out. According to Ramban, Isaac heard how well his father had done in *his* trip to Egypt and hoped to prosper there too. God must therefore intervene. Was wife snatching, then, a risk that he was willing to incur? Perhaps, he thought, it will happen anyway, no matter where I go—as in fact it did, in Gerar, where it had occurred to Abraham and Sarah. Always seeking a "sign for the children" in these narratives, Ramban finds in this exile to a place where Isaac's father had dwelt a hint of the future exile of Israel to the land of their fathers—Babylonia. Isaac's not losing Rebecca to Avimelekh, and his suffering only "exile" and its attendant "fear," thus foreshadowed the relatively painless character of that exile. Ramban seems to imply that in the first wife-sister story Pharaoh does sleep with Sarah. His thoroughgoing reading of every event as a portent of a later one is a mirror image of the approach of modern scholars, who believe that texts describing earlier events have been written, or at least edited, under the impact of the later history.

15. Rashi and Sforno agree that "this is the king." Shadal disagrees.

16. A description surely linked to the later Pharaoh's ideological defense for his anti-Israelite policies: cf. Ex. 1:9.

17. In the covenant which introduces the rite of circumcision (17:8), God has promised that Abraham's seed would one day receive "as an eternal possession" (*ahuza*) the "land of their sojourn" (*megurekha*—cognate to *ger* or "alien" and *gar* or "dwell"). Isaac, sending his son Jacob to their ancestral home to the northeast in order to find a wife, similarly transmits the promise that he and his seed would someday "possess the land where you are sojourning" (28:4). Speiser notes that a resident alien apparently could not acquire holdings routinely, hence the special negotiation recounted here and the exorbitant sum paid. Davies (*Gospel*, 23) attributes the story to P.

18. Neḥama Leibowitz directs us to this midrash in Genesis Rabba (79:7). "R. Judah b. R. Simon said: This is one of the three places regarding which the nations of the world cannot taunt Israel and say, 'Ye have stolen them.' These are they: the cave of Makhpelah, the [site of the] Temple, the sepulchre of Joseph." *Midrash Rabbah—Genesis*, vol. 2, tr. H. Friedman (London: Soncino, 1961). See Neḥama Leibowitz, *Studies in the Book of Genesis* (Jerusalem: World Zionist Organization, 1972).

19. Abraham's previous attitude to the Canaanite powers had been limited to a wary awareness. When his herdsmen quarrel with Lot's (13:7; cf. 12:6), the text's reminder that "the Canaanites and Perizzites were then dwelling in the land" strikes much the same tone as the distant drumbeats of hostile Indian tribes in films about American cowboys. Abraham, of course, has no supporting cavalry. Sforno makes a

similar point: because the Canaanites and Peruzzites were there, "an argument between two alien brothers would make them undesirable in the eyes of the natives—they would think them quarrelsome people."

20. Astour's study of this chapter (see Introduction, note 10)—a passage which he claims (p. 65) has attracted more attention from Biblicists than any other single chapter of the Pentateuch—is masterful. The attention has come, in his view, from the search for evidence which would document the historicity of Abraham.

21. Ramban, commenting on Jacob's appeasement of Esau (a similar case of prudence), points out that such pragmatism vis-à-vis gentile powers is a feature of exile that recurs time and again.

22. Abraham sends Isaac, and he Jacob, back "home" to the northeast to take wives among the people from whom the partners to the covenant had sprung. Ishmael by contrast can marry whomever he wishes, and Esau, having heard his father's injunction to Isaac against Canaanite women, only shows his unfitness for the covenant by comically hastening to marry—an Ishamelite (28:1, 6–9). For him, family is family. What could be wrong in marrying your cousin—as did your brother and father before you? We, however, understand the lesson that is beyond him. One can negotiate for a gravesite with the Hittites, one can trade and make treaties with them, but one cannot marry them. Political and economic alliances are inescapable. Family alliances are forbidden.

23. My preferred reading, and that of Leibowitz and Sforno. The latter speculates that trade was forbidden to aliens.

24. Ramban, alone among the commentators, raises the possibility of a third option: inducing the circumcised Shekhemites to join in the worship of Abraham's God, thereby following in the footsteps of Abraham, who "acquired souls [for God] in Haran." He is especially critical of Simeon and Levi, arguing that although the people of Shekhem and of all the seven nations of Canaan were idolaters and engaged in forbidden sexual relations and other abominations, and thereby worthy of execution, Jacob and his sons had no right to carry out that judgment—hence the curse of Simeon and Levi in Chapter 49. They alone murdered the townspeople. Sforno is more understanding, first claiming quite reasonably that Shekhem and his fellows only agreed to circumcision in the hope of gaining the Israelites' possessions, then arguing that Canaanites deserved to die because rapes such as this one were quite common among them and went unpunished.

25. It is inevitable that sex be the node at which conflict is joined, for two reasons. Most obviously, Israel's distinction will be preserved among a surrounding majority only if it refuses to intermarry with them. Equally important, sex as the most prominent of human desires comes to stand in this text—as in so many others, of whatever time and place—for the desires as a whole. The authors of Genesis are neither the first group nor the last to have attributed illicit or uncontrolled sexual desire to their neighbors. See especially Genesis 9:22–25; 19:4–9, 30–37; and 39:7–19. On the last case of "gentile" lust—that of Potifar's wife for Joseph—Rashi (drawing on the rabbis: Sotah 13b) even infers that Potifar himself desired sexual relations with Joseph. (It is perhaps noteworthy, given the stories of Noah and Lot on the one hand and much later associations on the other, that drunkenness does *not* play a role in the narratives of Canaanite or Egyptian lust.) It may be, of course, that these tales represent but one more example of a group projecting its own repressed desires onto outsiders whom it fears, a conjecture lent textual support by Reuben's incestuous liaison with his father's concubine (35:22) and Judah's relation with a "prostitute" who turns out to be his daughter-in-law (chapter 38).

26. Ramban: "because he did not want them to live as aliens in the land," though they had announced their intention "to reside temporarily . . . not to settle."

27. The traditional commentators even speculate that Joseph had the Egyptians moved "to remove the shame from his brothers—[now] no one would call them

exiles" (Rashi). He would thereby afford the brothers "consolation from their own estate of estrangement" (Abravanel). If Joseph's family had to be homeless, in other words, let all of Egypt be homeless with them. This reading, I think, stems more from the commentators' own feelings about exile and Gentiles than from the *pshat* of the text. Rashbam and Rashi are closer to the mark, explaining that the policy was designed to ensure that the Egyptian population could no longer lay claim to its lands. Rashbam even draws an analogy to the forced removals of Israelites carried out in 722 B.C. by Sennakharib of Assyria. Shadal argues that *"le-'arim"* should not be read "to cities" but "by cities," that is, moved group by group, with no loss of prior village ties. Speiser, who attributes the Joseph cycle to J and E, with marginal interpolations by P, reads *he'evid . . . la'avadim:* "he enserfed them." A transfer of population, in his view, would have been neither practicable nor useful. Like the traditional commentators, he finds nothing shocking in Joseph's actions, since Pharaoh was the de facto owner of Egyptian lands from the beginning. Of all the commentators Abravanel is the shrewdest in analyzing the story of Joseph, no doubt because of his own experience at the Spanish court—and his subsequent expulsion with the rest of Spanish Jewry. He notes, for example, that Pharaoh had Joseph marry Osnat so that her powerful family of priests could assist Joseph and strengthen his position. It was that marriage which first made Joseph famous. Abravanel also states, without textual basis, that while Egyptian officials at court could not speak against Joseph (Abravanel logically assumes that they wanted to!), he was in great danger during his travels through Egypt. Only by God's mercy did he remain unharmed.

28. The commentators, Abravanel included, refuse to see this, preferring to believe that God blessed all of Egypt—saw it through the famine—as part of Joseph's blessing. Egypt therefore survived because of the very policies which we find objectionable. I think, however, that we do not stray far from the *pshat* in surmising that Pharaoh has set Joseph over Egypt, at least in part, because the Hebrew alien can be trusted to carry out the ruler's policies without question. For Joseph, being an alien, has no power base from which to confront the king and can be disposed of whenever the situation warrants it.

29. Cf. Davies, *Gospel*, 12.

30. On the patriarchs' graphic nonpossession of the Land, see Von Rad, 169.

31. The term *sole power* and the point made here are Buber's. See Martin Buber, *Moses: The Revelation and the Covenant* (New York: Harper Torchbooks, 1958), 74–79. On the further moral dynamics of Israelite relations with outsiders, and specifically the theme of trust, see the fine analysis of the Judah-Tamar story (Gen. 38) in Robert Alter, *The Art of Biblical Narrative* (New York: Basic Books, 1981), 3–12.

32. This is the essence of the Deuteronomist philosophy of history, discussed further in the following chapter.

33. On Esther, see the Anchor Bible edition, introduced and translated by Carey A. Moore (Garden City: Doubleday, 1971) and Sandra Beth Berg, *The Book of Esther: Motifs, Themes and Structure* (Missoula: Scholars Press, 1979).

34. For an account of an anti-Semitic incident during the Middle Ages in which the various motifs discussed in this chapter figured crucially, see Yosef H. Yerushalmi, *Zakhor: Jewish History and Jewish Memory* (Seattle: University of Washington Press, 1982), 48.

II. Imagining Home: Deuteronomy

1. For a fine analysis of Deuteronomy's language and composition: see Robert Polzin, *Moses and the Deuteronomist: A Literary Study of the Deuteronomic History, Part One* (New York: Seabury Press, 1980), chapters 1–2, especially pp. 17, 26. Gerhard Von Rad, in his *Studies in Deuteronomy*, translated by David Stalker

(London: SCM Press, 1953), calls Deuteronomy "finished, mature, beautifully pro-portioned and theologically clear." See p. 37.

2. On the work's structure, see the masterful study by Moshe Weinfeld, *Deuteron-omy and the Deuteronomic School* (Oxford: Clarendon Press, 1972), preface and pp. 1–81; Von Rad, *Studies*, 53; S. R. Driver, *A Critical and Exegetical Commentary on Deuteronomy* (Edinburgh: T. and T. Clark, 1902), preface; Peter C. Craigie, *The Book of Deuteronomy* (London: Hodden and Stoughton, 1976), 22; Polzin, chapters 1–2.

3. On the dating of Deuteronomy's various strands see part 4 of this chapter and the notes cited therein.

4. The valley, called "House of Peor," is presumably the site where the idol was worshipped. I believe that the midrashic license I have taken here exposits the intent of the *pshat*. Cf. 4:46, where Moses locates the site of his *davar* as "opposite" (*mul*) Beth Peor, in the "land of Sihon," a king whom the Israelites had already defeated with God's help. Their location is thus doubly significant.

5. Von Rad, *Old Testament Theology*, 220.

6. As Von Rad notes (*Old Testament Theology*, 118), Israel is now pictured as a unit rather than a collection of tribes, and God judges it as such.

7. On the difficulty of Moses' task of persuasion compare Machiavelli, *The Prince*, chapter 6.

8. Polzin correctly notes (pp. 32–34, 61) that Deuteronomy's author draws upon the authority of Moses precisely as Moses drew upon God's. He is the sole transmit-ter and interpreter of the Message.

9. Rashi seems to have this in mind when at 11:13 he comments that the repetition of the word *hear* means: if you listen to the old, you will be able to hear the new. Polzin shrewdly observes (p. 19) that the dialectic between event and interpretive lens that we find in Deuteronomy—with far more space devoted to the latter than the former—holds true of the Deuteronomic history introduced by the book as a whole. In the overall effort, however, narration of events far outweighs interpreta-tion—for the key to understanding has already been provided, in Deuteronomy. The narrator, in Polzin's view, is claiming that his work is the true explanation of various events in Israel's history, from its "incursion" into the Land (!!) to its "exile" out of it. See Polzin, 63. According to Von Rad, Deuteronomy seeks to explain why Israel's exile is devoid of saving history (until God acts to end it). He goes on to say that Deuteronomy's emphasis upon interpretive theology rather than narrative history is a function of the fact that Israel had "no real history" during its exile and so was prone to "theological constructs." Von Rad, *Old Testament Theology*, 126, 344. As we will see, Zionist historians will make precisely the same claim.

10. As Ibn Ezra notes, with hindsight (4:10), Jews cannot observe the command-ments properly under pagan rule. I believe he had more in mind than the laws conditional upon residence in the Land.

11. Rashi, commenting on 11:12, writes that God is especially solicitous of the Land of Israel and through it, as it were, extends His care to all other lands.

12. See Chapter 1 of this book and Davies, *Gospel*, 15–16. As he points out (187, n. 26), the distinction between *eretz* and *adamah* is fluid. The text occasionally (cf. 11:17) uses one term when one expects the other.

13. See, for example, Von Rad, *Old Testament Theology*, 47, 178, 338; Moshe Weinfeld, "Deuteronomy: The Present State of Inquiry," *Journal of Biblical Litera-ture* 86 (1967): 256–61; and Jon D. Levenson, *Sinai and Zion* (Minneapolis: Winston Seabury Press, 1985).

14. As Von Rad puts it, if God is One, there can be only one revelation, one cult, and one Temple. See his *Old Testament Theology*, 227, and see 185 on God's one name.

15. This is, I believe, the definition of culture which Deuteronomy would provide

if pressed—and translated. For its contemporary articulation see Philip Rieff, *The Triumph of the Therapeutic* (New York: Harper Torchbooks, 1966), 1–27. Rieff is also the source of the term *sacred order,* the meaning of which he stipulates in a forthcoming book by that title.

16. JPS, following the Targum of Onkelos, translates "it will be to our merit" (Onkelos has *zekhuta*). Such a reading is supported by 24:13, but I think it loses the force intended by the text. For verses supporting my own reading see 9:4–6. As a rule, JPS understates, tones down, Deuteronomy's quite powerful rhetoric.

17. This is, I realize, a somewhat controversial claim on my part. I believe that it accords with the text's *pshat.* Polzin spends a good deal of time contrasting verses such as 4:2 and 13:1, which forbid addition to or subtraction from "the *davar* that I command you," with (1) the promise of a prophet who will provide new instruction and (2) God's own subsequent departure from the commandments, for example by permitting Israelites to retain booty captured in the conquest of Canaan. In his view the latter verses are intended to undermine the authority of Moses claimed by the former. See Polzin, 34–51 passim, and 59. I disagree. The *davar*—that is, the way of *mitzvah* here set forth, direction, the "word"—is to be followed literally. Cf. 5:29: "Be careful to do as the Lord has commanded you. Do not stray to the right or the left; follow only the path which the Lord your God has commanded you." The path is the *davar,* and it is this (13:1) which may not be altered. Any counter-*davar,* proposed by a false prophet (cf. 18:21–22) is to be ignored (a point missed by the JPS reading "oracle"). God's deeds on behalf of Israel in the wilderness as a *davar* (1:32). Forbidden acts in the Israelite camp sanctified by God's presence are called "*ervat davar*"—a *davar* which should not be seen, again missed by the JPS "unseemly." Out-and-out contradiction of the way's provisions is precluded. But the text does not preclude adjustment to altered circumstances. It provides, if you will, for an oral law, bounded by the circle of the way it inscribes. Moreover, as numerous lawgivers have testified, that which is most essential to a law code cannot be legislated. Cf. Rousseau, *Social Contract,* Book 2, chapter 12.

18. Ibn Ezra, sensitive to the disabilities of the weak, notes that the alien, orphan, and widow have no power to redress wrongs done them by the judicial system. See his commentary to 27:19. These commands, as Davies points out (*Gospel,* 24–25), also underscore that we and all we have belong to God.

19. There are two interpolations here—16:21–22 and 17:1—which forbid pagan poles or pillars and the sacrifice of sheep or oxen which have serious "blemishes" or defects.

20. A similar case could be made regarding the injunction against consuming the blood (or *nefesh,* "life force") of a creature—perhaps linked to the prohibition against "stealing a *nefesh*" (24:7), i.e., kidnapping.

21. The linguistic basis for this distinction is the fact that apportionment of the Land—inheritance by individual tribes—comes only once conquest is complete (cf. 3:2).

22. Rashi, following the rabbis of the Talmud and the Passover Haggadah, takes this as a reference to Laban's maltreatment of Jacob. Ibn Ezra believes that it refers to Jacob's poverty. Shadal reads it as the wandering of all the forefathers. Driver links it to Jacob as well and asserts that the text here disparages his foreign connections—a reading I find inexplicable. He notes that the root meaning of the verb *avod* applies to sheep who have strayed from the flock. See Driver, 289. Davies notes that by bringing first fruits (as by observing the sabbatical year), the Israelite testified to God's ownership of the Land. See Davies, *Gospel,* 24–25. Abraham Halkin, in a reading parallel to the one presented here, cites the "pictures of fulfillment" provided in Ps. 144:12–15 and 65:10–14. See the essay "Zion in Biblical Literature" in his anthology *Zion in Jewish Literature* (New York: Herzl Press, 1961), 20. Finally, on Deuteronomy's picture of homecoming in general, see the fine essay by Moshe Greenberg cited in Chapter 1, note 1.

23. At 4:26 and elsewhere, JPS translates *avod* as "perish," at 7:24 "vanish," at 9:3 and elsewhere "destroy," at 26:5 "fugitive"—an indication of the word's variety of connotations. *Avod* is the verb used by Deuteronomy to express what we, following Jeremiah and other texts, have come to call *galut*. See note 33.

24. The facts have all too often kept pace with Deuteronomy's rhetoric. I cite only one example, perhaps modeled to a degree on that rhetoric: the description by Josephus of the siege of Jerusalem in 72 A.D., as quoted by Michael Walzer in *Just and Unjust Wars* (New York: Basic Books, 1977), 161. "The restraint of liberty to pass in and out of the city took from the Jews all hope of safety, and the famine now increasing consumed whole households and families; and the houses were full of dead women and infants; and the streets filled with the dead bodies of old men. And the young men, swollen like dead men's shadows, walked in the market place and fell down dead where it happened. And now the multitude of dead bodies was so great that they that were alive could not bury them; nor cared they for burying them, being now uncertain what should betide themselves. And many endeavoring to bury others fell down themselves upon them. . . . And many being yet alive went unto their graves and there died. Yet for all this calamity was there no weeping nor lamentation, for famine overcame all affections. And they who were yet living, without tears beheld those who being dead were now at rest before them. There was no noise heard within the city."

25. "The stranger in your midst shall rise above you higher and higher"—the verb *aloh* is used four times!—"and you shall sink lower and lower" (28:43). Note the fear of the alien expressed by the text, the consequences of which Israelite aliens had themselves experienced—and would again.

26. Rashi, following Targum Onkelos, reads a related verse, 29:25, to say that the Israelites will worship gods who had done nothing for them—given them no "inheritance or portion." JPS rather reads "whom He [i.e., God] had not allotted to them." The fact that Israelites would pay tribute to gods who had not earned their gratitude is, in Rashi's view, only one more aspect of their shame. Ramban notes that all the awful punishments enumerated until this point were inflicted on the Israelites inside their Land, in order to drive them out. The only curse outside the Land is idolatry— that and the fear which inevitably accompanies exile: "Because of our fear in *galut* among the nations, who constantly impose evil decrees upon us." For the rest, Israel's condition would be like that of the Gentiles among whom they lived. God promises in the covenant mentioned here (28:69), Ramban believes, to preserve Israel so long as the exile endures—a reading unsupported by the *pshat*.

27. On this debate see, most recently, Edward Greenstein, "The Torah as She Is Read," *Response* 14:3 (1985): 17–40.

28. On the matter of authorship see Weinfeld, preface and 1–6, 52; Polzin, 9, 14, 18; Driver, preface and 93–94; Von Rad, *Studies*, 23, 37–41, 65–83. See also notes 1–2.

29. See Weinfeld, 69–81; Craigie, 22.

30. Weinfeld, 116–26. If he is correct, the Jew who came in the world's eyes and his own to be the symbol of the wandering alien had borrowed the imagery for that quite universal condition from a foreign source!

31. Plato, *The Republic*, translated by Desmond Lee (New York: Penguin Books, 1974), lines 498d, 492e, 501d, and 499c respectively.

32. Polzin, 71. Rashi notes that 30:3 could literally be read to mean "And the Lord your God will return you with your return and have compassion for you." Such a reading formed the basis of the rabbinic tradition that God had gone into exile with Israel and would return to the Land only when they did. The point will loom large in Chapter 3.

33. Cf. Solomon Mandelkern, *Concordantiae* (Jerusalem: Schocken, 1975), 363–64. About one-fourth of all usages in the Hebrew Bible occur in Jeremiah. Ezekiel, II Kings, Ezra, and Amos also recur to the word frequently. *Golah* refers to an exiled

population and not to the place of its exile: cf. Ezek. 3:11. *Galut* can refer to either the population or the act of exiling them, functioning as a gerund—cf. Jer. 24:5. Almost always it is Judah or Jerusalem or Israel which is exiled. Two usages refer to the removal of God's glory (I Sam. 4:21, Hos. 10:5). Mandelkern relates the verb *galoh* to the same root meaning "to reveal." The exile stands exposed in his weakness. More plausibly, Abraham Even Shoshan in his *Ha-milon he-ḥadash* (Jerusalem: Kiryat Sefer, 1977), relates the root to *galal* or *galgal*—to move or roll (see vol. 1, 341).

34. A text invoked by those who wish to stress the positive aspects of exile. See also Jer. 24 and Ezek. 17, cited by Davies, *Gospel*, 38. For a discussion of the idealization of the desert or the nomad in Israelite literature see Davies, 75–85, and Talmon, 31–37.

35. Cf. Talmon, 40, who also makes the "spatial" versus "temporal" distinction and distinguishes three different usages of *midbar*.

36. See, for one example of many, Ezekiel's term *midbar 'amim*, the "wilderness of the nations," and *midbar eretz mitzraim*, the "wilderness of the land of Egypt," 20:34–35. See Davies's discussion of those usages, *Gospel*, 83.

37. Davies, *Gospel*, 81–87; Talmon, 47, 60. The latter sees a progression: idealization of the desert period abates after the first destruction, possibly as a result of "the re-experience of actual wilderness-desolation conditions." In Deutero-Isaiah the "*rite de passage*" or "purification" connotations of *midbar* are overshadowed by the "divine benevolence theme." After the destruction, furthermore, the focal image of renewal is no longer the land itself, but Jerusalem and its monarchy and Temple.

38. I have borrowed this term from Gershom Scholem, who applied it to the reinterpretation of biblical and rabbinic terms by Hasidism. See "The Neutralization of the Messianic Element in Early Hasidism" in *The Messianic Idea in Judaism* (New York: Schocken Books, 1971), 200.

39. Davies, *Gospel*, 88.

40. For the logic of this consult Lev. 16, where the people's sins are carried off by a goat to the wilderness, or Ex. 32:20, where in order to utterly destroy the golden calf Moses has it burned, ground into powder, drowned in water—and then drunk by the Israelites. Following Davies (*Gospel*, 53, 101) we should note that the wilderness lay *beyond* the boundaries so carefully marked out by Deuteronomy. Now that the order within had become impure, the only true divine community, seeking purity, was forced to live in exile. On these "exiles of the desert" see Davies, 100–103, and Talmon, 61.

41. Davies, *Gospel*, 121.

III. Homeless at Home and Abroad: Avodah Zarah

1. The original formulation of many *mishnayot* may of course have taken place earlier, before the destruction. These too, however, would have reflected the struggle to resist Roman domination over the Jewish time and space of the Land. On the dating of the tractate, see Jacob Neusner, *Judaism: The Evidence of the Mishnah* (Chicago: University of Chicago Press, 1981), 62, 96, 144–46. Except for a few stipulations ascribed to the period "between the wars," that is to say between 70 and 135 C.E., most of the Order of Damages, which includes tractate Avodah Zarah, is attributed to the period after 135. The assumption here that the Mishnah as a whole can be understood as a response to the catastrophes of 70 and 135 is of course indebted to Neusner's pioneering work. See especially *Judaism*, 1–44.

2. W. D. Davies argues (*Gospel*, 4) that rabbinic theology, borrowing its philosophical tools and methods from Christianity, neglected "such awkward, particular" doctrines as the Land—part of an "unconscious concern to make Judaism in some way doctrinally comparable to Christianity." Yet he goes on to note (56) that fully

one-third of the Mishnah is preoccupied with the Land and that as much as nine-tenths of certain Mishnaic orders are devoted to that concern. Presumably for Davies law is unrelated to theology—a fundamental misreading of the rabbinic corpus. Gerson Cohen's claim that in most rabbinic theology Palestine is ignored as a "central pillar" is very different and, I believe, substantially correct. See parts 2 and 3 of this chapter and Cohen's essay "Zion in Rabbinic Literature," in Halkin, 38. It should be noted once again in this connection that in treating this tractate of the Mishnah I am not making the claim ascribed by Hyam Maccoby to Jacob Neusner (erroneously, I believe)—that the Judaism of the Mishnah's authors "can be fully described on the evidence of the Mishnah alone." See Hyam Maccoby, "Jacob Neusner's Mishnah," in *Midstream* (May 1984): 24–32, quote on 26.

3. It is paradoxical—but necessary, I believe, for reasons made clear in this chapter—to describe the situation of the people of Israel living in and upon the Land of Israel after 70 (and even before!) as a return to exile. Eliezer Schweid writes that exile in the full sense began only with the destruction, when "even the Land of Israel became more and more of a galut" (Schweid, *Homeland*, 37–39). The historian Gedaliah Alon, by contrast, insists that we regard the entire rabbinic period as one of transition to a true *galut* which began only with the Muslim conquest. Yet the conditions even before that conquest, by his own account, came perilously close to satisfying the sixfold definition of exile which he sets forth (Gedaliah Alon, *The Jews in Their Land in the Talmudic Age*, vol. I, tr. and ed. Gershon Levi [Jerusalem: Magnes Press of Hebrew University, 1980], 4–6). We, like the rabbis, cannot be so fastidious in our definition of Israel's situation; while preserving the distinction between Israel and other lands, they defined its condition in terms of the biblical depiction of exile, as we shall see. On the talmudic usages of the root *galoh* see Chaim Josua Kasowski, *Thesaurus Talmudis* (Hebrew) (Jerusalem: Ministry of Education and Culture, 1961), 231–36. Almost all the usages refer to expulsion—primarily from the Land, but also from one's native town to a "refuge city" or from one's home to another place (e.g., Berkhot 3a: "woe to the sons who are exiled from the table of the fathers").

4. Ephraim Urbach notes that the conventional doctrine of reward and punishment underwent a crisis during the Hadrianic persecutions. Not only did the righteous suffer, but their resolve to observe the commandments was itself the cause of their suffering or even death. See E. E. Urbach, *The Sages: Their Concepts and Beliefs*, tr. Israel Abrahams (Jerusalem: Magnes Press of Hebrew University, 1975), 442. Responses to this crisis of explanation were various and not our focus here. For a fine recent study see Mintz, chapter 2; and see Baruch Bokser, "Rabbinic Responses to Catastrophe: From Continuity to Discontinuity," *Proceedings of the American Academy for Jewish Research* 50 (1983): 39–61; idem, *The Origins of the Seder* (Berkeley: University of California Press, 1984), 1–10, 76–100.

5. Thus the famous *aggadah* (Menahot 29b) in which Moses, granted a vision of the great second-century scholar Akiba, asks why Akiba had not been privileged to receive the Torah instead of himself. "Be silent," God replies, "for this is the way I have determined it." Moses then asks to see Akiba's reward—and is shown Akiba's flesh "being weighed at the market stalls" after execution by the Romans for disobeying the ban on teaching Torah. When Moses questions God about this, he is again told, "Be silent, for this is the way I have determined it."

6. Neusner, *Judaism*, 78. The quotation below is from Jacob Neusner, *Method and Meaning in Ancient Judaism* (Missoula: Brown Judaic Studies/Scholars Press, 1979), 131.

7. We should note at the outset, with Neusner, the scriptural texts concerning idolatry on which the Mishnah relies: Exod. 22:13, 23:24, 23:32–33, 34:12–16, Deut. 7:11, 7:25–26, 12:2–3. See *The Talmud of the Land of Israel: A Preliminary Translation and Explanation. Vol. 33: Abodah Zarah*, tr. Jacob Neusner (Chicago: Univer-

sity of Chicago Press, 1982), 1–3. For Neusner's outline of the Tractate and its logic, see 3–6.

8. The reference is apparently to trade fairs at which idolatrous worship was routine. See Alon, 137–38. The passage recalls the Deuteronomic proscription on a king taking Jews on the road back to Egypt (17:16), a ban which God pointedly threatens (in the litany of curses) to defy (28:68; see also 28:27, 60).

9. *Basilicae.* Alon notes (211) that Jewish courts had no jurisdiction in capital cases.

10. The rabbis' intent, Alon writes (286), was apparently "to forestall the permanent settlement of foreigners in the Land of Israel, by preventing them from acquiring land and other economically important property (a description which did not apply to ordinary moveables)." The restrictions likely responded to the perceived danger, after 70, that large numbers of aliens would settle in Judea and displace the Jewish people from its native soil. Cohen notes (Halkin, 46) that much rabbinic legislation has an "irridentist flavor," the point being to keep Jews in Palestine and reclaim lands not already in the possession of Gentiles. The first great fact of Jewish history in talmudic times, he continues (50), was that Palestine was not entirely in Jewish hands and that a large percentage of the Jewish people was not in Palestine. Shmuel Safrai agrees with these assessments, noting that the battle to keep the Land in Jewish hands began in the second century and continued until the Arab conquest, spurred by the trend of Jewish emigration. Ruined towns were a feature of the landscape after 135, with the central hill land of Judea by and large bereft of Jewish population. See his essay "The Era of the Talmud: 70–640," in H. H. Ben Sasson, ed., *A History of the Jewish People* (London: Weidenfeld and Nicolson, 1979), 309, 334. Finally, we should observe, with Neusner, that the rabbis' concern with the lands of Israel and Syria betrays their larger concern with orders of sanctification, the demarcation of holy and profane. The Mishnaic stipulations dealt with a literal "ambiguity at the frontier"—the border of the Holy Land. Syria was both inside and outside the "frame" constructed by the rabbis' stipulations, and therefore required special attention. See Neusner, *Judaism,* 260.

11. There may have been grounds for such fears: see the article on "Inns, Restaurants" in the *Oxford Classical Dictionary,* 2nd edition, ed. N. Hammond and H. Scullard (Oxford: Clarendon Press, 1979), 547–48.

12. Cohen similarly attributes the rabbis' hostility toward Gentiles to the "humiliation and helplessness" of the Jewish nation. See Halkin, 48. But perhaps we should not ignore the factor of routine xenophobia, common to many peoples in the best of times. Strangers have rarely been welcomed, and rarely without fear. The same has been and remains true, to a degree, of travelers. See, for example, the survey of Japanese attitudes in Chie Nakane, *Japanese Society* (Berkeley: University of California Press, 1970), 134–35. As for the rabbis, Neusner (under)states their position succinctly: "Gentiles are assumed routinely to practice beastiality, bloodshed and fornication, without limit or restriction. This negative image finds expression in the text before us" (*Talmud,* 3). Finally, there may have been economic motives underlying or reinforcing some of the rabbis' restrictions, particularly those regarding trade in wine and oil. Alon (7, 164) observes that these two products dominated Israel's commerce. See also the classic study of these matters by Louis Ginzburg, *On Jewish Law and Lore* (Philadelphia: Jewish Publication Society, 1955), 79–86. Alon (277) attributes the prohibitions on selling Gentiles small cattle (1:6) to the age-old conflict between herdsman and farmer. The fields and orchards so basic to the Israelite economy required defense.

13. See the talmudic discussion (44b) where the rabbis, stimulated by Gamaliel's dubious reply to Proclus, become entangled in a series of apparently conflicting rulings which must be reconciled. The medieval commentators known as Tosafot are alert to this effort and join in. Rabban Gamaliel provokes a related controversy in the Yerushalmi (1:9) by reportedly praising the beauty of a Gentile woman. The rabbis

explain that he did not say, in blessing, "May no harm befall you" but only "blessed is he in whose world are beautiful creatures!"

14. The rabbis would of course have added the words "as it were" at this point, enabling them to articulate their dilemma and their doubt without trampling, theologically, on God's absolute freedom and transcendence.

15. Neusner sees the tractate's concluding preoccupation with libation wine as the principal illustration of its overriding concern: transactions with the gentile world. Avodah Zarah, he notes, follows upon three tractates devoted to maintaining "perfect stasis" *within* Israelite society. Its basic conception is implicit in scripture, but the problems dealt with in the tractate are an independent response to contemporary realities, libation wine being a case in point. Israelites believed idolaters capable of making such libations "on every possible occasion." Hence the "wholly Mishnaic . . . shape and interests" of the tractate, even if its "basic principle is Scriptural." See *Judaism*, 144, 202.

16. That is: Proclus in the bath, the elders at Rome, and a discussion (115) of a verse from the Song of Songs (1:2).

17. Neusner, *Method*, 1–2.

18. Neusner, *Judaism*, 28–47.

19. Neusner, *Judaism*, 257–61, 88, 78.

20. This, according to Neusner, is true of the Mishnah as a whole. See *Method*, 167.

21. Ironically, perhaps, Israel did *not* stand alone among the nations of Late Antiquity in its division between homeland and diaspora, "place" and "freedom from place." "Almost every religion in Late Antiquity occurred in both its homeland and in diasporic centers," according to Jonathan Z. Smith, whom Neusner cites (*Method*, 150–51).

22. These commandments include, by most enumerations (cf. Sanhedrin 56b), prohibitions on theft, bloodshed, forbidden sexual relations, and idolatry; the blessing of God's name; the establishment of courts of law; and abstention from the practice of eating flesh torn from a living animal. For further clarification of the concept see Maimonides, *Mishnah Torah, Hilkhot Isurei Bi'ah* 14:7; *Hilkhot Melakhim* 8:9–11, 10:3.

23. Eliezer Diamond points out (private communication) that these four figures also witnessed to Jewish loyalty to God in the face of oppression or temptation, according to scripture and/or midrash.

24. Note however that R. Joshua b. Levi, expounding (4b) the verse "The ordinances which I command thee this day to do them" (Deut. 7:11) is careful to explain that "this day is the time in which to do them, but not to be rewarded for them." That would have to wait for the world to come.

25. Two further comments in the Gemarra bear directly on our concerns. The rabbis discuss (5a) whether human beings, had they not sinned, would have been immortal—and as a result would have given no thought to having children. R. Yosi, in the course of this debate, offers the thought that Israel, rendered mortal like all men since the Garden, had accepted the Torah at Sinai so that the angel of death would no longer have dominion over them.

26. Neusner notes that the most striking feature of the rabbis' list of Persian festivals (8b) is its lack of information on the correct names of the holidays, their meaning to the Persians, or the nature of other holidays. See Jacob Neusner, *A History of the Jews in Babylonia. Vol. 2: The Early Sasanian Period* (Leiden: E. J. Brill, 1966), 88.

27. See also 21a where the question is whether it should be forbidden to rent Gentiles houses in Syria. Since renting is itself a safeguard, comes the reply, "shall we then go on making another safeguard to guard it?"

28. Recalling the idyllic relations of peaceful equality between Rome and Jerusa-

lem in the persons of the Roman ruler Antoninus and Rabbi Judah and the Prince, the codifier of the Mishnah. On the identity of Antoninus see the Soncino translation of the Talmud: *The Babylonian Talmud*, ed. and tr. I. Epstein (London: The Soncino Press, 1935), *Nezikin*, vol. 4, 50.

29. It is beyond our purview either to date the several strands of the Gemarra's discussion or to relate the picture of Jewish-Gentile relations presented in the tractate to the realities of life in "Babylonia"—that is to say, Persia of the third–fifth centuries. Suffice it to say that while Palestinian Jews in the early third century were enjoying relatively tolerant Roman rule, Babylonian Jews who had been accustomed to influence at court and participation in international affairs under the influence of the Parthians now found themselves, under the Sasanian dynasty, out of favor and "merely passive observers of events." The Sasanians, Neusner adds, were "far less accommodating of Jewish interests," particularly during a period of great intolerance at the start of the dynasty. Better relations ensued under Shapur I, depicted in rabbinic tales as a good friend of R. Samuel (see note 32). It was Samuel who formulated the Jews' acceptance of gentile rule in the famous dictum "the law of the land is the law." While Palestinian Jews could never grant legitimacy to a pagan ruler of the Holy Land, the Jews of Persia could accept the fact that they were "sojourners in a land not their own, though not possessed by anyone else either." Such *galut* harmony was of course not without its price. When the Jews of Caesarea were massacred in 260 as part of Shapur's assault on Palestine, Samuel refused to allow public mourning for fear of permanently alienating the ruler. Neusner notes that while Jews and Gentiles shared considerable economic and social interaction during this period, the rabbis continued to view pagans as "utterly estranged from God," regarding their rites as abominations and their lives as inherently immoral. For a fine sketch of these issues see Neusner, *History*, xii, 27–28, 39, 65–69, 79. The lesson of good Gentiles and bad is if anything clearer still in the Yerushalmi (2:3), which avoids speculation and fantasy, focusing instead on the details of Jewish-Gentile interaction. Qualifications of the Mishnah first introduced in the Tosefta (a collection contemporary with the Mishnah) are brought forward, including a teaching (T. Gitin 3:13–14) that if Israelites and Gentiles live in the same city and the latter contribute to charity, Jews are obligated to support the Gentiles' poor, visit their sick, console their mourners, and bury their dead—"all on account of peace." This interaction and the motive for it, however, do not extend to doing business with Gentiles on the days of their festivals. The text also cites stories of rabbis at gentile fairs and teaches (1:4, citing T.A.Z. 1:2) that if a Jew comes across a Gentile on the street, he should ask after the latter's health with due respect. As Neusner notes (*Talmud*, 30), "discrete trends of thought on the topic of the Mishnah" are evident here.

30. Cf. Roskies, 28–30.

31. Recall in this connection the story (16b) of R. Eliezer, arrested one day on the charge of heresy. When the governor asked him how such a wise man could occupy himself with such utter foolishness, he replied, "I acknowledge the Judge as right." The governor, the text tells us, mistakenly "thought that he referred to him—though he really referred to his Father in heaven." As a result of the misunderstanding, the rabbi is pardoned. The implication, of course, is that such confusion of ruling powers with Ruling Power is inherent in idolatry.

32. For more on Shapur, see Neusner, *History*, 7–9, 27–28, 70–71.

33. In Sanhedrin 104a we read that "because idolaters ate [at a Jew's] table, he caused *galut* to his children," and that "anyone who invites idolaters into his house and attends to him, causes his children to go into exile." The case in point is Hezekiah, the prooftext II Kings 20:16–18. Isaiah's warning that idolatry will result in exile is now extended to cover all sorts of intercourse with idolaters. Put another way: the need for demarcation in the wake of *galut* is argued on the grounds that failure to observe such demarcations had caused *galut* in the first place.

34. Logically enough, the discussion then turns to other sorts of defilement (37a–37b), to restrictions on various gentile foodstuffs (37b–38a, 39a–39b), and to specification of the amount of cooking by a Gentile without Israelite supervision which renders that food forbidden to Jews (38a–38b). The circles of prohibition are concentric: from that which cannot be consumed or traded, to that which cannot be eaten but can be traded, so that which can be eaten even though questions remain, and so on to the outer circles of prohibition.

35. *The Republic*, Book IX, 571–72. Recall the desire of Judah for Tamar in Genesis. Rashi, commenting on the prohibition on two women being alone in a room with one Israelite, explains that "women are frivolous, and two of them will turn modesty to transgression." The Gemarra's discussion of the point is long and involved, attempting to fathom and weigh the motives and urges of Gentiles who might be alone with Jews in a variety of situations.

36. Saul Lieberman, *Hellenism in Jewish Palestine* (New York: Jewish Theological Seminary of America, 1962), 120. The rabbis, he notes, never tried to refute idol worship; there was no need. "Unlike the earlier Hellenistic Jews the rabbis were no longer struggling with Gentile paganism. They mostly preached to Jews. To Judaism the mysteries represented no dangers." These comments on earlier generations apply to Amoraim as well. See also 116–18; all of 104–47 are crucial to understanding the rabbis' complex relation to their pagan surroundings.

37. Richard Rubenstein, in the course of a fascinating Freudian analysis of rabbinic *aggadah*, observes that the serpent legends are "paradigmatic. They contain intuitive reflections on the origins of the human community." In one legend (Avot de Rabbi Nathan, 1:5), the serpent plots to kill Adam and wed Eve, thereby becoming "king over all the earth." In a second *aggadah*, bearing directly on our concerns, the rape of Dinah is seen as illustrative of the consequences of sin as such. The prooftext is telling. "And whoso breaks through a fence, a serpent shall bite him" (Eccles. 10:8). The combination of text and commentary yields the association of the serpent with temptation, phallus, competition against Adam for Eve's sexual favors—and the angel of death. Richard Rubenstein, *The Religious Imagination: A Study in Psychoanalysis and Jewish Theology* (Boston: Beacon Press, 1971), 49, 53–54.
As further evidence of fear, see the discussion of whether snakes are afraid of persons who are asleep, during the day and/or at night—as clear a case of projection as one can encounter (30a). The angel of death is invoked explicitly at the end of this section of the Gemarra (35b). The Yerushalmi faces the matter squarely, telling stories of the deaths of the rabbis (3:1). It also (2:2) relates the two themes of snakes and death explicitly. We hear of one Eliezer b. Dama who came to a heretic for healing and dropped dead before he could prove to a critical R. Ishmael that his action was permissible. The prooftext, of course, is Eccl. 10:8, which the rabbi is said to have fulfilled. When the obvious objection is made—R. Eliezer did *not* break through the wall of rabbinic ordinance, death (the serpent) having prevented it, but *was* bitten by death's sting anyway, the unconvincing reply offered is: yes, but he won't be bitten in the world to come. Another serpent story is told on 2:3, provoking this statement of the rabbis' logic by Neusner (*Talmud*, 79). "What snakes will not drink idolaters will not use for a libation." Note the identification of idolaters with snakes (and so with temptation, sin, and death). Finally, see further references to serpents and venom in the Yerushalmi, 2:7 and 2:8.

38. We must recall, as we try to understand the rabbis' logic here, that Gentiles stood outside the system of purity and impurity and so by definition were impure, i.e., not subject to purification. They were not impure because of who they were, in other words, but because of what they were not—subject to the Torah's system of purification. However, more than simple defilement through contact was at work. The Tosefta, for example, notes that minors who do not understand idolatry cannot

render wine a libation. Intention, then, plays a role here. For further clarification on the rules concerning libation wine, see Neusner, *Talmud*, 178, 184, 212.

39. Mendelkern asserts the etymological link in his concordance. See Chapter Two, note 37.

40. *Mekhilta, Tractate Pisḥa*, chapter one. See the *Mekilta de-Rabbi Ishmael*, vol. 1, ed. and tr. Jacob Lauterbach (Philadelphia: Jewish Publication Society, 1976), 5–7 (lines 57–82).

41. Cf. Sanhedrin 10:1, the prooftext for which comes from Isaiah 60:21. "All Israel have a share in the world to come, as it is said: 'Thy people shall all be righteous, they shall inherit the land for ever; the branch of My planting, the work of My hands, wherein I glory.'" For a similar account of the rabbis' objectives, see Schweid, *Homeland*, 37–46.

42. Davies, *Territorial Dimension*, 39. Davies draws an analogy (119–22) between the Land and the episcopate in Christianity, which was seen by some as the very essence (*esse*) of the Church, but to others was only a means to the well-being (*bene esse*) of the Church. The land, in the rabbis' view, was likewise not essential (*esse*) to the existence of Judaism, but a precondition of its full realization (*bene esse*); a great blessing to Jews, in other words, but far from a matter of life and death in the interval between the destruction and the Messiah. Davies is correct here, I believe, and in his larger point (91) that there is no simple or simplistic territorial doctrine of Judaism.

43. Judah Halevi, *The Kuzari: An Argument for the Faith of Israel* (New York: Schocken Books, 1964), 294. See also the claims made for the unique properties of the Holy Land in part one, 78. See also Baer, chapters 5 and 6.

44. Scholem, *Messianic Idea*, 42–48. See also 180–202; and Shalom Rosenberg, "Exile and Redemption in Jewish Thought in the Sixteenth Century: Contending Conceptions," in Bernard Dov Cooperman ed., *Jewish Thought in the Sixteenth Century* (Cambridge: Harvard University Press, 1983), 399–430. See also Baer, chapter 10.

45. The most succinct argument of this position—containing the exposition of Lurianic kabbalah summarized crudely here—comes in Gershom Scholem, *On the Kabbalah and its Symbolism*, tr. Ralph Mannheim (New York: Schocken Books, 1965), pp. 109–17. The last quotation can be found on 112.

46. Scholem, *On the Kabbalah and its Symbolism*, 116.

47. Scholem, *On the Kabbalah and its Symbolism*, 116.

48. Ham Hillel Ben Sasson, "Galut and Redemption in the eyes of the Spanish Exiles" (Hebrew) in *Yitzhak Baer Jubilee Volume*, ed. Shmuel Ettinger and Salo Baron et al. (Jerusalem: Historical Society of Israel, 1960), 222, 227.

49. These developments are traced brilliantly by Jacob Katz in *Exclusiveness and Tolerance* (New York: Schocken Books, 1962), 24–47.

50. Yerushalmi, 57–63. This section of the present study is greatly indebted to his work. See also Baer, chapters 12–14.

51. Haim Hillel Ben Sasson, "The Generation of the Spanish Exiles on its Own Condition" (Hebrew) in *Tzion* 26 (1961): 53–59. Ironically, the lost home lamented by many exiles was not the Land of Israel but their real home—Spain, where security, dignity, and, in some cases, great wealth had been theirs.

52. Ben Sasson, "Generation," 34–47. The quotation from Ben Sasson is on 45.

53. On the *reservatio mentalis* see Katz, 50.

IV. Homecoming: The Revival of the Spirit

1. Theodor Herzl, *The Jewish State*, in Arthur Hertzberg, ed., *The Zionist Idea* (New York: Harper Torchbooks, 1966), 213, 225.

2. Herzl, 222.

3. For a concise statement of its aims see Benedict de Spinoza, *A Theologico-Political Treatise*, tr. R. H. M. Elwes (New York: Dover, 1951), 6.

4. Spinoza, 245: the title of Chapter 19.

5. See Leo Strauss, *Spinoza's Critique of Religion* (New York: Schocken, 1982).

6. Spinoza, 46.

7. Spinoza, 101–102. Spinoza does not seem to take this possibility of a reborn Jewish state very seriously.

8. Spinoza, 44.

9. For more on Spinoza and Jewish return to Zion consult Yosef H. Yerushalmi, "Spinoza on the Existence of the Jewish People" (Hebrew), *Proceedings of the Israeli Academy of Sciences* 6: 10 (1983).

10. Moses Mendelssohn, *Jerusalem* (New York: Schocken, 1969), 61. On the context of Mendelssohn's reinterpretation of galut see Jacob Katz, "The Impact of Jewish Emancipation on the Concepts of Galut and Geulah—Exile and Redemption," *Yearbook of the Central Conference of American Rabbis* (1976): 119–30.

11. Except as a "symbolic script." See Mendelssohn, 71–91.

12. Mendelssohn, 102. On this point see the commentary on *Jerusalem* by Alexander Altmann in the new edition of the work translated by Allan Arkush (Hanover: University Press of New England, 1983), 232–34. On 235 Altmann observes, in agreement with the reading of the text offered here, that in Mendelssohn "the hope to achieve civic equality in exile pushed the messianic expectation of a return to the Holy Land into the background." See also, on this matter, his *Moses Mendelssohn: A Biographical Study* (Philadelphia: Jewish Publication Society, 1981), 207, 424–26.

13. Mendelssohn, 104.

14. Altmann, *Mendelssohn*, 314.

15. Samson Raphael Hirsch, *The Nineteen Letters on Judaism*, tr. Bernard Drachman (New York: Feldheim, 1969).

16. Nachman Krochmal, *Guide for the Perplexed of the Time*, in *The Writings of Nachman Krochmal*, ed. Simon Rawidowicz (Hebrew; Waltham: Ararat Publishing Society, 1961), chapters 8–9; see especially pp. 50–51.

17. Abraham Geiger, *Judaism and its History*, tr. Charles Newburgh (New York: Bloch, 1911), 68. See Geiger's tracing of the mission in chapters 1–6, and, for a periodization of Jewish history, "A General Introduction to the Science of Judaism" in Max Wiener, ed., *Abraham Geiger and Liberal Judaism* (Philadelphia: Jewish Publication Society, 1962), 149–54.

18. Heinrich Graetz, "The Structure of Jewish History" in *The Structure of Jewish History and Other Essays*, ed. and tr. Ismar Schorsch (New York: Jewish Theological Seminary of America, 1975), 65, 69.

19. Moses Hess, *Rome and Jerusalem*, tr. Meyer Waxman (New York: Bloch, 1943), 68.

20. Isaiah Berlin, "The Life and Opinions of Moses Hess," in *Against the Current: Essays in the History of Ideas* (New York: Penguin Books, 1982), 216.

21. The preceding summary is Berlin's.

22. Moses Hess, *Die Heilige Geschichte der Menschheit* (Stuttgart, 1837), 311. In a later essay entitled "Jugement dernier du vieux monde social" (1851), Hess wrote that the Jewish people wanders "like a ghost across the centuries as a just punishment for its *spiritualistic* aberrations." Quoted in Martin Buber, *On Zion: The History of an Idea* (London: East and West Library, 1973), 116. On Hess' early writings as a whole see Jonathan Frankel, *Prophecy and Politics* (Cambridge: Cambridge University Press, 1981), 7–20.

23. Hess, *Rome and Jerusalem*, 43.

24. Hess, *Rome and Jerusalem*, 57–58.

25. Hess, *Rome and Jerusalem*, 62–64.

26. Hess, *Rome and Jerusalem*, 55, 43.

27. Hess, *Rome and Jerusalem*, 40.

28. Buber, 117–18.

29. Hess, *Rome and Jerusalem*, 115–16.

30. Hess, *Rome and Jerusalem*, 157.

31. Hess, *Rome and Jerusalem*, 165–67.

32. Hess, *Rome and Jerusalem*, 260–62.

33. Hess, *Rome and Jerusalem*, 262.

34. Ahad Ha'am, *Complete Writings* (Hebrew; Tel Aviv: D'vir, 1965), 11–14. Most of the essays cited can be found in *Selected Essays of Ahad Ha'am*, ed. and tr. Leon Simon (Philadelphia: Jewish Publication Society, 1962).

35. Ahad Ha'am, *Complete Writings*, 20–22.

36. Ahad Ha'am, *Complete Writings*, 23–26.

37. Ahad Ha'am, *Complete Writings*, 80; *Selected Essays*, 77.

38. Ahad Ha'am, *Complete Writings*, 43–44.

39. Leo Pinsker, "Auto-Emancipation: An Appeal to his People by a Russian Jew," in *Zionist Idea*, 181–98.

40. Pinsker bowed to general pressure on the matter of Eretz Israel, but his own position remained unchanged. See Vital, *Origins of Zionism*, 140.

41. Ahad Ha'am, *Complete Writings*, 45–48.

42. Ahad Ha'am, *Complete Writings*, 1–3.

43. *The Writings of Micah Joseph Bin Gurion (Berdiczewski)* (Hebrew; Tel Aviv: D'vir, 1960), 33. On Berdiczewski's ambivalent relationship to Ahad Ha'am see Arnold Band, "The Ahad Ha'am and Berdyczewski Polarity," in *At the Crossroads: Essays on Ahad Ha'am*, ed. Jacques Kornberg (Albany: State University of New York Press, 1983), 51.

44. Ahad Ha'am, *Complete Writings*, 159–64.

45. Ahad Ha'am, *Complete Writings*, 313–20.

46. Berdiczewski, *Writings*, 38, 106–107.

47. Berdiczewski, *Writings*, 99.

48. Berdiczewski, *Writings*, 20.

49. Berdiczewski, *Writings*, 19, 30, 35–36, 101.

50. Berdiczewski, *Writings*, 20, 27.

51. Berdiczewski, *Writings*, 28. See also 44.

52. Cf. Roskies, 46, 68–70, 75–77, and Mintz, 8, 118–54.

53. Berdiczewski, *Writings*, 64; for Berdiczewski's comments on the need for sovereignty, see 74–79 and 111, and for his critique of Herzl and Dubnow, 81–82, 95, 113.

54. Sigmund Freud, *The Interpretation of Dreams*, tr. James Strachey (New York: Avon Books, 1965), 230.

55. Ahad Ha'am, *Complete Writings*, 154–59.

56. Ahad Ha'am, *Complete Writings*, 406–407.

57. Berdiczewski, *Writings*, 41–42.

58. Simon Dubnow, "Letters on Old and New Judaism" in *Nationalism and History: Essays on Old and New Judaism*, ed. Koppel S. Pinson (Philadelphia: Jewish Publication Society, 1958), 74, 111, 138, 166–68, 175.

59. Dubnow, 131–41, 159–60, 176–78.

60. Dubnow, 176; see Ahad Ha'am's essay "Three Steps" (1897–98) in *Complete Writings*, 150–53.

61. Ahad Ha'am, *Complete Writings*, 399–403, in part conveniently available in Hertzberg, 270–77. For Dubnow's response see "Letters," 175, 180, 188. On the debate between the two friends see Robert Seltzer, "Ahad Ha'am and Dubnow," in *Crossroads*, 60–72.

62. Ahad Ha'am, *Selected Essays*, 254; *Complete Writings*, 174.

63. Ahad Ha'am, *Complete Writings*, 393–94, 421. These arguments are reiterated

in Ahad Ha'am's parting essay "In Sum" (1912), *Complete Writings,* 421–28, which is framed in terms of Moses' parting message to Israel in Deuteronomy.

64. *Selected Essays,* 254; *Complete Writings,* 174.

65. A fitting sobriquet by Arthur Hertzberg; see *Zionist Idea,* 247. See also the critique of Ahad Ha'am's caution by his disciple Menahem Ussishkin, cited by Stanley Nash in "Ahad Ha'am and Ahad Ha'amism: The Onset of Crisis," in *Cross-roads,* 82.

66. A. D. Gordon, *The Nation and Labor* (Hebrew; Jerusalem: World Zionist Organization, 1952), 167–68, 173, 176–77; see also 108, 134, 140–42.

67. See, for example, Gordon, 106, 127, 134, 207, and, for an especially striking passage, 282, where Gordon writes: "Here, before us today, life has revealed the disease of parasitism in all its ugliness and rot. All our strength devoted to healing the nation must be centered in this labor of cure, of surgery, of cleansing of the air." The image is of course Nietzschean, transmitted perhaps by Jewish Nietzscheans such as Berdiczewski.

68. Gordon, 198, 91.

69. Gordon, 257.

70. Gordon, 493–500, 517–21.

71. Gordon, 140, 144, 185, 208, 335. Professor Anita Shapira points out (private communication) that Gordon's position on *avodah zarah* and his use of the term were common among Labor Zionists of his day.

72. Gordon, 190–97, 234, 348.

73. Gordon, 188.

74. Gordon, 447.

75. Gordon, 350–53.

76. Gordon, 501.

77. Gordon, 261, 265.

78. Gordon, 494–97.

79. Gordon, 364.

80. Gordon, 318, 321, 335.

81. See the assessment by kibbutz intellectual Muki Tzur in *Lelo K'tonet Pasim* (Doing it the hard way; Tel Aviv: Am Oved, 1976), 80–84. Tzur comments (82) that Gordon became the symbol among kibbutznikim of the worker and of opposition to intellectual life, a man convinced that his teaching could not be transmitted intellec-tually. For a sophisticated and sympathetic evaluation of Gordon see Eliezer Schweid, *Ha-yahid* (The single one; Tel Aviv: Am Oved, 1970).

82. See the "Three Addresses on Judaism" in Martin Buber, *On Judaism,* ed. Nahum Glatzer (New York: Schocken, 1972), 11–55. Buber's strongest denunciations of *galut* can be found on pp. 29–31.

83. "Three Addresses on Judaism," 18.

84. "Three Addresses on Judaism," 30.

85. "Three Addresses on Judaism," 53, 85, 128–34.

86. See, in particular, Martin Buber, *I and Thou,* tr. Walter Kaufmann (New York: Scribners, 1970); *Israel and the World: Essays in a Time of Crisis* (New York: Schocken, 1963) and *Paths in Utopia* (London: Routledge and Kegan Paul, 1949). On Buber's Zionism see also Laurence J. Silberstein, "Martin Buber: The Social Para-digm in Modern Jewish Thought," *Journal of the American Academy of Religion* 49: 2: 211–23.

87. See for example, "The Man of Today and the Jewish Bible" and "Hebrew Humanism" in *Israel,* 89–102, 240–52; and the recent collection, *A Land of Two Peoples: Martin Buber on Jews and Arabs,* ed. Paul R. Mendes-Flohr (New York: Oxford University Press, 1983), particularly the writings from 1947 to 1949.

88. Martin Buber, "Zion, the State and Humanity: Remarks on Hermann Cohen's

Answer," in Arthur A. Cohen, ed., *The Jew: Essays from Martin Buber's Journal "Der Jude," 1916–1928* (University, Ala.: University of Alabama Press, 1980), 93–96.

89. Buber, *Paths*, 139.

90. Buber, *On Zion*. On the "mystery" of Israel's relation to the Land, see especially xx.

91. Martin Buber, "Religion and Philosophy," in *Eclipse of God* (New York: Harper Torchbooks, 1957), 34.

92. Martin Buber, *Hasidism and Modern Man* (New York: Harper Torchbooks, 1966), 59, 159.

93. Buber, *Eclipse*, 34.

94. Roskies, 276.

95. On this point see the superb study by Marthe Robert, *As Lonely as Franz Kafka*, tr. Ralph Manheim (New York: Harcourt Brace Jovanovich, 1982), 16–20, and Chapter 8 of this book.

96. Cited by Roskies, 72.

97. Shlomo Avineri, *The Making of Modern Zionism* (New York: Basic Books, 1981), 199–200. The essay from which this quotation comes is entitled "From Class to Nation."

98. David Ben-Gurion, "The Imperatives of the Zionist Revolution," in Hertzberg, 606–609.

99. Ben-Gurion, 607, 611–12, 618–19.

V. Homecoming: The Resurrection of the Body Politic

1. Herzl, 204–215.

2. Herzl; quotations on 205, 225, 220, 206 respectively.

3. Herzl, 223.

4. Herzl. For evidence of Herzl's appeal among the East European masses rather than among Western Jews (the constituency he first sought) see Vital, *Origins*, 12–13; and David Vital, *Zionism: The Formative Years* (Oxford: Clarendon Press, 1982), 97, 258–64. On messianism among secular Zionists, see Jacob Katz, "Israel and the Messiah," *Commentary* 36 (1982), 34–41.

5. Herzl, 225.

6. Alex Bein, *Theodor Herzl: A Biography*, tr. Maurice Samuel (Philadelphia: Jewish Publication Society, 1945), 12.

7. Bein, 13–14.

8. Ahad Ha'am, *Complete Writings*, 314–24.

9. Theodor Herzl, *Altneuland*, tr. Paula Arnold (Haifa: Haifa Publishing Company, 1960), 8, 20.

10. Herzl, *Altneuland*, 30–37.

11. Herzl, *Altneuland*, 49–78, 107–109.

12. Herzl, *Altneuland*, 184.

13. Berdiczewski, 76, 82.

14. Herzl, *Altneuland*, 218.

15. Jacob Klatzkin, *Teḥumim* (Hebrew; Jerusalem: D'vir, 1928), 45–54.

16. Klatzkin, 52–54.

17. Klatzkin, 77–80.

18. For a vivid example in the work of a leading Israeli historian see Shmuel Ettinger, "The Modern Period," in Haim Hillel Ben Sasson, ed., *A History of the Jewish People* (London: Weidenfeld and Nicolson, 1976), 727–1096. Note especially chapter 54: "The Failure of Emancipation, the Struggle for Survival and National Rebirth (1881–1848).

19. Klatzkin, 76–77, 98.

20. Klatzkin, 81–83.

21. Klatzkin, 64–68.

22. Klatzkin, 73–75, 86–94, 100–102.

23. Klatzkin, 105.

24. For two analyses see Janet Koffler O'Dea, "Israel With and Without Religion: An Appreciation of Kaufmann's *Golah Ve-Nekhar*," *Judaism* (Winter 1976): 85–97; and Laurence Silberstein, *History and Ideology: The Writings of Yehezkel Kaufmann*, unpublished dissertation, Brandeis University, 1971.

25. Yehezkel Kaufmann, *Golah Ne-nekhar*, vol. I, preface, 6. Chapter one takes up issues such as Marxist materialism, freedom of the will, the independence of culture from economic and political forces, and, briefly, the notion of ethnicity and religion.

26. Kaufmann, chapter 2. The contrasting position on the primacy of language is found on pp. 108 and 120.

27. Kaufmann, 126, 132, 139. See also 146, where full nationhood is said to be based in common ethnicity, blood, and language, as well as a shared high culture.

28. Kaufmann, 151–61, 164.

29. Kaufmann, 166.

30. Kaufmann, 171–202. The point about language is found on 187.

31. Kaufmann, 205–207.

32. Kaufmann, 187, 475, 479, 501; II, 12, 94, 321–27.

33. Kaufmann, I, 501.

34. Kaufmann, I, 204.

35. Kaufmann, I, 205.

36. Kaufmann, I, chapter 5. See especially 214–18; 217 (a particularly apologetic passage which sees Yehudah Halevi's treatment of the Jewish role in the world as "balanced"), 252–55 (a very problematic distinction between *aggadah*—said to be particularist—and *halakhah*—said to be universalist), and 287.

37. Kaufmann, I, 283, 319–21.

38. Kaufmann, I, 321, 330, 338. See also 304, 310–12, 341, 354, 410–11.

39. Kaufmann, I, 333, 433. It should be noted in this connection that Jesus was a preoccupation of many Jewish thinkers in the late nineteenth and early twentieth centuries. See the comments by Roskies, 126–27, 158, 264–72, 280–89.

40. Yehezkel Kaufmann, *The Religion of Israel*, tr. and abridged by Moshe Greenberg (Chicago: University of Chicago Press, 1960), chapters 3–4; *Golah*, vol. 1, 257.

41. Kaufmann, *Golah*, I, 434.

42. See, for example Kaufmann, *Golah*, I, 434, 436, and II, 31, 213.

43. Kaufmann, *Golah*, I, 300.

44. Kaufmann, *Golah*, I, 288, 293, 295.

45. Kaufmann, *Golah*, I, 458–59, 462, 481.

46. Kaufmann, *Golah*, I, 543, 552; II, 173.

47. Kaufmann, *Golah*, I, 472, 505–507.

48. Kaufmann, *Golah*, I, 176, 507–14, 528, 530.

49. Kaufmann, *Golah*, II, 216; see also 194, 218.

50. Kaufmann, *Golah*, I, 45. The idea of Israel's mission was a doctrine of assimilation, Kaufmann charges (75).

51. Kaufmann, *Golah*, II, 8n, 90, 100–104, 303–27.

52. Aviad, 88.

53. Kaufmann, *Golah*, II, 110, 199, 243. Kaufmann, like Klatzkin, also distinguishes *among* the various sorts of exiles in which Jews lived, finding four distinct categories: South Europe, the Anglo-Saxon countries, Germany, and the Slavic nations (220). However, he denies the premise, contained in negation of the diaspora, that assimilation can put an end to galut (227–28, 243). The decline of religion, among Jews *and* Gentiles, would not help in this regard.

54. Kaufmann, *Golah*, II, 421.

55. Kaufmann, *Golah*, II, 470.
56. Kaufmann, *Golah*, II, 275–79, 352–59, 367–69, 379–80.
57. Kaufmann, *Golah*, I, 202.
58. Kaufmann, *Golah*, II, 402.
59. Yehezkel Kaufmann, "The National Will to Survive" (1920) in David Hardin, ed., *Sources: Anthology of Contemporary Jewish Thought* (Jerusalem: World Zionist Organization, 1971), 120–21.
60. Kaufmann, *Golah*, II, 440.
61. Here we see the basis of Vladimir Jabotinsky's extension of Herzl's political Zionism to new heights both of rhetoric and realpolitik. Jabotinsky's masterful addresses combined flights of oratory with simple statements of the realities. The Jews had to leave Europe at once. It was only natural for the Arabs to resist Jewish immigration: never in history had any group of inhabitants agreed to new settlers. The Arabs had not misunderstood the Zionists, but perceived them only too clearly. The only apparent solution was a Jewish homeland under the protection of British guns. Let us then make the necessary political arrangements. Spirit could wait. Jewish bodies needed to be saved. Realpolitik was the only way to save them, the way chosen by every other nation; the way, in other words to normalization. See Ze'ev Jabotinsky, *Medinah Ivrit: Pitaron She'elat Ha-yehudim* (A Jewish state: A solution to the Jewish question) (Hebrew; Tel Aviv: T. Kopp, 1937), 73–74; Vladimir Jabotinsky, *The Jewish War Front* (Westport, Conn.: Greenwood Press, 1978), 214–22 (originally published 1940). See also Avineri, 161–80.
62. An idea therefore criticized by Zionists of every stripe. See Herzl's denunciation in *Altneuland*, 107–109, and Kaufmann's in *Golah*, II, 75. Ahad Ha'am's most famous critique of the Jewish mission comes in his essay "Slavery under Freedom." See the original in *Complete Writings*, 64–69, or the English translation in *Selected Essays*.
63. Kaufmann Kohler, *Jewish Theology: Systematically and Historically Considered* (New York: Macmillan, 1928), 7–8. See also his *Hebrew Union College and Other Addresses* (Cincinnati: Ark Publishing Company, 1916), 24 ("The Jew has at all times been the true cosmopolitan"), 196 (on America as the "God-blessed land of liberty"), and 204 (on America as Zion).
   More sophisticated non-Zionist positions do not differ from Kohler's in substance. For Hermann Cohen (d. 1918), the Jews' "stateless isolation" was itself a symbol for the unity of the confederation of mankind which constituted the "ultimate value" of world history. Indeed, Deuteronomy had taught that Israel's national history was but an idealization from the point of view of its historic task, an opportunity to depict the people's sin in repeatedly relinquishing the true God. See Hermann Cohen, *Religion of Reason out of the Sources of Judaism*, tr. Simon Kaplan (New York: Frederick Ungar, 1972), 254, 263. Realization of the "idea of messianic mankind" was the task of the Jewish people. The Zionists, by contrast, believed that Judaism could be preserved only by an "all-encompassing nationalism." Their writings "abounded in frivolous derisions "of [the] supreme idea of the Jewish religion" and charged that liberal Jews such as Cohen himself were "deluded for feeling at home in the civilized countries in which we are living." Cohen's reply was twofold. First, "no restriction of civil rights must be allowed to make us waver in our sense of obligation and total commitment to the country we claim as our own." (See Hermann Cohen, "A Reply to Dr. Martin Buber's Open Letter to Hermann Cohen" in Alfred Jospe, ed. *Reason and Hope* [New York: W. W. Norton, 1971], 164–70.) The stated objective of a "legally recognized homeland" should be altered by the addition: "for those Jews who have no other homeland." (See "Religion and Zionism," in *Selected Essays from Judische Schriften* [Hebrew; Jerusalem: Bialik Institute, 1977], 89.) Second, "we regard the moral world as it unfolds throughout history as our Promised Land." ("Reply"). This was the only land of any consequence to Cohen besides his own,

Germany. "We must deepen and strengthen our relation to Judaism just as we are commanded to strengthen our relationship to Germanism" ("Religion," 91).

64. Quoted in S. Z. Abramov, *Perpetual Dilemma: Jewish Religion in the Jewish State* (Rutherford, N.J.: Fairleigh Dickenson University Press, 1976), 74.

65. *Franz Rosenzweig: His Life and Thought*, ed. Nahum N. Glatzer (New York: Schocken Books, 1976), 354–56.

66. *Franz Rosenzweig*, 358.

67. Franz Rosenzweig, *The Star of Redemption*, tr. William W. Hallo (Boston: Beacon Press, 1972), 298–301.

68. Rosenzweig, 301–303.

69. Rosenzweig, 331–32.

70. Rosenzweig, 298–99.

71. The star is composed of two triangles: the three "elements" God, world, and humanity; and the three terms of their interrelations: creation, revelation, redemption. Judaism is the fire burning at the star's core; Christianity, the other true faith, is the rays going forth from the star to the world, "ever on the way" between the two.

72. Rosenzweig, 358, 354.

73. On Rosenzweig's relation to Zionism see also Yaakov Fleischman, "Franz Rosenzweig's Blessing of Zionism" (Hebrew) in Akiba Ernst Simon, ed., *On Franz Rosenzweig* (Jerusalem: Magnes Press of Hebrew University, 1956), 54–73.

74. Cf. Berdiczewski, *Writings*, 33.

75. Cf. Abraham Isaac Kook, *Orot* (Lights) (Hebrew; Jerusalem: Mosad Ha-rav Kook, 1963), 151. (The work originally appeared in 1921.) Kook's is the most profound and most influential statement of the messianist positions. For nonmessianist statements by key figures such as Yitzhak Reines, see Aviezer Ravitzky, "The Foreseen: And Freedom Is Provided" (Hebrew) in *Israel—Towards the 21st Century*, edited by Aluf Hareven (Jerusalem: Van Leer Institute, 1985), 135–37, 187–88.

76. The reborn state of Israel is described as such in the prayer for the state added to Sabbath prayers by the Orthodox rabbinate in Israel and now standard throughout the Orthodox world.

77. For a good introduction to Kook's work in English, see Abraham Isaac Kook, *The Lights of Penitence* (and other works), ed. and tr. Ben Zion Bokser (New York: Paulist Press, 1978). For a sympathetic exposition of Kook's oeuvre—tendentious in its liberal reading of Kook's teachings, I believe—see Tzvi Yaron, *The Philosophy of Rav Kook* (Hebrew; Jerusalem: World Zionist Organization, 1979).

78. See the pertinent selections in Hertzberg, 104–114.

79. For an account see Vital, *Formative Years*, 213–29.

80. Abramov, 67–74.

81. See, for example, Kook, *Orot*, 126–27.

82. See, for example, Abraham Isaac Kook, *Ḥazon Ha-geulah* (The vision of redemption) (Hebrew; Jerusalem: Association for Publishing the Works of the Chief Rabbi A. I. Kook, 1941), 275.

83. Kook, *Ḥazon*, 35, 56, 61, 74, 87, 169—but a few examples.

84. Kook, *Ḥazon*, 231, 233.

85. See for example Kook, *Orot*, 9, 20, 77, 88–89, 100–104, 151; *Ḥazon*, 69–70, 78, 85. On pp. 261–62 Kook's routine use of the word *holy* is apparent in the phrases "It is a holy duty to propose" and "the holy connection" (between the Yishuv and Orthodox party in Europe, Agudat Israel).

86. Kook, *Orot*, 9–12, 20, 62, 84.

87. Kook, *Orot*, 22, 34, 59, 100. See also Ravitzky, 148–52, 155–57.

88. Kook, *Orot*, 9, translated in Hertzberg, 419.

89. Kook, *Ḥazon*, 87–90.

90. Kook, *Ḥazon*, 70–72, 76–78, 85; *Orot*, 45–47, 49, 66.

91. Kook, *Ḥazon*, 87.

92. Kook, *Orot*, 77–80; *Lights*, 127.

93. Kook, *Orot*, 82.

94. Kook, *Ḥazon*, 275.

95. Kook, *Orot*, 85.

96. Kook, *Orot*, 44.

97. Kook, *Orot*, 58.

98. On the kabbalistic usage of *gevurah* see Gershom Scholem, *Major Trends in Jewish Mysticism* (New York: Schocken, 1941), 213; and *Kabbalah* (Jerusalem: Keter, 1974), 106–113, 121–23, 163. In Lurianic Kabbalah, Scholem notes, the figures of Cain and Abel represent the forces of *gevurah* and *hesed* respectively, the "restrictive and the outgoing" forces of creation. At present the latter had the upper hand but in the redeemed state or *tikkun* or perfection the ordering would be reversed.

99. Kook, *Ḥazon*, 85.

100. Kook, *Orot*, 59.

101. Kook, *Ḥazon*, 74.

102. Kook, *Ḥazon*, 38–39.

103. Kook, *Ḥazon*, 128.

104. Kook, *Ḥazon*, 71.

105. Kook, *Ḥazon*, 188–96.

106. On this point see Scholem, "Messianic Idea."

107. Kook, *Ḥazon*, 96. For a critique of Kook at this point by an anti-Zionist rabbi, see Ravitzky, 181.

108. Kaufmann, *Golah*, II, 425.

109. Kook, *Orot*, 56.

110. On "statism" see the following chapter and Charles Liebman and Eliezer Don-Yehiya, *Civil Religion in Israel* (Berkeley: University of California Press, 1983), chapter 4.

VI. Between Homecoming and Redemption

1. I rely here and in what follows on the account by Leibman and Don-Yehiya. See also Amnon Rubinstein, *From Herzl to Gush Emunim and Back* (Hebrew; Tel Aviv: Schocken, 1980). The work has recently been issued in somewhat revised form in English under the title *The Zionist Dream Revisited* (New York: Schocken, 1984).

2. *The World Ideological Conference* (Hebrew), *Hazut*, vol. 4 (Jerusalem: Sifriyah Tzionit, 1958), 168.

3. *World Ideological Conference*, 166–67, 202–205.

4. *World Ideological Conference*, 142, 167.

5. See Moshe Davis, ed., *The Yom Kippur War: Israel and the Jewish People* (New York: Arno Press, 1974).

6. See Leibman and Don-Yehiya, chapter 5.

7. See Janet Aviad, *Return to Judaism: Religious Renewal in Israel* (Chicago: University of Chicago Press, 1983).

8. See Chapter 7 of this book.

9. Yeshayahu Leibowitz, *Judaism, the Jewish People and the State of Israel* (Hebrew; Jerusalem: Schocken, 1976), 121–28.

10. Leibowitz, 128–37.

11. Leibowitz, 36–49, 138–47.

12. Cf. Leibowitz, 113–14, 120; and see Chapter 4 of this book.

13. I cannot enter in this context into the thorny subject of Leibowitz's debt to Kant, a matter which has received considerable critical attention elsewhere. See most recently the excellent summary by Enzo Nafi in *Ha'aretz* (April 11, 1985): 16–17; Leibowitz's response in the issue of May 24, 1958: 18–19; and Naomi Kasher, "Leibowitz's Concept of Morality" in *Sefer Yeshayahu Leibowitz* (Hebrew; Tel Aviv:

Students' Organization of Tel Aviv University, 1982), 20–34. Suffice it to say that just as Kant requires that we subordinate our desires to performance of our duty because and only because it is our duty, so Leibowitz requires that Jews subordinate all else to the service of God and perform that service because and only because God requires it. See for example Leibowitz, 22–29, 57–66, and Yeshayahu Leibowitz, *Faith, History and Values* (Hebrew; Jerusalem: Akademon of Hebrew University, 1982), 11–19, 57–66, 74. Hence the presumption that faith can never be a means to any end outside itself, lest it serve us rather than God. Hence, too, the belief that assuming one's obligations to God represents the pinnacle of human responsibility, the only source of human worth. On this point see, for example, Leibowitz, *Judaism*, 22–29.

14. Leibowitz, *Judaism*, 205.

15. Leibowitz, *Judaism*, 145.

16. Leibowitz, *Judaism*, 181–89, 268–73.

17. Leibowitz, *Judaism*, 74–81, 173–75, 268. See especially 173–74, where Leibowitz quotes Ben-Gurion as saying that he wanted the joining of Judaism and the state so that the latter could hold the former firmly in its hand.

18. Leibowitz, *Judaism*, 119; *Faith*, 128–30.

19. Aharon Lichtenstein, "Religion and State: The Case for Interaction," *Judaism* (Fall 1966): 387–89.

20. Lichtenstein, 389–95.

21. Leibowitz, *Judaism*, 91. The essay from which the assertion is taken, "Days of Remembrance" (1949), is an especially lucid example of Leibowitz's thinking.

22. Leibowitz, *Judaism*, 92–93.

23. Leibowitz, *Judaism*, 406–407.

24. Leibowitz, *Judaism*, 167–69, 338–44; *Faith*, 140–44, 166–67. See also the illuminating exchange in *Faith*, 146–55; the essay which follows, 156–63; and *Judaism*, 14–21, 414–15.

25. Scholem, *Messianic Idea*, 3–4.

26. Zevi Yehudah Ha-Cohen Kook, *To the Pathways of Israel* (Hebrew; Jerusalem: Menorah, 1967), 35–36; see also 13.

27. The issue is more than academic among Gush Emunim settlers who follow the teachings of the elder Kook but not those of his son. See David Hanshka, "What is Happening to the *Lights* of Rav Kook?" (Hebrew), *Nekudah* 79 (Marḥeshvan 1983): 12–13, 28.

28. Kook, *Pathways*, 89. On the relation between the thought of father and son, compare Ravitzky, 153–54.

29. Kook, *Pathways*, 171, 188.

30. Kook, *Pathways*, 160; and see the note which follows.

31. Leibman and Don-Yehiya, 198. In a statement (no date given) reprinted in Simon Federbush, ed., *Torah and Kingship* [or "Government"] (Hebrew; Jerusalem: Mosad Harav Kook, 1961), 102–103, Zevi Yehudah contrasts those who "speak of 'the beginning of redemption'" with his own opinion that "this is already the middle of redemption. The beginning occurred hundreds of years ago." What was most needed now was the faith "to recognize the reality" in which Israelis found themselves. Because that reality was one of redemption, Israel's defense forces were "absolutely holy . . . the symbol of the people of Israel's rule over its land. . . . The kingdom of heaven reveals itself in this government—even if it is the government of Ben Gurion." Let us hope, he adds, that we are worthy of seeing Jerusalem rebuilt and whole.

32. Z. Y. Kook, "Clarification," *Amudim* 369 (Tamuz 1976): 380–81; and the statement in Federbush, 102–103. See also Yisrael Ariel, "Is This Really a Rebellion against Authority (*malkhut*)?" (Hebrew), *Nekudah* 73 (May 1984): 16–17, 28. Janet Aviad quotes a statement by Kook that "a war may be required" to prevent return of

the conquered territories. "Our bodies, our lives, all of us is required." See her "Gush Emunim: Roots and Ambiguities," *Forum* 23 (Spring 1975): 39–50.

33. Z. Y. Kook, "Clarification."

34. Uriel Tal, "The Land and the State of Israel in Israeli Religious Life," *Proceedings of the Rabbinical Assembly of America* (1976): 1–40. The essay includes a valuable bibliography of Hebrew sources on this issue. See also Uriel Tal, "Jewish Self-Understanding and the Land and State of Israel," *Union Seminary Quarterly Review* (Summer 1971): 351–82; and Ravitzky, 160–62.

35. Yehudah Amital, "The Ascents from the Depths," quoted in Rubinstein, 112.

36. Z. Y. Kook, *Pathways*, 36. For anti-Zionist readings of the same signposts, see Ravitzky, 168–79.

37. Shlomo Goren, *Torat Ha-Moadim* (Tel Aviv: Avraham Tzioni Publishers, 1964), 312–14, 563–67.

38. See note 34.

39. Yaakov Ariel, cited in Uriel Simon, "Fear of Heaven Without Fear of Sin," *Nekudah* 75 (July 1984): 29.

40. Kook, *Orot*, 9–11.

41. Ephraim Urbach, *On Zionism and Judaism: Reflections and Addresses* (Hebrew; Jerusalem: Sifriyah Tzionit, 1985), 47, 51, 77, 235.

42. Urbach, 49, 52.

43. David Hartman, *Joy and Responsibility: Israel, Modernity and the Renewal of Judaism* (Jerusalem: Ben Zvi Posner and the Shalom Hartman Institute, 1978), 6–7.

44. Hartman, 68, 259–86. See also Leibowitz's critique of the book in *Petaḥim* (Adar 1979): 82–88, and Hartman's reply in the following issue (Elul 1979): 78–83. Hartman's approach accords with that of Ravitzky, 185–97.

45. Hartman, 276. See also the comparison of the diaspora to "spring training," making Israel the major leagues, on 271.

46. Hartman, 256.

47. Compare Leibman and Don-Yehiya, chapters 3–4. They describe Ahad Ha'am as "the unacknowledged founder of Israeli civil religion" on p. 232. See also Eliezer Schweid's observation on the "crisis in secular Israeli culture" in *Judaism and Secular Culture* (Hebrew; Tel Aviv: Kibbutz Ha-me'uḥad, 1981), 222–23.

48. "Towards a Social Zionism" (*Tzionut Ḥevratit*), published by the Seminar for Social Zionism, 1984.

49. A. B. Yehoshua, *On Behalf of Normality* (Hebrew; Jerusalem: Schocken, 1980), 52–53, 66, 129. The work has since been issued in English under the title *Between Right and Right*, tr. Arnold Schwartz (Garden City, N.Y.: Doubleday, 1981).

50. Rubinstein, 151–68.

51. Amos Oz, *Under this Blazing Light* (Hebrew; Tel Aviv: Sifriat Hapoalim, 1979), 74–78. "Grandfather Israel" (*Yisrael Saba*), a term derived from Bialik, connotes Jewish tradition in general and the shtetl in particular—not without a negative resonance.

52. Oz, 74, 144–45; and Amos Oz, *In the Land of Israel*, tr. Maurie Goldberg-Bartura (San Diego: Harcourt Brace Jovanovich, 1983), 135–36.

53. Oz, *Land*, 134–38, 140–42, 149–50; *Light*, 79, 87, 96–99.

54. Oz, *Light*, 99; *Land*, 130–31.

55. Oz, *Land*, 148; *Light*, 75–76.

56. Oz, *Land*, 129–31, 138–40, 148–50.

57. Oz, *Light*, 76–77.

58. Oz, *Land*, 239–40.

59. Oz, *Light*, 147–49.

60. Nathan Rotenstreich, "Reflections on the Contemporary Jewish Condition" (Jerusalem: Institute for Contemporary Jewry of the Hebrew University, 1975), 28.

61. Nathan Rotenstreich, *Tradition and Reality: The Impact of History on Modern Jewish Thought* (New York: Random House, 1972), 98–99, 106, 113–18, 129.

62. Nathan Rotenstreich, *Reflections on Contemporary Zionism* (Hebrew; Jerusalem: Hasifriya Hatzionit, 1975), 74–80, 89–90, 138–40.

63. Rotenstreich, *Tradition*, 107–108, 119–30; and Nathan Rotenstreich, "Secularism and Religion in Israel," *Judaism* (Summer 1966): 259–83.

64. Schweid, *Secular Culture*, 244; compare Rotenstreich, *Tradition*, 122.

65. Eliezer Schweid, *Homeland*. See especially 37–41, 214–21, 228–30.

66. Schweid, *Secular Culture*, 233.

67. Schweid, *Secular Culture*, 231–46. See also Eliezer Schweid, *From Judaism to Zionism, From Zionism to Judaism* (Hebrew; Jerusalem: Hasifriya Hatzionit, 1984), 37–54. On *"Mishpat Ivri,"* see the classic work of that title by Menachem Elon (Hebrew; Jerusalem: Magnes Press of Hebrew University, 1973).

68. See, for example, Schweid, *Secular Culture*, 223–24, 229–30.

69. Schweid, *Homeland*, 230.

70. Gershom Scholem, *Devarim B'Go (Explications and Implications: Writings on Jewish Heritage and Renaissance)* (Hebrew; Tel Aviv: Am Oved, 1976), I, 74.

71. Gershom Scholem, *On Jews and Judaism in Crisis*, ed. Werner J. Dannhauser (New York: Schocken, 1976), 22.

72. Scholem, "Jews and Germans" (1966), *Crisis*, 90.

73. Scholem, "Reflections on Jewish Theology" (1974), *Crisis*, 275.

74. Scholem, "Reflections," 275.

75. "With Gershom Scholem, An Interview" (1975), *Crisis*, 34, 36.

76. Scholem, "Israel and the Diaspora" (1969), *Crisis*, 257.

77. Scholem, "A Speech Concerning Israel" (1974), *Devarim*, 128.

78. Scholem, *Crisis*, 22, 250.

79. Scholem, "Israel and the Diaspora," *Crisis*, 248.

80. The following account concurs with and expands upon that of David Biale, *Gershom Scholem: Kabbalah and Counter History* (Cambridge: Harvard University Press, 1979).

81. Scholem, *Messianic Idea*, 3–4.

82. Scholem, *Crisis*, 1–17, 61–92.

83. Scholem, *Messianic Idea*, 35.

84. Scholem, *Crisis*, 286–89.

85. Scholem, *Crisis*, 2.

86. Scholem, *Crisis*, 43.

87. Scholem, *Crisis*, 45.

88. Scholem, *Messianic Idea*, 35.

89. Ismar Schorsch, "On the History of the Political Judgment of the Jews" (New York: Leo Baeck Institute, 1976).

90. Biale, 172.

91. Scholem, *Messianic Idea*, 35–36; cf. Scholem, *Crisis*, 26: "I am not an anti-messianist. I have a strong inclination toward it. I have not given up on it." Biale notes (184) that Scholem edges up to the messianic abyss, but is ever careful to keep a prudent distance.

92. Scholem, *Crisis*, 289.

93. Scholem, *Crisis*, 22.

94. Gershom Scholem, "Who is a Jew," *Yearbook of the Central Conference of American Rabbis*, 1970, 134–38.

95. Leibman and Don-Yehiya, chapter 5.

96. Haim Hazaz, "The Sermon," tr. Ben Halpern, in Robert Alter, ed., *Modern Hebrew Literature* (New York: Behrman House, 1975), 273–77.

97. Hazaz, 282.

98. Hazaz, 284.

99. Cf. Leibman and Don-Yehiya, chapter 8.

100. Sanhedrin 98a, cited in Scholem, *Messianic Idea*, 13.

101. See the varying perceptions of the museum's message by Nahum Goldmann, Abba Kovner, and Rachel Arbel in *Beth Hatefutsoth—The First Years*, edited by Geoffrey Wigodor (Tel Aviv: Beth Hatefutsoth, 1983), 5–9, 30–32.

VII. Between Homecoming and Diaspora

1. Rotenstreich, "Jewish Condition," 35. On Buber's addresses see Chapter 4 of this book.

2. Gershom Scholem, "The Galut Now Emptied of the Spark of Redemption," 220.

3. Jakob Petuchowski, *Zion Reconsidered* (New York: Twayne, 1966), 88.

4. Ben Halpern, *The American Jew: A Zionist Analysis* (New York: Theodor Herzl Foundation, 1956).

5. Mordecai M. Kaplan, *A New Zionism* (New York: Theodor Herzl Foundation, 1955).

6. See below, sections 2 and 3; and compare Moshe Davis, ed. *Zionism in Transition* (New York: Herzl Press, 1980), 57–77.

7. Leibowitz, *Judaism*, 243. Rotenstreich makes a similar admission in the wake of the Yom Kippur War. See his *Reflections*, 89–90.

8. Rotenstreich, *Reflections*, 79.

9. Scholem, *Crisis*, 250.

10. See Chapter 6.

11. See the discussion in this book, 126–29.

12. Talmud Torah Hebron, in the Gush Emunim settlement of Kiryat Arba, emphasizes the significance of the Land in its curriculum by focusing on the Bible in the early years of schooling and postponing study of the Talmud until high school—a radical departure from the normal pattern of yeshivah education. "We are a school for the children of Eretz Israel. . . . Our job is to create an authentic Eretz Israel education, not to borrow the ideas and methods of the Galut." Yossi Klein Halevi, "Hebron: The Roots of Jewish terror," *Moment* (April 1985): 41. See the portrait of the school's founder and principal, Dan Be'eri, a member of the Jewish terrorist underground, in *Nekudah* 76 (August 1984), 20–21, 29.

13. Leibowitz, *Judaism*, 249.

14. Rotenstreich, *Zionism*, 31–33, 229; and Nathan Rotenstreich, "The Zionist Idea at This Hour" (Hebrew; Jerusalem: Institute for Contemporary Jewry of Hebrew University, 1972), 28.

15. Scholem, *Crisis*, 255–56.

16. Scholem, *Crisis*, 22.

17. Schweid, *Lonely Jew*, 79–82.

18. Schweid, *From Judaism*, 121–37.

19. Schweid, *From Judaism*, 136.

20. Schweid, *From Judaism*, 152.

21. Schweid, *From Judaism*, 155–63. See also Eliezer Schweid, "The Rejection of the Diaspora in Jewish Thought: Two Approaches," *Studies in Zionism* (Spring 1981): 43–69.

22. Schweid, *From Judaism*, 166–67, 181–206.

23. See for example Mordecai Bar-On, "The Lesson for Zionism of the Holocaust" (Hebrew), *Kivvunim* (May 1981): 15–34. Schweid's response, "Yes, Negation of the Diaspora," is cited in the preceding note. A stance similar to Bar-On's can be found in Arye Carmon, "The Need for a Dialogue" (Le Semana Publ. Co. and the Moshe Sharett Institute, 1983). Schweid's answer to my own criticism can be found in *From Judaism*, 196–200: only the State, and not the *golah*, has a secure future.

24. Scholem, *Devarim*, 219.

25. Yehoshua, *Normality*, 27–38.

26. Hillel Halkin, *Letters to an American Jewish Friend* (Philadelphia: Jewish Publication Society, 1977), 12, 24–27.

27. Halkin, 73, 182, 197–98.

28. Halkin, 71, 116.

29. Halkin, 146–51.

30. See the praise for Herzl and condemnation of Ahad Ha'am as an obscurantist who "insisted that the desired effect must also be used as its own cause" by urging the priority of a cultural center. Horace Kallen, *Zionism and World Politics* (Garden City: Doubleday, Page and Company, 1921), 5–6, 76–78, 132–33. Kallen's horror at the religious significance lent the return by marchers at a Jewish parade in New York in 1920 is well expressed on p. 276.

31. Kaplan, *Zionism*, 13.

32. Melvin Urofsky, *American Zionism from Herzl to the Holocaust* (Garden City: Doubleday Anchor, 1975), 128n. On the alleged correspondence between Zionist and American ideals see 129–31, 427–29, and see also Ben Halpern, *The Idea of the Jewish State* (Cambridge: Harvard University Press, 1909), 281.

33. Louis Brandeis, "The Jewish Problem and How to Solve It" (1915) in Hertzberg, *Zionist Idea*, 519–22.

34. Remarkable not only in content but because it was issued despite opposition to the Zionist movement on the part of the Board to whom Schechter was responsible as Chancellor of the Jewish Theological Seminary.

35. Solomon Schechter, "Zionism: A Statement" (1906) in *Seminary Addresses and Other Papers* (New York, Burning Bush Press, 1959), 91–97.

36. Schechter, 97, 102–104.

37. On both the community's self-definition and the thought of Kaplan, see Arnold Eisen, *The Chosen People in America* (Bloomington: Indiana University Press, 1983), chapters 2, 4.

38. Mordecai M. Kaplan, *Judaism as a Civilization: Toward a Reconstruction of American Jewish Life* (New York: Schocken, 1967), 215–16, 267, 273–78. On Dubnow see chapter 4 in this book.

39. Mordecai M. Kaplan, *The Future of the American Jew* (New York: Macmillan, 1948), 124–30, part of Kaplan's discussion of "The Role of Eretz Israel in the Life of Diaspora Jewry." He opposes negation of the diaspora in his chapter on American Jewish education, 433–38, insisting that there be a "two-fold norm" for Jewish life.

40. Kaplan, *Zionism*, 13, 18–20, 41.

41. Kaplan, *Zionism*, 119, 130–31, 139.

42. Kaplan, *Zionism*, 84–124. Zionism was the "remaking of the Jewish people through the remaking of its land," not a "nation on the way" (Herzl) or "the Jewish people on its way back to the land" (Ben-Gurion); 149. See also Kaplan's similar statement before the conservative rabbinate: "Ideological Evaluation of Israel and the Diaspora," *Proceedings of the Rabbinical Assembly* (1958): 137–48.

43. Abba Hillel Silver, *The World Crisis and Jewish Survival* (New York: Richard R. Smith, 1941), 117, 14–42; and *Vision and Victory* (New York: Zionist Organization of America, 1949), 13–16, 212, 218–22, 225–29.

44. Citations from the translation of Simon Rawidowicz's conclusion to *Babylon and Jerusalem* by Frank Talmage, published under the title "Jerusalem and Babylon" in *Judaism* (Spring 1969): 131–42.

45. "The Meaning of Galut in America Today: A Symposium," *Midstream* (March 1963): 3–9. See the response by Nathan Rotenstreich, *Zionism*, Chapter 1.

46. See the opening paragraph of this chapter.

47. *Midstream*; see for example the remarks of Samuel Grunzweig and C. Bezalel Sherman.

48. *Midstream*, 20–23; Ben Halpern, *American Jew*, 12–13, 26–33, 63–67.

49. Halpern, *American Jew*, 38–40, 50, 63–67, 87, 93.

50. Petuchowski, 15–17.

51. Petuchowski, 30–34, 57, 65, 70–76.

52. Petuchowski, 87, 108. We should also note that Petuchowski's anti-Zionism is exceeded by that of the Satmar rebbe. See Allen L. Nadler, "Piety and Politics: The Case of the Satmar Rebbe," *Judaism* (Spring 1982): 135–51.

53. Jacob Neusmer, *Israel in America—A Too Comfortable Exile* (Boston: Beacon Press, 1985), 15.

54. For an especially interesting statement of the consensus position see David Polish, "The Tasks of Israel and Galut," *Judaism* (Winter 1969): 3–16.

55. Arthur Hertzberg, "America is Different" in Arthur Hertzberg, Martin E. Marty, and Joseph N. Moody, *The Outbursts That Await Us* (New York: Macmillan, 1963), 140–63.

56. Arthur Hertzberg, "America Is Galut," *Jewish Frontier* (May 1964): 7–9.

57. Jacob Neusner, *Stranger at Home: "The Holocaust," Zionism and American Judaism* (Chicago: University of Chicago Press, 1981), 1–4.

58. Hertzberg, "America Is Galut."

59. Jacob Neusner, "The Jewish Condition after Galuth" in Elan Levine, *Diaspora: Exile and the Jewish Condition* (New York: Jason Aronson, 1984), 280.

60. Neusner, *Stranger*, 5–6, 10–11, 31, 40–41, 47–48, 103; "Jewish Condition," 274–75.

61. Neusner, "Jewish Condition," 280.

62. Neusner, *Israel*, x.

63. Neusner, *Israel*, 101–105, 144, 160–61, 274–80.

64. For Neusner's rejection of Israeli claims to spiritual centrality, see 143–49, 153.

65. Ben Halpern, "Exile and Redemption: A Secular Zionist View," *Judaism* (Spring 1980): 178–84. See also "The Jewishness of Secular Judaism," *Judaism* (Spring 1981): 225–27, and the reply in the same issue of *Judaism* by Robert Gordis, "Does Secular Judaism Have a Future," 228–32. For pieces written between these and the *American Jew* see Halpern's contributions to Rotenstreich, "Zionist Idea," 9–11; and to "Negating the Diaspora: A Symposium," *Jewish Frontier* (December 1979): 9–10. In the latter he disputes Klatzkin's contention that the *golah* does not deserve to survive, arguing that one cannot say this of any group. We can negate only galut, the condition of exile, and not a *golah* or exilic community.

66. Joseph Soloveitchik, "The Lonely Man of Faith," *Tradition* (Summer 1965): 10.

67. Joseph Soloveitchik, *Halakhic Man*, tr. Lawrence Kaplan (Philadelphia: Jewish Publication Society, 1984).

68. Soloveitchik, "Lonely Man," 10–30.

69. See in particular Soloveitchik, "Lonely Man," 8, 56; and *Halakhic Man*, 41–42, 142–43.

70. Joseph Soloveitchik, *"Kol Dodi Dofek"* in *In Aloneness, In Togetherness* (Hebrew), ed. Pinchas Peli (Jerusalem: Orot, 1967), 333–40, 350–54. See Ravitzky, 149, 192, for usages of this same motif by A. I. Kook—and Yehudah Halevi.

71. Soloveitchik, *"Kol Dodi Dofek,"* 354–62.

72. Soloveitchik, *"Kol Dodi Dofek,"* 362–67.

73. Soloveitchik, *"Kol Dodi Dofek,"* 368–80, 390–400.

74. Compare the fine analysis by Michael Rosenak, "The Jewish Person and the State," (Hebrew) in S. Yisraeli et al., eds., *Jubilee Volume in Honor of Rabbi Joseph Dov Halevi Soloveitchik* (Jerusalem: Mosad Harav Kook, 1984), I, 152–69.

75. Joseph B. Solovetchik, *The Rav Speaks: Five Addresses* (Jerusalem: Tal Orot Institute, 1983), 26–32.

76. Solovetchik, *Rav Speaks*, 36.

77. Solovetchik, *Rav Speaks*, 73–74, 155–56, 198.

78. Solovetchik, *Rav Speaks*, 76–77.

79. Solovetchik, *Rav Speaks*, 47.

80. Joseph Soloveitchik, "*Ma Dodekh Mi-Dod*" in *In Aloneness*, 239–45.

81. Cited by Rosenak, 153.

82. Joseph Soloveitchik, "Concerning Love of the Torah and Salvation of the Soul of this Generation," *In Aloneness*, 424–30.

83. Rosenak, 168.

84. Soloveitchik, "Love of Torah," 430–32.

85. Abraham Joshua Heschel, *The Earth is the Lord's*, in *The Earth is the Lord's and the Sabbath* (New York: Harper Torchbooks, 1966), 13.

86. Heschel, *The Sabbath*, 3, 9, 48, 108.

87. Abraham Joshua Heschel, *Israel: An Echo of Eternity* (New York: Farrar, Straus and Giroux, 1967), 44, 51.

88. Heschel, *Israel*, 113, 115.

89. Heschel, *Israel*, 127–28.

90. Heschel, *Israel*, 130–31.

91. Heschel, *Israel*, 137.

92. Heschel, *Israel*, 136.

93. Heschel, *Israel*, 202.

94. Abraham Joshua Heschel, "*Yisrael: Am, Eretz, Medinah* (People, Land, State): An Ideological Evaluation of Israel and the Diaspora," *Proceedings of the Rabbinical Assembly of America* (1958): 118–19.

95. Heschel, *Yisrael*, 121.

96. Heschel, *Yisrael*, 122–35.

97. But see the reflections on the significance of history for truth in Emil Fackenheim, *Encounters between Judaism and Modern Philosophy* (New York: Basic Books, 1973), 73–76, 87–88.

98. Emil Fackenheim, *God's Presence in History* (New York: Harper Torchbooks, 1972), 6–14. The conceptualization leans heavily on Buber.

99. Fackenheim, 25–30, 67–98.

100. Emil Fackenheim, *The Jewish Return into History* (New York: Schocken, 1978), 131, 184, 228, 231, 282.

101. Fackenheim, *Return*, 40.

102. Fackenheim, *Return*, 23.

103. Fackenheim, *Return*, xii.

104. Fackenheim, *Return*, 282.

105. Fackenheim, *Return*, 160.

106. Fackenheim, *Return*, 113. But see p. 178 on the "imperfect relation" between the theological and political dimensions.

107. Emil Fackenheim, *To Mend the World: Foundations of Future Jewish Thought* (New York: Schocken, 1982), 13–14, 146n, 284–85.

108. Fackenheim, *Mend*, 93–95, 146n, 284–85.

109. Fackenheim, *Mend*, 266, 289–90, 300–302. Fackenheim recognizes that this claim is "the pivotal point of the developing argument of this whole work."

110. Fackenheim, *Mend*, 143–44, 303, 312–13. Arthur Cohen writes that Fackenheim's argument in *To Mend the World* "utterly collapses" on the "other side" (i.e., ours) of the Holocaust. It is all but "drowned" in unsorted examples. That those who took a stand for life thereby began the work of *tikkun* is an excellent device of rhetoric, but is as nothing in the face of Fackenheim's rage, in the first part of the book, before philosophy and its deceptions. Such "patchwork argument" can hardly lay the "foundations of future Jewish thought." Arthur Cohen, "On Emil Fackenheim's *To Mend the World: A Review Essay*," *Modern Judaism* 3: 2 (May 1983): 231–35.

111. Fackenheim, *Return*, 40.

112. Fackenheim, *Mend*, 28.
113. See this book, 148, 151.
114. See this book, 151.
115. See this book, 152–53.
116. Abraham Joshua Heschel, "The Theological Dimension of Medinat Yisrael," *Proceedings of the Rabbinical Assembly* (1968): 102.

Conclusion: "K," "Pariah," Zionist, Jew

1. The following discussion draws extensively on the researches into Orthodoxy of Charles Liebman. See, most conveniently, *Civil Religion in Israel*, chapters 7–8. The American situation is treated in my *Chosen People*, chapters 6–7.
2. Joseph Soloveitchik, "Confrontation," *Tradition* (Winter 1964): 18–23.
3. Cited by Scholem, *Crisis*, 82.
4. George Steiner, "Our Homeland, The Text," *Salmagundi* 66 (Winter–Spring 1985): 13–16.
5. Steiner, 13.
6. Walter Benjamin, "Franz Kafka: On the Tenth Anniversary of His Death," in *Illuminations*, ed. and tr. Hannah Arendt (London: Collins/Fontana Books, 1973), 128; "Max Brod's Book on Kafka," *Illuminations*, 146. The following discussion of Kafka is heavily indebted to these two masterful essays.
7. Franz Kafka, *The Castle*, tr. Willa and Edwin Muir (New York: Vintage Books, 1974), 31.
8. Kafka, *Castle*, 31–32.
9. Kafka, *Castle*, 92.
10. Kafka, *Castle*, 114.
11. Franz Kafka, "The Great Wall of China," tr. Tania and James Stern, in *The Complete Stories*, ed. Nahum Glatzer (New York: Schocken Books, 1971), 238–39. For Kafka's use of the "China" motif and its link to Rosenzweig, see Benjamin, 120, 132. Marthe Robert points to the story as one with obvious reference to the Jews and Judaism in her *As Lonely as Franz Kafka* (New York: Harcourt Brace Jovanovich, 1982), 20.
12. Kafka, "Great Wall," 240–41.
13. Kafka, "Great Wall," 247–48.
14. Robert, 27. See also 14–20.
15. Franz Kafka, "Investigations of a Dog," in *Complete Stories*, 283–85. The passage discussed here concerns the "musical artists."
16. Kafka, "Investigations of a Dog," 316.
17. Max Weber, "Science as a Vocation," in *From Max Weber*, ed. Hans Gerth and C. Wright Mills (New York: Oxford University Press, 1969), 156.
18. Weber, "Science."
19. See, for example, Salo W. Baron, *A Social and Religious History of the Jews (in three volumes)*, vol. 3 (New York: Columbia University Press, 1937), 5; and Ephraim Shmueli, "The 'Pariah People' and its 'Charismatic Leadership': A Revaluation of Max Weber's Ancient Judaism," in *Proceedings of the American Academy for Jewish Research* 36 (1968), 167–247.
20. Max Weber, *Economy and Society: An Outline of Interpretive Sociology*, tr. and ed. G. Roth and C. Wittich (New York: Bedminster Press, 1968), 493.
21. Weber, "Science," 156.
22. Weber, "Science," 148.
23. Weber, "Politics as a Vocation," in *From Max Weber*, 115–121.
24. Steiner, 24.
25. Steiner, 23.
26. Steiner, 17.
27. Scholem, *Crisis*, 82–83.
28. Benjamin, *Illuminations*, 148.

SELECTED BIBLIOGRAPHY

Modern Primary Sources

Aḥad Ha'am. *Complete Writings* (Hebrew). Tel Aviv: D'vir, 1965.
————. *Selected Essays*. Edited by Leon Simon. Philadelphia: Jewish Publication Society, 1962.
Bar-On, Mordecai. "The Lesson for Zionism of the Holocaust" (Hebrew). *Kivvunim* (May 1981): 15–34.
Ben-Gurion, David. "The Imperatives of the Zionist Revolution" in *The Zionist Idea*. Edited by Arthur Hertzberg. New York: Harper Torchbooks, 606–19.
Berdiczewski, Micah Joseph. *Writings* (Hebrew). Tel Aviv: D'vir, 1960.
Brandeis, Louis. "The Jewish Problem and How to Solve It." In Hertzberg, *Zionist Idea*, 519–22.
Buber, Martin. *The Eclipse of God*. New York: Harper Torchbooks, 1957.
————. *Israel and the World: Essays in a Time of Crisis*. New York: Schocken, 1963.
————. *On Judaism*. Edited by Nahum Glatzer. New York: Schocken, 1972.
————. *Paths in Utopia*. Boston: Beacon Press, 1958.
————. *On Zion: The History of an Idea*. London: East and West Library, 1973.
————. "Zion, the State and Humanity: Remarks on Hermann Cohen's Answer." In *The Jew: Essays from Martin Buber's Journal "Der Jude," 1916–1928*. Edited by Arthur A. Cohen. University, Ala.: University of Alabama Press, 1980.
Carmon, Arye. "The Need for a Dialogue." Le Semana Publishing Company/Moshe Sharett Institute, 1983.
Cohen, Hermann. *Religion of Reason out of the Sources of Judaism*. Translated by Simon Kaplan. New York: Frederick Ungar, 1972.
————. "Religion and Zionism," in *Selected Essays from Jüdische Schriften* (Hebrew). Jerusalem: Bialik Institute, 1977, 87–91.
Dubnow, Simon. *Nationalism and History: Essays on Old and New Judaism*. Edited by Koppel S. Pinson. Philadelphia: Jewish Publication Society, 1958.
Elon, Ari. "As Much Heaven as One Could Stand" (Hebrew). *Shdemot* (Sivan 1980): 11–19.
Fackenheim, Emil. *God's Presence in History*. New York: Harper Torchbooks, 1972.
————. *The Jewish Return into History*. New York: Schocken, 1978.
————. *To Mend the World*. New York: Schocken, 1982.
Federbush, Simon, ed. *Torah and Kingship* (Hebrew). Jerusalem: Rav Kook Institute, 1961.
Geiger, Abraham. *Judaism and its History*. Translated by Charles Newburgh. New York: Bloch, 1911.
Glatzer, Nahum N., ed. *Franz Rosenzweig: His Life and Thought*. New York: Schocken, 1976.
Gordon, Aaron David. *The Nation and Labor* (Hebrew). Jerusalem: World Zionist Organization, 1952.
Goren, Shlomo. *Torat Ha-Moadim*. (*Laws of the Festivals*). Tel Aviv: Avraham Tzioni Publishers, 1964.
Graetz, Heinrich. *The Structure of Jewish History and Other Essays*. Edited by Ismar Schorsch. New York: Jewish Theological Seminary, 1975.
Halkin, Hillel. *Letters to an American Jewish Friend*. Philadelphia: Jewish Publication Society, 1977.

Halpern, Ben. *The American Jew: A Zionist Analysis.* New York: Theodor Herzl
     Foundation, 1956.
————. "Exile and Redemption: A Secular Zionist View." *Judaism* (Spring 1981):
     225–27.
Hartman, David. *Joy and Responsibility: Israel, Modernity and the Renewal of
     Judaism.* Jerusalem: Ben Zvi Posner/Shalom Hartman Institute, 1978.
Ḥazut. The World Ideological Conference (Hebrew). Vol. 4, 1958.
Hertzberg, Arthur. "America Is Different." In *The Outbursts That Await Us.* By
     Arthur Hertzberg, Martin E. Marty, and Joseph N. Moody. New York:
     Macmillan, 1963.
————. "America is Galut." *Jewish Frontier* (May 1964): 7–9.
Herzl, Theodor. *Altneuland.* Translated by Paula Arnold. Haifa: Haifa Publishing
     Company, 1960.
————. *The Jewish State.* In Hertzberg, *Zionist Idea,* 204–26.
Heschel, Abraham. *Israel: An Echo of Eternity.* New York: Farrar, Straus and
     Giroux, 1967.
————. "Yisrael: Am, Eretz, Medinah: An Ideological Evaluation of Israel and the
     Diaspora." *Proceedings of the Rabbinical Assembly of America* (1958): 118–
     36.
————. "The Theological Dimension of Medinat Yisrael." *PRAA* (1968): 91–103.
Hess, Moses. *Die Heilige Geschichte der Menschheit.* Stuttgart, 1837.
————. *Rome and Jerusalem.* Translated by Meyer Waxman. New York: Bloch,
     1943.
Hirsch, Samson Raphael. *The Nineteen Letters on Judaism.* Translated by Bernard
     Drachman. New York: Feldheim, 1969.
Jabotinsky, Vladimir. *A Jewish State: A Solution to the Jewish Question* (Hebrew).
     Tel Aviv: T. Kopp, 1937.
Kafka, Franz. *Complete Stories.* Edited by Nahum Glatzer. New York: Schocken,
     1971.
Kallen, Horace. *Zionism and World Politics.* Garden City: Doubleday, Page and
     Company, 1921.
Kaplan, Mordecai. *The Future of the American Jew.* New York: Macmillan, 1948.
————. *Judaism as a Civilization.* New York: Schocken, 1967.
————. *A New Zionism.* New York: Theodor Herzl Foundation, 1955.
Kaufmann, Yehezkel. *Golah Ve-Nekhar* (Hebrew). 2 vols. Tel Aviv: D'vir, 1962.
————. "The National Will to Survive." In *Sources: Anthology of Contemporary
     Jewish Thought.* Edited by David Hardin. Jerusalem: World Zionist Organi-
     zation, 1971.
Klatzkin, Yaakov. *Teḥumim* (Hebrew). Jerusalem: D'vir, 1928.
Kohler, Kaufmann. *Jewish Theology: Systematically and Historically Considered.*
     New York: Macmillan, 1928.
Kook, Abraham Isaac Ha-cohen. *Ḥazon Ha-ge'ulah. (Vision of Redemption.)* Jerusa-
     lem: Association for Publishing the Works of the Chief Rabbi A. I. Kook,
     1941.
————. *Orot. (Lights.)* Jerusalem: Rav Kook Institute, 1963.
Kook, Zevi Yehudah Ha-cohen. *Lenetivot Yisrael. (To the Pathways of Israel.)*
     Jerusalem: Menorah, 1967.
Krochmal, Nachman. *Guide for the Perplexed of the Time* (Hebrew). Edited by
     Simon Rawidowicz. Waltham: Ararat, 1961.
Leibowitz, Isaiah. *Faith, History and Values* (Hebrew). Jerusalem: Akademon of
     Hebrew University, 1982.
————. *Judaism, the Jewish People and the State of Israel* (Hebrew). Jerusalem:
     Schocken, 1976.

Mendelssohn, Moses. *Jerusalem*. Translated by A. Jospe. New York: Schocken, 1969.

Midstream. "The Meaning of Galut in America Today: A Symposium" (March 1963): 3–45.

Neusner, Jacob. "The Jewish Condition After Galuth." In *Diaspora: Exile and the Jewish Condition*. Edited by Etan Levine. New York: Jason Aronson, 1984, 271–82.

———. *Israel in America—A Too Comfortable Exile?* Boston: Beacon Press, 1985.

———. *Stranger at Home: "The Holocaust," Zionism and American Judaism*. Chicago: University of Chicago Press, 1981.

Oz, Amos. *In the Land of Israel*. Translated by Maurie Goldberg-Bartura. San Diego: Harcourt Brace Jovanovich, 1983.

———. *Under this Blazing Light* (Hebrew). Tel Aviv: Sifriat Hapoalim, 1979.

Petukhowski, Jacob. *Zion Reconsidered*. New York: Twayne, 1966.

Pinsker, Leo. "Auto-Emancipation." In Hertzberg, 181–98.

Ravitzky, Aviezer. "The Foreseen: And Freedom is Provided—Messianism, Zionism, and the Future of Israel, According to Competing Israeli Religious Perspectives" (Hebrew). In *Israel—Towards the 21st Century*. Edited by Aluf Hareven. Jerusalem: Van Leer Institute, 1985.

Rawidowicz, Simon. "Conclusion" to *Babylon and Jerusalem. Judaism* (Spring 1969): 131–42.

Rosenzweig, Franz. *The Star of Redemption*. Translated by William W. Hallo. Boston: Beacon Press, 1972.

Rotenstreich, Nathan. *Reflections on Contemporary Zionism* (Hebrew). Jerusalem: Hasifriya Hatzionit, 1975.

———. *Tradition and Reality: The Impact of History on Modern Jewish Thought*. New York: Random House, 1972.

Rubinstein, Amnon. *The Zionist Dream Revisited*. New York: Schocken, 1984.

Schechter, Solomon. *Seminary Addresses and Other Papers*. New York: Burning Bush Press, 1959.

Scholem, Gershom. *Devarim B'Go. (Explications and Implications: Writings on Jewish Heritage and Renaissance)*. Two volumes. Tel Aviv: Am Oved, 1976.

———. *On Jews and Judaism in Crisis*. Edited by Werner Dannhauser. New York: Schocken, 1984.

Schweid, Eliezer. *From Judaism to Zionism. From Zionism to Judaism* (Hebrew). Jerusalem: Hasifriya Hatzionit, 1984.

———. *Judaism and Secular Culture* (Hebrew). Tel Aviv: Kibbutz Hame'uhad, 1981.

———. *Judaism and the Solitary Jew* (Hebrew). Tel Aviv: Am Oved, 1975.

Soloveitchik, Joseph B. *Halakhic Man*. Translated by Lawrence Kaplan. Philadelphia: Jewish Publication Society, 1984.

———. *In the Secret of Aloneness and Togetherness*. Edited by Pinchas Peli. Jerusalem: Hetza'at Orot, 1979.

———. "The Lonely Man of Faith." *Tradition* (Summer 1965): 5–67.

———. *The Rav Speaks: Five Addresses*. Jerusalem: Tal Orot Institute, 1983.

Spinoza, Benedict. *Theologico-Political Treatise*. Edited by R. H. M. Elwes. New York: Dover, 1955.

Steiner, George. "Our Homeland, the Text." *Salmagundi* (Winter–Spring 1985): 4–25.

Urbach, Ephraim. *On Zionism and Judaism: Reflections and Addresses* (Hebrew). Jerusalem: Sifriyah Tzionit, 1985.

Yehoshua, A. B. *Between Right and Right*. Translated by Arnold Schwartz. Garden City: Doubleday, 1981.

Secondary Sources on the Modern Period

Abramov, S. Z. *Perpetual Dilemma: Jewish Religion in the Jewish State.* Rutherford, N.J.: Fairleigh Dickenson University Press, 1976.

Altmann, Alexander. "Commentary" to *Jerusalem.* By Moses Mendelssohn. Hanover: University Press of New England, 1983.

Avineri. Shlomo. *The Making of Modern Zionism.* New York: Basic Books, 1981.

Band, Arnold. "The Ahad Ha'am and Berdyczewski Polarity." In *At the Crossroads: Essays on Ahad Ha'am.* Edited by Jacques Kornberg. Albany: State University of New York Press, 1983.

Benjamin, Walter. *Illuminations.* Edited and translated by Hannah Arendt. London: Collins/Fontana Books, 1973.

Berlin, Isaiah. "The Life and Opinions of Moses Hess." In *Against the Current: Essays in the History of Ideas.* New York: Penguin Books, 1982, 213–51.

Biale, David. *Gershom Scholem: Kabbalah and Counter-History.* Cambridge: Harvard University Press, 1979.

Eisen, Arnold. *The Chosen People in America: A Study in Jewish Religious Ideology.* Bloomington: Indiana University Press, 1983.

Fleischman, Yaakov. "Franz Rosenzweig's Blessing of Zionism" (Hebrew). In *On Franz Rosenzweig.* Edited by Akiba Ernst Simon. Jerusalem: Magnes Press of Hebrew University, 1956.

Katz, Jacob. "The Impact of Jewish Emancipation on the Concepts of Galut and Geulah—Exile and Redemption." *Yearbook of the Central Conference of American Rabbis* (1976): 119–30.

Kornberg, Jacques. *At the Crossroads: Essays on Ahad Ha'am.* Albany: State University of New York Press, 1983.

Liebman, Charles, and Eliezer Don-Yehiya. *Civil Religion in Israel.* Berkeley: University of California Press, 1983.

O'Dea, Janet-Koffler. "Israel With and Without Religion: An Appreciation of Kaufmann's *Golah Ve-Nekhar.*" *Judaism* (Winter 1976): 85–97.

Robert, Marthe. *As Lonely as Franz Kafka.* Translated by Ralph Manheim. New York: Harcourt Brace Jovanovich, 1982.

Rosenak, Michael. "The Jewish Person and the State" (Hebrew). In *Jubilee Volume in Honor of Rabbi Joseph Dov Halevi Soloveitchik.* Edited by S. Yisraeli, et al. Volume 1. Jerusalem: Rav Kook Institute, 1984, 152–69.

Roskies, David. *Against the Apocalypse: Responses to Catastrophe in Modern Jewish Culture.* Cambridge: Harvard University Press, 1984.

Schweid, Eliezer. *Ha-yahid.* (*The Single One.*) Tel Aviv: Am Oved, 1970.

———. *The Land of Israel: A Homeland or Land of Destiny?* New York: Herzl Press/Associated Universities Press, 1985.

———. "The Rejection of the Diaspora in Jewish Thought: Two Approaches." *Studies in Zionism* (Spring 1981): 443–69.

Strauss, Leo. *Spinoza's Critique of Religion.* New York: Schocken, 1982.

Tal, Uriel. "Jewish Self-Understanding and the Land and State of Israel." *Union Seminary Quarterly Review* (Summer 1971): 351–82.

———. "The Land and State of Israel in Israeli Religious Life." *Proceedings of the Rabbinical Assembly of America* (1976): 1–40.

Urofsky, Melvin. *American Zionism From Herzl to the Holocaust.* Garden City: Doubleday Anchor, 1975.

Vital, David. *The Origins of Zionism.* Oxford: Clarendon Press, 1975.

———. *Zionism: The Formative Years.* Oxford: Clarendon Press, 1982.

Weber, Max. "Science as a Vocation." In *From Max Weber: Essays in Sociology.* Edited by Hans Gerth and C. Wright Mills. New York: Oxford University Press, 1969, 129–56.

Yaron, Tzvi. *The Philosophy of Rav Kook* (Hebrew). Jerusalem: World Zionist Organization, 1979.

Other Secondary Sources

Alon, Gedaliah. *The Jews in their Land in the Talmudic Age.* Vol. 1. Translated and edited by Gershon Levi. Jerusalem: Magnes Press of Hebrew University, 1980.

Alter, Robert. *The Art of Biblical Narrative.* New York: Basic Books, 1981.

Baer, Itzhak. *Galut.* New York: Schocken Books, 1977.

Ben Sasson, Haim Hillel. "Galut and Redemption in the Eyes of the Spanish Exiles" (Hebrew). In *Yitzhak Baer Jubilee Volume.* Edited by Shmuel Ettinger and Salo Baron, et al. Jerusalem: Historical Society of Israel, 1960, 216–27.

———. "The Generation of Spanish Exiles on Its Own Condition" (Hebrew). *Tzion* 26 (1961): 23–64.

Bokser, Baruch. "Rabbinic Responses to Catastrophe: From Continuity to Discontinuity." *Proceedings of the American Academy for Jewish Research* 50 (1983): 39–61.

Buber, Martin. *Moses.* New York: Harper Torchbooks, 1958.

Davies, W. D. *The Gospel and the Land: Early Christianity and Jewish Territorial Doctrine.* Berkeley: University of California Press, 1974.

———. *The Territorial Dimension of Judaism.* Berkeley: University of California Press, 1982.

Halkin, Abraham, ed. *Zion in Jewish Literature.* New York: Herzl Press, 1961.

Hoffman, Lawrence, ed. *The Idea of the Land of Israel.* South Bend: Notre Dame University Press, 1986.

Kasowski, Josua. *Thesaurus Talmudis* (Hebrew). Jerusalem: Ministry of Education and Culture, 1961.

Lieberman, Saul. *Hellenism in Jewish Palestine.* New York: Jewish Theological Seminary of America, 1962.

Mandelkern, Solomon. *Concordantiae.* Jerusalem: Schocken, 1975.

Mintz, Alan. *Ḥurban: Responses to Catastrophe in Hebrew Literature.* New York: Columbia University Press, 1984.

Neusner, Jacob. *A History of the Jews in Babylonia.* Vol. 2: *The Early Sasanian Period.* Leiden: E. J. Brill, 1966.

———. *Judaism: The Evidence of the Mishnah.* Chicago: University of Chicago Press, 1981.

———. *Method and Meaning in Ancient Judaism.* Missoula, Mont.: Brown Judaic Studies/Scholars Press, 1979.

———. *The Talmud of the Land of Israel: A Preliminary Translation and Explanation.* Vol. 33: *Abodah Zarah.* Chicago: University of Chicago Press, 1982.

Polzin, Robert. *Moses and the Deuteronomist: A Literary Study of the Deuteronomic History. Part One.* New York: Seabury Press, 1980.

Rosenberg, Shalom. "Exile and Redemption in Jewish Thought in the Sixteenth Century: Contending Conceptions." In *Jewish Thought in the Sixteenth Century.* Edited by Bernard Dov Cooperman. Cambridge: Harvard University Press, 1983, 399–430.

Safrai, Shmuel. "The Era of the Talmud; 70–640." In *A History of the Jewish People.* Edited by Haim Hillel Ben Sasson. London: Weidenfeld and Nicolson, 1979, 307–82.

Scholem, Gershom. *Kabbalah.* Jerusalem: Keter, 1974.

———. *On the Kabbalah and its Symbolism.* Translated by Ralph Manheim. New York: Schocken, 1965.

————. *The Messianic Idea in Judaism and Other Essays on Jewish Spirituality*. New York: Schocken, 1971.

Urbach, Ephraim. *The Sages: Their Concepts and Beliefs*. Translated by Israel Abrahams. Jerusalem: Magnes Press of Hebrew University, 1975.

Von Rad, Gerhard. *Studies in Deuteronomy*. Translated by David Stalker. London: SCM Press, 1953.

Weinfeld, Moshe, *Deuteronomy and the Deuteronomic School*. Oxford: Clarendon Press, 1972.

————. "Deuteronomy; the Present State of Inquiry." *Journal of Biblical Literature* 86 (1967): 256–61.

Yerushalmi, Yosef H. *Zakhor: Jewish History and Jewish Memory*. Seattle: University of Washington Press, 1982.

INDEX

ARNOLD M. EISEN, senior lecturer in Jewish Philosophy at Tel Aviv University, is the author of *The Chosen People in America: A Study in Jewish Religious Ideology* (Indiana University Press, 1983).